STUDIES IN MEDIEVAL HISTORY

PRESENTED TO

R.H.C. DAVIS

RALPH HENRY CARLESS DAVIS

STUDIES IN MEDIEVAL HISTORY

PRESENTED TO

R.H.C. DAVIS

EDITED BY

HENRY MAYR-HARTING AND R.I. MOORE

THE HAMBLEDON PRESS
LONDON AND RONCEVERTE

Published by The Hambledon Press 1985

35 Gloucester Avenue, London NW1 7AX (U.K.)

309 Greenbrier Avenue, Ronceverte,
West Virginia 24970 (U.S.A.)

ISBN 0 907628 68 0

© The contributors 1985

British Library Cataloguing in Publication Data

Studies in medieval history presented to R.H.C. Davis
   1. Europe – History – 476-1492
   I. Davis, R.H.C.   II. Mayr-Harting, Henry
   III. Moore, R.I.
   940. 1'7   D117

Library of Congress Cataloging-in-Publication Data

Main entry under title:

Studies in medieval history presented to R.H.C. Davis

Bibliography: pp. xv-xviii
1. England – Economic conditions – Addresses, essays, lectures.
2. England – History, Local – Addresses, essays, lectures.
3. Davis, R.H.C. (Ralph Henry Carless), 1918-.
I. Davis, R.H.C. (Ralph Henry Carless), 1918-.
II. Mayr-Harting, Henry.
III. Moore, R.I. (Robert Ian), 1941-.
HC257.E5S78 1985   942.01   85 – 17750
ISBN 0 907628 68 0

Typeset by Chambers Green Ltd, Southborough, Kent

Printed and bound by Hartnoll (1985) Ltd, Victoria
Square, Bodmin, Cornwall

Contents

List of Illustrations		vii
Preface		ix
Henry Mayr-Harting and R. I. Moore		
Ralph Davis: A Personal Appreciation		xi
Martin Roberts		
Bibliography of R. H. C. Davis		
1	Byzantine Porridge	1
	Anthony Bryer	
2	Currency and Freedom: Some Problems in the Social History of the Early Middle Ages	7
	H. R. Loyn	
3	Beyond the Edge of Excavation: The Topographical Context of Goltho	21
	Steven Bassett	
4	The Royal Anglo-Saxon 'Chancery' of the Tenth Century Revisited	41
	Pierre Chaplais	
5	Lawyers' Time: History and Memory in Tenth- and Eleventh-Century Italy	53
	Chris Wickham	
6	The Miracles of St Benedict: A Window on Early Medieval France	73
	D. W. Rollason	
7	Towns and Cottages in Eleventh-Century England	91
	Christopher Dyer	
8	Guibert of Nogent and his World	107
	R. I. Moore	
9	Henry I and the Invisible Transformation of Medieval England	119
	C. Warren Hollister	
10	Henry I and Wales	133
	R. R. Davies	
11	The Scots Charter	149
	G. W. S. Barrow	
12	The First English Pilgrims to Santiago de Compostela	165
	D. W. Lomax	

13	Prester John and the Three Kings of Cologne *Bernard Hamilton*	177
14	Functions of a Twelfth-Century Shrine: The Miracles of St Frideswide *Henry Mayr-Harting*	193
15	Peter of Blois and the Third Crusade *Sir Richard Southern*	207
16	Magna Carta and the Common Pleas *M. T. Clanchy*	219
17	Titles to Orders in Medieval English Episcopal Registers *R. N. Swanson*	233
18	The Organization and Achievements of the Peasants of Kent and Essex in 1381 *Nicholas Brooks*	247
19	How Much did it Cost to Found a Jeronimite Monastery in late Medieval Spain? *J. R. L. Highfield*	271
20	War and Peace in Fifteenth-Century Castile: Diego de Valera and the Granada War *John Edwards*	283
21	Did Politics Change in the late Middle Ages and Renaissance? *Denys Hay*	297
List of Subscribers		309

List of Illustrations

Ralph Henry Carless Davis   *Frontispiece*

Maps

1a	Estates in the Bullington area in 1086	23
b	Ecclesiastical and civil parishes in the Bullington area	23
2	The putative mid Saxon Estate of Bullington	25
3	Early landscape elements surviving into the late nineteenth century (1883–8) in the vicinity of Bullington and Goltho	33
4	Places associated with the 'Miracles of St Benedict'	75
5	Wales at the time of Henry I	132
6	The Beginning of the Revolt (30 May–4 June)	253
7	Preparation and Dissemination of the Revolt (6–9 June)	257
8	The Approach to London (10–12 June)	261

Plates

1a	Charter of David I for Robert de Brus	
b	Charter of David I for Arnolf of Swinton	148
2	Charter of Malcolm IV for Durham Cathedral Priory	159
3	Charter of William I for Hexham Priory	161
4	Charter of William I for Kelso and Melrose Abbeys	163

Acknowledgements

The plates are reproduced by the kind permission of the following: J. C. Blackett Ord (3); The Trustees of the British Library (1a, 4); The Dean and Chapter of Durham Cathedral (1b, 2).

Preface

R. H. C. Davis's contribution to scholarship is too well known to need elaborate description. His edition, in collaboration with H. A. Cronne, of the charters of Stephen's reign, is a major addition to medieval learning. Continuing and completing his father's project to edit the charters of the Norman kings, it represents the highest standards in collection, dating, criticism and publication. It will provide a permanent foundation for the study of a generation in English history. Ralph's own scrutiny of these and other materials for Stephen's reign, conducted with a combination of common sense and bold imagination, has enriched our understanding not only of that reign but also of kingship and government in general during the high Middle Ages. Yet if this is unquestionably Ralph's major achievement, the list of his lesser ones would have been sufficient to place him among the leading historians of his generation. For instance, two papers across the years, one an estimate of the nature and extent of Danish settlement in England, the other an unravelling of the treaty between Alfred and Guthrum, have issued in radical reinterpretations of central problems in Anglo-Danish history. His exploration of the chronicle accounts of the early Normans produced, in *The Normans and their Myth*, not only a dramatic revision of accepted views, but also a searching appraisal of the nature of historical memory itself, and of the role of the historical imagination in the definition of communities and the articulation of power. Two papers on twelfth-century Oxford have been important contributions in bringing to life the subject of urban history in the Middle Ages. One of them has a positively devilish explanation for the origins of Oxford University. It has not been too much noticed, perhaps because it was published in a local journal, and even perhaps because it was not very gratifying to those who would see themselves against a lofty background. In any case, it is singularly difficult to dispose of. In these papers he has repaid a debt to his home town. The motto of Oxford city is *fortis est veritas*; surely quite as good a motto for Ralph as the *Dominus illuminatio mea* of the university.

It may seem hardly relevant to an appreciation of Ralph as a scholar and teacher to mention his courage and commitment during the war, when he served with the Friends' Ambulance Corps in the Middle East, North Africa and France, and won the Croix de Guerre. One of his contemporaries who read 'Greats' at Oxford both before and after the war has observed that the teaching in Ancient History of those tutors who had done service of various kinds in the war had a grip and a direction which he could not recollect previously. It is hard to doubt that this observation has always applied to Ralph. His study of History has always been informed by real human concerns. In this, as in his zeal for the visual remains of History, wherever he has found himself, from the Oxford region with its masons' marks to Cairo with its mosques he has never been like some medieval bishops, content so long as the details were written down somewhere.

Everyone who has been in touch with Ralph or read his writings will know that high amongst his priorities in the study of History are the pleasures of the chase. In other words, he loves and excels in the function of a detective. He has found the charter which shows who Jocelin of Brakelond really was, the charter which shows how difficult it was in reality for barons to change sides in the wars of Stephen's reign, and the dates of the charters which show what Geoffrey de Mandeville's real game was. He has tracked down step by step – this with dazzling brilliance – the person who must have been the author of the *Gesta Stephani*, and so has made possible the controlled use of that vital source. The audience of undergraduates who first heard this last-mentioned piece of detective work, when characteristically he stopped short of naming the person and invited his hearers to send him suggestions for the following week, sat listening with open mouths and unblinking eyes. It should be emphasized, however, that these discoveries, and others like them, never remained purely archival insights. They were indeed only possible, and their full interest was elicited, because of Ralph's sense of what was important in the widest historical perspective.

Two special characteristics are common to all his work. First, it has invariably been the product of a fresh reading of the primary sources and the ability to ask of them the fundamental questions. Second, the results have been presented in language and reasoning of great directness, with the minimum of apparatus and complete abstention from all display of erudition or intellectual power. He possesses, in remarkable measure, the 'noble simplicity' which for Marc Bloch enabled a scholar 'to speak in the same tone to savants and schoolboys alike'.

We have not thought it desirable to arrange this volume around a theme or confine it to a short period within the Middle Ages. This has not been a decision of principle, but one of pure pragmatism. When we surveyed the varied interests of Ralph's former pupils and close colleagues, it virtually imposed itself. Nonetheless we believe there is not one contributor who cannot thank him for some helping hand given in a wholly unpatronizing way, or some interest taken, or some encouragement shown, in the kind of work here presented. In that sense, as well as in the more general sense of his friendship and stimulus, we all reflect something of him, and we all join together with many others to express to him our gratitude and affection.

Ralph Davis: A Personal Appreciation

Martin Roberts

I must first have met Ralph in September, 1947. I do not remember the meeting, being, I suspect, much more interested in the imminence of my sixth birthday. He had just joined the staff of Christ's Hospital where my father was Head of History. Though he only stayed at the school a year before moving to University College, London, my parents and he became firm friends, the more so if anything after he married Eleanor.

In his short time at Christ's Hospital he made his mark. My mother remembers how he both stimulated and disconcerted the Oxbridge candidates (among whom she thinks was Bryan Magee) by asking them seemingly simple questions which proved to be very demanding and refusing even to outline a possible answer until they had themselves thoroughly wrestled with the problem.

My parents clearly held him in high regard as a historian. So too did Michael Cherniavsky, a friend and contemporary of his at Balliol who was my sixth-form history teacher at Christ's Hospital. I first began to understand why in 1957 when I was studying for 'A' level. In that year Ralph published his *History of Medieval Europe from Constantine to St. Louis,* and Michael Cherniavsky made sure that our sixth-form library was stocked with a number of copies. Before long Davis was proving as rich a mine of material for our essays as Pirenne, Previté-Orton and Z. N. Brooke. Not many scholars attempt outline histories for undergraduates and sixth-formers. It is arguable that they are significantly harder to write than monographs. You can assume no prior knowledge from your readers, must write in a clear but unpatronising style and cover the major themes within the number of words agreed in advance with the publisher. Being a conservative sixth-former, I did not know at first quite what to make of Davis. I expected such books to be difficult and include plenty of -isms. Davis was not like that. It was unusually clear and easy to read, yet managed to present familiar themes in a new light. It soon became a favourite of Christ's Hospital sixth-formers. Its quality as an introduction to medieval history is reflected in the fact that twenty seven years after publication, not only is it in print but, my Longman spies tell me, is selling nicely both at home and abroad. A third edition is in preparation at the moment.

Christ's Hospital generally and Michael Cherniavsky particularly were expert at getting pupils into Oxbridge, so, in 1960, I found myself at Merton. The tutorial team there was exceptional. Starting with Michael Wallace-Hadrill, we moved on to Ralph, then to Roger Highfield and finally to John Roberts. They were all fine teachers with splendidly contrasting styles. Ralph's approach was, I suspect, not that dissimilar from the one which disconcerted the Christ's Hospital Oxbridge candidates back in 1947. It certainly disconcerted some of us first-year undergraduates when we met it for the first time. Instead of the parade of impressive specialist knowledge, there were the unusual and deceptively simple questions which, on reflection, were most difficult to answer. The approach and the experience of adjusting to it were both stimulating. His methods of criticism were also individual and effective. One week I had an essay on King Stephen. For one reason or another it got low priority and emerged a mediocre offering, very much a late-night black coffee production. This was an especially poor piece of timing, since Stephen's reign was then Ralph's major research interest. In my reading of the essay I did my utmost to make it sound much more perceptive than it really was, only to realise to my chagrin that Ralph had fallen asleep.

Eleanor and Ralph were extremely hospitable. We were regularly invited to their home in Lathbury Road for lunch or tea or charades. What in the first year seemed a summons became a genuine pleasure in the second and third years. You came to realise that they both had a genuine concern for your personal welfare. I would discuss the affairs of the world and college with Ralph and the things that really seemed to matter with Eleanor. As it happens I often now walk or cycle along Lathbury Road on my way to work. Number 16 has not changed much. The garden seems a little less well-tended, the garage paintwork has faded and the noisy St Clare's girls and their escorts are very much in evidence.

Many of the readers of this book will be, like me, former pupils of Ralph. Perhaps the foregoing will have encouraged some memories to surface. Other readers will be departmental and faculty colleagues from London, Oxford and Birmingham or friends and teachers from other universities or fellow medievalists from overseas. They will be much better able than I to estimate his achievements as a historian. However, I should like to draw attention to two characteristics of his writings which have caught my unscholarly eye. The first is its range. Not only are there major editions like *The Kalender of Abbot Samson* or the *Regesta Regum Anglo-Normannorum* but also important books like *King Stephen* and *The Normans and Their Myth*. In addition there are numerous articles for *E.H.R.* and *History* and papers on local history, particularly that of Oxford. His subjects have also been varied. His first published article, when he was still only 19, was on *Mason Marks in Oxfordshire* (1938). This was followed in 1944 by *The Mosques of Cairo* which he researched during his spare time while on war-service in North Africa with the Friends Ambulance Unit. Most recently he has written on 'Alfred and Guthrum's Frontier' in *E.H.R.* (1982), while a major research interest in 1983 and 1984 has been 'the Medieval Horse'. The second characteristic is his readiness to undertake tasks which most would regard as chores but are of great utility to other historians – bibliographies, articles on photographic facilities available to historians, on record societies and the like.

The study of history is not however just the concern of university specialists and their students. It is of considerable interest to a much wider audience and a matter of national significance, difficult though it may be to define the nature and extent of this significance. Few historians alive today have devoted as much time as Ralph to the task of reaching this wider audience. Partly he has communicated through his own writing, to school pupils through *English History in Pictures: the Early Middle Ages* or to the general public through contributions to the series *The History of the English Speaking Peoples* which appeared initially in weekly magazine form. More important have been his efforts for the Historical Association, first as editor of *History* from 1968 to 1978 and then as President from 1979 to 1982. The H.A. passed through a serious crisis in the early 1970s. Rapid inflation caused severe financial difficulties and there were organisational problems too. That it survived was due to the wise leadership of a number of senior members of whom Ralph was one. During his presidency the Association moved into calmer waters. He encouraged it to look afresh at its role and, as its confidence and financial situation improved, to undertake new initiatives so that it could meet more effectively the requirements of its members and attract new ones. Only in the H.A. have I had the opportunity actually to work with Ralph. In that context he is someone who not only does things himself to a continuously high standard but is skilled at getting the best out of others. He is a firm but kindly committee chairman with a clear grasp of the practical and the impractical.

One might have thought that as he neared retirement he might leave potential battlefields to younger generals. This has not been the case. In the last few years when the place of history in universities and in schools has become increasingly threatened, the most effective defence to date has been that mounted by the History in Universities Defence Group (H.U.D.G.). It has organised lively, well-attended and effective conferences all over the country and is stimulating schoolteachers who, hitherto, have been a trifle disorganised into active consideration of the most appropriate responses to their vulnerable situation. Ralph has now handed over the lead of the H.U.D.G. to others but I know that it is accurate to describe it as very much his creation, and that it has achieved what it has on a tiny budget and minimal secretarial support. If, in the years ahead, we are able first to safeguard and then improve the standing of history in education (as I am sure that we will), then we and future generations will be greatly in his debt. If we fail (which at the time of writing remains a possibility), we shall not later be able to argue that we had no-one to give us a lead.

No appreciation of Ralph would be complete without mention of Eleanor. In her cheerful, no-nonsense and by no means uncritical way, she takes great pride in his achievements whether she is recounting anecdotes from his youth or from his experiences as Birmingham University's Public Orator. She is also an essential partner both in high ceremonial, as when the Queen honoured the H.A. with her presence on its 75th Anniversary during Ralph's Presidency, and in providing hospitality for a never-ending stream of visitors, university colleagues and students. With Ralph and their sons Christopher and Timothy (not to mention Prince, the dog) she has created wherever they have been homes which are always welcoming. It is certainly no platitude to say that in Ralph's case his successes would not have been so manifold without his wife's support and understanding.

Ralph taught me much about history. He has also been my best adviser. On the innumerable occasions when I have sought his advice, I have usually taken it, and regretted those occasions when I did not. In a manner which I find hard to categorise, which is apparently prosaic and quite unpretentious, he gets to the heart of a matter and explains it in an unusual yet illuminating way. At my initial interview for admission to Merton, I was asked by the panel about Florentine art and history. Could I recommend a good guide which gave some insights not only into the artistic masterpieces but into the society which produced them? I floundered unhappily and the interviews mercifully passed on to their next question. Later that day I found on the table in my room a copy of *Romola* with a note from Ralph saying 'you might enjoy reading this'. That gesture, which he will have long forgotten, seems to me twenty-five years later absolutely typical – stimulating, generous, thoughtful and different.

Bibliography:
The Writings of R. H. C. Davis (to 1983)

Book reviews are not included

1938
'Masons' Marks in Oxfordshire and the Cotswolds', *Oxfordshire Archaeological Society*, lxxxiv, 68–83.

1944
The Mosques of Cairo (Cairo).

1946–7
'The Chronology of Perpendicular Architecture in Oxford', *Oxoniensia* xii–xiii, 75–89.

1951
'Charlemagne's Empire', *History* xxxvi, 171.

1954
'Balliol College: the Buildings', *C.V.H. Oxfordshire* iii, 90–95.
'A Catalogue of Masons' Marks as an aid to Architectural History', *Journal of the British Archaeological Association*, 3rd series xvii, 43–76.
The Kalendar of Abbot Samson of Bury St. Edmunds and related documents, Camden Third Series (London, Royal Historical Society), lxxxiv.

1954–57
'The Early Middle Ages, 500–1200', *The Annual Bulletin of Historical Literature*, xl, 12–15; xli, 13–17; xlii, 12–15; xliii, 11–15.

1955
'East Anglia and the Danelaw', *Transactions of the Royal Historical Society*, Fifth Series, v, 23–39
'The Monks of Bury St. Edmunds in the Eleventh and Twelfth Centuries', *History*, xl, 227–239.

1957
A History of Medieval Europe from Constantine to St. Louis (London; Second edition 1970).

1960

Revised edition of H. W. C. Davis, *Medieval Europe*, with Epilogue (Oxford).

'King Stephen and the Earl of Chester revised', *E.H.R.* lxxv, 654–660.

1962

'The authorship of the *Gesta Stephani*, *E.H.R.* lxxvii, 209–232.

'Treaty between William Earl of Gloucester and Roger Earl of Hereford', *A Miscellany for Doris Mary Stenton* (London, Pipe Roll Society, New Series xxxvi), 139–146.

'Brixworth and Clofesho', *Journal of the British Archaeological Association* 3rd series, xxv, 71.

1963

European History, 395–1500: a select bibliography (London, Historical Association; Second revised edition 1968; Third revised edition, *Medieval European History: a select bibliography*, 1977).

With R. W. Hunt, revised edition of H. W. C. Davis, *A History of Balliol College* (Oxford).

1964

'Introduction', H. Busch and B. Lohse, *Romanesque Europe*, iii–iv (London).

'Geoffrey de Mandeville reconsidered', *E.H.R.* lxxix, 299–307.

'What happened in Stephen's reign', *History*, xlix, 1–12.

English History in Pictures: the Early Middle Ages (London, Historical Association).

1966

'The Norman Conquest', *History* li, 279–288. (Reprinted in C. Warren Hollister, ed., *The Impact of the Norman Conquest*, New York, 1969.)

1968

'An Oxford charter of 1191 and the beginnings of municipal freedom', *Oxoniensia*, xxxiii, 53–65.

'Photographic Services in British Libraries and Archives', *History* liii, 247–253.

With H. A. Cronne, *Regesta Regum Anglo-Normannorum*, iii, (1135–54), (Oxford).

1969

With H. A. Cronne, *Regesta Regum Anglo-Normannorum*, iv, *Facsimilies* (Oxford).
King Stephen (London).
'English Kingship', *The History of the English Speaking Peoples* No. 8, 252–260.
'Anarchy in England', *ibid.* No. 11, 350–356.

1971

'Alfred the Great: Propaganda and Truth', *History* lvi, 169–182.
'An Unknown Coventry Charter', *E.H.R.* lxxxvi, 533–547.
'Local History and Ancient Monuments', *History* lvi, 59–65.
Good History and Bad: Inaugural Lecture (Birmingham).

1973

'Why have a Historical Association?', *History* lviii, 233–239.
'William of Tyre', *Relations between East and West in the Middle Ages* ed. Derek Baker (Edinburgh), pp. 64–76.
'The Ford, the River and the City', *Oxoniensia* xxxviii, 258–267.

1974

'The College of St. Martin-le-Grand and the Anarchy, 1135–54', *London Topographical Record*, xxiii, 9–26.

1975

'Record Societies in England', *History* lx, 239–246.

1976

The Normans and their Myth (London).
With K. R. Potter, *Gesta Stephani*, second, revised edition (Oxford).
The Early History of Coventry (Dugdale Society Occasional Paper No. 24) (Oxford).

1978

'The Carmen de Hastingae Proelio', *E.H.R.* xciii, 241–261.

1980

'William of Jumièges, Robert Curthose and the Norman Succession', *E.H.R.* xcv, 597–606.

1981

With J. M. Wallace-Hadrill (ed.) *The Writing of History in the Middle Ages: Essays presented to Richard William Southern* (Oxford).

'William of Poitiers and his History of William the Conqueror', *ibid.* pp. 71–100.

'The Content of History', *History* lxvi, 361–375.

1982

'Alfred and Guthrum's Frontier', *E.H.R.* xcvii, 803–810.

1983

'The Medieval Warhorse', *Horses in European Economic History: a preliminary canter*, ed. F. M. L. Thompson (London, British Agricultural History Society), pp. 4–20.

1

Byzantine Porridge

Anthony Bryer

'Dis-moi ce que tu manges, et je te dirai ce que tu es.'
Anthelme Brillat-Savarin (1755–1826)

Pastoralists subsist on the meat and milk of their flocks. Without fixed ovens or fields, bread is not a staff of life. But medieval pastoralists who also had access to grain devised various gruels as a substitute: *kashk* in the Persian epic Shāh-nāma, the *kishk* of the Lebanon, Russian *kashi* and Spanish *gachas* are examples of a dish to which English liberal shepherds gave a grosser name: 'hasty pudding'.[1] The modern Greek variety is usually called *trachanás*; it is *tarhana* in modern Turkish, *turkhana* in Bulgarian and *tar(h)ana* in Serbian.[2] Arabella Boxer describes it as an 'instant soup mix made by Greek peasants in late summer. It is formed from coarsely ground wheat mixed to a dough with goat's milk or yoghurt, then left in the sun for several days until as dry as powder' (but grittier). 'It is then stored, usually in the form of small rolls, and used to make a delicious and nourishing soup . . .'[3] I first encountered it being

---

[1] Although I have been preparing this bowl of Byzantine porridge for Ralph Davis for almost as long as the editors of his *Festschrift* have been planning the greater feast, I confess that, while I first ventured the connections put forward here in 1979, I was discouraged by a sequence of articles in the periodical *Petits Propos Culinaires (PPC)*, which seemed to pre-empt my conclusions. In 'What was tracta?', *PPC*, 12 (1982), 37–39, the learned Charles Perry took the matter from Apicius to Athenaeus. In 'Tracta and Trahanas', *PPC*, 13 (1983), 76–77, Caroline Conran proposed a direct leap from one to the other. In 'Tracta/Trahanas/Kishk', *PPC*, 14 (1983), 58–59, Charles Perry returned with an emphatic Persian origin for *trachanás*. I think that Lady Caroline Conran was right to make her connection, and while I cannot dispute Charles Perry's Middle Eastern information, am relieved to find that another, and Byzantine, bowl of porridge remains worth serving up. See also R. Levy, *The Epic of the Kings* (London, 1967), p. 150; R. E. F. Smith, 'Russian diet', *National and Regional Styles of Cookery. Oxford Symposium 1981*, ed. Alan Davidson (London, 1981), p. 134 (on *kashi*); Gerald Brenan (to whom I am grateful for correspondence on *gachas*), *South from Granada* (Harmondsworth, 1963), p. 180; Raphaela Lewis, 'Turkish cuisine', *Oxford Symposium 1981*, p. 118; A. A. M. Bryer, 'The estates of the Empire of Trebizond. Evidence for their resources, products, agriculture, ownership and location', *Archeion Pontou*, 35 (1979), p. 412 = *The Empire of Trebizond and the Pontos* (London, 1980), Study VII.

[2] Phaidon Koukoules, *Byzantinon Bios kai Politismos*, V (Athens, 1952), p. 40; *Rječnik hrvatskoga ili srpskoga Jezika*, XVIII (Zagreb, 1962–66), s.v. *tarana*.

[3] Cited, without reference which I cannot find, in Conran, *PPC*, 13 (1983), p. 76.

prepared and dried on balconies and roofs of lowland villages around Trebizond one September. There it is made from *bulgur* wheat, cracked in a mortar, carefully husked, and then rolled in the palms of the hands into rough nodules the size of Greek *kephtedes* or English dumplings, using milk as a binder – creamy *kaymak*, skimmed *ayran*, or just yoghurt. I first enjoyed this porridge (there is no other word for it) in a *yayla* encampment on an upland pasture above Trebizond the following summer. Its consistency is formidable: a boxwood spoon will stand up in it. Its taste is unforgettable: nutty and sour from the fermented milk in which the nodules were soaked months before and may be cooked in again. It is a peculiarly refreshing way in which to start a day in the boundless summer pastures.

The attraction of *trachanás* and like porridges to pastoralists is that its cooking is elementary and that it can be preserved from the lowland autumn to take up to the highland summer. But it needs a pastoral symbiosis with agriculture, which is why in the Pontos at least it is especially the food of transhumants.

Most people are not shepherds, which does not however stop most people who enjoyed *trachanás* being lowlanders or even townsmen: indeed it has recently appeared on the menu of the most expensive Greek restaurant in London. Nor, beyond the basic principles of the food, does there seem to be any more conformity of preparation or cooking than there is for Anglo-American-Scottish porridge. It does not figure in any of the common Greek or Turkish cook-books, but, like Frankish porridge, is widely known and arouses strongly-held opinions. A casual enquiry of a group of Greek Birmingham Byzantine students as to how their mothers made *trachanás* brought down a Babel of conflicting advice, from Aetolia, Crete, Cyprus, Epirus and Thessaly.[4] The wheat is special, but need not be *bulgur* (even maize can be employed); it can be ground in a hand quern rather than crushed in a mortar; it is made in September not just because of the harvest but because goats' milk is richer and abundant then; it is frankly best when fresh, rather than stored for shepherds. Some follow an old-attested practice and add *feta* cheese to the brew.[5] None know whether it could be kept dry for more than a year, for by then it had all been eaten. All (save the Cretan) agree that the Cretan version is too sharp. But all maintain that their local *trachanás* is distinct from any other and the best.

Charles Perry states that *trachanás* is 'a Persian word. In Persian it is spelled *tarkhāna* or *tarkhīna*; the Turks spread it through Anatolia and the Balkans (the spelling with an aspirated *t* in Armenian makes this fairly certain). In Greek the word was altered first with the inflexional ending -*s* and then by the transposition of the second and third letters, under the

---

[4] I am grateful to George Calofonos, Anna Frangedaki, Catia Galatariotou, Aglaia Kasdagli, Marianna Spanaki and Dimitris Tziovas.

[5] Cf. Koukoules, V, p. 119.

influence of a folk etymology connecting the foreign word with the native adjective *trachýs*, "rough". The oldest literary reference to *tarkhāna* seems to be the fourteenth-century Bushaq' (Fakr al-Din Ahmad b. Halladji Abu Ishak, d. 1424 or 1427).[6]

I do not question that the modern Tukish and Greek *tarhana/trachanás* share a Persian name, which was conveniently close to an existing Byzantine word, but I do not think that the Greek was derived from *trachýs*, do not know if it was the Turks who imported the Persian word, and will propose that the porridge has another and older history than Bushak.

That the Turks introduced crops and a cuisine from the Islamic world into the lands they conquered, settled and grazed in the Byzantine world is an attractive proposition, often ventured but more rarely demonstrated. That there may be something cultural about *trachanás* in particular, as the mark of the Turkish pastoralist as opposed to the diet of the Christian agriculturalist, is hinted at in a Serbian version of an Ottoman proverb: '*Tarhana* is Moslem food: cabbage and bacon are infidel food'.[7] It is an equally attractive proposition that Anatolian Turkish names for agricultural processes and implements tend to be derived from the Greek peasants whom the Turks converted, supplanted or married, but that they brought their own terms for pastoral and transhumant activities. But such equations may not be so simple. To begin with, the Byzantine world preceded, and was in agricultural and culinary touch with, the Islamic one long before the Turks, and it was not a one-way exchange. The Byzantines wore turbans and had prayer carpets before they met the Seljuks, while '*Murri* Byzantine style' (an awesome condiment made from barley dough that has been rotted for forty days) is among Byzantium's contributions to medieval Arabic cook-books.[8] Here are some more snags in the argument.

It has been proposed, for example, that Asiatic rice (which was to be a staple to the commissariat of the Ottoman army) was introduced to

---

[6] Perry, *PPC*, 14 (1983), p. 59; cf. *The Encyclopaedia of Islam*, I (Leiden-London, 1960), p. 1342.

[7] See *RHISJ* in n. 2. Other proverbs cited are 'Turks say: "*Tarhana* is food, all *raya* are cabbage and bacon"; "The old fame (glory, or beauty) has gone out of fashion as *tarana* when it is warmed up"; and a saying quoted by Vuk: "My mother and his mother dried their *tarana* under the same sun".' M. Benson and Biljama Šljivić-Šimšić, *Serbo-Croatian – English Dictionary* (Pennsylvania, 1974), s.v. *tarana*, cites the saying 'to leave as *tarana* in the pot' = 'to take French leave' (this sounds very obscure). I am grateful to Dr Zaga Gavrilović for these references.

[8] Cyril Mango, 'Discontinuity with the classical past in Byzantium', *Byzantium and the Classical Tradition. University of Birmingham Thirteenth Spring Symposium of Byzantine Studies 1979*, ed. Margaret Mullett and Roger Scott (Birmingham, 1981), pp. 51–52; Charles Perry, 'Three medieval Arabic cook books', *Oxford Symposium 1981*, pp. 96, 98 and n. 5 on p. 103.

Anatolia by the Turks in the fourteenth century at the earliest.[9] This does not explain why Geoffrey of Langley, Edward I's envoy to the Mongol Ilkhan of Persia, was able to buy 16 aspers'-worth of rice in Byzantine Trebizond in 1292.[10] It is true that Byzantines had their own words (which the Turks did not inherit) for transhumance, whereas the Turks borrowed numerous essential agricultural terms from Greek – such as *düğen* (Modern Greek *dókane*, Byzantine *týkane*, Latin *tribulum*) for the threshing sledge which tribulates the peasant's corn.[11] But it is hard to envisage a Türkmen pastoralist without peering through the smoke of his dung-cake fire upon which he stirs his *tarhana*. Yet his name for the fuel, *tezek*, is derived not from Turkic words, such as Mongol *argols*, but apparently from Byzantine *zarzakon* – the fumes of which perhaps asphyxiated the Emperor Jovian in the cold Galatian highlands on the night of 16–17 February 364. Similarly *tarhana* is not a Turkic word; it may be just as likely that the Turks inherited it from the Greek as the Persian.[12]

A familiar problem is that neither Byzantine nor Islamic people wrote of the banausic things they used every day. Indeed *zarzaka*, or dung-cakes, are attested only once in the whole of Byzantine literature, and that by a desperate tenth-century highland bishop who wanted to bring his plight home to his emperor, Basil II.[13] But *trachanás* is better attested, in a pre-Turkish form. The clue to its etymology lies in the way it was pronounced until recently by Greeks on Imbros (*trachanós*) Euboea (*traganós*) and in the Pontos (*tragáni*).[14] It may be clinched by the tenth-century edition of the *Geoponica*, which claims to have been

---

[9] N. Beldiceanu and Irène Beldiceanu-Steinherr, 'Riziculture dans l'empire Ottomane (XIVᵉ – XVᵉ siècle)', *Turcica*, 11 (1978), p. 15; A. M. Watson, *Agricultural Innovation in the Early Islamic World; the Diffusion of Crops and Farming Techniques, 700–1100* (Cambridge, 1983), pp. 15–19.

[10] Bryer, Study VII, p. 390.

[11] A Tietze, 'Griechische Lehnwörter im Anatolischen Türkischen', *Oriens*, 8 (1955), pp. 204–57; S. Vryonis, Jr., *The Decline of Medieval Hellenism in Asia Minor and the Process of Islamization from the Eleventh through the Fifteenth Century* (Berkeley-Los Angeles-London, 1971), p. 476; A. A. M. Bryer, 'Greeks and Türkmens: the Pontic exception', *Dumbarton Oaks Papers*, 29 (1975), pp. 139–40 = Study V.

[12] L. Robert, 'Les kordakia de Nicée, le combustible de Synnada et les possons scies. Sur les lettres d'un Métropolite de Phrygie au Xᵉ siècle. Philologie et réalités', *Journal des Savants* (juillet-septembre 1961), pp. 115–37; C. Foss, 'Late Antique and Byzantine Ankara', *Dumbarton Oaks Papers*, 31 (1977), p. 42 and n. 53. On Erzurum *tezek*, see R. Curzon, *Armenia* (London, 1854), pp. 110–13; and on Mongol *argols*, see M. Huc, *Travels in Tartary, Thibet, and China during the years 1844–56* (London, n.d.), p. 23. I am grateful to Dr Michael Ursinus for checking the absence of *tezek* and *tarhana* in early and east Turkic vocabularies.

[13] Jean Darrouzès, *Epistoliers Byzantins du Xᵉ siècle* (Paris, 1960), pp. 198–99.

[14] Koukoules, V, p. 40 and n. 3; A. A. Papadopoulos, *Historikon Lexikon tes Pontikes Dialektou*, II (Athens, 1961), s.v. *tragáni*. N. P. Andriotes, *Etymologiko Lexiko tes Koines Neoellenikes* (Athens, 1951), s.v. *trachanás* got the point by deriving it from both Turkish *tarhana* and Byzantine *traganós*.

commissioned by Constantine VII Porphyrogenitus, and gives a recipe for *trágos* which echoes Arabella Boxer's description of the modern porridge:

The making of *trágos*

One must take wheat called Alexandrinos, and one must soak, separate [sc. in nodules] and dry it in the heat of the sun; and in doing that, discard the husks, shells and fibrous parts of the wheat. One must dry and store the *trágos* [made] from *olyra* wheat of superior strain.[15]

The recipe given immediately before that for *trágos* in the *Geoponica* is for *chóndros*, or gruel. In his dream book, Artemidorus equates *chóndros* with *trágos*, and there is a scattering of other references to *trágos*, or Latin *tragum* in Galen and in Dioscorides, the first-century Cilician botanist.[16] Tellingly, the modern Cretan word for *trachanás* is *xynóchondros*. Most important, however, is that Hesychius, the fifth-century Alexandrian lexicographer, defines *chóndros* gruel as *traganós* in his dictionary.[17]

Trachanás to *traganós*, by way of *tarhana* or not, is an easy leap. *Traganós* and *trágos* are clearly related. Greek *trágos* is a goat, and that etymology leads to tragedy. But *trágos* is also spelt, the coarse ancient grain.

I am more cautious about the next leap back, which is from *traganós* and *trágos* to Latin *tracta*, because Athenaeus has the word in Greek, as *trákta*, rather than *traganós* in the third century. In his Deipnosophists, he writes:

In making the so-called *artoláganon* (wheat wafer), a little wine, pepper, and milk are introduced, along with a small quantity of oil or lard. Similarly into *kapýria*, called by the Romans *trákta*, are put mixtures as into the wheat-wafer.[18]

---

[15] Cassianus Bassus Scholasticus, *Geoponica sive De re Rustica Eclogae*, ed. H. Beckh (Leipzig, 1895), p. 95 (III, 8; cf. V, 30, iii; XV, 1, xxxv; XVII, 9). Despite the superior strain (*eugenoûs olýras*) of the 'rice-wheat' here, our porridge is made from coarse grain or spelt in most accounts. Its consistency may be the same as today, but its ancient and medieval quality and taste is irrecoverable: see, for a start, N. Jasny, *The Wheats of Classical Antiquity* (Baltimore, 1944).

[16] Artemidorus Dablianus (Daldanius), *Onirocriticon libri v*, ed. Roger A. Pack (Lepizig, 1963), p. 75; cf. the same's *The Interpretation of Dreams: Oneirocritica*, trans. R. J. White (New Jersey, 1975), p. 52: 'Groats of wheat and spelt, because they provide nourishment, signify profit.' Magnus Hippocratus Cous, et Claudius Galenus, *Opera*, ed. R. Charterius (Chartier) (Paris, 1679), VI, 321; XII, 14F; Pedanius Dioscorides Anazarbeus, *De materia medica*, I (Berlin, 1958), p. 206 (IV, 51).

[17] Hesychius Alexandrinus, *Lexicon*, ed. M. Schmidt, IV (Halle, 1862; reprinted Amsterdam, 1965), p. 293, s.v. *chóndros*.

[18] Athenaeus, *The Deipnosophists*, ed. C. D. Gulick, II (London-Cambridge, Mass., 1967), pp. 32–33 (III, 113). Cf. Marcus Cato, *De Agri Cultura*, LXXVI.

Psellos makes clear that *kapyrídia* were flat dried cakes, from which Charles Perry concludes that *tracta* were dry biscuits or crackers to be eaten with wine.[19] I think we are on a different track here, which I suggest ends up with *ta'amia* or *falafel*, rissoles made today from the dried white broad bean, which are claimed as an ancient Coptic dish. Claudia Roden has an enticing description of them served in her, and Athenaeus's, native Egypt.[20] Egyptian Birmingham Byzantine students have served them fresh-made and Oriental groceries have a packet variety (made in Israel). They are indeed delicious, but are not our porridge.

The justification for a leap from Byzantine *traganós* to Latin *tracta* is, once more, in a recipe. Among the recipes for dormice in honey in the first-fourth century cook-book of the Roman gourmet, G. Gavius Apicius, appear *tracta*. His *tracta* (sometimes mistaken as the first reference to Italian *pasta*) were evidently used to thicken sauces. They are certainly not the *trakta* rissoles of the Deipnosophists. Apicius's *Pultes tractogalatae* is much closer to medieval and modern accounts of our porridge and is, appropriately, served with lamb from the pastures:

> Put a [pint] of milk and a little water in a new saucepan and bring it to the boil over a small fire. Crumble three nodules (*orbiculos*) of dried *tracta* and put the crumbs into the milk. Stir to prevent it burning, adding water. When it is cooked, pour it over lamb.[21]

I am not worried about the fact that Apicius's nodules sound rather large: home-made *trachanás* today comes in all shapes and sizes and must indeed be crumbled before reviving in milk. Apicius also recommends *tracta* for *Pullus tractogalatus* (chicken with *tracta* sauce) and *Porcellus assum tractomelinum* (roast sucking pig with *tracta* and honey stuffing).[22]

Roman *tracta*, Byzantine *traganós*, Turkish *tarhana*, must be the oldest surviving form of pastoralists' packet porridge. I offer a bowl of it to my pastor, Ralph Davis. Now largely dried and packaged in Cyprus, Eleanor and Ralph may find *trachanás* in Greek groceries within half a mile of Balliol, Merton, University College London and, even, of their own University of Birmingham.

---

[19] Perry, *PPC*, 12 (1983), p. 39.

[20] Claudia Roden, *A Book of Middle Eastern Food* (Harmondsworth, 1970), pp. 60–62. I am grateful to Drs Samira Abdel-Kader, Wesam Farag, and Abdulrahman Salem for practical demonstrations of *falafel*.

[21] Apicius, *Decem Libri cui dicuntur de re Coquinari et excerpta a Vinidario conscripta*, ed. Mary E. Milham (Leipzig, 1969), p. 37 (V, i, 3); cf. Barbara Flower and Elisabeth Rosenbaum, *The Roman Cookery Book* (London, 1958), pp. 124–25.

[22] Apicius, ed. Milham, pp. 51, 71 (VI, viii, 13; VIII, vii, 5); ed. and trans. Flower and Rosenbaum, pp. 154–55, 194–95.

2

Currency and Freedom:
Some Problems in the Social History of the Early Middle Ages

H. R. Loyn

There is a special delight and also a corresponding difficulty in contributing an essay to a volume that honours a scholar whose range is as wide as R. H. C. Davis's. His work has illumined so many aspects of medieval history that there is inevitable agony of choice to decide which theme to approach and to attempt to exploit. He has shown himself a master both of the precise, pointed essay that makes positive addition to knowledge and also of the wider interpretative book or essay that makes positive addition to thought. A note on the current attitude to the sokeman of the Danelaw, the latest view on Ethelred or Cnut, or an essay on who after all were the Normans might be equally appropriate. There are some matters, however, of underlying concern to nearly all the themes that he has made distinctively his own, and it is in relation to two of these that the following paper is constructed. For currency and freedom haunt us when we turn to so many of the social problems of the age that runs from the end of the Roman Empire in the West to the central Middle Ages of the twelfth and thirteenth centuries.

It is more than fifty years since Marc Bloch in the very first number of the *Annales d'histoire économique et sociale* declared that what was needed for the serious student of the early Middle Ages was a better understanding of the currency and of freedom.[1] With his usual perspicacity he recognised similarities in the type of evidence associated with both themes, a patchiness and uncertainty that defied easy synthesis. He also recognised that there was an element of close relationship between the two themes, again not easy to define and variable from century to century and community to community.

Our concern will be primarily with the manifestation of the relationship in England, especially in the later Anglo-Saxon period, and a fine text which serves as a suitable starting-point for discussion occurs in the *Rectitudines Singularum Personarum*, a statement in Anglo-Saxon of the

---

[1] M. Bloch, *Annales*, 1 (1929), 256. Bloch returned time and time again to the problems of freedom and slavery as will be seen in his posthumously collected papers *Mélanges Historiques* (Paris, 1963), some of which are translated in *Slavery and Serfdom in the Middle Ages* ed. W. R. Beck, (Berkeley and Los Angeles, 1975).

rights and duties of the inhabitants of a great estate, surviving in a manuscript of the later eleventh century but referring to pre-Conquest conditions.[2] We are told that the cottar's right varied according to the custom of the estate, that in some he had to work for his land each Monday throughout the year or three days each week at harvest time and that in others he worked all through August, keeping an acre of corn or half-an-acre of wheat for his own use together with the allotment made to him by the lord's servant or the reeve. He did not pay rent for his land and was expected to have at least five acres. He was also instructed to give his hearth-penny on Holy Thursday (Ascension Day) even as each freeman ought. Church dues were to be paid at Martinmas.[3] The revealing phrase is 'even as each freeman ought' (*ealswa ælcan frigean men gebyreð*). It was the mark of a freeman that he paid his proper taxes.

We deal, of course, with a period of history that for long stretches knew no true taxation and that for shorter but still significant stretches knew no true currency. How then do we approach these highly complicated matters of currency and freedom? Is it legitimate to attempt to reconsider them together? Let us start by disentangling them and treating each in turn. In many ways the problem of the currency presents the more practical and straightforward side of the picture. There are three points at which investigation of the European currency has improved and refined acceptable conclusions over the last generation and we are now better aware of the dramatic changes in the seventh century, the stabilization of the late eighth and the surge forward that took place in the late tenth and early eleventh.

The last quarter of the seventh century witnessed one of the most startling developments in Western European monetary history. Put at its simplest Western Europe ceased to rely on gold for its native minted currency and ceased substantially to strike a regular gold coinage. This did not mean to say that the area ceased to know and value gold. Indeed gold coins from Byzantium and from the Moslem world continued to circulate: but native rulers and native ecclesiastical princes did not find it to their taste nor in their interest to strike their own gold coins.[4]

England was affected by this phenomenon as well as the Continent

---

[2] F. Liebermann, *Die Gesetze der Angelsachsen*, vol. i (Halle, 1903), pp. 444–53; a good translation in *English Historical Documents*, vol. ii, ed. D. C. Douglas and G. W. Greenaway (London, 1953), pp. 813–16.

[3] Liebermann, p. 446, *Rectitudines* 3.4.

[4] There is a good recent discussion of the problem as seen in England by Ian Stewart 'Anglo-Saxon Gold Coins' *Scripta Nummaria Romania: Essays presented to Humphrey Sutherland*, ed. R. A. G. Carson and C. M. Kraay (London, 1978), pp. 143–72. Dr. Stewart points out that the end of English gold coinage in the seventh century came swiftly, though with some uncertainty about boundaries with silver *denarii* (pp. 152–3). D. M. Metcalf, *Coins and the Archaeologist*, ed. John Casey and Richard Reece (B.A.R., 1974), pp. 215–6, has aired the possibility that the disappearance of gold may have occurred earlier than is normally assumed, perhaps in the 660s or even a shade earlier.

and English numismatists in their concern for accurate interpretation of the Sutton Hoo and Crondall finds have secured genuine advance in our understanding of it.[5] For we know now that England, to meet first royal and then the new ecclesiastical needs after a long period with no native coinage whatsoever, revived the use of coins towards the end of the sixth century and further, from the early seventh century to about 670, struck a native coinage in gold. The Sutton Hoo coins, it so happens, were all struck in Continental mints from all parts of Merovingian Frankia, but the coin habit was established. Evidence has accumulated to suggest a large tract of country in the south-east and east of England fully accustomed to the use of coin with a dominant mint at London. The likelihood is that the striking was substantial, much more substantial than a simple concentration on the number of coins surviving would allow. The number of known dies as distinct from the number of coins was considerable.[6] By mid-century much of newly Christianized England was once again experienced in the use of gold currency of respectable quality, increasingly in demand for royal courts, gift-exchanges, ecclesiastical needs, a universal medium of exchange enough to take bishops to Rome, ambassadors to Paris, or to buy books at Lyons. But then within one generation, at a time when by apparent paradox English ecclesiastical activity reached a peak, there occurred this dramatic and quite abrupt change, the flight from gold. Why should this be?

The natural and surely correct tendency has been to associate this monetary move with wide-ranging alterations in the balance of European political and economic power. Henri Pirenne attributed the change directly to Moslem advance.[7] Native gold currency may have dwindled to a mere trickle but Byzantine and Moslem gold continued to circulate. Gold currency was associated with inter-regional trade on a world scale and specifically with control of the Mediterranean. Others, including Bloch himself, threw more weight on technical reasons, interpreting the crisis of the late seventh century as a culmination of the process of steady drain of bullion to the east. The quantity of gold in the

---

[5] C. H. V. Sutherland, *Anglo-Saxon Gold Coinage in the Light of the Crondall Hoard* (Oxford, 1948) remains a standard guide. Modifications to chronology have come about largely through work on the Merovingian series, notably that by Jean Lafaurie 'Le Trésor d'Escharen' *Revue Numismatique*, VI serie 11, pp. 153–210, and by the application of his findings to the Sutton Hoo coins by John Kent, *The Sutton Hoo Ship Burial*, vol. i, ed. Rupert Bruce-Mitford (London, 1975), pp. 578–653, with important ancillary information by W. A. Oddy and M. J. Hughes and historical analysis by Stuart Rigold and P. V. Hill.

[6] Sutherland, pp. 60ff., and also in his later survey *English Coinage, 600–1900* (London, 1973), p. 4.

[7] H. Pirenne, *Mahomet and Charlemagne* (London, 1939), especially pp. 107–17. An influential statement on the role of gold had been made by Marc Bloch 'Le problème de l'or au moyen âge', *Annales*, 5 (1933), pp. 1–34.

West, argued Bloch, should be thought of as a sack to be emptied rather than as a field to be tilled. Again arguments have been half-formulated (but not fully worked out) to represent the currency changes in terms of developments in state authority in the West, a switch from a Merovingian world still recognisably Roman as Byzantium was Roman, to a new early 'Carolingian' rusticated West. To Pirenne's dramatic isolation of the fall of Carthage to the Moslems in 698 as the symbolic end of the ancient Classical World was countered the victory of Pippin the Old, Mayor of the Palace of Austrasia, ancestor of Charlemagne, at Tertry in 687, a swing away from the golden Mediterranean to the silver-loving German. The most productive line of general thought today, as I see it, is the more purely economic and agrarian which reads the currency change as a final stage in the ruralization of the West, a long continuous process from the second to the eighth century AD, from Roman villa to medieval manor, with the peasant fixed on his plot under the legal fictions of the late Roman agrarian laws in some areas and under modifications of Germanic custom in others. We move firmly in the eighth century into a recognizably medieval world, into a world of a so-called denarial economy, an economy of pence.[8]

Within that new world there appeared the second of our monetary phenomena that demands some consideration. The successor native silver currencies that overlapped with gold and finally triumphed were initially far from impressive. There was a degree of artistic merit, notably in the traders' series used between Frisia and England, but overall the coinage was not of high standard. To judge from surviving coins alone economic prospects in early eighth-century Europe were bleak. Reform came, and with it a straightforward association of political and economic stability, in the reign of Charles the Great (768–814). Already in 755 or soon after his father, Peppin the Short, had sanctioned a revision of the currency which resulted in the production of larger, thinner silver coins, near the size of what came to be the normal silver *deniers* or pennies of the Middle Ages. He also introduced the custom (at this stage no more than custom) of placing the king's initials R.P. (*Rex Pippinus*) or R.F. (*Rex Francorum*) on the obverse. He standardized the weight of the pound of silver at 327 grains from which the moneyers were expected to strike 264 silver pence (240 plus 10%), that is to say 22 sous or shillings of 12 pence, of which the moneyer might be expected to retain one and the royal officers another. Charles himself carried the reform further. He increased the weight of the pound of silver by 50%, to 491 grains, a standard which remained in force to the time of the French Revolution, and he acknowledged and

---

[8] A clear general account is to be found in R. Latouche, *Les origines de l'économie occidentale* (Paris, 1956), translated E. M. Wilkinson, *The Birth of Western Economy* (London, 1961).

authorized the value of the sou or shilling, no coin but a unit of account, at the rate of 12 pence a shilling. What was to remain the natural currency for much of the West for the following millenium and more, pounds, shillings and pence, can be traced back firmly to the time of the early Carolingians. Little gold was struck. This was essentially a silver currency, though the rate of exchange, 12 to 1, silver to gold, was employed in many accounting devices.[9]

At the same time as these Carolingian reforms, even possibly preceding it in some ways, there was a major reform of the English currency. Two minor Kentish kings, Heaberht and Ecgberht, seem to have initiated it, but the process was carried through by the great Offa of Mercia and, as Mr Christopher Blunt has taught us, it was during Offa's reign (757–96) that the larger, thinner penny appeared 'which was to remain effectively the sole denomination in England (outside Northumbria) for the next five hundred years'.[10] In both Carolingian Europe and in the England of King Offa similar economic needs prompted similar political reactions from powerful authorities, the creation of a stable, and incidentally at its best beautiful, silver currency, well adapted to the needs of a ruralized but not unprosperous West where the dominant institutions were kingship and landlordship and where marketing was intense but local. Royal theocracy and the medieval manor are the two concise phrases historians use to describe institutions; and the manor was indeed both a centre of production and a centre of exchange.

The final phenomenon we need to consider manifests itself naturally in the new institutional moulds, particularly in relation to the English currency. A generation of able numismatists, inspired by Sir Frank Stenton and ably led by Christopher Blunt and the late Professor Dolley, have uncovered a rather special development in the history of the coinage in England. From the end of the reign of Edgar to the Conquest and beyond (for political change only scratched the surface of economic reality) England enjoyed a managed currency of unusual sophistication and precocity.[11] There was a systematic change of

[9] P. Grierson provides the best account of the coinage of Charles the Great in 'Money and Coinage under Charlemagne', *Karl der Grosse*, vol. i, ed. W. Braunfels (Dusseldorf, 1965), pp. 501–36. Grierson comments (p. 501) that the division of the pound into twenty sous of twelve deniers apiece antedated the reign of Charles. See also *The Carolingian Coins in the British Museum*, ed. R. H. M. Dolley and K. F. Morrison (London, 1966).

[10] C. E. Blunt, 'The Coinage of Offa', *Anglo-Saxon Coins*, ed. R. H. M. Dolley (London, 1961), p. 39.

[11] R. H. M. Dolley's work remains fundamental to our understanding of the late Anglo-Saxon coinage. A memorial volume for Dolley edited by Mark Blackburn will bring together current thought. Important introductions to the problems include C. S. S. Lyon, 'Some Problems in interpreting Anglo-Saxon Coinage', *A.S.E.*, 5 (Cambridge, 1976), pp. 173–224, and D. M. Metcalf, 'Continuity and Change in English Monetary History, c. 973–1086, pt. 1', *British Numismatic Journal*, 50 (1980), pp. 20–49, and pt. 2 B. N. J., 51 (1981), pp. 52–90.

coinage, referred to in Domesday Book as a *renovatio monetae*. The money was changed, coins were recalled and reminted, at regular intervals from 973, about every six years initially falling back to every two or three under the Confessor. The king took profit when the moneyers paid for their dies, at times at regional die-cutting centres but increasingly at one main workshop at London. There were some sixty or seventy mints, some large and more or less in permanent operation, some temporary only. Standards were maintained by a rigorous control of dies and by ferocious legal penalties.[12] Elsewhere in Europe coinage did not reach the same standard, though in Germany and the Low Countries similar efforts were made. Attempts to reduce the numbers of mints to nine in ninth-century Frankia had failed and feudal debasement became the order of the day. The fortunate combination of effective royal authority over a relatively compact and defined kingdom, technical achievement, and a secure economic base in agriculture and the wool trade to Flanders prompted successful refinement and organization of currency in late Anglo-Saxon England.

The work of the last generation has enabled us to understand a little better these critical developments in the history of the currency. The flight from gold has been placed firmly in the context of the move away from concentration of aristocratic wealth in the hands of some few men and institutions, royal courts and the great churchmen, in Merovingian Europe. The stabilization of the silver Carolingian currency has been associated with the stabilization of a rural economy under royal leadership. The refinements of the late tenth and early eleventh centuries, notably in late Anglo-Saxon England have been linked to institutional growth within feudal monarchies. The penny and the writ are the two planks in the platform of those who speak for strength in the English monarchy. Yet what has this to do with freedom? Were Bloch's instincts right or wrong in attempting to associate the two? Here we tread on delicate ground indeed. Freedom can be, and is to us, a sophisticated concept bred from a highly sophisticated political and legal organisation. There is an immense range of acknowledged semantic and significant meaning to the term. In the early Middle Ages there were the same difficulties of range. *Liber* and *nobilis* were often closely linked and even used as virtual synonyms.[13] Words denoting freedom had the tang of nobility to them. Responsibility and freedom were also intimately associated: more was expected from a freeman than from others. And it is too easily forgotten that unfreedom also had

---

[12] H. R. Loyn, *Anglo-Saxon England and the Norman Conquest* (London, 1962), pp. 122–24.

[13] L. Génicot, 'La noblesse au moyen âge dans l'ancienne "Francie": continuité, rupture, ou evolution', *Comparative Studies in Society and History*, 5 (Ann Arbor, 1962), pp. 52–9. Translation in *Lordship and Community in Medieval Europe*, ed. F. L. Cheyette (N.Y. and London, 1967), pp. 128–36.

a very wide range of meaning, openly expressed in the laws in terms of degrees of servitude, half-free, *coliberti, laets,* thralls, *theows,* and slaves. The earliest English laws to survive, dated from the early seventh-century, refer to no fewer than three grades of slave-woman attached to a *ceorl* for whom compensation is due if a man unlawfully lies with them, six shillings for the first grade, 50 pence for the second, and 30 pence for the third.[14] The diversity is vast indeed when one considers the whole wealth of experience of early medieval Europe. Distinctions of the first order exist, for example, in real as well as in terminological terms between the chain-gang type of slavery in urban Roman settings, the *familia rustica* of Rome, gangs of slaves who cultivated great estates on the grand scale for aristocratic landowners, and the household thralls of the settled agrarian communities of north-west Europe or the new colonizing ventures to the Northern Isles of Scotland, the Faroes, Iceland and points even further west.

Yet in slowly Christianized Western society, in spite of all the diversity, some tenuous but clear legal threads help to illuminate the path of freedom. A freeman was he who was entitled in his social group to bear arms in his own defence and in defence of his community. A freeman was he who was entitled to take part in legal deliberations, in the court life of his locality, to judge issues, above all to testify. A freeman was a man whose oath was judged of value. And a freeman was he who paid as a freeman should; church dues, regular alms, liturgical dues, payments for Rome, secular dues, geld against the Danes, geld to support the army. It may be that in recent years we have made most advance towards understanding this problem of freedom by an awareness that, not only in England but especially in England, social development had moved far along the path from the idea of a free kinsman to the idea of a free subject. A freeman was increasingly thought of not as a simple member of a small kin group but as a member of a territorial group that was not only a fighting group but a paying group. Some of the incongruities of the early medieval world as well as those of high feudal society can be resolved in terms where the ideal expresses service in warlike forms but the reality involves payment.

At the simplest level therefore one can see how the association of coinage and freedom is easily made. In elaborate territorial communities the expression of the responsibilities and duties of freemen was barely possible without the use of currency. There are deeper levels also where modern investigation is proving helpful. The English situation again provides something of a touchstone. The older basic interpretation of the English social scene was of a movement

---

[14] Liebermann, vol. i, Ethelbert 16, p. 4: gif wið ceorles birelan man geligeþ, VI scillingum gebete; æt þære opere ðeowan L scetta; æt pare priddan XXX sceatta.

whereby a peasantry originally free was transformed to dependence in the face of rising kingship and lordship in secular society and in the church. The process was still incomplete in the eleventh century. The villeins and the bordars and the cottars of Domesday Book might be heavily encumbered by lordly rights and dues but they were still legally free in contrast to the many slaves, free and therefore subject to the many obligations that lay on the freeman. The weakness of the interpretation lay in its failure always to stress the presence of powerful lordships over the soil even in the earliest days of the Anglo-Saxon kingdoms but behind it was an assumption, still substantially acceptable, of a relatively simple process of expanding and deepening agrarian settlement from c.600 to 1066 with a lull in the eighth and ninth centuries. The simplicity itself, insofar as it ever existed, is now disappearing. We hear of impermanence as well as permanence in agrarian settlement, of multiple estates at a very early stage, of flexibility of settlement pattern.[15] Some evidence has been brought forward to suggest shifting rather than growing settlement with the somewhat unexpected result that more of a dynamic is ascribed to kingship and secular lordship in the early Saxon period. In those early days kingdoms most certainly did not in the strict sense embrace wholly coherent populations. The social groups of the eighth-century Tribal Hidage retained their identity late.[16] Secular lords with free dependants, variously burdened, helped to knit together a complex social fabric which still relied heavily on free kinsmen groups. Freedom as well as unfreedom had many gradations. We touch on one of the strangely neglected problems in modern historiography, the transition from classical slavery to medieval serfdom. Bloch laid down the challenge here again when he argued in a classic essay, published posthumously in 1947, that serfdom was a new, an original, creation even though some of the servile impositions laid on the peasantry in early medieval Europe were rooted in the law of Rome.[17] There have been few to take up the challenge and there are many fuzzy intermediate areas both in terminology and chronology. *Servus*, alas, can mean slave or serf according to context and retains its fearsome ambiguity at least until the twelfth-century. The chronology is exceedingly complex. Classical slavery did not disappear with the Germanic invasions and the Germans brought with them their own heavily negative view of the unfree as men deprived of rights to arms and to counsel. The focal point of interest and discussion lies in the Carolingian period. We all remember

---

[15] *Medieval Settlement: continuity and change*, ed. P. H. Sawyer (London, 1976), especially G. R. J. Jones, 'Multiple Estates and Early Settlement', pp. 15–40.
[16] Wendy Davies and Hayo Vierck, 'The context of the Tribal Hidage: Social Aggregates and Settlement Patterns', *Frühmittelalterliche Studien*, 8 (1974), pp. 223–93.
[17] Marc Bloch, 'Comment et pourquoi finit l'Esclavage Antique', *Annales*ESC (1947), pp. 30–40.

Eileen Power's magnificent picture of Bodo, the Carolingian peasant, in *Medieval People*.[18] Tied to the soil, the heir of the Roman *colonus* not the slave, he fed himself and was responsible for a multiplicity of free obligations: field work, hand-work, plough-work, army dues and services at wood and wine, poll-tax, rents in produce. Slaves continued to exist in the Carolingian empire but were comparatively few in number. Military, social and to some extent religious trends were against them. Bodos predominated. As Eileen Power said with characteristic charm and strength 'History is largely made up of Bodos!'[19] It is indeed a question of preponderance, of heavy preponderance, serf against slave; and the moment when the social process tilted decisively in the favour of the serf appears to have been in the eighth-century, in Carolingian Europe. In a mysterious way this is associated with our currency changes. Classical slavery as a dominant institution seems to depart from the West with the native gold currency.[20]

In this respect England provides both parallels and contrasts. The main lines are identifiable, a time of conflict and confusion between burdened freemen, and unfree peasants and slaves. Alfred in his laws made provision for public holidays. The freemen did quite well with twelve days at Christmas, February 15th, March 12th, seven days at Easter and seven after, June 29th, the first week in September, and November 1st. The slaves (*theows*) and the unfree labourers (*esnewyrhtan*) did not so well. They were to have the Wednesdays in the four Ember weeks, but significantly these were specifically to sell what they could of what they had been given or what they could earn in their leisure moments. Slaves could make a profit; and freedom could be bought.[21]

Perhaps more than anything else the Scandinavian complications affected the scene. The Vikings were slavers and accustomed to slavery in their social institutions and in their agrarian practices. They adapted themselves to English customs and were in time assimilated but slavery persisted both in English England and in the Danelaw, negative and Germanic, to merge finally into drab uniform villeinage to all appearance under the impact of the great inflation of 1180–1220.[22] Already by 1066 however, slaves were heavily in the minority among the peasantry and became increasingly vestigial in the Anglo-Norman world. Two social processes, colonization and urbanization, helped to accelerate the decline; both are much bound up in matters concerning

---

[18] Eileen Power, *Medieval People* (London, 1924): 'The Peasant Bodo', pp. 1–23.
[19] *Ibid.*, p. 23.
[20] Latouche, *The Birth of Western Economy*, pp. 120–24, and 129–31.
[21] Liebermann, vol. i, Alfred 43, p. 75: *English Historical Documents*, vol. i, ed. Dorothy Whitelock (London, 1955, second ed. 1979), p. 416.
[22] P. D. Harvey, 'The English Inflation of 1180–1220', *P.P.*, 61 (1973), 3–30.

coinage and currency, and yet neither has received adequate attention in relation to problems affecting these subtle gradations between slavery and serfdom.

Colonization presents many puzzles and apparent paradoxes. Some of the best attested evidence for slavery comes from colonizing ventures. This is especially true of the Scandinavian, Moslem and Magyar outbursts of the Viking Age, but may also reflect conditions in the massive folk-wandering of the fifth and sixth centuries. Iceland presents a particularly interesting example. Slaves from the Celtic world, the Hebrides, Ireland and Wales helped to bring fresh land under cultivation in the inhospitable North and it is interesting to note that modern work on bloodgroups helps to confirm the presence of substantial Celtic elements within the modern population.[23] In a rough crude way slave labour was needed to open up new lands but only of course as long as discipline could be maintained. And yet when we turn further to the eleventh and twelfth centuries, times of general expansion, our records tell a different story. Assarting, taking in land from the waste, the opening up of the Black Forest, perhaps even the bordars of Domesday Book, certainly the tenancies held of great houses in the Île de France, the hôtises, the Germain *Hufe*, all leave evidence of colonizing enterprise; and the colonisers under a mixture of strong dominical pressure and protection often win their freedom. Grant of free status to the unfree was often the bait to uproot.[24]

The apparent paradox of colonising encouragement of slavery and colonising urge towards freedom is easily resolved and the resolution is directly associated with the state of the currency. In the early days before coins flowed freely at local level (and this varied greatly from the sixth to the twelfth century even in the tightly-knit West) unfreedom was emphasized as new land was taken in. Colonisation stressed the breach between the warrior protectors and the tillers of the soil. As society settled and developed, and especially in Bloch's 'Second Feudal Age', c.1050–1250, freedom was the gift to the enterprising; and currency is the best symbol and index in time and space of the processes of settlement and development. Lordship was more elaborate, more divorced from the soil, often non-resident, more anxious for profit, more attuned to expression of profit in hard cash. It is recognised, of course, that such a view implies a developing society rather than a shifting society, a Western Europe where more land was under

---

[23] A good account of the British evidence and of the possibilities and limitations is given by T. W. Potts, 'History and Blood-Groups in the British Isles', *Medieval Settlement*, ed. P. H. Sawyer (London, 1976), pp. 236–53; the Icelandic data is discussed on pp. 250–1. The basic work was done by A. E. Mourant and his collaborators, *The Distribution of Human Blood-Groups* (London, 1954) and *The Distribution of the Human Blood-Groups and other Polymorphisms* (Oxford, 1976).

[24] G. Duby, *Rural Economy and Country Life in the Medieval West* (London, 1968), p. 218.

cultivation, a greater population maintained and fed, and more and more elaborate means of organisation in force for keeping order, supporting kingship, stabilising courts and mintage, the striking and regulating of currency.

The concept of a developing society brings into play another important social theme, the process of urbanisation. The tag 'Stadtluft macht freie' haunts us when we turn to the medieval scene, but there is more to it than that. Ancient cities flourished on slavery, though these cities, as we are often reminded, were not as much centres of production as centres for consumption, for conspicuous expenditure. The difference comes with the economic base. Where the base is overwhelmingly agrarian the town represents a long stride forward in the organisation of human society. Clues appear from the beginning of our records of the early Middle Ages. Take, for example, the practical matter of providing good witness for sale and purchase, the process of vouching to warranty. Barbarian lawcodes, notably among the Anglo-Saxons, show a demand for definition of places where good witness can be obtained. By the tenth century England had many little towns, scattered among the community, fortified, with a court, good witness, a market and a mint where coins were struck. As society grew more peaceful local marketing became more complex, and an important social development began to take place. From about 900 onwards an increasing number of men and women came to owe their position in society less to status and more and more to function. Charlemagne had already clearly anticipated when he instructed his stewards that they should see that his estates were provided with 'good workmen, namely blacksmiths, goldsmiths, silversmiths, shoemakers, turners, carpenters, shield-makers, fishermen, falconers, soapmakers, brewers, that is people who knew how to make beer, cider, perry or any other suitable beverage, bakers to make bread for our use, netmakers who can make good nets for hunting or fishing or fowling, and all the other workmen too numerous to mention'.[25] Aelfric's ploughman might well lament that his lot was harder because he was not free, but the teacher's concern was with his function as a ploughman – and so with the fisherman, hayward, bee-keeper, cheese-maker, and other rural craftsmen and specialists.[26] The complexity and concentration on function were exaggerated in the towns of late Anglo-Saxon England and indeed throughout continental Europe. New or newly flourishing urban communities were a vital element in the elaborate processes of social change that end with the disappearance of slavery. Let me point a contrast. In Merovingian Frankia, gold-loving and gold-using, coins were struck at something like 2,000 separate places, churches, villas,

---

[25] Capitulary *De Villis*, cl. 45 in H. R. Loyn and John Percival, *The Reign of Charlemagne* (London, 1975), p. 70.
[26] *Ælfric's Colloquy*, ed. G. N. Garmonsway (London, 1939).

vici, abbeys, as well as declining Roman towns, places served by a network of slaves and dependants tied to the soil. In late Anglo-Saxon England there were indeed some 60–70 minting-places but all of borough status, where inhabitants were substantially free. Function not status was the determining mark of social position.

It is appropriate to finish with a comment on one aspect of late Anglo-Saxon society that again is somewhat neglected. The general flow of social movement in England is now interpreted in a straightforward manner. It is seen as a predominantly agrarian society slowly recovering from disaster in the sixth century, Christianised and stabilised in the seventh and eighth centuries and suffering a time of tribulation and doubt with the Danish invasion and successes of the late ninth. The recovery under Alfred and his successors is variously interpreted according to continental analogues, Carolingian and late or Ottonian and early! The Danes were absorbed. The Benedictine revival, led by St Dunstan, was deep-rooted and deeply effective. The coronation of Edgar at Bath, a mere eleven years after that of Otto the Great at Rome, indicates the continental parallel. The institutional growth of late Anglo-Saxon England, its managed currency, local government and advanced vernacular culture have been matter for strong comment. There also exists a formidable corpus of dependable record of manumission side by side with evidence of an effective reformed currency.[27] Bishop Theodred freed the men of Tillingham. Penal slaves on episcopal land were freed by bishop Aelfsige. Aelfgifu freed the penal slaves at Risborough. Archbishop Aelfric freed those who had been reduced to slavery. Thurketil Heyng freed his men – those who would work for it. A great Anglo-Saxon lady, Aethelgifu, whose will, dating from the 980s, was brought to light only in 1948, manumitted at least sixty individuals, along with two households and six sets of children.[28] Gradations are recognised: those who are half-free, penal slaves, freedmen.[29] It seems likely that the disruptions and hardships caused by Scandinavian invasions had led to a temporary increase in slavery that the more settled and literate tenth century put to rights. Men were freed in wills, at crossroads, above all in return for an

---

[27] Dorothy Whitelock, *Anglo-Saxon Wills* (Cambridge, 1930) provides the best collection of evidence (no. 1, Theodred's will; no. 4, bishop Ælfsige's; no. 8, Ælfgifu's; no. 18, archbishop Ælfric's; no. 25, Thurketil Heyng's; and *passim* for references to freed penal slaves and others.

[28] Dorothy Whitelock discusses manumission generally in her comment on this document. *The Will of Æthelgifu*, ed. Lord Rennell (Roxburghe Club, Oxford, 1968), pp. 34–5. She notes both the large number of slaves bequeathed by Æthelgifu and her special concern to free the younger generation.

[29] D. Pelteret, 'The *Coliberti* of Domesday Book', *Studies in Medieval Culture* XII (Toronto, 1979), pp. 43–54, suggests that *coliberti*, a term restricted in use geographically to Wessex and Western Mercia and a possible equivalent of *geburas*, represented tenants who ranked as the lowest in the hierarchy of those of free status.

acceptable sum in good silver. Solid silver and trustworthy currency make free.

Work from many sources and many disciplines is serving to erect the basic structures. Modifications in climate are taken seriously. Place-name experts refine our views of the two great migrations of early medieval England, the Anglo-Saxon and the Scandinavian. Historical geographers link the whole European world and teach us to look for multiple estates with a tendency to fission as an important element in settlement patterns. Urban archaeology is helping to make more real the physical picture of the decay of town life in the early period and revival in the tenth and eleventh centuries. Among the main lines of social change that characterised the early Middle Ages proper attention should be paid to the process by which classical slavery disappeared. The division of society into those who fought, those who prayed, and those who worked represented a higher ideal than that represented by the crude division into free and slave.

3

Beyond the Edge of Excavation: The Topographical Context of Goltho★

Steven Bassett

The name Goltho is rightly famous in medieval archaeology. A small civil parish 15 km. east-north-east of Lincoln, it contained the site of a large depopulated village, complete with motte-and-bailey castle and church, in which Mr Guy Beresford excavated extensively in 1970–4. His reports[1] show that from the ninth century a sizeable agricultural community developed on the former site of a Romano-British settlement. A sequence of late Anglo-Saxon manor houses lay within an increasingly strongly fortified enclosure which, during the Norman period, was converted into a motte. Although this manorial centre was abandoned around the middle of the twelfth century, the village continued to be occupied until the fifteenth century.

Mr Beresford's results are of great importance, not least for the light they throw on the origins of medieval rural settlement and on the development of private fortifications in England. What they unavoidably lack is information about the place of the excavated site in the historical development of its district. That is beyond the scope of archaeological excavation. Other sorts of historical evidence, however, may be able to supply the necessary details. This paper is an attempt to use such evidence to reconstruct something of the wider landscape – both tenurial and administrative – in which the village of Goltho stood; and, second, to clarify its status within that area.

Goltho does not appear in Domesday Book or in the early twelfth-century Lindsey Survey. The close ecclesiastical and other ties, however, which it later shows with Bullington adequately demonstrate that Goltho would have lain within the area of that name at the time of the two surveys. Domesday Book records three separate estates at

---

★Ralph Davis himself encouraged me to write this paper, and gave valuable comments on its first draft. It arose out of a day's fieldwork at Goltho, one of many such outings with him from which I have had great benefit and pleasure.

[1] G. Beresford, *The Medieval Clay-Land Village: Excavations at Goltho and Barton Blount*, (Society for Medieval Archaeology Monograph Series, no. 6), 1975; G. Beresford, Goltho: The Development of an Early Medieval Manor *c*. 850–1150 (forthcoming).

Bullington, each held as a manor (Table 1). One, held in 1086 by Odo from Ivo Taillebois, was assessed at 5 bovates. The other two were held by Nigel from the bishop of Durham and by Colsuan from earl Hugh respectively, and were each assessed at 3½ bovates (Map 1).[2]

TABLE 1

Estate	DOMESDAY BOOK (1086)			LINDSEY SURVEY (1115–18)	
	Tenant-in-chief (subtenant)		Bovates	Tenant-in-chief	Bovates
BULLINGTON	Bishop of Durham (Nigel)		3½	Bishop of Durham	8
BULLINGTON	Earl Hugh (Colsuan)		3½	Earl Richard	6
BULLINGTON	Ivo Taillebois (Odo)		5	Ranulf Mischin	5
NEWBALL	Earl Hugh (Osbern)		24	Earl Richard	18
APLEY	William de Perci		7 ⎫		
APLEY	William de Perci		7 ⎬	Bishop of Durham	16
APLEY	William de Perci		2 ⎭		
KINGTHORPE	Ivo Taillebois (Odo)		2⅔	Ranulf Mischin	2⅔
KINGTHORPE	Ivo Taillebois (Odo)		7⅓	(omitted)	
KINGTHORPE	Erneis de Burun		2⅓	Geoffrey fitz Payne	2
KINGTHORPE	Rainer de Brimou		3	Ralf de Criol	2¹¹⁄₁₂
STAINFIELD	William de Perci		12 ⎫	Bishop of Durham	24
STAINFIELD	William de Perci		12 ⎭		
			91⅔		84⁷⁄₁₂

Just south of Bullington were three estates at Apley, all consisting of sokeland. Two, assessed at 7 bovates each, belonged to (*in*) Stainfield and Barlings respectively; the third, assessed at 2 bovates, belonged to Bullington.[3] All three were held in 1086 by William de Perci. The bishop of Durham, however, claimed the soke of 2 bovates on the grounds that Aluric, his predecessor at Bullington, had held it, and the wapentake agreed that 'he himself ought to have it as belonging to Bullington'.[4] The bishop was clearly successful in his claim; indeed in 1115–18 the Lindsey Survey shows him as the only holder of land in Apley, with his 2 carucates there clearly representing the three former sokes of 7, 7, and 2 bovates respectively.[5]

There can be no doubt that the existence by 1086 of two or more estates of the same name in one district reflects the earlier fragmentation of a single estate, a process which has for a long time been recognised as a

---

[2] Trans. & ed. C. W. Foster & T. Langley, *The Lincolnshire Domesday and the Lindsey Survey* (Lincoln Record Society, vol. 19) (1924), p. 85, no. 14/57; p. 31, no. 3/8; p. 76, no. 13/26. (One carucate consists of 8 bovates.)

[3] *Lincs. Domesday*, p. 102, nos. 22/18, 22/19, 22/20.

[4] 'Ipse debet habere in Bolintone'. *Lincs. Domesday*, p. 213, no. 69/32.

[5] *Lincs. Domesday*, p. 255, no. 16/2.

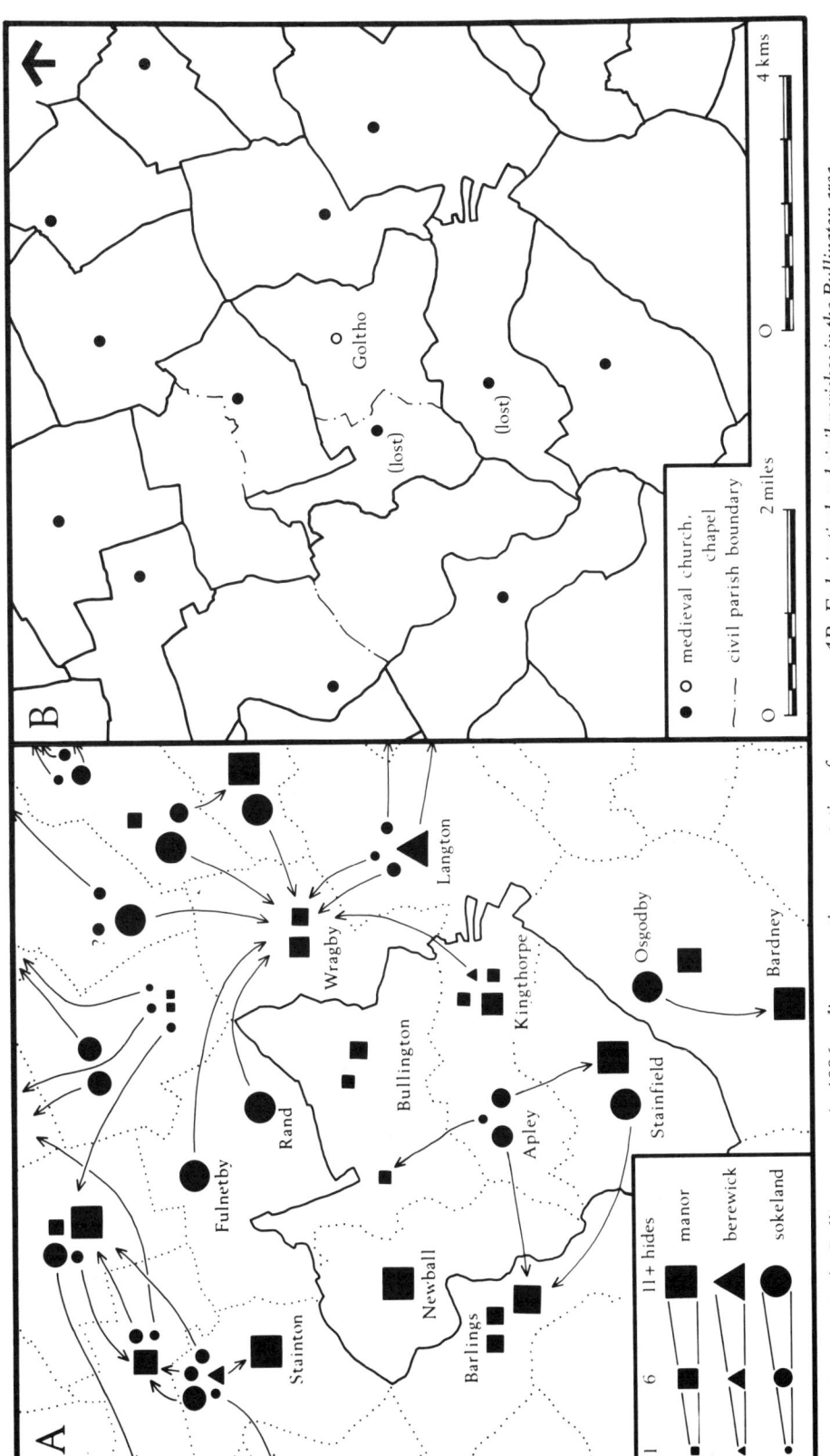

Map 1A. Estates in the Bullington area in 1086: a diagrammatic representation of their relative sizes and of the links between them reported in Domesday Book.

1B. Ecclesiastical and civil parishes in the Bullington area.

common occurrence in many parts of later Anglo-Saxon England.[6] It is therefore clear that the three manors called Bullington once formed parts of the same estate; a similar explanation probably lies behind the existence of three sokes called Apley. There may, however, have been a yet earlier stage in the process of estate fragmentation in this area. One of the three sokes of Apley was anciently subordinate to a Bullington manor, and the details incompletely recorded by Domesday Book and the Lindsey Survey may well show that all three once belonged to Bullington. This would be consistent with the former existence of an estate centred on Bullington which was far more extensive than the combined area of the three Domesday manors of that name. The district called Apley would originally have been part of it, but then, with other outlying areas, would have begun to be broken up into lesser holdings. Some of these would eventually have become manorially independent of Bullington, while others were held to the ancient centre by links of one sort or another, usually as sokes or berewicks.[7] If all the Apley sokeland did once belong to Bullington, then it is likely that its reattachment to the bishop of Durham's manor there by 1115–18 indicates that the latter was the senior of the three Bullington manors, that is the one in which the manor-house and church of the putative original, unfragmented, estate would have lain.

Bullington and Apley lie close to the River Witham, within the catchment area of two sizeable tributaries. In the same area other Domesday estates indicate similar processes of fragmentation. Domesday Book lists four estates called Kingthorpe, three of them manors of 7⅔, 3, and 2⅔ bovates respectively, and the fourth a berewick of 2⅓ bovates which in 1086 was probably attached to Erneis de Burun's manor of Wragby.[8] The four together are likely once to have formed a single estate assessed at 2 carucates.[9] The association of one of these with Wragby might be thought to indicate that the whole area called Kingthorpe had once been subordinate to Wragby. The great majority, however, of that area was, or would soon come to be, in the eastern part of the ecclesiastical parish of Apley, which could prove a significant indication of Kingthorpe's early attachment to Apley and, therefore, to Bullington.[10]

Similarly there were two Domesday estates called Stainfield, just south of Apley, both held by Wiliam de Perci.[11] One was a manor of 12

[6] See, for example, C. C. Taylor, *Dorset* (1970), ch. 2.

[7] These links are best described in F. M. Stenton, 'Types of Manorial Structure in the Northern Danelaw' in ed. P. Vinogradoff, *Oxford Studies in Social and Legal History*, ii (1910), esp. 3–55.

[8] *Lincs. Domesday*, p. 88, no. 14/91; p. 160, no. 40/10; p. 85, no. 14/59; p. 152, no. 34/23.

[9] The four Domesday estates total 15⅔ bovates, ⅓ bovate short of 2 carucates.

[10] Kingthorpe is further discussed below. p. 36.

[11] *Lincs. Domesday*, p. 102, nos. 22/16, 22/17.

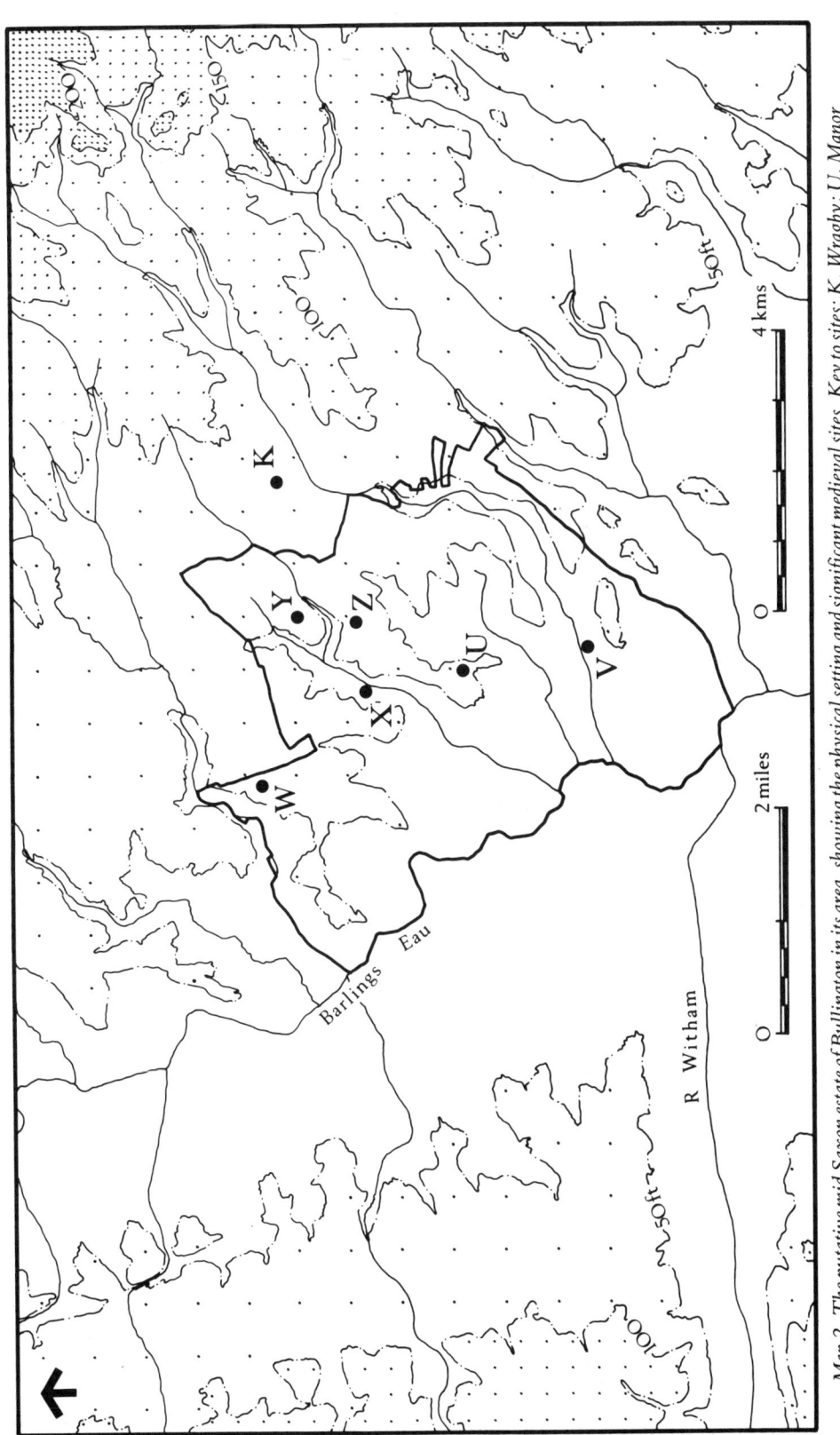

Map 2. The putative mid Saxon estate of Bullington in its area, showing the physical setting and significant medieval sites. Key to sites: K, Wragby; U, Manor Farm, Apley; V, Stainfield Hall and Priory; W, Bullington Hall; X, ringwork in Cocklode Wood; Y, Goltho: the excavated manorial centre and village; Z, Goltho Hall.

bovates. The other was sokeland, also of 12 bovates, which in 1086 was said to belong to Barlings; this was, however, contested successfully by Gilbert de Gant, who also claimed Barlings's soke of 7 bovates in Apley.[12] Yet although Gilbert's son Walter had succeeded him by 1115–18 in his estates at Bardney, Osgodby and Southrey,[13] just to the south of Stainfield, both of these sokes had passed to the bishop of Durham by then. This might mean no more than that the two sokes belonged to the manor of Barlings – one of three whose total assessment was 21 bovates – which in 1086 was held by the bishop of Durham. In 1115–18, however, those three manors were all held by Robert de Haia, who was Walter de Gant's subtenant there for a further 3 bovates.[14] Had the two sokes in question belonged anciently to Barlings, one would certainly have expected them to stay attached to it, in view of the enquiry about them which Domesday Book records. On the contrary, by 1115–18 they were the bishop's, as too was the manor of Stainfield which William de Perci had held in 1086.[15]

From all this one gains the impression that a lot of land to the south of Bullington had an ancient association with that place, even though in most cases the link had been considerably weakened during the long process of estate fragmentation which produced the pattern shown by Domesday Book. One can add greatly to this impression by noting other evidence of several sorts.

First, it is clear from Map 2 that the ecclesiastical parishes of Bullington (with Goltho) and a number of adjacent places together formed a coherent block of land along the north-eastern bank of the River Witham. Barlings Eau, a major tributary of the Witham, gave an obvious western limit to this area; while to the south-east a long, broken ridge between two further tributaries separated the Bullington area from Bardney and its medieval appendages. In general the block of land corresponded to the lower catchment area of three closely adjacent tributaries of the Witham which rise further to the north-east in the area of higher ground dominated by Wragby. Most of the medieval estates within this area have been mentioned already: those at Bullington (including Goltho), Apley, Kingthorpe, and Stainfield. To them must be added one at Newball, lying between Bullington and the river. In 1086 there was a single estate of 3 carucates there, held by earl Hugh of Chester; in 1115–18 his son earl Richard was holding an estate of 2 carucates and 2 bovates there (i.e. 18 bovates), with no other reference made to the place in the Survey.[16] It can be seen that these estates

[12] *Lincs. Domesday*, p. 213, nos. 69/30, 69/31.
[13] *Lincs. Domesday*, pp. 106–7, nos. 24/17, 24/18, 24/19; p. 256, no. 16/7.
[14] *Lincs. Domesday*, p. 241, no. 3/4; p. 242, no. 3/19. These 3 bovates appear to have been overlooked in Domesday Book. Together with the 21 bovates recorded there, they suggest an original, unfragmented estate at Barlings assessed at 3 carucates.
[15] *Lincs. Domesday*, p. 255, no. 16/2.
[16] *Lincs. Domesday*, p. 78, no. 13/45; p. 255, no. 16/1.

together comprised a compact, subrectangular block of land of about 25 square kilometres, whose boundary conformed well to the prevailing natural topography of this part of Lindsey.

A second source of evidence clearly underlines the ancient unity of this amalgamation of eleventh- and twelfth-century estates. All of them lay within the wapentake of Wraggoe, as both Domesday Book and the Lindsey Survey demonstrate. The latter, however, adds some invaluable information about the administrative subdivisions of this and all the other wapentakes of Lindsey. In a rubric beneath the heading *In Wraghehou wapentake* we are told that 'there are reckoned to be 9 hundreds, [and] in each [hundred] 12 carucates of land'.[17] There is of course no guarantee that these hundreds represented anything more than artificial groupings of adjacent estates made for fiscal purposes at some fairly recent point in the past. Certainly that was what Stenton assumed in his Introduction to *The Lincolnshire Domesday and the Lindsey Survey*, while at the same time admitting that he was puzzled by them and unable to account for their origins.[18] Unfortunately there are no Anglo-Saxon documentary references to these estates to indicate by when any of them had gained the assessments which the two Norman surveys list, nor are there such records of other estates in this part of the shire. In other parts of England, however, such administrative and fiscal associations of estates have been found to mirror a much earlier (often mid Saxon) pattern of extensive and as yet unfragmented estates of the sort which may once have surrounded Bullington. The area of an eleventh-century hundred has often proved to be coterminous with a former large estate and the parish of its church.[19]

So it is interesting to note that the total assessment of all the estates in this area which are listed in the Lindsey Survey (Table 1) is 10 carucates and $4^{7}/_{12}$ bovates, an amount which is 1 carucate and $3^{5}/_{12}$ bovates short of 12 carucates; while in Domesday Book the total is 11 carucates and $3^{2}/_{3}$ bovates, only $4^{1}/_{3}$ bovates short. The chief reason for the difference between the two totals is the omission from the Lindsey Survey of one of the three manors which Domesday Book records at Kingthorpe, one of $7^{2}/_{3}$ bovates held in 1086 by Odo of Ivo Taillebois. As Ivo's only other estate in the area, his 5 bovate manor at Bullington, reappears in the later survey with an unchanged assessment,[20] it is most unlikely that the Kingthorpe land is included as part of a different estate.

This is the only omission by the later survey of a Domesday estate, but several changes of assessment are apparent. Most notably, the two

---

[17] *Lincs. Domesday*, p. 255 (folio 21).

[18] Pp. xi–xv; in 'Types of Manorial Structure', pp. 89–90, he suggested that they had been imposed on the Danelaw in the late tenth or early eleventh century.

[19] Ed. R. H. C. Davis, *The Kalendar of Abbot Samson of Bury St Edmunds* (1954), pp. xliv–xlvi.

[20] *Lincs. Domesday*, p. 255, no. 16/10; held then by Ranulf Mischin.

other Bullington manors had increased their assessment – the bishop of Durham's from 3½ bovates to 1 carucate, and the earl of Chester's from 3½ to 6 bovates – while the manor of Newball's had decreased from 3 carucates to 2 carucates and 2 bovates. Very slight changes in the assessment of two of the four estates at Kingthorpe accounted for a decrease of 5/12 bovate. These various alterations within no more than about 30 years may reflect considerable fluidity in the pattern of landholding in the area, or may merely indicate imperfections in one or both of the surveys.[21] In either case it seems that the information which the two surveys contain can be taken to represent advanced stages in the fragmentation of a single extensive estate and the continual, if normally slow, interaction between the many resultant land-units.

As Stenton demonstrated, studying the assessments given by Domesday Book for estates of the same name in Lincolnshire (and elsewhere) clearly shows that, in each case, the whole area of land of that name was originally assessed at a round number of carucates.[22] For example, in Wraggoe wapentake close to Bullington we have already seen that the three estates of Apley had a combined assessment of 2 carucates and the two of Stainfield had one of 3 carucates, while the four at Kingthorpe were together only ⅓ bovate short of 2 carucates.[23] Elsewhere in the wapentake, the six Domesday estates of Hainton were together assessed at 6 carucates,[24] the seven estates of Ludford at 6 carucates,[25] and the five estates of Reasby at 3 carucates.[26] By contrast some estate names only occur once in the Domesday record of this wapentake. For instance, in the area around Bullington, Stainton-by-Langworth was a single estate of 3 carucates, as also were Fulnetby, Newball and Rand.[27]

From all this it seems that assessments must have been imposed on the different estates of Wraggoe wapentake long before 1086, at a time before the processes of fragmentation were far advanced. Otherwise separate parts of a formerly unified area, which by 1086 were often associated with two or more different manors, would not have carried

---

[21] A great many additions and interlineations, some contemporary but most of them probably either later twelfth- or fifteenth-century, occur in the Lindsey Survey. These often provide important explanations of the recorded assessments or give further information about them.

[22] Lincs. Domesday, pp. xi–xiv.

[23] For these, see notes 3, 11, and 8 respectively.

[24] Lincs. Domesday, p. 27, no. 2/23; p. 42, no. 4/46; p. 91, nos. 16/12, 16/14; p. 160, no. 40/9.

[25] Lincs. Domesday, p. 85, no. 14/61; p. 102, nos. 22/21, 22/22, 22/23; p. 117, no. 25/18; p. 161, no. 40/16.

[26] Lincs. Domesday, p. 19, no. 1/37; p. 76, no. 13/25; p. 101, no. 22/13; p. 102, no. 22/15; p. 133, no. 28/26.

[27] Lincs. Domesday, p. 76, no. 13/24; p. 152, no. 34/20; p. 78, no. 13/45; and p. 152, no. 34/21 respectively.

assessments which so often combine to form a neat total of carucates. Further calculations suggest that they were imposed at a time when subdivision had not proceeded so far that the existence of the original extensive estates had been forgotten, (as had clearly happened in most instances by 1086). Indeed it seems certain that, as in other parts of England, those estates had been transformed by 1086 into the hundreds of which each wapentake was composed – or, rather, had lost their territorial identity in every respect except the exercise of hundredal administration. This is borne out by adding together the assessments of all the estates, wapentake by wapentake, which the Lindsey Survey lists, and then comparing each total with the total 'reckoned to be there'. Table 2 shows that in seven of the seventeen wapentakes for which this calculation can be made,[28] the discrepancy between the actual total and the official total is less than two per cent, and in four more it is less than four per cent. So it appears that in almost two-thirds

TABLE 2

	TOTALS		DISCREPANCY		
Wapentake	Reckoned	Actual	+	−	%
1 MANLEY	? 174	179–5½+	? 5–5½		?3.2
2 ASCALOE	90	92–0⁷⁄₃₀	2–0⁷⁄₃₀		2.2
3 LAWRESS	144	133–6		10–2	7.7
4 CORRINGHAM	60	59–6		0–2	0.4
5 AXHOLME	48	? 48–0			0
6 WELL	84	104–6	20–6		19.9
7 WALSHCROFT	96	96–4¹⁄₁₂	0–4¹⁄₁₂		0.4
8 HAVERSTOE	90	89–2⁷⁄₁₂		0–5⁵⁄₁₂	0.8
9 BRADLEY	42–3	59–0⁵⁄₁₂	16–5⁵⁄₁₂		28.3
10 LUDBOROUGH	36	34–7		1–1	3.2
11 YARBOROUGH	168	216–7⅚	48–7⅚		22.6
12 BOLINGBROKE	96	96–2	0–2		0.3
13 GARTREE	72	70–7⅔		1–0⅓	1.4
14 CANDLESHOE	120	122–4½	2–4½		2.0
15 CALCEWATH	120	119–3½		0–4½	0.4
16 WRAGGOE	108	129–4¹¹⁄₁₂	21–4¹¹⁄₁₂		16.6
17 HILL	72	73–2	1–2		1.7
18 LOUTHESK	120	122–6⅓	2–6⅓		2.2
19 HORNCASTLE	78	93–5	15–5		16.6
	?1818–3	1943–1½+	138–6	13–7⅓	

[28] It cannot be done for two more. The actual total for Manley is about 180 carucates, but perishing of the surface of the MS has reduced the rubric to 'There are reckoned to be . . . hundreds and a half'. The entire section on Axholme consists of the statement, 'There are reckoned to be 4 hundreds, [and] in each [hundred] 12 carucates of land. And Nigel de Albeneio holds them in demesne.'

(65 per cent) of the wapentakes of Lindsey the regular pattern of assessment initially established had been maintained into the twelfth century, though perhaps after some revision in a few cases.[29] In a minority, however, that pattern had been badly distorted. The actual total of the assessments of estates in Wraggoe wapentake is 129 carucates and $4^{11}/_{12}$ bovates, far in excess of the reckoned total of 108 carucates. This represents a difference of 16.6 per cent. Discrepancies of between 16 and 29 per cent also occur between the reckoned and the actual totals of another four wapentakes.[30]

Nevertheless, even within these latter it is still possible to reconstruct many of the separate original estates whose extent was perpetuated in the hundreds which the Lindsey Survey records. As we have seen, Bullington was in all probability at the head of one of them.[31] Table 1 shows that Domesday Book assigns 11 carucates and $3^{2}/_{3}$ bovates to a group of thirteen estates in the Bullington area which, on both tenurial and topographical grounds, were closely associated. Of them, only the three at Bullington itself did not have a combined assessment which is a round number of carucates; instead they were assessed at $1\frac{1}{2}$ carucates. It may, however, be possible to raise this figure to almost exactly 2 carucates, thereby in effect producing a total for the whole group of 12 carucates, the assessment of a hundred. The extra $4\frac{1}{2}$ bovates which the bishop of Durham's Bullington estate had gained by 1115–18 presumably did not come from the transfer of a sizeable piece of any adjacent land-unit of which we know,[32] since the descent of each of the Domesday estates here can be fairly satisfactorily accounted for. It is much more likely to represent something else overlooked by the compilers of that survey but noticed in 1115–18.[33] If $4\frac{1}{2}$ bovates can authentically be added to the combined assessment in 1086, its total becomes 12 carucates and $\frac{1}{6}$ bovate, near enough to the exact assessment of a hundred for the difference not to matter.

---

[29] The reckoned total for Bradley is $3\frac{1}{2}$ hundreds and 3 bovates, which suggests that there has been some alteration of the original scheme. In all, five wapentakes are reckoned at so many hundreds and a half, perhaps again indicative of revision.

[30] When the sum of the actual totals for the 19 wapentakes is compared with the sum of their reckoned totals (allowing a maximum of $14\frac{1}{2}$ carucates to Manley and 4 to Axholme), the former is 124 carucates (or just over the equivalent of 10 hundreds) in excess of the latter. According to Darby's calculations, the assessments for Lindsey recorded in Domesday Book amount to 2034 carucates, 91 more than in the Lindsey Survey: H. C. Darby, *The Domesday Geography of Eastern England* (1971), p. 39.

[31] Further study suggests that adjacent estates were centred on Nettleham to the west, Wragby to the north-east, and Bardney to the south.

[32] Whereas the earls of Chester's possession of Newball and another of the Bullington manors may well help to explain their altered assessments. (Newball's fell from 3 carucates to 2 carucates and 2 bovates, while Bullington's rose from $3\frac{1}{2}$ to 6 bovates.)

[33] Cf. the estate of 3 bovates at Barlings (note 14).

The place names of the area also accord well with the concept of an extensive estate which slowly disintegrated during the later Anglo-Saxon period. Bullington is an Old English name meaning 'the estate of *Bula's people',[34] one which is entirely appropriate for a large land-unit in existence before the Scandinavian settlement of eastern England began in the ninth century. The other important place names of this area are all typical of secondary settlement in such an estate, often in woodland or on other underdeveloped land which was being brought into full agricultural use. Apley, 'apple wood', Goltho, 'enclosure where marigold grew', and Stainfield, 'stony open land', may well indicate colonisation of the outer parts of the estate.[35] Kingthorpe, 'the king's farm', and Newball, 'new homestead', may similarly denote small settlements dependent on a neighbouring estate centre.[36]

It is curious that the Old English name Goltho should not appear in Domesday Book. There can be no doubt that at least one of the three Bullington manors listed there was later on called Goltho, and probably two of them.[37] A possible explanation is that the name was of very late formation; but if so, it would be difficult to account for its attachment to *two* estates which were both already manorially independent by 1066. On etymological grounds, moreover, it is a name which seems likely to belong to a much earlier period in the area's history. On the other hand, if those two manors had been formed by the subdivision of a single estate called Goltho (to distinguish it from other parts of the former, unfragmented estate of Bullington), one would expect them to be recorded by that name in Domesday Book and the Lindsey Survey. There may, however, be a simple solution to this problem. Professor Davis has shown that two of the three manors called Bullington in the surveys had been reamalgamated by the late twelfth century, and that they were probably both within the area covered by the modern parish of Goltho.[38] He suggests that, on the abandonment of the manorial site which Mr Beresford excavated, a centre for the united estate was established on a different site, in the vicinity of the present Goltho Hall. This may well have been a new site, located near the common boundary of the two former manors for greater convenience in their administration as one estate. Whether or not it was new, the existing name of the locality, Goltho, would quickly have come to distinguish

---

[34] E. Ekwall, *The Concise Oxford Dictionary of English Place-Names*, fourth ed. (1960), p. 73.
[35] Ekwall, pp. 11, 200, 436. All three are essentially OE names, though Stainfield has a Scandinavianised form.
[36] Ekwall, pp. 278, 339. Both these names show Scandinavian influence: Old Scand. *thorp* is a very common element in the place names of eastern England, and Newball is wholly Old Scand.
[37] R. H. C. Davis, 'Goltho – the manorial history', in Beresford, Goltho: The Development of an Early Medieval Manor.
[38] Davis, *ibid*.

this manorial centre from those of the bishop of Durham and the priory a little to the west at Bullington.

There is another important source of evidence for the history of the medieval estates and settlements of this part of Lindsey. In both its present landscape and the early Ordnance Survey maps there is a great amount of information about the area's physical development. By using the techniques of topographical analysis,[39] it is possible to discover the remains of a framework of roads and fields covering the majority of the area which, allowing for considerable local variations in the natural topography, is consistently rectilinear throughout. Here, as in other parts of England where similar underlying patterns have been identified in the modern landscape,[40] piecemeal alterations and additions to the framework stand out as nonconformities. Occasionally one of these can be dated, thereby providing a *terminus ante quem* (if only a distant one) for the creation of the rectilinear framework itself.[41] Map 3 shows a number of landscape elements which all appear on the Ordnance Survey Six-Inch Survey (first edition) of the area. Almost every field boundary illustrated on the figure lies more or less parallel or at right-angles to all the others in its vicinity. Many of the local roads and tracks, as well as sections of some throughroutes, clearly conform to the same alignments; and where they have now moved away from them, footpaths and field boundaries often continue the lines which mark their former courses.[42] Good examples of this are provided by roads 4, 5, 10 and 13. All of them are discontinuous in the modern landscape, but their earlier routes can be reconstructed with some accuracy from evidence on the ground and on the earlier maps.

The full extent of the survival of this rectilinear framework has not been established. To the south it does not cross the long finger of higher ground which separates the areas dependent on Bullington and Bardney. Again, to the east and north-east the system begins to break down on the lower slopes of the Lincolnshire Wolds. To the north-west, however, it continues well beyond the limits of the study area, perhaps

---

[39] Explained in detail and demonstrated in S. R. Bassett, 'Medieval Lichfield: a topographical review', *Trans. South Staffs. Archaeol. & Hist. Soc.*, 22, 1980–1, (1982).

[40] Bassett, 'Medieval Lichfield', pp. 95–8; W. J. Rodwell, 'Relict Landscapes in Essex', in ed. H. C. Bowen & P. J. Fowler, *Early Land Allotment in the British Isles*, (Brit. Archaeol. Reports, Brit. Series, no. 48) (1978), 89–98; S. R. Bassett, *Saffron Walden: Excavations and Research, 1972–80*, (Council for Brit. Archaeol. Research Report 45) (1983), pp. 5–9 & Fig. 3.

[41] Though, of course, it will not necessarily postdate the establishment of every surviving boundary within the framework; many of them will be much later subdivisions of these early fields.

[42] Boundaries not illustrated on Map 3 are those on markedly different alignments, very often parallel or at right-angles to the nonconformist roads (some of which are also not shown).

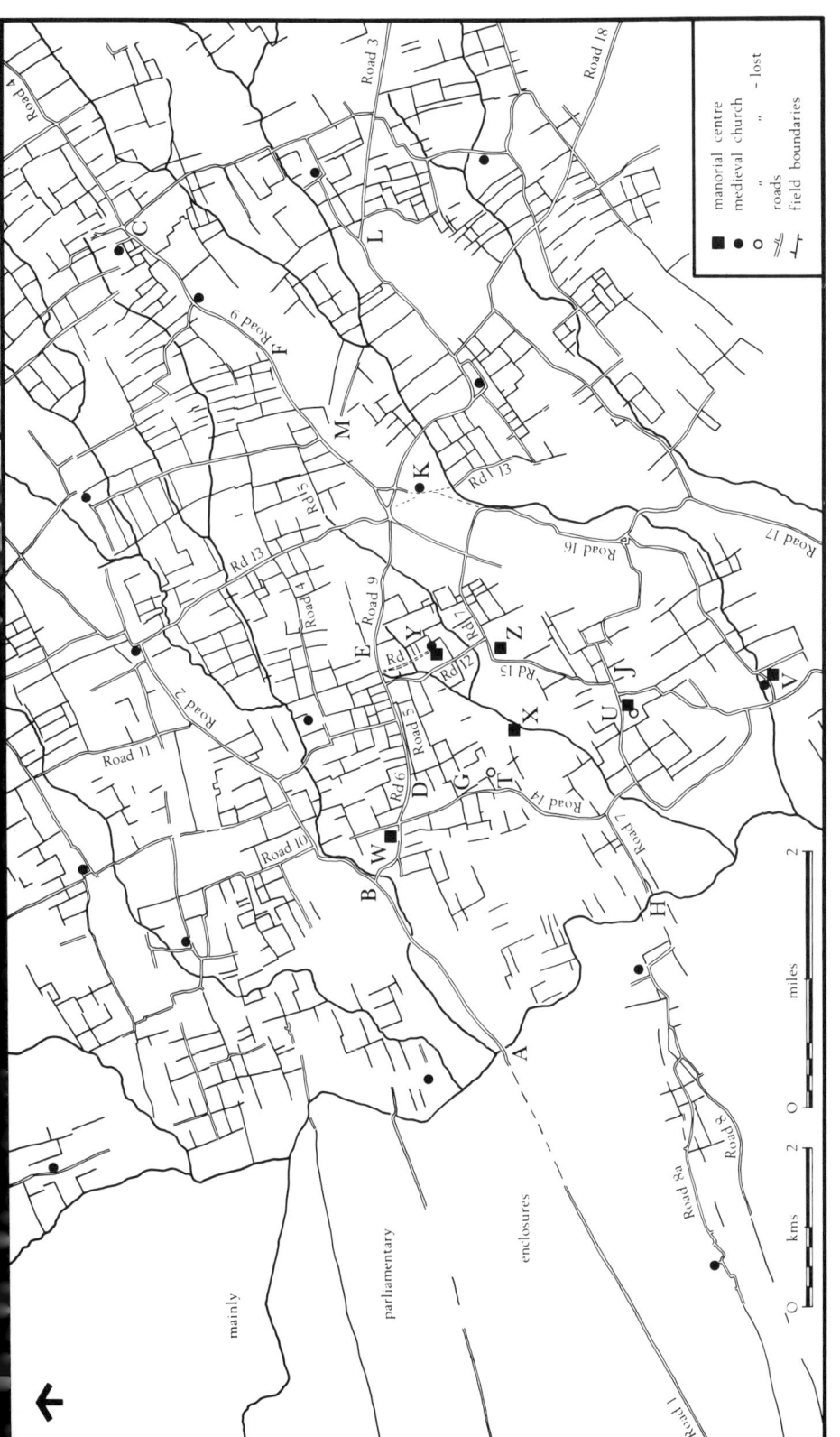

Map 3. Early landscape elements surviving into the late nineteenth century (1883–8) in the vicinity of Bullington and Goltho.

extending over the majority of the Boulder Clay of the southern part of the Clay Vale of Lindsey.[43]

Two or more Roman roads cross the area. Margary described what is well known about them;[44] but more can now be added from topographical analysis. The road which he labelled 27, running from Lincoln to Burgh-le-Marsh via Bullington, is in fact two roads, numbered 1 and 3 on Map 3, (or perhaps three, depending on how these two roads were joined). Road 1, for the most part followed by the modern A158, crosses Barlings Eau at Langworth.[45] It then runs on for a further 2.5 km., after which its course disappears in the northern part of Bullington parish. The rest of Margary's route 27 is a separate road (3 on Map 3) whose course westwards disappears on the southern boundary of Panton, though its continuation after a short interval may be marked by one or other of two nearly parallel lengths of track and field boundary (at M).[46] This road is clearly nonconformist, cutting diagonally across a block of fields and local roads which are an integral part of the area's rectilinear framework. As it is generally held to be Roman (but has not yet been more closely dated), road 3 gives the framework a Roman *terminus ante quem*. So early a date for the existence of this framework of fields and roads is not entirely unexpected. Elsewhere in lowland Britain – for example, at Little Waltham, Essex – topographical studies have proved that similar rectilinear systems had already been laid out by the later first century BC.[47] At Goltho, moreover, the recent excavations showed that the boundaries of a Romano-British rural settlement and of the later Anglo-Saxon settlement which overlay it were both on the alignment of the rectilinear system of the whole area.[48]

The course of Margary's other Roman road (his route 272) has not been quite so definitely determined.[49] There can, however, be no doubt about its line through the parishes immediately north and north-east of Bullington, where it too is demonstrably nonconformist. One fact of particular interest about these Roman roads emerges from Map 3. Road 1 (from Lincoln) crosses Barlings Eau at the point (A) aimed for by road 5, one of the more obvious routes belonging to the rectilinear framework. A little to the north, another of these conforming routes, road 4, heads directly for the place (B) where Margary's road 272 approaches one of the tributaries of Barlings Eau before veering away

---

[43] Information about the physical regions is from Darby, pp. 85–9.
[44] I. D. Margary, *Roman Roads in Britain*, third ed. (1973), pp. 192, 238–41.
[45] Margary, p. 239.
[46] Margary, p. 239.
[47] P. J. Drury, *Excavations at Little Waltham 1970–71*, (Council for Brit. Archaeol. Res. Report 26) (1978), pp. 134–6.
[48] Beresford, Goltho: The Development of an Early Medieval Manor.
[49] Margary, p.241.

again to the north-east. Roads 4 and 5 are both sufficiently prominent within the framework to be considered original elements of it. Points A and B may therefore represent established river crossings which the new Roman roads from Lincoln utilised. Indeed there can be no doubt that the network of existing roads, both local and long-distance, would have continued in use throughout the Roman period and in many instances – Map 3 demonstrates – thereafter. So it is very likely that road 3 (the continuation of Margary's road 27) would have run west to meet road 5 (or perhaps 4) and have been connected thereby to road 1. A third river crossing at point H seems to have been approached by a road from the west – road 8, perhaps subsequently diverted onto part of 8a. Its line was continued eastwards by road 7.

Several roads on a generally north-south alignment can also be reconstructed from Map 3. Two of these are particularly important to the present study. Road 10 survives almost continuously for over 5 km. through Snelland, Fulnetby, and Bullington parishes, passing by (or through) the alleged deserted medieval village at Bullington Hall (W).[50] Field boundaries now carry its line southwards for a further 0.9 km. to where it would have run beside the traditional site of Bullington priory (T)[51] and only a short distance west of a large ringwork in Cocklode Wood (X). The road's course further south is not obvious; but, according to Map 3, it can be presumed to have passed very close to Manor Farm, Apley, (U) and to Stainfield priory and the adjacent moated site now occupied by Stainfield Hall (V). The movement away from this line by the roads still in use today was no doubt a result of the abandonment of the ringwork (which was probably the manorial centre of the bishops of Durham's Bullington estate for a while,[52] and on or close to the site of its Anglo-Saxon predecessor), and of the dissolution of the two priories. Nonconformist road 14 allows modern traffic to avoid the two Bullington sites. On the other hand road 15 must have developed to provide easier access between Apley (and beyond) and the moated site just west of Goltho Hall (Z), which may have replaced the manorial centre (Y) which Beresford excavated.

The courses of other nonconformist roads similarly suggest the changing importance of individual sites (though not the timescale of such changes). Two instances are of particular interest. The first is the line of road 6, which provides a direct link between road 5 and the probable river crossing at B, passing en route the site of the alleged deserted village at Bullington Hall. Only excavation could establish whether road 6 or the settlement itself was the earlier. In the second

---

[50] Ed. M. W. Beresford & J. G. Hurst, *Deserted Medieval Villages* (1971), p. 193.
[51] T. Allen, *The History of the County of Lincoln*, ii (1834), p. 64, seems to be the earliest source for this tradition.
[52] Davis, 'Goltho – the manorial history'.

instance, however, it seems clear that the growing importance of Wragby caused a major dislocation of the road network in its vicinity. Road 9 presumably developed to enable traffic on throughroutes 4 and 5 to reach Wragby more conveniently; indeed it may well be simplest to see road 6 as the western continuation of 9. From the south-west roads 16 and 17 also cut diagonally across the area's rectilinear framework, providing a direct route between Wragby and Bardney; while road 18 (which could be Roman) links Wragby with Horncastle. Again the date of these changes is unknown, though they may have begun quite early in the medieval period, if the etymological link between the names Wragby and Wraggoe (the wapentake) is any indication of the former's role as a major Anglo-Saxon administrative centre.[53]

In view of this it is especially interesting to note that Wragby lies within one of the largest areas shown on Map 3 from which the rectilinear framework is entirely absent. Most of these nonconformist areas can easily be explained by reference to medieval woodland. Today there is still quite a lot of woodland at the southern end of the Clay Vale of Lindsey, though certainly not as extensive a cover as in the Norman period. Domesday Book records a very considerable amount of woodland there and a relatively low density of plough-teams.[54] Most, if not all, of this may have developed in the first medieval centuries, when some of the poorer land in the area can be expected to have gone out of agricultural use, as both local population levels and the market demand for surplus produce fell. (The corollary of this is, of course, that the areas where the rectilinear framework has survived cannot ever have fallen out of agricultural use for more than relatively short periods of time.)

The majority of the nonconformist area in which Wragby lies was clearly occupied by woodland in the earlier medieval period. Much of this must have remained in 1086, when the four Kingthorpe estates, for example, which carried a high assessment relative to their size and number of plough-teams, had between them 340 acres of woodland.[55] As the great majority, perhaps all, of these estates' land lay within the nonconformist area, it is likely that Kingthorpe originated in the later Anglo-Saxon period as a colonising settlement in extensive woodland on the eastern fringes of the putative original Bullington estate. Other encroachments into this woodland seem to have been made from the direction of Goltho, Wragby, and Langton, as is shown by the courses

[53] 'Wraghi's settlement', 'Wraghi's burial mound': Ekwall, p. 537. Wraghi is an Old Danish personal name; both second elements, *by* and *haugr*, are Old Scand.

[54] Darby, Fig. 7 on p. 48 and Fig. 12 on p. 61. Within the area of the putative original estate of Bullington, 840 acres of woodland were recorded in 1086 and 620 acres of underwood (refs. in notes 1, 3, 8, 11, 16).

[55] *Lincs. Domesday*, p. 88, no. 14/91; p. 160, no. 40/10; p. 85, no. 14/59; p. 152, no. 34/23.

of their parish boundaries (Map 2) and by the local place names. In such circumstances small, relatively newly formed estates could much more easily have moved from one ancient centre's sphere of influence to another's, as happened in the case of the land of 2⅓ bovates at Kingthorpe which was a berewick of Wragby in 1086. Even Wragby itself may have begun as a settlement on marginal land (though doubtless at a much earlier date), since only a small part of its parish's layout conforms to the rectilinear framework.[56]

Large parts of Newball and also the southern half of Stainfield were probably heavily wooded in the early medieval period. Both have large acreages of woodland recorded in Domesday Book,[57] and both contain a lot of land from which the rectilinear framework is absent. Finally, one much smaller nonconformist area is worth discussion. This is centred on the ringwork (X) at the eastern edge of Bullington parish, and is in effect a western extension of the much larger area in which Wragby lies. It stretches as far west as the traditional site of Bullington priory, and to the east includes the moated site at Goltho Hall. Today the majority of the area is woodland (though much of this may be quite recent). Some of it is likely to have lain within a park first recorded in the mid twelfth century. Simon fitz William, subtenant of the bishop of Durham's manor of Bullington, founded a priory c. 1155 in his park of Bullington, and gave to it part of the park and lands to the north and east of it.[58] The probable site of the priory church is known (T); it lies just west of a surviving length of earthwork boundary formed of a substantial bank with a ditch on its southern side. This runs around the north-west side of Cocklode Wood, and formerly seems to have continued westwards from the wood at least as far as to road 14.[59] There can be little doubt that this was a park boundary, presumably established here to separate the surviving part of Simon fitz William's park from what he had given to the priory. The full extent of the park is unknown, but it may have contained all the southern part of Bullington parish, most of which is defined by streams. The remainder of this nonconformist area – the part in Goltho parish – has not been examined on the ground. Much of it may have belonged to the large tract of woodland which, it has been suggested above, developed hereabouts in the first medieval centuries.

[56] There is no record of it having been subject to parliamentary enclosure, which might otherwise account for its nonconformity, according to W. E. Tate, *A Domesday of English Enclosure Acts and Awards*, ed. M. E. Turner (1978).

[57] Newball (500 acres): *Lincs. Domesday*, p. 78, no. 13/45. Stainfield (381 acres): ibid., p. 102, nos. 22/16, 22/17.

[58] Ed. F. M. Stenton, *Transcripts of Charters relating to the Gilbertine Houses of Sixle, Ormsby, Catley, Bullington, and Alvingham*, (Lincoln Rec. Soc., vol. 18), 1920 (1922), p. 91.

[59] Seen by Prof. R. H. C. Davis and the author as well defined cropmarks (visit in mid July, 1984).

This paper has examined several sorts of evidence for the medieval history of Goltho and its environs. These have provided information about the human geography of the area within which the excavated village developed, and have shown something of its status. The paper's main conclusions can be summarised as follows. In the later Anglo-Saxon period there was a large estate centred on Bullington which consisted of a geographically coherent block of land alongside the River Witham. It was one of the nine hundreds, each assessed at 12 carucates, which were amalgamated to form Wraggoe wapentake, and would almost certainly have represented the *parochia* of Bullington church. By 1086 dependent settlements, often initially involved in colonising outer parts of the estate, had gained varying measures of territorial independence. Of the 13 land-units into which the estate had fragmented by then (many of them separate manors and some in newly formed parishes), one or two lay in the area now called Goltho. Although still called Bullington in 1086, this area developed an increasingly distinct identity, epitomised by the place name Goltho and by aspects of its landscape, as well as by the history of its church.[60]

The paper has also shown something of an even earlier period of land-use in this part of Lindsey. Techniques of topographical analysis have been used to demonstrate the partial survival of an extensive rectilinear framework of roads and fields, which is proved to be early Roman or earlier in origin by the superimposition of several Roman roads built primarily for military purposes. Where the framework persists in the modern landscape it can be presumed to have remained in more or less continuous use from the Roman period.

This last point has implications of great importance for the early history of the excavated site at Goltho. The first settlement found there was of the period *c.* 50 to *c.* 200, consisting (in the excavated area) of three circular houses in all, with associated enclosures.[61] A spread of later pottery and coins on the site, together with roof and flue tiles and sections of a stone pillar, indicates that a large and sophisticated masonry building stood close by during the third and fourth centuries. There is, however, no need to imagine that this Romano-British settlement – apparently an important farmstead – ceased to be occupied after the fourth century. It may well have persisted through a long but effectively aceramic period, as one of a number of British centres in the district from which agriculture continued to be organised, if on a greatly reduced scale.[62] In that case the ninth-century occupation of the excavated area would represent the expansion of a surviving core,

---

[60] S. R. Bassett, 'Bullington priory, Bullington parish church, and Goltho chapel' (*in preparation*).
[61] Beresford, Goltho: The Development of an Early Medieval Manor.
[62] Cf. Bassett, *Saffron Walden*, pp. 5–11.

brought about by mid Saxon demographic recovery, rather than the recolonisation of a long abandoned site.

Only by a great deal more investigation on the ground could one hope to test the further hypothesis which this suggests. That is that the Romano-British settlement at Goltho was a villa estate centre, that the chief settlement in it of immigrant Anglo-Saxons lay somewhere not too far away to the west, and that the hybrid English-speaking population which emerged eventually renamed the estate Bullington, 'the estate of *Bula's people'.

4

The Royal Anglo-Saxon 'Chancery' of the Tenth Century Revisited

Pierre Chaplais

In an important book published in 1980, Dr Simon Keynes argued that, from a date not later than the reign of Athelstan (AD 924–39) and possibly earlier, royal Anglo-Saxon diplomas were produced in a royal office centred upon the king's household.[1] The royal secretariat, which moved around with the king, drafted and wrote the diplomas on the occasion of a meeting of the witan. Such a view, it is claimed, is supported by the analysis of the witness-lists (i.e. the non-autograph subscriptions) which are attached to the diplomas. The charters issued in the name of King Eadwig in 956, for example, can be divided into four groups according to their witness-lists, which are identical in the documents assigned to each group. It is therefore likely that each group consists of diplomas produced at the same meeting of the witan. In addition, since at least two of the groups share a number of diplomatic features, it is reasonable to assume that the same central agency was responsible for both. This agency, which had to be mobile and to operate wherever the witan met, could not have been a static ecclesiastical scriptorium. Besides, the uniformity of the diplomas in external design and formulation over long periods suggests a permanent office likely to have been attached to the king's household rather than an *ad hoc* organization involving different ecclesiastics and their staff. Dr Keynes admits that there may have been cases in which diplomas were drawn up by ecclesiastics, whether these ecclesiastics were directly, indirectly or not at all interested in the transaction, but this is unlikely to have happened without the king's express authorization.

Unlike Richard Drögereit, who in 1935 had already expressed the view that there was a royal Anglo-Saxon chancery in the tenth century, Dr Keynes does not think that the office had disintegrated before the end of Edgar's reign.[2] Indeed he believes that the situation which had existed ever since Athelstan's time had not altered substantially by Æthelred II's

---

[1] Simon Keynes, *The Diplomas of King Æthelred 'The Unready', 978–1016* (Cambridge Univ. Press, 1980), pp. 39–83, 134–53.
[2] R. Drögereit, 'Gab es eine angelsächsische Königskanzlei?', *Archiv für Urkundenforschung*, xiii (1935), 335–436; Keynes, *op. cit.*, pp. 79, 134–53.

reign: then royal diplomas were still produced by a central, royal agency as they had been ever since the 930s. The office of chancellor, 'the exalted official with responsibilities for producing written documents' may even have been known in Anglo-Saxon England, since the word *cancellarius* is included in an Abingdon glossary of the first half of the eleventh century.[3]

Regrettably, the evidence of the Abingdon glossary does not strengthen the case for the existence of a royal chancery or central agency for producing diplomas in Anglo-Saxon times. The glossarist himself makes it plain that by *cancellarius* (or *scriniarius*) he understood a keeper of a treasure-chest (*scrinium vel cancellaria; hordfæt* in English), not an official responsible for writing documents. The *cancellarius* was a *burthen*, that is to say an official of the chamber, not a chancellor in the post-Conquest sense of the word. The glossarist also implies that the office of *cancellarius* was held by more than one person at a given time, since he refers to a *primiscrinius* or senior *burthen*.[4] It is clear therefore that, if we are to find an answer at all to the question of the existence or otherwise of a royal chancery in the tenth century, we must turn once again to the documents which that office is supposed to have produced, that is to say the diplomas: an examination of the script of extant originals may help us to locate their scribes, while a study of the formulae found in both originals and trustworthy copies may give us valuable clues to the identification of their draftsmen. As Dr Keynes has rightly pointed out, one should never assume that a diploma was necessarily drafted by its scribe, although it may have happened from time to time.

Nobody would seriously suggest that a diploma could have been produced without the knowledge or permission of the king whose grant it recorded. Nor would anyone deny that the royal grant was normally made or at least confirmed at a meeting of the witan. The king as grantor and the members of the witan as *testes videntes et consentientes* could be expected to be interested in having the grant recorded in writing accurately, but this does not mean that the drafting and actual writing of the document had necessarily to be completed while the witan was in session. Some preliminary drafting, of course, had to be done on the spot. This would include noting down the names of the grantee and land granted as well as the extent and conditions of the grant, and making a list of those present at the meeting.[5] But for

---

[3] *Ibid.*, pp. 145–7.

[4] *Journal of Eccl. Hist.* xxxv (1984), 263–4.

[5] Sometimes the list of witnesses was transferred to the original inaccurately or incompletely: in P. H. Sawyer, *Anglo-Saxon Charters* (London, 1968) [henceforth cited as Sawyer], no. 795, the name of a bishop has been erased; *ibid.*, no. 416, two subscriptions were added at the foot of the last column in a different, but contemporary hand.

each of Athelstan's long diplomas of the 930s the writing alone is likely to have taken hours. The time spent to complete the twenty shorter diplomas of Group 2 issued in 956 must also have been considerable. Sometimes, the bounds of the land granted were not known to the scribe when he started writing the diploma; they had to be obtained from wherever the land granted was situated, and to be inserted later *by the same scribe* either at the end of the document or, more often, in a blank space left for that purpose before the dating clause and subscriptions.[6] Are we to suppose that such busy men as bishops and ealdormen had to remain in attendance until the whole of the work had been finished? It may be argued that several scribes and possibly several draftsmen could have been detailed to carry out whatever work had to be done at each meeting of the witan: we do know, for example, that two scribes were in 956 involved in the writing of the diplomas of Group 2;[7] even so, the issue of twenty documents cannot have been a speedy operation.

The production of diplomas might have taken long enough to try the patience of the members of the witan, if they really had to wait for the completion of the documents before returning home, but hardly long enough to make it a full-time occupation even for one person and even if that person was made responsible for both drafting and writing. If we take again as an example the diplomas issued in the name of King Eadwig in 956, a particularly productive year in so far as diplomas are concerned, the text of just under sixty documents is still extant for the whole year. Assuming that they all are genuine and making allowances for probable losses, it seems unlikely that more than one hundred diplomas were originally produced in that year. The whole of the work connected with their issue cannot possibly have taken more than fifty days to complete. Since we know that two scribes were involved in writing diplomas in 956, we come to the surprising conclusion that they cannot have been occupied in that task for more than one month each. If they were royal scribes, what did they do for the rest – that is to say most – of the year? Perhaps they were employed writing royal correspondence and administrative documents, but the amount of royal correspondence is unlikely to have been very large and Anglo-Saxon administrative documents, unlike their continental counterparts, were probably all written in the vernacular, thus requiring a literacy in English only rather than in both English and Latin.[8] The drafting of

---

[6] In Sawyer, no. 535, the boundary clause was certainly written later than the subscriptions in a space left blank; *ibid.*, no. 684, the clause is at the foot of the charter.

[7] Sawyer, nos. 624, 636; Keynes, *op. cit.*, p. 54; *Prisca Munimenta*, ed. Felicity Ranger (London, 1973). p. 41.

[8] James Campbell, 'Observations on English Government from the tenth to the twelfth century', *Transactions of the Royal Hist. Soc.*, Fifth Series, vol. 25 (1975), 42–3; F. E. Harmer, *Anglo-Saxon Writs* (Manchester Univ. Press, 1952), p. 6.

diplomas entailed a competent knowledge of Latin; so did their writing (although to a lesser degree) as well as a reasonable penmanship. The first of these qualifications would have been wasted on documents connected with royal administration. Are we not therefore entitled to ask whether it would not have been extravagant for the king to employ a permanent staff for the sole purpose of producing diplomas, when there were ecclesiastics around who could be asked to do the work and were capable of doing it? It is worth noting in this connexion that the only royal scribe mentioned by name in an Anglo-Saxon charter, a certain Ælfwine to whom Æthelred II granted land in Lew (Oxon.) in 984, is described in the document itself not only as *meo scriptori*, but also as *ministro*.[9] As Dr Keynes has suggested, he is likely therefore to have been a layman; this does not necessarily mean that he knew no Latin, but there is a strong possibility that his literacy was restricted to the vernacular,[10] and that he would have been more competent to deal with administrative documents than with Latin diplomas. It is true that the same conclusion could not be extended to Felix, the man to whom, in a letter addressed to King Æthelwulf of Wessex a century and a half earlier, Lupus of Ferrières referred as *qui epistolarum vestrarum officio fungebatur*;[11] but the word *epistolarum*, if Lupus used it literally, would have been singularly inappropriate as an allusion to royal diplomas, whereas it would have been the correct description for royal correspondence.

A few royal diplomas of the tenth century make the statement that they were drafted or written (or both) by a known ecclesiastic. Such is, for example, the charter of 949 in which King Eadred granted the monastery of Reculver and its lands to the cathedral church of Archbishop Oda of Canterbury: in one of its subscriptions, Abbot Dunstan of Glastonbury is made to claim that, at the king's bidding, he composed the document (*dictitando conposui*) and wrote it with his own fingers (*propriis digitorum articulis perscripsi*).[12] Such is also the grant of liberties made by King Æthelred II in 994 to Bishop Ealdred of Cornwall: in this case, the dating clause declares that the diploma was written (*scripta*) by Sigeric, archbishop of Canterbury.[13] Since the Reculver diploma from beginning to end, including its subscriptions, is written in a hand which is quite unlike what is believed to be Dunstan's own hand, the claim that we have here an autograph of the great abbot has to be rejected.[14] We must therefore be wary of accepting too hastily the statement that Sigeric wrote Æthelred's diploma of 994: a grant of

---

[9] Sawyer, no. 853.
[10] For the comments of Dr Keynes, see *op. cit.*, pp. 135–6, 147, 149, 160.
[11] *Mon. Germ. Hist.*, *Epist.* VI. i (Berlin, 1902), no. 13.
[12] Sawyer, no. 546.
[13] Sawyer, no. 880.
[14] *Prisca Munimenta*, ed. Ranger, p. 47.

liberties to a bishop and his church was of so much concern to the metropolitan that we might expect the latter to be extremely interested in the correct wording of the charter, but can we really believe that such an important person as an archbishop would write a long charter with his own hand? Scepticism is all the more justified as one subscription to the same document makes Bishop Ordbriht of Selsey tell the standard untruth that he 'consolidated' the charter with his own hand (*propria chyra*); some intriguing resemblance which has been noticed between the hand of the charter and another found in the Lanalet Pontifical, which seems to have belonged to the bishop of Cornwall, does not help to dispel our doubts.[15] It cannot be denied, however, that both this document and the Reculver diploma are written in a contemporary hand, thus deserving to be treated as originals unless or until they can be irrefutably proved to be otherwise. In so far as the Reculver diploma is concerned, a Canterbury forger of a later date might have had the ingenious idea that, by associating such a famous and saintly man as Dunstan with the writing of the document, he would wave suspicion away from his handiwork, but the hand is not that of a later age.[16] There are in addition diplomatic links of an unusual kind between the document and Glastonbury charters of varying repute, which gives us valid grounds for thinking that Dunstan may have played a role in the drafting of the diploma and entrusted its actual writing to someone else.[17] The same conclusion does not seem out of place regarding Æthelred's charter of 994, which may have been composed by Archbishop Sigeric or at least under his active or nominal supervision. Throughout the Middle Ages, everywhere in the West, acting through a deputy, with or without acknowledgements, was standard practice in almost every walk of life.[18] Neither of the two charters, at any rate, can possibly be listed among the products of a royal chancery.

We find here and there a definite proof that one particular diploma was written by the beneficiary or some member of his staff. Such is the charter of 997 in which Æthelred II grants land at Sandford (Devon) to Bishop Ælfwold of Crediton: the charter is written in the same hand as the bishop's will. The claims which have been made that the extant single-sheet is not an original, but a slightly later and faulty copy of the original, are in my view totally unfounded.[19]

It would be wrong to assume, however, that, in tenth-century England, *any* beneficiary of a royal grant might have been allowed to

[15] *Bull. Inst. Hist. Res.*, xxxix (1966), p. 21, lines 5–7.

[16] See the comments of Nicholas Brooks in *The Early History of the Church of Canterbury* (Leicester Univ. Press, 1984), pp. 234–36.

[17] *Prisca Munimenta*, ed. Ranger, pp. 48 (n. 34), 65 (n. 9).

[18] See, for example, *Liber Eliensis*, ed. E. O. Blake (Camden Third Series, xcii, 1962), p. 147, lines 5–6.

[19] P. Chaplais, *Essays in Medieval Diplomacy and Administration* (Hambledon Press, London, 1981), XV Add.

have it drafted and/or written down by anyone he pleased. The example of the Sandford charter concerns an ecclesiastical beneficiary of the highest order, who not only had the staff facilities for drafting and writing diplomas, but also held a holy office, which made documents produced by him or under his control just as worthy of unimpeachable trust as entries in gospel-books were at the time – unwisely, as it turned out – assumed to be. Indeed it is likely that high ecclesiastics such as bishops and abbots were sometimes allowed by the king to draft and write royal grants made in their favour because of their 'authenticity' *ratione officii* rather than because of their drafting and writing capabilities. It must not be forgotten that the royal Anglo-Saxon diploma, unlike its continental equivalent, displayed no outward and permanent mark of validation, neither seal nor autograph subscriptions or *signa*, which could have been compared with other similar marks of the same date after the death of the witnesses had made the ephemeral guarantees of authenticity which their subscriptions had provided while they were still alive unverifiable and therefore useless. The religious sanctity, which the relevant bishop or abbot had conferred upon the land-book drafted and written by him or under his supervision, made up for the visible, civil authenticity which the document lacked. Membership of the witan, which the bishops and abbots of the tenth century, or some of them, seem to have enjoyed, was an additional bonus, since it was at the *witenagemot* in the course of which a particular royal grant was made that the king is likely to have ordered or authorized such and such a bishop or abbot in attendance to cause the grant to be recorded in writing.

The same remarks could not be made about those in whose favour the vast majority of Anglo-Saxon diplomas of the tenth century were issued, namely the thegns and other laymen. Some of them, too, were members of the witan, but neither did they have at their disposal the same literate facilities as bishops and abbots nor could they claim the religious authenticity of their episcopal and abbatial colleagues. Since they were neither able nor allowed to write down themselves the royal grants made in their favour, what other means was there than a royal chancery of satisfying their need for written records? To this knotty problem the scribes of bishops and religious communities had already provided the perfect answer long before the reign of Athelstan. We may cite as an example the famous diploma in which, in 858, Æthelberht, [sub]king [of Kent], granted to the thegn Wulflaf land at Wassingwell (Kent) in exchange for some other land at Mersham (also in Kent).[20] Although the document is not subscribed by Archbishop Ceolnoth, it was undoubtedly drafted in Canterbury, as its dispositive words alone 'dabo et concedo' indicate; its hand is that of the Christ Church scribe who wrote, among other charters, an assignment of food-rent made by Lufu, 'God's handmaid', to Christ Church itself on her property at Mongeham

[20] Sawyer, no. 328.

(Kent) (AD 843–63).[21] One of the two endorsements which the Christ Church scribe himself wrote on Æthelberht's charter resembles in appearance, though not in wording, the outside address of letters close: it is written upside down as compared with the text on the face of the charter and it is divided into two by a fairly wide gap:

+ ðis siondan [blank] ðes landes boc
et was – [blank] – singwellan.

This is likely to mean that the charter was sent from the place of writing (presumably Canterbury) to some other place, perhaps by the scribe of the charter to its original draftsman for checking (? before dispatch to the beneficiary).[22]

An interesting point about the endorsement on Æthelberht's charter is that it is virtually identical *mutatis mutandis* with the dorsal note found on a diploma issued by Athelstan in 931, the earliest original document of the tenth century for which a chancery origin has been claimed. Athelstan's charter, which records a grant of Ham (Wilts.) to the thegn Wulfgar, has a dating-clause which states that it was written (*perscripta*) at Lifton (Devon) on 12 November 931;[23] its scribe [my scribe 1; Drögereit's Athelstan A] also wrote another original charter of Athelstan, which granted land at *Derantune* (Kent) to another thegn, Ælfwold; this second charter claims to have been written (again *perscripta*) in Winchester on 28 May 934.[24] The first charter comes from the archives of the Old Minster, Winchester, which, according to the will of Wulfgar, the grantee, was to acquire Ham after the death of the testator's wife; the second charter comes from the archives of Christ Church, Canterbury.

Since hardly any trustworthy Anglo-Saxon diploma has survived for the fifty years or so which preceded Athelstan's reign, it is impossible to evaluate the diplomatic changes which our two originals might otherwise illustrate. Their general structure follows the pattern which had been evolved for the Anglo-Saxon diploma over the centuries: pictorial invocation, proem, dispositive clause, boundary clause, sanction, date, corroboration and subscriptions. Examined in detail, however, the two diplomas display features which are not encountered in earlier extant originals. The proem is much longer and written in the hermeneutic style of Latin which has been studied by Dr Michael Lapidge.[25] The dating clause is much more elaborate, mentioning the

---

[21] Sawyer, no. 1197.
[22] See *Medieval Scribes, Manuscripts and Libraries; Essays presented to N. R. Ker*, ed. M. B. Parkes and A. G. Watson (London, 1978), p. 16.
[23] Sawyer, no. 416.
[24] Sawyer, no. 425.
[25] For example, in *Anglo-Saxon England*, vol. 4 (1975), pp. 67 ff.

year of the Incarnation, the indiction, the king's regnal year, the epact, concurrents and age of the moon, as well as the day (according to the Roman calendar) and place of 'writing' of the charter. The subscriptions, much more numerous than those of earlier diplomas, are all drawn up in the form: 'Ego . . . consensi et subscripsi' and arranged in neat columns of equal length.

The strange Latin vocabulary, largely made up of latinized forms of Greek words is matched by equally strange spellings of vernacular words and personal names. In both diplomas, the boundary clause begins with the rare form *ærast* for *ærest*. In the charter of 931, connected with land in Wiltshire, the Mercian forms *ondlong* and *ðonon* occur regularly in the description of the bounds; the name of one witness is given the Kentish spelling *biorhtsige*, while other names are in their West-Saxon form, for example *beorhtric* and *beornstan*; other curious spellings of names include *ælferd, ælfheh, burherd, ðeoderd* and *uhterd*. In the charter of 934, which concerns land in Kent, it is not surprising to find Kentish words to describe the bounds, for example *biorh* and *dionu*, but the spellings *ðonon* and *ðonan* occur side by side; personal names are generally given a Kentish spelling, e.g. *biorhtelm, biorhtsige, biornstan* (also *biorhstan*) and *ðiodred*, but the apparently Mercian form *ælfhæh* (for *ælfheah*) also occurs as well as *wulfheh*. In both charters, the letter *h* was sometimes omitted and later corrected above the line, for example in the Latin words *dehiscentibus* and *his* as well as in the vernacular words and personal names *biorhtsige, ealhhelm* with one *h* (once left uncorrected), *hlinc* and *hlinces*. The greater part of the fifth line in the charter of 934 is written over an erasure. Finally, in the charter of 931, the scribe omitted two subscriptions, which were supplied by another contemporary scribe at the foot of the last column.

Although there is no doubt that the same scribe wrote both charters, his hand changed slightly from 931 to 934: in the earlier charter, the tail of the letter *g* is open, whereas it is closed in the later one. It cannot be firmly established that the scribe should be definitely associated with the Winchester scriptorium, but the style of his hand is at least consistent with the script practised there: judging by the general appearance of the writing and by the forms of some letters, for example *a* (either square, or rounded at the bottom and pointed at the top with a straight back rising well above the letter) and *y* (sometimes shaped like *f*), the hand might be regarded as intermediate between Hand 1 and Hand 2 in the Parker Chronicle, of Winchester origin;[26] it could also be compared profitably with one of the Winchester hands in Cotton MS. Galba A. xviii of the British Library.[27]

The same draftsman composed not only our two originals, but also a group of other charters, which have survived in copies only and are

[26] N. R. Ker, *Catalogue of Manuscripts containing Anglo-Saxon* (Oxford, 1957), p. 58.
[27] E. Temple, *Anglo-Saxon Manuscripts, 900–1066* (London, 1976), plates 15–17.

spread over the period 929–34.[28] Whether the mixture of vernacular dialects should be attributed to him or to the scribe is debatable. If he was responsible for it, it might be suggested that he was of foreign origin and that he worked in Christ Church, Canterbury. This suggestion would explain the large number of Kentish forms of names.

The charter of 934, said to have been written at Winchester, has no contemporary endorsement, whereas that of 931, 'written' at Lifton, was endorsed by the scribe of the text: 'þis is þæs landes boc æt hamme'. The fact that the charter written at Winchester has no endorsement may be significant, but since the endorsement on the charter written at Lifton follows the Canterbury pattern of Æthelberht's charter of 858 which has been discussed above, while it is written in the West-Saxon dialect, it would be futile to speculate further.

Regarding the charters of the period 939–57, written by the scribes whom, in 1965, I called Scribes 2, 3, 4, 5, 7 and 8 and whom I assigned, following the lead of N. R. Ker, to the Winchester scriptorium,[29] Dr Keynes has argued that they were royal scribes. In particular, he believes that Scribe 4, who wrote the 951 annal in the Parker Chronicle as a Winchester scribe, may have been in the king's service when he wrote a charter of 956.[30] In fact, a close examination of the chronicle shows that the scribe wrote the 951 annal between 955 and 958, that is to say during the period in which he wrote the charter. There is therefore no reason to doubt that he was still at Winchester when he wrote the charter. Nor can we accept the argument that, because Scribe 3, who wrote five royal charters between 944 and 949, was also responsible for noting in Cotton MS. Tiberius A. ii that it was a gift from Athelstan to Christ Church, Canterbury, he must have been a royal scribe at the time.

In so far as Scribe 6 [Drögereit's Edgar A] is concerned, there is every reason to think that he was an Abingdon scribe and not a royal one. This can be deduced from one of the charters which he wrote, Edgar's grant of Ringwood to the abbey of Abingdon (AD 961).[31] Scribe 6 wrote the first part of the charter, from the initial chrismon to the end of the boundary clause, in his usual hand (insular minuscule), while a second scribe wrote, in caroline minuscule, the dating-clause and the subscriptions. It is evident that, if the scribe of the first part was a royal scribe, whoever wrote the date and subscriptions must *a fortiori* have also been in the king's service. This second scribe, however, describes Edgar in the royal subscription as 'Eadgar Britanniae Anglorum

---

[28] See Drögereit, *art. cit.*, p. 434.
[29] *Prisca Munimenta*, ed. Ranger, p. 41.
[30] Keynes, *op. cit.*, p. 25.
[31] Sawyer, no. 690. See T. A. M. Bishop, *English Caroline Minuscule* (Oxford, 1971), no. 11.

monarchus', a style which is only found in charters connected with Abingdon.[32] This suggests that the second scribe was an Abingdon monk, who not only wrote, but also drafted the second and vital part of the charter, in which case Scribe 6, who wrote the first part, must also have been connected with the abbey. In addition, the hand of Scribe 6 is very similar to that of a *pancarta* granted by Edgar to the abbey of Pershore in 972.[33] In this *pancarta* the king subscribes with the unusual style 'Eadgar Brittannię Anglorum monarchus' which we found in the Ringwood charter, and Osgar, abbot of Abingdon, uses the form 'Ego . . . dictaui' in his own subscription, indicating that he had drafted the charter. If the abbot took the responsibility of drafting the charter for Pershore, it is likely that one of his scribes wrote it, and therefore Scribe 6, who wrote a similar hand, must also have been associated with the abbey of Abingdon. It should be added that Scribe 6 did not endorse the Ringwood charter, whereas he did endorse others; in this respect, however, he was not consistent.

The subscription of Abbot Osgar of Abingdon on the Pershore *pancarta* brings us to the question of the *dictavi* formula sometimes used by a witnessing bishop or abbot in his subscription. Although I agree with Dr Keynes that the word *dictavi* may sometimes have meant simply 'I asserted', that is to say a virtual synonym of *consensi, roboravi* etc., there are cases, like that of the Pershore *pancarta*, in which it was meant to be understood as 'I drafted' [the charter].[34] It cannot be by accident that Bishop Cenwald of Worcester, who undoubtedly drafted a whole group of alliterative charters of the mid-tenth century, subscribed another charter, not alliterative, but diplomatically connected with the group, in the form: 'Ego Cenwald episcopus dictavi'.[35] It is equally certain that Bishop Ælfwold of Sherborne used the words 'scribere iussi' in the same sense: two original charters of Edgar, granting lands to laymen respectively in Dorset and in Somerset, have the rare wording 'hæfð gebocod' in their contemporary endorsement and share other diplomatic features.[36] Since one of these charters has the subscription 'Ego Alfwold episcopus scribere iussi', it is clear that the bishop drafted both. Here the bishop chosen by the king to draft the charters was the diocesan. Dr F. E. Harmer has also shown that the royal practice of allowing a bishop to 'dictate' a land-book connected with a grant of land situated in his diocese was occasionally followed by Edward the Confessor.[37]

The problem of the existence or otherwise of an Anglo-Saxon

---

[32] Sawyer, nos. 688, 689; no. 811, of Winchester origin, is not genuine.
[33] Sawyer, no. 786.
[34] Keynes, *op. cit.*, pp. 26–8, 63, 121.
[35] Sawyer, no. 574.
[36] Sawyer, nos. 697, 736.
[37] Harmer, *Anglo-Saxon Writs*, pp. 245, 281, 432.

chancery is obviously a difficult one, but I contend that the evidence points in one direction: Anglo-Saxon kings did not find it necessary or economic to set up a royal chancery in order to deal with their Latin charters; they preferred to use instead bishops and a few favoured abbots. The choice of one bishop rather than another might vary from one meeting of the witan to another according to circumstances. We may conclude with a remark about a royal book, the MacDurnan gospels, which Athelstan presented to Christ Church, Canterbury. In this manuscript (Lambeth Palace, MS. 1370), the inscription recording Athelstan's gift is written in a vocabulary so close to that of the alliterative charters of the mid-tenth century that there is little doubt that Bishop Cenwald of Worcester drafted it just as he did the charters.[38] If Cenwald was responsible for drafting such a record in a book given to Christ Church, why should we reject the evidence that a Winchester scribe wrote an inscription of the same nature, recording a grant of the same king to the same church?

---

[38] Keynes, *op. cit.*, p. 26, n. 37; p. 82, n. 165. Dr Keynes is preparing a paper on the books of Athelstan which he kindly allowed me to read.

5

Lawyers' Time: History and Memory in Tenth- and Eleventh-Century Italy

Chris Wickham

Ralph Davis, in his remarkable essay *The Normans and their Myth*, asked: 'if a nation without history is a contradiction in terms, can it be that the only way to create a nation is by the creation of a myth?'[1] Let us look at how this insight can be pursued in the kingdom of Italy between the end of Carolingian rule and the appearance of the city communes – in the history, that is, of a state that failed, a nation that broke up, a country with, by all appearances, notably little in the way of myth-making.[2]

Myth when used in this sense has nothing to do with the stories of gods and heroes, nor with the closely-defined narratives analysed in structuralist anthropology; it has to do with collective representations of social groups, their legitimising traditions, the beliefs and unanalysed assumptions that give societies their meaning. In medieval Europe (until the fourteenth century, at least), beyond the level of the village, such myths were the concern of élites: the definitions of all social systems were structured by what their élites themselves believed. The tenth-century Anglo-Saxon aristocracy, for example, were increasingly persuaded – or persuaded themselves – that they were part of an English kingdom, rather than of Wessex, Mercia, and so on. Even if this process was not yet complete in 1000, it was fully recognised by the new military aristocracy ruling England in the generations after 1066, and never contested again; Hastings was not the less a myth because it was a real event, and it did as much for the myth of the coherence of the English state as it did for that

---

[1] R. H. C. Davis, *The Normans and their Myth* (London, 1976), p. 16. Cf. the type-analysis by Georges Duby, *Le dimanche de Bouvines* (Paris, 1973), pp. 160–215, and some of the discussion in E. J. Hobsbawn and T. Ranger (eds.), *The Invention of Tradition* (Cambridge, 1983). I am most grateful to Ceridwen Lloyd-Morgan and to Patrick Wormald for reading a first draft of this text and for suggesting a number of important improvements, and to James Fentress for stimulating my interest in the nature of memory.

[2] The kingdom of Italy in 900 included northern Italy, Tuscany, and the duchy of Spoleto in central Italy. I will exclude the latter from my discussions; its history and historiographical traditions were closer to those of Rome and the south Italian states, which were genuinely very different in type. For the political and social developments that underpin the following discussion, see G. Tabacco, *Egemonie sociali e strutture del potere nel medioevo italiano* (Turin, 1979); C. J. Wickham, *Early Medieval Italy* (London, 1981).

of the Normans themselves.[3] In the Italian kingdom, by contrast, the same period showed an almost constant decline in the perceived relevance of the kings to the ordinary political life of the Italian upper classes; neither the 'national' kings of the period to 962, nor the German king-emperors of the following century and a half, succeeded in imposing themselves as political foci in the way that English kings did from Alfred onwards. Yet the Italian state in 950, say, was the most sophisticated in Western Christendom, with a complex legal-administrative system that ran courts and collected dues across the Po plain and Tuscany in a more systematic manner than any other part of the Carolingian empire, and certainly far more systematically than in England. Its kings, though feeble enough, were also the richest in the West, and if they got overtaken later it was only because of the new resources available to the German kings through the opening up of the Harz silver-mines and to the English kings through the organisation of Danegeld.

The paradox of the failure of the Italian kings, despite the continuing coherence of the Italian state, will not be fully resolved here; it has to do with the interrelationship – and slow separation – of national and local power, with changes in state structures, with the increasing importance for churchmen and aristocrats of more local political rewards. But the ideology of kingship was a crucial element in this history. Where all power is based on land, the position of rulers is more directly dependent than elsewhere on the attitudes of their immediate servants, whose power base is the same as their lords'. Kings, to be successful, do not only need to offer rewards; they need the recognition of their counts, bishops, vassals, that the rewards they had to give were worth having. The ideology surrounding kings was not, of course, the only element in medieval royal power; but the success and failure of political power is incomprehensible without it. Bearing this in mind, I propose to discuss the failure of the Italian kingdom in the tenth and eleventh centuries in the context of an analysis of the processes of historical memory; for what people remember of the past – and what they forget – is one of the key elements in their unconscious ideology. Let us consider this a little more closely.

Different groups of people remember things in different ways. There is a wealth of difference in social and political attitudes between people who remember 1974 as the year of the second miners' strike and those who put the accent on Labour's election victories. Time, above all

---

[3] For some discussions of the mechanisms of this development see C. P. Wormald, 'Bede, the *Bretwaldas* and the origins of the *Gens Anglorum*' in *idem* (ed.), *Ideal and Reality in Frankish and Anglo-Saxon Society* (Oxford, 1983), pp. 120–9, and the pioneering article by R. H. C. Davis, 'Alfred the Great: Propaganda and Truth', *History*, lvi (1971), 169–82. For the post-Conquest period, see, emblematically, E. Searle (ed.) *The Chronicle of Battle Abbey* (Oxford, 1980), at pp. 178–82.

remembered time, is not a constant; it is given meaning in cultural contexts that change from social group to social group. Social groups tend to identify and legitimate themselves through systems of collective memory, that can vary not only in their interpretation of given historical events, but in what events, what type of events, are seen as historically significant at all. There has been some anthropological work on this, but the issue has not really been systematically discussed since Maurice Halbwachs' work in the 1920s–30s. Halbwachs wrote in a Durkheimian framework, and his discussions of dream, and individual versus social perception, would not satisfy us now; but his insight that shared memory plays a large part in the self-definition of social groups is crucial.[4] We are used to looking at historians (and writers in general) in the medieval period in terms of their conscious views on what History was: its literary genre, its rules of causation, its cycles, its relation to eschatology.[5] Only recently, principally in France, has much attention been paid to the mental schemata that determined which events in the remembered past were of historical significance, the pins on which a framework of historical memory was hung.

Contrast, for instance, the focus of English history-writing in the central middle ages on events in the kingdom as a whole, with the French tendency towards the legitimation, through historical and genealogical memory, of ever smaller principalities – Normandy and Gascony in the eleventh century, Guines by the twelfth. A twelfth-century history of Norfolk, or even a marcher earldom, would have been inconceivable; even William Marshal's personal epic has no interest in his lordships for themselves, as opposed to their importance for his status in the kingdom and at the court.[6] That this also represents a real contrast in political scale is not the point; real relationships are

[4] M. Halbwachs, *Les cadres sociaux de la mémoire* (Paris, 1925), esp. pp. 241–96; idem, *La mémoire collective* (Paris, 1950; Eng. ed. *The Collective Memory*, New York, 1980), esp. ch. ii. Cf. E. J. Hobsbawm, 'The Social Function of the Past', *Past and Present* 55 (1972), 3–17. A guide to some modern works is P. Joutard, 'L'histoire dans l'imaginaire collectif', *L'Arc*, lxxii (1978), 38–42. For anthropological work, see the seminal conspectus and bibliography in M. T. Clanchy, 'Remembering the Past and the Good Old Law', *History*, lv (1970), 165–76; and W. MacGaffey, *Custom and Government In the Lower Congo* (Berkeley, 1976); cf. also the discussions in C. Lévi-Strauss, *The Savage Mind* (London, 1972), pp. 232–42, 254–64. The key historical text is of course J. Le Goff, 'Au moyen âge: temps de l'église et temps du marchand' (1960), now trans. in idem, *Time, Work and Culture in the Middle Ages* (Chicago, 1980), pp. 29–42, 289–93.

[5] Some guides: B. Guenée, *Histoire et culture historique dans l'occident médiéval* (Paris, 1980); R. W. Southern, arts. in *Transactions of the Royal Historical Society* fifth ser. xx (1970), 173–96, xxi (1971), 159–79, xxii (1972), 159–80, xxiii (1973), 245–63; R. D. Ray, 'Medieval Historiography through the 12th Century', *Viator*, v (1974), 33–59.

[6] Cf., for example, G. Duby, *Hommes et structures du moyen âge* (Paris, 1973), pp. 267–98; B. Guenée, 'Temps de l'histoire et temps de la mémoire au moyen age', *Annuaire-bulletin de la société de l'histoire de la France* (1976–7), 25–35. For William, see P. Meyer (ed.), *L'histoire de Guillaume le Maréchal*, 3 vols. (Paris, 1891–4). For an Italian parallel, overtaken too soon by the rival territorialisation of the city communes, see n. 21.

always mediated by perception, and cannot be understood unless perception is analysed separately. The convergence on kings of the historical memory of English élites will remain as a constant contrast to my Italian examples. Memory does not just provide contrasts in national consciousness, either; élites can be broken down into their component parts as well. Take, for example, a recent article by Françoise Autrand. She has shown in a subtle analysis of the proceedings of the Paris Parlement in 1350–1450 what were the mental points of reference for the judges involved there: some of the major events of the English Wars, certainly; the Jacquerie; but above all the taking and retaking of Paris in 1418 and 1436, which in each case involved the milieu of the *robe* directly and often disastrously. '1418, pour les gens de robe, c'est un peu ce que fut Azincourt pour la noblesse.' Agincourt is mentioned casually in these texts, without a date; 1418, however, becomes a symbol, 'the year 18'.[7] This sort of difference between professionals and aristocrats, in their framework of historical relevance, in what was important enough to remember, is crucial. Similar differences in group consciousness between two components of the Italian élite, educated churchmen and lawyers, will be a key feature of this analysis.

The early medieval kingdom of Italy did not produce a great mass of history-writing. Indeed, given the relatively high level of literacy there, lay as well as clerical, it is striking how little literary work of any type was produced.[8] Not only the overall shortage of texts concerns us here, however, but what they say; and, in particular, what they do not say. The historians of the Italian kingdom were not only few, but brief; they often give little of what we conventionally consider useful, or even plausible, historical information. This is not necessarily because the historians were inept, although they sometimes were, but because they often had so very little to go on. Paul the Deacon himself, whose *Historia Langobardorum* of the 790s remained, for better or for worse, the major historical model for subsequent Italian writers for many centuries, only had access to a few nuclei of material – for Alboin,

---

[7] F. Autrand, 'Les dates, la mémoire et les juges', in B. Guenée (ed.), *Le métier de l'historien au moyen âge* (Paris, 1977), pp. 157–82; quote from p. 174. Compare the bureaucratic framework around all Chinese historiography, written 'by functionaries for functionaries', with resultant distortions: W. G. Beasley and E. G. Pulleyblank (eds.), *Historians of China and Japan* (London, 1961), esp. E. Balazs, 'L'histoire comme guide de la pratique bureaucratique', pp. 78–94. Many of the best recent discussions of historical memory can be fouund in *Temps, mémoire, tradition au moyen-âge* (Aix, 1983).

[8] R. Bezzola, *Les origines et la formation de la littérature courtoise en Occident* ii (Paris, 1960), p. 82; W. Wattenbach & R. Holtzmann, *Deutschlands Geschichtsquellen im Mittelalter* i (re-ed. F. -J. Schmale, Weimar, 1967), pp. 313–4; G. Arnaldi, 'Liutprando e la storiografia contemporanea nell'Italia centro-settentrionale', *Settimane di studio*, xvii (1969), 497–519, at 497–500.

Agilulf, or Grimoald – to string together into a coherent text.[9] But it is Andreas of Bergamo, who wrote a brief continuation of Paul the Deacon in the 880s, whose ignorance can best serve to introduce my theme.

Andreas was an honest compiler: he took Italian history from the ending of Paul's *Historia* in 744 up to the 860s when his own experience began, with recourse to *series litterarum* and the testimony of *antiqui homines*. They did not help him much; his significance is that he admits this. We can guess that, unusually among medieval historians, Andreas wrote down more or less all he knew. He knows the dates of the kings, and how many laws they issued in the north Italian manuscript tradition (king-lists were appended to many legal texts; presumably this was his *series litterarum*). Apart from that, he knows little. Pippin's invasions of Italy, for example, have been entirely forgotten. Charlemagne's conquest has not, and Andreas preserves a schematic and garbled account of the events leading up to it. The blinding of King Bernard in 818, the enmity between Lothar I and Louis the Pious in the 830s, and, rather more briefly, the battle of Fontenay in 841, are recorded, too, more or less schematically; apart from these, nothing until 859. This certainly shows how little impact the Carolingians made on Italian historical consciousness, at least up to Louis II (850–75), Andreas' chief subject. It is also, however, worth stressing that historical memory (Andreas' *antiqui homines*) had focussed on one or two events of dynastic history as the only thing it was relevant to remember. Charlemagne's conquest in 774 persisted for a century as a major point of reference in popular memory, as court-cases show; but it did not create the sense of historical change and of a lost past that 1066 did for the historians among the defeated in England, except, perhaps, for Paul himself. Andreas' dynastic anecdotes are without a historical context to give them meaning, such as might have been provided by the collective memory of his own family, or by a sense of the history of the Italian court or of the Italian state. These were evidently unavailable. Instead, the anecdotes appear in the principal way in which such isolated stories

---

[9] Paul, *Historia Langobardorum* and Agnellus, *Liber Pontificalis*, both ed. in M[onumenta] G[ermaniae] H[istorica] S[criptores] R[erum] L[angobardicarum et Italicarum] (Hannover, 1878), pp. 45–187, 275–391; for recent analyses see *Settimane di studio* xvii, 357–86, 457–95.

tend to be remembered in Europe, through the narrative morphology characteristic of 'folktale'.[10]

The structures of oral tradition and the role of folktale motifs in them cannot be discussed here; the precise ways that memory and oral transmission pattern and adapt events are a different problem to mine. But the absence in Andreas of any overall organising framework, apart from internal narrative pattern, is important. Paul had turned similarly thin material into a coherent text with its own literary structure; but Paul had both the intelligence and the literary models to enable him to do this. Andreas failed. But Andreas' incapacity is more useful for an understanding of how history in Italy was *constructed*. It is, above all, the absence of any sense of the structure of the Italian state, and the continuity of the Italian court, that I will wish to emphasise. Bede could find a great mass of material, often orally transmitted, about kings in England a century and more before he wrote; although secular history was not his principal interest, it was an essential base for the complex historical analysis he produced. So it was for Orderic Vitalis and William of Malmesbury, even leaving aside their sophisticated use of literary and documentary material.[11] The evidence available to Paul and Andreas and their successors, and, subsequent to Paul's exceptional achievement, the interpretative framework available to Italian historians, was wholly different in type. In Italy oral history was, above all, contemporary history; the past quickly became forgotten.

Andreas' history, however thin, was the last attempt at a history of the Italian kingdom. Italy plays a leading role in some of the major histories of the later period, but none of them is centred on Italian history, either of the *regnum*, or, still less, the peninsula, as a subject in its own right. Bearing this in mind, let us look briefly at three historians working in the tenth and eleventh centuries, in particular through their concept of the Italian kingdom: what sort of things they are concerned to relate about the kingdom and the kings, in the context of their own

---

[10] Andreas, *Historia*, ed. *M.G.H.SRL*, pp. 221–30, cf. Wickham, p. 51. 'Folktale' is an inexact category in ordinary English, but see, e.g., S. Thompson, *The Folktale* (New York, 1946), esp. pp. 263–71, as a very basic introduction. North Italian oral traditions of the Carolingians were already by the 880s far inferior to those across the Alps: contrast the rich collection in Notker der Stammler, *Taten Karls des Grossen*, ed. H. F. Häfele (Berlin, 1962), and see ii. 17 for a highly dramatic conquest of Italy. Popular memory of 774 in ninth-century Italy, as opposed to that of the élite, is evidenced in inquests, where it is the only political event referred to by witnesses: C. Manaresi (ed.), *I placiti del regnum Italiae*, i (Rome, 1955), nn. 38, 56, Inquest vi, vii. The true parallel to 1066, however, lies in the Norman conquest of southern Italy, which spawned histories and chronicle-cartularies, just as in England.

[11] M. Chibnall (ed.), *The Ecclesiastical History of Orderic Vitalis* i (Oxford, 1980), pp. 56–92; R. M. Thompson, 'William of Malmesbury as historian and man of letters', *Journal of Ecclesiastical History*, xxix (1978), 387–413.

separate preoccupations, and, most important, what sort of things they leave out.[12]

Liutprand of Cremona's *Antapodosis* was written around 960. *Antapodosis* means 'Tit for tat', and in effect expresses Liutprand's theory of history; Girolamo Arnaldi has argued persuasively that Book I, covering the period 888–98, was posed as an exemplification of divine retribution for misdeeds, those in particular of Arnulf and Berengar I.[13] Liutprand's theory was neither subtle nor original, but it had already become too complex to employ when he came to explain the early death of one of his few heroes, King Lambert, in 898, and he settled for a personalisation of the same theory: his history was to deal out praise and venom in return for good and bad deeds, notably those done to himself and his kin. The *Antapodosis* dealt largely with Italian affairs, for that was Liutprand's world, until he fled to Otto I in the 950s; his good and bad patrons were Hugh and Berengar II, successive Italian kings. The prologue, however, makes it clear that the focus is, in theory, all Christian Europe, and perhaps a third of the book covers Germany and Byzantium; Liutprand moves in and out of the three countries he knows best with no comment beyond phrases meaning 'at the same time'. Liutprand's own sense of identity was somewhat unclear: he sees himself, when living outside Italy, as *in captivitate seu peregrinatione*, and he generalises about the nature of Italians; but in Constantinople in 968, admittedly as legate for Otto I, he aligns himself as a Lombard with the German peoples north of the Alps in opposition to the Romans. The Italian kingdom is an important organising concept in Liutprand's mind, but it is never the focus of his synthesising interest.[14]

Liutprand was explicitly writing recent history, and he knew a lot more about it than Andreas had done; over half the *Antapodosis* predates Liutprand's own experience as an eye witness in Hugh's and Berengar II's court. There are, nonetheless, significant gaps in his knowledge and interest. Liutprand tells us about civil wars and revolts, jealousies and betrayals, who was supposedly sleeping with whom. But he says nothing that illuminates the ordinary processes of royal rule. Between 905, when Berengar I blinded Louis of Provence, and 921, when Berengar's aristocrats revolted against him, there was stable government in the Italian kingdom. Liutprand has almost nothing to say about the period at all. Similarly, the rule of Hugh (926–47), which Liutprand mostly witnessed from close to, is reduced entirely to wars, conspiracies, and royal reprisals against nobles. Hugh is learned, brave, and cunning, a patron of the poor, churchmen, and scholars, but

---

[12] Full lists in Wattenbach-Holtzmann, i. 313–33; iii (Köln, 1971), 918–36.
[13] Liutprand of Cremona, *Antap[odosis]*, in *Liudprandi opera*, ed. J. Becker (third ed., Hannover 1915); Arnaldi, pp. 507–12.
[14] Liutprand, *Antap.* i. 1, 37, 44, ii. 17, iii. 1, 38, 39, iv. 15, *Legatio* 7, 12 for citations.

lustful, nepotistic, and harsh to his aristocrats. Liutprand does not mention justice and government, even in the most conventional terms, although they were commonplace in contemporary historiography.[15] His kings are active; but they are isolated from the framework of the Italian state. This is important. It can certainly be argued that the traditional Lombard-Carolingian framework of the Italian state was breaking down in Hugh's time; that legislation and capillary intervention in local affairs, frequent and legitimate in the ninth century, were no longer possible. But Liutprand was a courtier; he became Berengar II's secretary for a time, and twice acted as ambassador to Constantinople. And, despite the breakdown of royal hegemony in Italy, the king's palace remained, throughout the tenth century, a coherent administrative focus, active, legally sophisticated, and rich. Liutprand of course knew this; but it did not seem relevant to a history. Arnaldi has commented on the absence of court-oriented monastic chronicles in the kingdom of Italy, despite the number of monasteries around the permanent capital of Pavia. Reto Bezzola notes that not only do the tenth-century Italian kings not seem to have patronised court literature, but they did not even manage to get epitaphs for themselves.[16] Pavia, for all its sophistication, did not succeed in producing a court culture like that of the Ottonians in Germany, or the English kings, or even the early Capetians. Nor can this be explained simply through the ephemerality of the kings before 962, the discontinuity of their political traditions as king overthrew king, or their absence for most of the time after 962; each of these can be matched point by point in the history of England between (say) 1000 and 1135, without its stopping English (and Anglo-Norman) chroniclers, even the most locally oriented, from seeing the kingdom as a continuous structure and as a crucial narrative focus. What was lost in post-Carolingian Italy was any conception of the historical centrality of the court and government traditions of the capital, or of the kings as rulers; of, to follow Ralph Davis' usage, the 'myth' of the Italian kingdom.

Liutprand's failure to represent his kings in this light is not necessarily a failure of collective memory, of course, for Liutprand witnessed much of his account personally; but it is certainly a gap in his own perceptions. Such an absence cannot be seen as peculiarly his fault. I shall argue, in fact, that it is because a consciousness of the Italian state was in effect in the hands of legal specialists – who did not include

---

[15] Liutprand, *Antap*. iii. 19, iv. 1, v. 18. For Berengar I see ii. 32–73. Liutprand's only reference to justice comes in incidental references to two disloyal judges in Pavia (iii. 39–41); it is they who judge, not Hugh. (For Hugh's own more problematic attitude to judging, see the *Miracula S. Columbani*, ed. H. Bresslau, *M.G.H.S[criptore]s*, xxx. ii (Leipzig, 1934), pp. 997–1015.) Liutprand does mention Berengar II taxing in *Antap*. v. 33, a special case. Arnaldi, p. 506, ascribes Liutprand's standpoint to a 'palace', not a 'court', culture; the distinction seems to me misleading.

[16] Arnaldi, p. 498; Bezzola, ii. 213–6.

Liutprand, close though he was to the kings – that that absence was so complete. Before attempting to account for it, however, let us consider two other historians, both rather farther in narrative focus, if not location, from the problems of the Italian kings.

The *Chronicon Novaliciense* was written in around the early 1050s in Breme, only some 40 km. west of Pavia, whither the monks had moved when the Arabs of La Garde Freinet sacked Novalesa itself. The Chronicle is a fascinating ragbag of a text, full of folk-tales about kings and monks, including an epitome of (and extracts from) the Latin heroic poem *Waltharius*. It includes, entwined with this, what passes for a general account of Italian history from the eighth century onwards, again with especial attention to Charlemagne's conquest, which has a mass of legendary accretions by now. Getting into the century up to 1050, this account becomes more detailed, but startlingly ill-informed. Hugh's lusts are remembered, but the fact that he fell to an invasion led by Berengar II is forgotten; instead, Hugh drowns, as a punishment for sleeping with his son's wife Adelaide. Berengar's own pursuit of Adelaide is described, and her romantic escape to Canossa, from which Otto I delivered her, but Otto is not a Saxon, or even a king; he is duke of the Bavarians. It is not Otto II, but Otto III, who gets defeated by the Arabs in Calabria. And so on. The anonymous chronicler has a clear conception of writing *acta vel gesta regum*, within which he explicitly interlaces discussion *de vassis* (the marquises of Turin, major enemies of the monastery) and of monastic history. One could say that he recognised as possible a history of the Italian kings, and perhaps even of the kingdom. But the details of royal history, even where relevant to a monastic chronicle, are lost or garbled; their only precision, as with Andreas of Bergamo, tends to be in dating, for the monks clearly had a dated king-list, and tried off and on, rather vaguely, to add royal dates to their monastic narratives. There is certainly no notion of any specific function for kings, other than that of issuing charters to the monastery, or, more wickedly, ceding power over Breme to lay and ecclesiastical lords; kings no longer act, they merely legitimate.[17]

My final example is Landulf senior, writing a history of Milan in the years up to 1110, though his narrative stops in 1085. Landulf was not the first historian of Milan – his elder contemporary was Arnulf, who had a much more sober competence – but Landulf's very inaccuracies make him more interesting for us. He is rhetorical, shrill, inventive, a firm supporter of the Ambrosian tradition and of the married clergy in Patarine Milan; to give an Ambrosian origin to his political line, he took his history back to the fourth century. Milan was always a major

---

[17] Most recent ed. is *Cronaca di Novalesa*, ed. G. C. Alessio (Turin, 1982), with useful notes; see also G. Penco, 'Tradizione mediolatina e fonti romanze nel *Chronicon Novaliciense*', *Benedictina*, xii (1958), 1–14. Citations: *Cron. Nov.* v. 2–4, 8, 10–12, Appx. 15, 17.

political centre of the Italian kingdom, and histories of the city and its archbishops were likely to devote much space to kings. Arnulf had had a fair amount of accurate material about them, going back to Hugh, where he began his account; Landulf, however, had not, despite (if we are to believe him) extensive archival research.[18] Landulf invents a sack of Milan by King Lambert, and transposes it from 896 (when Lambert executed Count Maginfred of Milan) back into the sixth century, before the Lombard invasion. Berengar II has been totally lost, his place taken, as a fantasy king of the Roman Empire, by his son Adalbert, Landulf makes these extraordinary statements (as well as more ordinary errors) in the context of a conscious manipulation of his source material far greater than that of any historian previously cited. Brian Stock, in a sophisticated and (in the main) convincing structuralist analysis shows how he patterned his material to bring out a series of formal oppositions – Lambert's attack on Milan, for instance, described as a *clandestina pestis*, prefigures Landulf's vision of the Pataria, the chaos of the forest opposing the civilisation of the city. But this source manipulation does not lessen the effect of Landulf's lack of knowledge. It would have made no difference to his argument to put Lambert back in 896–8; Landulf does not *know* when Lambert reigned. Arnulf, doubtless, would have done, and others in Milan in 1100 certainly did; but it was possible for entirely distinct networks of knowledge of the past to coexist in the same city, and in the traditions Landulf had at his disposal the precise dates of Lambert's attack on Milan and of his resultant death (the same story, more or less, as in Liutprand, modified by a century and a half of transmission) were unknown.[19]

I have been discussing ignorance, but the ignorance concerned is of various kinds, and they must be kept apart. First, it is an absence of written narrative sources. These historians had king-lists at their disposal, for the most part; law-codes, sometimes; saints' lives, sometimes; and, above all, documents. But, after Paul and the Roman *Liber Pontificalis*, they had no narrative histories; none of them had

---

[18] Landulf, *Historia Mediolanensis*, eds. L. C. Bethmann, W. Wattenbach, *M.G.H. SS*, viii (Hannover, 1848), pp. 37–100 (cf. Arnulf, *Gesta archiepiscoporum Mediolanensium*, ibid., pp. 6–31). Landulf's research: p. 37 and iii. 2; see L. A. Ferrai, 'I fonti di Landolfo seniore', *Bull. dell' Ist. Stor. Ital. per il Medioevo*, xiv (1895), 7–70. (Landulf did not know Arnulf's work.) Commentary: O. Capitani, 'Storiografia e riforma della chiesa in Italia', *Settimane di studio*, xvii (1969), 557–629, at 564–6; B. Stock, *The Implications of Literacy* (Princeton, 1983), pp. 163–215.

[19] Landulf, ii. 2, 16; Stock, pp. 174–83. Cf. Liutprand, *Antap.* i. 42. It must be emphasised that the lack of historical knowledge in Landulf's circle cannot be established by the argument, still so common, that 'had Landulf thought his audience knew otherwise, he would not have written as he did.' This argument is almost *never* valid – look at any daily newspaper. A good parallel for history, even accurate history, being written as, and thus becoming, myth (in a Lévi-Straussian sense) can be seen in C. Carozzi, 'Le dernier des Carolingiens: de l'histoire au mythe', *Le moyen âge*, lxxii (1976), 453–76.

visible access to any contemporary accounts.[20] The history of the kings was filled out with oral tradition, a tradition at best fitful: Hugh was remembered for his lust, Berengar II for his pursuit of Adelaide – itself evidently a self-standing oral narrative, but increasingly important politically as it became tied in with the origins and political legitimacy of the house of Canossa, particularly in the entourage of the Countess Matilda up to her death in 1115. The frequent factual inaccuracy of these traditions is not necessarily surprising for oral history, or even necessarily important – 'false' history can be just as valid and certainly just as interesting as 'true' history – but does nonetheless emphasise the lack of narrative complexity in the oral material drifting across the Po plain. But the most important absence in these writers' works is that none of them sees in the actions of kings anything approaching a concern, or even a lack of concern, for the government of the kingdom; this is equally true of the other major historical narratives of the period, like Arnulf's history of Milan, or Donizo's history of Matilda.[21] Kings no longer rule the kingdom; they engage in political activity in the historian's field of interest. They no longer underpin justice; they make judicial decisions (preserved because of the survival of documents) with respect to the claims of the archbishop of Milan, or of the abbot of Novalesa-Breme. And, above all, the remembered actions of kings are divorced from any coherent narrative context. The kingdom still exists in these texts, and is important; but kings themselves are outsiders, beneficent or maleficent, with a discontinuous impact on 'real history', which has become localised, in a monastery, a city, or a principality. And the localisation of 'real history', for the Italians, was one arena in which the failure of the Italian kings, both before and after the Ottonian conquest of 962, very clearly lay.[22]

---

[20] Paul existed in over a hundred manuscripts (*M.G.H. SRL*, pp. 28–43), the *Liber Pontificalis* in 86, no other Italian historian over 16 (Guenée, *Hist. et cult. historique*, pp. 250–2) and Liutprand's MS tradition was mostly transalpine (*Liudprand*, ed. Becker, pp. xxiv–xxxv).

[21] Donizo, *Vita Mathildis*, ed. L. Simeoni, *Rerum italicarum scriptores nova ed.*, v. ii (Bologna, 1930); see M. Nobili, 'L'ideologia politica in Donizone', *Studi Matildici* (Modena, 1978), pp. 263–79; idem, 'La cultura politica alla corte di Matilde di Canossa', *Le sedi della cultura nell'Emilia Romagna. L'alto medioevo* (Milan, 1983), pp. 217–36. Donizo, as Nobili shows, was trying to establish the legitimacy of the Canossa and their principality as a rival to the kingdom; the latter is still recognised as a crucial legitimising element for the Canossa themselves, but the kings are merely seen acting as princes, in rivalry with Boniface and Matilda, and on the same level.

[22] Arnulf is an exception, in that he saw Milan's interests as being *in themselves* the interests of the kingdom; he discusses the latter as a continuous narrative as a result, but its reality is brought down to the eye-level of the city, much as Donizo does for the princes. (cf. Capitani, 564f.) The monasteries of south-central Italy, too, maintained an interest in the kings, as defenders of their rights, even as founts of justice; but very much as outsiders nonetheless: C. J. Wickham, *Studi sulla società degli Appennini nell' alto medioevo* (Bologna, 1982), p. 60f.

I have been characterising this failure as being inside the framework of the collective memory available to history-writers in the tenth and eleventh-century Italian kingdom, principally ecclesiastics, from a wide range of environments: royal and local courts, cathedrals, rural monasteries. But these historians did not exhaust the range of the literate élites of early medieval Italy. In particular, none of them came from one important group, the lawyers: that is to say, for the purposes of this article, the judges and notaries of the Italian central bureaucracy, the professionals of the state administration, and the jurists of the Pavia law-school, themselves generally judges in the capital. A professional group like this could be expected to have a collective memory structured along rather different lines from that, say, of clerics or aristocrats; and indeed the political perceptions of these lawyers, most visible in their view of the past, were in many respects rather different from those we have looked at hitherto.

So, what do lawyers remember? Not a lot, one could reply. Law originates in the past, but its validity, its relevance, is determined by its situation in an eternal present of legal applicability. Out-of-date law is not explained or justified by a past historical context; it is merely no longer binding. Certainly, the world of Roman law of the twelfth century onwards, for all its strong idealist streak, recognised the existence of historical change and historical explanation; but it was not a predominant attitude. And the experience of reading through the corpus of Lombard-Carolingian law, the great achievement of the Pavese jurists, either the collection of texts and glosses that forms the *Liber Papiensis* of the mid tenth century onwards, or the *Expositio* and commentaries of the late eleventh and twelfth, will not convince many people that the Pavese lawyers had any great interest in the past: laws, however old, are immanent; they do not need explanation, only interpretation. The chronological order of the *Liber Papiensis* is reduced to a mathematical series; only some of Otto I's legislation is seen in historical terms, in that it is criticised as bad law, and even then the historical ascription of the text, to Leo of Vercelli, is wrong, for Leo was an adviser to Otto III.[23]

Lawyers meet the past not in the ideology of their subject-matter, but in the history of themselves as a group. Otto's laws threatened lawyers as a group, for they legitimated the challenge of documents by duel, a frontal attack on the complex interweaving of legal norms that gave jurists their raison d'être. One obvious text is the product of such a group ideology, the so-called *Honorantiae Civitatis Papiae*, written in the

---

[23] *Liber papiensis*, ed. A. Boretius, *M. G. H. Leges*, iv (Hannover, 1868); p. 572 for comments on Otto I; the classic exercise in legal interpretation is on Rothari 153, pp. 317–23. (The *Lombarda* commentaries are much the same; see n. 29). Lawyers and history: Guenée, *Hist. et cult. historique*, pp. 33–5, 311; for a defence, D. R. Kelley, 'Clio and the lawyers', *Medievalia et humanistica*, N.S., v (1976), 25–49.

1020s, which is a description of, and in part a lament for, the traditional glories of the capital city, the predominance of its palace, palace tribunal, and legal schools, and the wealth that came into the city from state duties on trade and artisans' workshops: these have declined from their glory under Hugh and Otto I, thanks to venality and neglect. The text is transparently written by a palace administrator, and is our major source for the institutions of Pavia as capital; *none* of them are evidenced in Liutprand of Cremona. Kings come and go very fleetingly; they only impinge when they appoint wicked administrators who sell off the rights of the crown.[24] This is important, for we are here not dealing with Breme or Milan, but with the institutions of state; the kings are scarcely relevant even to them.

Let us at this point return to our English parallel. The classic text for the consciousness of lawyers/administrators is the *Dialogus de scaccario* of the late 1170s. Richard Fitz Neal was, of course, trying to write history even less than the author of the *Honorantiae* was; but the history the *Dialogus* contains is instructive. It is above all history as seen by men with a particular training and collective experience. The points of historical reference (after the Conquest itself) are Domesday book, the development of dues in money, the development of the Exchequer under Roger of Salisbury and its decline in the wars of Stephen's reign. The wars themselves do not appear except as a context for administrative changes. This is not entirely surprising; the *Dialogus* is about administration. But the history Richard refers to is clearly the product of oral tradition, about the history of Danegeld, or the origins of Domesday book. The traditions are inaccurate, but this does not matter, except in that it shows us the *independence* of this oral culture; no other historian of twelfth-century England makes similar statements. In most societies there is more than one body of oral tradition available at a time; this one was the product of the collective memory of Henry II's administrators. Italy does not have anything like this text. But the *Dialogus* certainly matches the sort of consciousness found in the *Honorantiae*, and indeed throws it into higher relief. And there is one major difference: the kings, William I and Henry I, by implication Henry II, are direct actors in Fitz Neal's historical excursus; they are crucial points of reference, their actions themselves conferring legitimation. The administrative system of England, unlike that of Italy, was closely related to, and dependent on, the kings, and recognised it.[25]

---

[24] Group memory for lawyers: Halbwachs, *Cadres sociaux*, pp. 243–9. 'Honorantiae' ed. A. Hofmeister, *M.G.H. SS*, xxx. ii, 1450–9.

[25] *Dialogus de Scaccario*, ed. with fullest commentary by A. Hughes, C. G. Crump, C. Johnson (Oxford, 1902), i. 4, 7, 8, 10, 16. For Domesday memory, see comments in M. T. Clanchy, *From Memory to Written Record* (London, 1979), pp. 11f, 18.

Lawyers in Italy nonetheless had the law-code, which conveyed something of the kingdom's past, for anyone who wished to read the text in that light, through the successive edicts of successive kings. Legal manuscripts tend to consist of the law-code alone, in one of its many variants, occasionally along with other legal texts. But around a third of them also append a set of catalogues of the Italian kings. These are stark lists, with precise and generally correct reign-lengths, sometimes exact to months and days, and with *interregna* and co-rulership duly listed. Such catalogues also frequently occur in various other sorts of manuscript compilation in the centuries before 1200. They rarely include any incidental detail, although sometimes a half-sentence or so slips in, especially from periods closest to the compiler – Otto II's defeat in the South, Henry II's overthrow of Arduin, and the like. These are not annals, included for historical or antiquarian interest; they are tools. They are the texts that judges and notaries needed to date and compare documents.[26] We have hundreds of Italian court-cases from the period up to 1100; the results of nearly all of them hang on documents, read out in court. Kings are very often referred to; but always in the context of surviving documents. This is lawyers' time; it is less concerned with any sort of historical consciousness than with legitimation, by the lawyers, above all of rights of property.

Historical memory is, in general, functional; the past is remembered in order to legitimate activity in the present. Icelandic historical memory in the twelfth and thirteenth centuries, complex and sophisticated as it was, was given one of its major frameworks by a need to legitimate property claims (whether true or false) by a traceable descent from the original ninth-century landtaking, the founding myth of Icelandic history. The property element in rival versions of orally transmitted material has been stressed, too, by several African anthropologists. In Italy, this element in historical memory was hardly necessary, there were so many documents around. Even in court, oral evidence, though fully admissible at law, was relatively rarely used

---

[26] Manuscripts (of the Lombard code to 774, the *Liber Papiensis*, and the *Lombarda*): M. G. H. *Leges*, iv, xii–xliii, liii–lxii, xcix–cx. Catalogues: most are conveniently collected in *M.G.H. SRL*, pp. 490–523. For a parallel, see J. P. Genet, 'Droit et histoire en Angleterre', *Annales de Bretagne*, lxxxvii (1980), 319–66, at 329–31, against the overall thrust of his argument. Some MSS. of the Lombard code had an attached history of the Lombards; that belonged to an earlier stage in legislation. For the establishment of the code and of the right to legislate by the kings – see C. P. Wormald, '*Lex scripta* and *verbum regis*', in P. H. Sawyer and I. N. Wood (eds.), *Early Medieval Kingship* (Leeds, 1977), pp. 105–38, esp. p. 121.

after 900 or so.[27] In Catalonia, recent work has emphasised that the continued dating by the kings of France in tenth and eleventh-century documents, despite their complete political irrelevance, derives simply from a persistent desire for the legitimation of land tenure; even the constant reference in charters to a historical event, the 985 Arab sack of Barcelona, can be described as the result of a 'maniacal' concern for written law – the Arabs having destroyed so many documents.[28] Italian legal experts redimensioned their kings in a similar way; kings, effective or ineffective in real life, became simply the abstract legitimations of a legal system and a structure of land tenure, in an array of interconnected local societies that had otherwise totally escaped royal control. The existence of widespread (if partial) lay literacy and of so many documents virtually allowed the Italians to forget their kings; the documents, and the structure of law, were good enough on their own. The process culminated in the historical tradition about the Lombards appended in the early twelfth century by the jurist Ariprand to his commentary on the *Lombarda* (the version of the Italian law-code taken out of chronological order and divided into topics along Roman lines). Ariprand's Lombard kings have undergone a startling transformation; the twenty-five rulers in Italy between 568 and 774 have been reduced to six, Queen Gambara, who led the invasion, and her successors Rothari, Grimoald, Liutprand, Ratchis, and Aistulf: the five lawgivers. Their successors are similarly those Carolingian and German emperors who legislated. Not surprisingly, the major acts of Gambara and Rothari are to create the law, in imitation of and as a challenge to the Justinianic code. Here, the whole of history has been telescoped into the law-code. The past, as a framework in its own right, barely exists at all.[29]

The Italian state was strong, coherent, and rich, well into the eleventh century. Despite its legal-administrative force, however, this state was barely relevant to the historical consciousness of the very few historians Italy produced in the tenth and eleventh centuries. Where the state impinged was on the consciousness of lawyers and administrators.

---

[27] For Iceland, see *The Book of Settlements. Landnámabók*, trs. H. Pálsson & P. Edwards (Manitoba, 1972), with the comments of S. Rafnsson, *Studier i Landnámabók* (Lund, 1974), pp. 140–2, 150–1; cf. J. Benediktsson, 'Some problems in the history of Iceland', in T. Andersson & K. Sandred (eds.), *The Vikings* (Uppsala, 1978), pp. 161–5. Africa: MacGaffey, *ubi supra* n. 4; cf. also L. Bohannan, 'A Genealogical Charter', *Africa*, xxii (1952), 301–15. Courtcases: C. J. Wickham, 'Land disputes and their social framework in Lombard-Carolingian Italy', in W. Davies & P. J. Fouracre (eds.), *The Settlement of Disputes in Early Medieval Europe*, forthcoming.

[28] R. J. H. Collins, *Early Medieval Spain* (London, 1983), p. 259; M. Zimmermann, 'La prise de Barcelone par Al-Mansûr et la naissance de l'historiographie catalane', *Ann. Bretagne*, lxxvii, 191–218.

[29] *M.G.H. SRL*, pp. 591–602; for Ariprand, 592–6. Cf. A. Anschütz, *Die Lombarda-Commentare des Ariprand und Albertus* (Heidelberg, 1855), pp. 1–13; Albertus, Ariprand's successor, amplifies Ariprand's historical fantasy, but then adds an epitome of Paul.

They knew the rules, even if no-one else did. (The Pavesi told an unconvinced Conrad II that they were acting within their rights when they burned down his royal palace in 1024, as there was technically an *interregnum* before his coronation.) The legal-administrative structure of the kingdom looms large in normative texts. But lawyers' time does not, under normal circumstances, extend to a historical consciousness about the *politics* of the kingdom. Historical origins tend to matter to lawyers only when the legitimation of an entire political and legal system explicitly depends on them, in a way that few systems do after a generation or so of normalisation and stability (think of Soviet Russia), and tenth and eleventh-century Italy certainly did not.[30] The Italian state, to the lawyers, existed in itself; it was not determined by the importance of the Italian kings, only by the existence of kingship; the kings thus lost contact with the structure of their own state. This does not, however, imply that the failure of the kings *derived* from their failure to keep control of the processes of historical consciousness. Indeed, the survival of a vision of kingship as a basis for the Italian state preserved a certain legitimacy for the activity of the kings themselves, when backed by German armies, right the way from Otto I to Henry IV, and up to Barbarossa. Nonetheless, the framework of memory throws into relief the *context* in which the tenth-century Italian kings failed to keep control either of local society (so difficult anyway to control in the tenth-century world), or even of the state and its resources. When kings ceased to be relevant to people, they, and their activities, were lost.

But there is more than this. Kings in Europe could be very weak, poor, and politically circumscribed – the early Capetians are an obvious example – and still remain a lasting focus of historical attention, at least in their immediate entourage. The failure of the Italian kings was also a failure to establish a court culture. The court of Pavia was, by 900, a complex organism with a long history. It was heavily sectorialised. The king's entourage, men like Liutprand and the major court aristocrats, were different from the administrators and judges who ran the major offices of the capital and the palace law-court. Tenth-century Pavia was already sophisticated enough to have more than one social category with a group consciousness. It must indeed have had several – Liutprand is, after all, cynical enough about the lay aristocracy to underline that their world-view was rather different (it was almost totally a non-literate one, and so much less clearly visible).[31] This

[30] Wipo, *Gesta Chuonradi*, ed. H. Bresslau (Hannover, 1919), c. 7 for the Pavesi. In the communal period, of course, lawyers were not only interested in city history, but virtually controlled its recording (cf. below, nn. 34, 35). But it is the communes that are the exception; their uncertain identity and continuing constitutional instability entailed constant legitimation by calls on the past, and the political and professional position of lawyers themselves was directly dependent on this.

[31] *Antap.*, i. 37.

complexity led to a diffuseness in the ideology projected from the court. But this was not in itself the cause of its failure. The point can be best seen by returning to the court of Henry II of England, probably the first in the West to match Pavia in complexity.

Henry's court is badly served if regarded as a coherent unit; bewildering enough even to insiders, it must have been incomprehensible to most outsiders. The later twelfth-century court literature from England is quite other than homogeneous: Howden, the *Policraticus*, the *Dialogus*, Walter Map in the *De nugis curialum* speak entirely different languages. Indeed, the juxtaposition of the *Dialogus* and Walter Map matches rather well the juxtaposition of the *Honorantiae* and Liutprand, in the complete mutual exclusion, a mutual irrelevance rather than a respective ignorance, of their historical points of view, the administrator failing totally to communicate with the courtier, to say nothing of outsiders. But there is a contrast. Reading Walter Map is not, apart from the entertainment value, like reading Liutprand. Map, like most people in England in all probability, was not very interested in Henry II's legal and administrative reforms; but Henry was his fixed point of reference in a way no king, even Otto I, was for Liutprand. And Henry was this for each one of his court writers: the point at which each of their various identities met, just as Henry I and William I were for each of their various excursions into the past. In this sense, Henry *had* a court; Map presented it as an entire world, his version of hell.[32] The Italian kings did not. Even when Henry was away, the justiciar maintained a social as well as governmental focus; the count of the palace in Ottonian Italy, though an active administrator and a powerful noble (he was usually count of Bergamo), remained a political cipher. The Italian court, at least after Louis II's death in 875, never fused into the cohesive framework that would focus the diverse sectoral loyalties and world-views of the court of twelfth-century England.

To an extent Henry II managed this because he inherited (and resolutely reinstated) the myth of the English state that had existed since 1066 and, in many ways, since Alfred. But this only restates the problem of how it was the Italian kings never had a myth. The contrast between Italy and England, in large part, comes back to lawyers' time. The underpinning of the Italian state was, and had been since the seventh century, more secular than in any other country in Europe. Nowhere else were there so many lay notaries and legal professionals, and indeed nowhere else were clerical notaries and legal professionals so fully part of

---

[32] W. Map, *De nugis curialum*, eds. M. R. James, C. N. L. Brooke, R. A. Mynors (Oxford, 1983), esp. i. 1–10, v. 1–7. (Map does not say much about Henry as a legal reformer, but he does appear as a judge: v. 7, p. 508f.) No useful overall discussion of Henry's court cultures exists. The best survey is Bezzola, iii. i (Paris, 1963); see also E. Türk, *Nugae curialum* (Geneva, 1977).

a lay administrative *cursus*. Every other political system in Europe before the thirteenth century relied on clerics, trained by other clerics. But ecclesiastical cultures of every kind contained a direct access to historical tradition, indeed a great many strands of historical tradition. The legal culture of Pavia, of Milan, later of Bologna, did not. So Italy had no Howden, or even an *Anglo-Saxon Chronicle*, to give perspective and narrative line to the *Honorantiae*, or a sense of the role of the state to Liutprand. The past was not symbolic to lawyers, so it was forgotten. The legal orientation of literate culture in pre-communal Italy makes it one of the few to fully justify Ammon's famous fears that writing would 'implant forgetfulness in men's souls': it is quite possible that the more literate Italian laymen were, the less history they remembered.[33] These men controlled the framework of the Italian court, and its culture; the court thus lived strictly in the present. This was fine while Italian kings were continuously powerful, as (by and large) they were up to Louis II; but the ideology of the court lost its coherence as soon as royal power went into eclipse. By Liutprand's time it was already too late. The kings, who could elsewhere have relied on a historical perspective for the legitimation of their politics, thus drifted out of memory the moment they ceased to maintain a direct impact on Italian society; they could never regain it.

What happened to the kings thereafter cannot be pursued here; we would find ourselves in the arid beginnings of the city chronicles, the products of a local notarial culture at last to an extent interested in the past, at least insofar as it offered (uncertain) legitimation for the new reality of the communes. The very existence of the kingdom became dependent on local concerns for the political status of cities and of rural aristocrats, at least as much as on the still continuing importance of the kings as validators of law and documents. But as the twelfth century got under way, as the communes began to stake their claims more boldly, as urban institutions appeared that did not in some way represent the state, as local statutes began to be issued by the cities, as documents began to be dated by the Incarnation, even that existence began to weaken. Twelfth-century judicial inquests show that the points of historical reference for Italian local élites had simply become the wars undertaken by their own

---

[33] Plato, *Phaedrus* 274E–5C; cf. Clanchy, 'Remembering the past', p. 176, among many.

cities against their enemies; here the state has finally gone.[34] The irony is that Barbarossa and his successors ended up by being recognised by almost no-one except the lawyers.[35]

[34] City chronicles: G. Martini, 'Lo spirito cittadino e le origini della storiografia comunale lombarda', *Nuova rivista storica*, liv (1970), 1–22, at 20–22; P. Classen, '*Res gestae*, Universal History, Apocalypse', in R. L. Benson, G. Constable (eds.), *Renaissance and Renewal in the twelfth century* (Oxford, 1982), 387–417, at 393–8; I have not seen G. Arnaldi, 'Il notaio-cronista e le cronache cittadine in Italia', *Atti del 1° cong. internaz. della Società Ital. di storia del diritto* (Florence, 1966), pp. 293–309. Inquests: J.-P. Delumeau, 'La mémoire des gens d'Arezzo et de Sienne à travers des dépositions des témoins', *Temps, mémoire, tradition*, pp. 45–67, esp. 52–3; see further U. Pasqui, *Documenti per la storia della città di Arezzo*, ii (Florence, 1916), pp. 124, 136, 137, 147; L. Passerini, 'Documenti che illustrano la memoria: una monaca del secolo XIII', *Archivio storico italiano*, 3 ser., xxiii (1876), 205–17, 385–403, at 208, 211, 217, 385, 388–9, 396–7. (Contrast, for example, Manaresi, *Placiti* 51 for 851.) It should not be forgotten that these witnesses were all clerics and small aristocrats – and some merchants in Manaresi 51; peasants would have been little touched by any of the argument in this article. Thus, in Languedoc – although not necessarily elsewhere – peasant historical consciousness of any type was very limited in depth: M. Gramain, 'Mémoires paysannes', *Ann. Bretagne*, lxxxiii (1976), 315–24; E. Le Roy Ladurie, *Montaillou* (Paris, 1975), pp. 424–31. See further as a mise-en-scène Y. Grava, 'La mémoire, une base de l'organisation politique des communautés provençales au XIVe siècle', *Temps, mémoire, tradition*, pp. 69–94. In fourteenth-century England, by contrast, peasants could have a sense of the past that extended back to before 1066, not entirely inaccurately: R. Faith, 'The "Great Rumour" of 1377 and Peasant Ideology'; in R. H. Hilton and T. H. Aston (eds.), *The English Rising of 1381* (Cambridge 1984) pp. 43–73. There is much to be done in this field.

[35] Lawyers still tended to regard the kingdom as the field of action of the law. The establishment of the communes and their own law remained in the world of the informal for a long time, and greatly complicated legal historical consciousness. Indeed, most Italian archives show some lawyers, well past 1200, keeping fast to their imperial (or in *interregna*, royal) titles, despite a century of communal history. Peter Classen's unfinished survey of twelfth-century Italian legal culture shows how complex the issues are, and how much there is still to be done: *Studium und Gesellschaft im Mittelalter* (Stuttgart, 1983), 27–126. The other group who still needed the kingdom, to legitimise their titles, were the surviving great rural aristocrats, such as the Obertenghi, the Guidi, the marquises of Monferrato. The actual political *alignments* of Barbarossa's time are a different matter, however; see, as a guide, P. Brezzi, 'Gli alleati italiani di Federico Barbarossa (feudatari e città)', in R. Manselli & J. Riedmann (eds.), *Federico Barbarossa nel dibattito storiografico in Italia e Germania* (Bologna, 1982), pp. 157–97.

6

The Miracles of St Benedict:
A Window on Early Medieval France

D. W. Rollason

Accounts of the posthumous miracles of saints form a significant proportion of the surviving Latin literature of the Middle Ages.[1] They are extant either as chapters forming part of accounts of the translations or elevations of saints' relics or as free-standing collections of miracle-stories, sometimes of considerable bulk. Into this last category falls one of the best-known collections of miracle-stories, that concerned with miracles supposedly worked by the intercession of St Benedict for the abbey of Fleury (Saint-Benoît-sur-Loire) and its dependencies chiefly from the ninth to the twelfth century.[2] This St Benedict was none other than the sixth-century Italian holy man and compiler of the Rule of St Benedict whose relics the Fleury monks claimed (probably rightly) to

---

[1] See, for example, R. C. Finucane, *Miracles and Pilgrims: Popular Beliefs in Medieval England* (London, 1977), B. Ward, *Miracles and the Medieval Mind* (London, 1982) and P. R. Morison, 'The Miraculous and French Society, c.950–1100' (unpubl. D. Phil. thesis, University of Oxford, 1983). I am grateful to Dr Morison for permission to consult her thesis, which will soon be published in an expanded form. The results of her research, although comparable to the conclusions presented here, are of much wider scope and are quite independent. Work for the present paper was made possible by the Leverhulme Trust, which awarded me a European Studentship to enable me to study in Paris during the academic year 1976–7, and by grants from the University of Durham Committee for Staff Travel and Research. I am grateful to Professor G. Duby for guidance at the outset and to the Sunderland Branch of the Historical Association and the Oxford University Stubbs Society for inviting me to deliver earlier versions of this paper as lectures.

[2] The collection was edited by E. de Certain, *Les miracles de saint Benoît écrits par Adrevald, Aimoin, André, Raoul Tortaire et Hugues de Sainte Marie, moines de Fleury*, Société de l'Histoire de France (Paris, 1858) (hereafter *MSB*). On the deficiencies of this edition see A. Vidier, *L'historiographie à Saint Benoît-sur-Loire et les Miracles de Saint Benoît* (Paris, 1965), pp. 152–3, 182–3, 198–201 and 210; references to earlier editions are here given. Four miracle-accounts overlooked by De Certain are edited on pp. 227–8 (cf. pp. 184–91). A better edition of sections of the first book of the collection is given by O. Holder-Egger, *Monumenta Germaniae Historica, Scriptores*, xvi (Hanover, 1887), 474–500. A new edition of the whole collection is shortly to be published under the direction of Mr F. Charpin of the University of Limoges. For convenience, page-references will here be given to De Certain's edition.

have translated from Monte Cassino to their own abbey in the late seventh or early eighth century.[3]

The renown of this miracle-collection is entirely justified, for its characteristics and the circumstances of its composition render it of exceptional importance. Firstly, its sheer length is noteworthy: it occupies 371 pages of the printed edition and is one of the longest collections extant. Secondly, it was composed over a long period of time. Book I was written probably in the late 860s and an appendix of two chapters was added later in the ninth century: it is thus set in the period of fragmentation of the Carolingian Empire, the end of the reign of Charles the Bald and the period of Viking attacks. Books II–VII by contrast take us into the period of the early Capetian kings, a time of great royal weakness. Books II and III were written at the beginning of the eleventh century, Books IV–VII by different hands in the middle years of that century. Book VIII belongs to the late eleventh or very early twelfth century and the fragmentary Book IX to the first quarter of the twelfth, a period in which the Capetian kings were able to some extent to consolidate their power.[4] Although lacking a tenth-century contribution, the miracle-collection thus forms a remarkable cross-section of French history, all the more so because successive authors regarded it as an evolving compilation and referred back to their predecessors' work.[5] Thirdly, Fleury, where the collection was made, was an influential place. Obscure as its history is in the two centuries after its supposed foundation in 651, it seems likely that even then it was an important abbey in the southern borders of the heartland of royal power. Its prominence under the Carolingians is reflected by grants of land and privilege made to it and it emerged in the tenth century as a centre of reformed monasticism whose influence extended as far as England. The early eleventh century, however, seems to have been an especially brilliant period of its history, for nearby Orléans was a favourite residence of the Capetian kings, Fleury's abbots included Abbo and Gauzlin and it was producing a series of distinguished scholars and writers.[6] Fourthly, the compilers of the miracle-collection include men of high calibre who have in several cases left other works. Adrevald, the compiler of Book I, was also the author of a life of St Aigulf, a treaty on

---

[3] See, for example, H. Leclercq, 'Fleury-sur-Loire', *Dictionnaire d'archéologie chrétienne et de liturgie*, v (Paris, 1923), cols.1709–60, and *Studia Monastica*, xxi (1979).

[4] Vidier, pp. 157–8, 163–4, 183–4, 202–4, 212 and 214.

[5] Vidier, pp. 139–40.

[6] See, for example, C. Brühl, *Fodrum, Gistum, Servitium Regis*, 2 vols. (Köln and Graz, 1968), pp. 237–8 and Maps 4 and 5; J. Laporte, 'Fleury', *Dictionnaire d'histoire et de géographie ecclésiastique*, xvii (1971), cols. 441–76 (with further references); P. Cousin, *Abbon de Fleury-sur-Loire* (Paris, 1954), and *André de Fleury, Vie de Gauzlin, abbé de Fleury*, ed. and trans. R-H. Bautier and G. Labory (Paris, 1969), pp. 15–16 and *passim*.

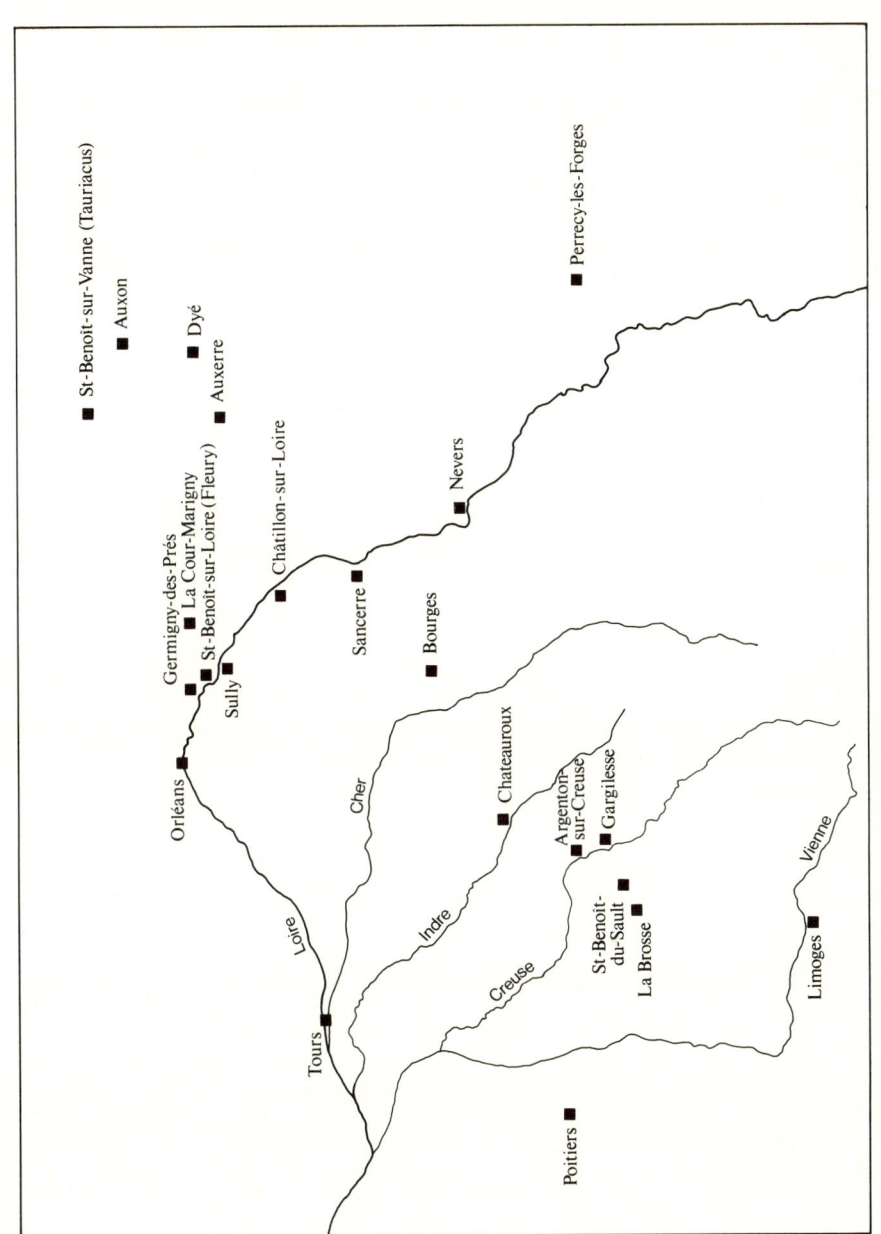

Map 4. Places associated with the Miracles of St Benedict.

the Eucharist and perhaps an account of the translation of St Benedict.[7] Aimoin, the compiler of Books II and III, was the companion and biographer of Abbo and author of an unfinished *Historia Francorum* and a now lost history of the abbots of Fleury.[8] Andrew, the compiler of Books IV–VII, has left a biography of Gauzlin, abbot of Fleury;[9] and Ralph Tortarius, who compiled Book VIII, was a noted writer of hagiography, letters and poetry, including a metrical version of the Miracles of St Benedict which survives.[10] The fragmentary Book IX may be the work of no less a figure than the historian Hugh of Fleury although this is less certain.[11] Only Adelerius, the compiler of the appendix to Book I, is otherwise unknown to us.[12] The Miracles of St Benedict therefore merit the closest attention. The problem is that of knowing how best to exploit from an historical viewpoint a source dealing chiefly with the miraculous and with events connected with miracles. What sort of information can be expected and how can it be extracted?

A prominent characteristic of the Miracles of St Benedict is the extent to which they include material which is incidental or, in some cases, unrelated to the miracles described. Much attention is lavished on the history of Fleury, whole chapters being devoted to the career and translation of St Benedict, the course of Norman devastation, the careers of the abbots, whose succession can largely be traced by reference to the Miracles, and other aspects of the abbey's affairs. But the writers' horizon extended beyond Fleury and its properties to take in the history of Western Francia. Adrevald draws, for example, on Einhard's Life of Charlemagne to paint a picture of the later Merovingians and the accession of the Carolingians; and his successors devote chapters to the transference of power to the Capetians, the heresy which arose in Orléans and was condemned in 1022, the troubles of Henry I with his mother Constance and so on.[13] The reader frequently has the impression of dealing with a chronicle rather than with a miracle-collection, an impression reinforced by the inclusion of

---

[7] Vidier, pp. 153–8 and addendum to p. 158. On the *Historia translationis* cf. Holder-Egger, pp. 474–5.

[8] Vidier, pp. 183–4, and K. F. Werner, 'Die literarischen Vorbilder des Aimoin von Fleury und die Entstehung seiner *Gesta Francorum*', *Medium Aevum Vivum: Festschrift für Walther Bulst*, ed H. R. Jauss and D. Schaller (Heidelberg, 1960), pp. 69–103.

[9] Vidier, pp. 201–3, and Bautier and Labory, *passim*.

[10] Vidier, pp. 210–12, where further references are given. See also F. Bar, 'Raoul le Tourtier moine de Fleury et poète latin à la fin du XIe siècle', *Etudes ligériennes d'histoire et d'archéologie médiévales*, ed. R. Louis (Auxerre, 1975), pp. 1–8.

[11] Vidier, pp. 213–14.

[12] *Ibid.*, pp. 163–4.

[13] *Ibid.*, pp. 159–60, 194–5, 206–7 and 212–13, and R-H Bautier, 'La place de l'abbaye de Fleury-sur-Loire dans l'historiographie française du IXe au XIIe siècle', *Etudes ligériennes*, ed. Louis, pp. 28–30.

The Miracles of St Benedict 77

information about eclipses, floods and famines which are standard elements in full-blown chronicles.[14] Adrevald and Aimoin seem aware that they are often writing history rather than simple accounts of miracles, for they apologise for doing so.[15] All this suggests that the Miracles of St Benedict are potentially a source of great value for the understanding of provincial viewpoints on the history of early medieval France. Some examples must serve to demonstrate the possibilities. In Book I, Adrevald devotes a long section to the wars in 834 between Odo, count of Orléans, and the former count of Orléans Matfrid, the latter supported by Lambert, count of Nantes, and their Neustrian allies.[16] Adrevald adds information about this campaign otherwise unrecorded and his account has rightly been used by historians. Thus he describes Odo's summoning of reinforcements from Burgundy and the ravaging committed by this army during its three-day journey down the Loire.[17] But it should also be noticed that his attitude is very parochial. Odo was in this campaign a supporter of the emperor Louis against insurgents fighting in the interests of his rebellious son Lothar and Adrevald clearly knew this. Odo, one would have expected, would have had the Fleury monks' support but, because as count of Orléans he had attempted to infringe Fleury's immunity, his defeat and death were evidently regarded as desirable and were supposed to have been foretold by St Benedict himself in a vision. A second and no less striking example of what appears to be a provincial viewpoint is that of Andrew of Fleury on the Peace of God league organised in or before 1037 by Aimo, archbishop of Bourges.[18] According to Andrew, Aimo's league was notable in that it required a peace-oath to be sworn by all male inhabitants of the archdiocese over the age of fifteen years, who thus bound themselves to pursue those who broke the peace – with military force if necessary.[19] The league was a success for a time but it ultimately failed, partly because it was infected with bribery and corruption, partly as a result of the deaths of a large number of people who were sheltering in a castle which the peace militia stormed. In a battle between Aimo's militia and Odo of Déols, a heavenly thunderbolt is supposed to have struck the former and many were

[14] See, for example, *MSB*, III.9 (pp. 150–3), V.1 (p. 192), VI.11 (pp. 233–6), VI.21 (p. 248) and VII.3 (p. 252).
[15] *MSB*, I, 27 (p. 61) and II.1 (p. 95).
[16] *MSB*, I. 20–1 (pp. 47–51). Cf. L. Halphen, *Charlemagne et l'empire carolingien* (Paris, 1947), pp. 297–8.
[17] B. Simson, *Jahrbücher des fränkischen Reichs unter Ludwig dem Frommen*, 2 vols. (Leipzig, 1874–6), ii, 102–5, especially 103 nn. 9 and 10, and 104 n.l.
[18] *MSB*, V. 2–4 (pp. 192–8). See B. Toepfer, *Volk und Kirche zur Zeit der beginnenden Gottesfriedensbewegung in Frankreich* (Berlin, 1957), p. 78, and H. Hoffmann, *Gottesfriede und Treuga Dei*, Schriften der Monumenta Germaniae historica, xx (Stuggart, 1964), pp. 106–9. Cf. G. Devailly, *Le Berry du Xe siècle au milieu du XIIIe; Etude politique, religieuse, sociale et économique* (Paris, 1973), pp. 142–8.
[19] *MSB*, p. 193.

killed, including Aimo himself. Andrew's account of this Peace is thus ultimately unfavourable to it. It may be, as Duby has argued, that he was distressed by the apparent novelty of enlisting peasants as well as knights in the peace militia.[20] But it is also possible that he, like Gerard, bishop of Cambrai, had misgivings about the Peace itself.[21] If so, his testimony is valuable evidence for attitudes at Fleury which, with its position on the Loire, looked both south to the homeland of the Peace of God and north where it spread later from the south.[22]

The keen interest in historical writing displayed by the compilers of the miracle-collection is significant in relation to other aspects of its content. For these writers, who clearly thought themselves as much historians as hagiographers and who could use historical methods, were led by the nature of their material to consider a wider social spectrum than usually came within the purview of the medieval historian. The courts of kings and princes are by no means the predominant subject; and relatively little attention is devoted to the monastic life and the monks themselves. Instead the miracle-accounts offer a range of vivid scenes from the life of the laity of early medieval France.[23] Historians have not been slow to exploit the best of this material and some examples must serve to emphasize its richness. F. L. Ganshof has drawn attention to the importance of a miracle-account in Book I, in which a salt ship sailing up the Loire to Fleury was detained by toll-collectors at Orléans.[24] The captain showed his document exempting Fleury's ships from paying toll but the toll-collectors would not accept its validity and the ship was handed over to the procurator of the port and impounded in the *portus fiscalis*. This is a precious account of the working of toll-collection and the salt trade on the Loire and we possess it simply because the incident in question was thought to have called forth the miraculous intervention of St Benedict. On Sunday morning, Adrevald tells us, the unmanned ship moved out into the river of its own accord and sailed upstream. Equally striking is Andrew's account of the serf Stabilis who resented his servitude and escaped to Burgundy where he lived as a free man.[25] He prospered to the extent that he could set himself up as a knight with horses, hawks, dogs, young followers and a noble wife. This sidelight on social mobility in the mid-eleventh century was also preserved because it formed part of a miracle-story.

[20] G. Duby, *The Three Orders: Feudal Society Imagined*, trans. A. Goldhammer (Chicago and London, 1978), pp. 185–91.
[21] *Ibid.*, pp. 21–43.
[22] Toepfer, *Volk und Kirche*, p. 66.
[23] J. Leclercq, 'Violence et dévotion à Saint-Benoît-sur-Loire au Moyen Age', *Etudes ligériennes*, ed. Louis, pp. 247–56, especially p. 254.
[24] *MSB*, I.19 (pp. 46–7); F. L. Ganshof, 'A propos du tonlieu à l'époque carolingienne', *La città nell' Alto Medioevo*, Settimane di Studio del Centro Italiano sull' Alto Medioevo, vi (Spoleto, 1959), 485–90.
[25] *MSB*, VI.2 (pp. 218–21).

When challenged by the prior of Fleury's possession at Dyé, Stabilis denied his servitude and elected to prove his freedom in trial by battle before the Count of Troyes. Through St Benedict's miraculous intervention, the coin which represented his dues as a serf and which he had in his sleeve grew to enormous size and forced him to give way. As a final example, we might take a story from Book VIII concerning a noble called Seguin who ravaged Fleury's lands and stole pigs. When messengers were sent to remonstrate with him they found him in his wooden tower and specifically in the upper storey (*solarium*) where he lived with his family. The floor was made of beams and below there were cellars and food-stores. This picture of an early twelfth-century fortified dwelling comes to us, like the other accounts, because it is part of a miracle-story. As Seguin declined to make amends, the floor collapsed beneath him and he fell into the cellar to his death.[26]

To exploit the full potential of the Miracles of St Benedict in this area, however, it is necessary to do more than merely pull out the 'plums' of information which they contain. Attention must be focused on what the compilation as a whole has to tell us about French society. For, as we have seen, the Miracles cover a long time-span from the ninth to the twelfth century and, although we must regret the lack of a tenth-century section, they offer us a uniquely long-running series of observations. These observations are, it is true, of limited value in the study of changes in that society – for the miracle-stories are necessarily selective and can scarcely be expected to give us a balanced picture. They do, however, afford some indication of changing attitudes on the part of the monks to the laity and we should certainly ask whether the image of society projected by the miracle-stories changes over this highly formative period of French history. The full potential of this approach becomes apparent if we consider for a moment the construction of the miracle-collection as a whole. As stated above, it is in its present form the work of various writers. Further study of the contents and their presentation suggests strongly that these writers were in fact acting more as editors than as authors and that they were dealing with material of three types. Firstly, it is reasonable to assume that the clearly historical sections and the essentially historical judgments discussed above are the contribution of the writers themselves. Aimoin's historical passages, for example, have all the hallmarks both in language and in content of being his own work.[27] Secondly, there are rather bald accounts of cures, exorcisms, escapes from falling and similar miracles which are rarely elaborated and often

---

[26] *MSB*, VIII.16 (pp. 298–300). See G. Fournier, *Le château dans la France médiévale: Essai de sociologie monumentale* (Paris, 1978), pp. 65–80, espcially p. 70.

[27] Werner, pp. 72–3.

deal with anonymous persons.²⁸ These may well have been derived from records of shrine-keepers and indeed our writers often lament that, as for example in the time of Abbot Odo, those who should have kept records of miracles had not done so.²⁹ Thirdly, there are more extended and elaborate miracle-stories of the sort recounted above. These have a great wealth of circumstantial detail and often constitute narratives of some power. A good example is the story in Book I of how Raho, count of Orléans, tried to lure the abbot of Fleury to his death and how the latter was informed in the nick of time by a dwarf at the place where the count was staying. The thwarted Raho retired to bed with his concubine and received a vision of St Benedict who struck him on the head and thus marked him out for death. The names of the dwarf (Gauringisus) and the concubine (Deutheria) are given, even though the incident occurred almost a century before Adrevald was writing, and this and the vividness of the story suggest that it represented a living tradition.³⁰ Another good example is Andrew's account of the Breton knight and his companions who raped a divorcee and her daughter and were duly seized by demons.³¹ Stories of this complexity and verve may have been written down or they may have been told to our authors directly. An examination of the geographical origins of the stories serves to emphasize their value as a source for contemporary attitudes. Some of these stories clearly emanate from Fleury itself or from properties adjacent to it such as La Cour-Marigny, Bouzonville, Germigny-des-Près and Yèvre-la-Ville.³² Others, however, come from the farther-flung dependencies and cells of Fleury. In particular consecutive blocks of stories emanate from Châtillon-sur-Loire where the relics of St Posennus had been discovered,³³ from

---

²⁸ Such accounts predominate in Book IX but are found throughout. Examples include I.23 (pp. 53–5), I.29–31 (pp. 66–9), II.12 (pp. 114–15), II.19 (pp. 124–5), III. 17–18 (pp. 164–6), IV.3 (pp. 178–9), VII. 5–6 pp. 254–8),VIII. 8–9 (pp.285–6), (for cures and exorcisms); II.11 (pp. 113–14), and VIII.30 (pp. 327–8)(for escapes from the effects of falls); and VI.6 (pp. 226–7) and VIII.8 (pp. 264–5) (for miraculous escapes from gaol).

²⁹ *MSB*, II.4 (p. 101) and VIII.38 (p. 340).

³⁰ *MSB*, I.18 (pp. 43–6).

³¹ *MSB*, VII.7 (pp. 259–64). The source for this is said to have been one of the participants (p. 260).

³² For example, *MSB*, VII.5–14 (pp. 254–72) (Fleury); VIII.15–16 (pp. 296–8) and VIII.37 (pp. 339–40) (La Cour-Marigny); VIII.24 (pp. 314–17) (Yèvre-la-Ville); VI.6 (pp. 226–7) and VIII. 32–3. (pp. 329–33) (Bouzonville); VI.13 (pp. 237–40) and VIII.1–5 (pp. 277–82) (Germigny-des-Près). The identifications of these and other placenames are derived from J. Soyer, *Recherches sur l'origine et la formation des noms de lieux du département du Loiret* (Orleans, 1932–52) and, for regions outside the Loiret, from De Certain's admittedly inadequate foot-notes to *MSB*.

³³ *MSB*, V.5–15 (pp. 198–213), and VIII.34–6 (pp. 333–9).

Saint-Benoît-du-Sault,[34] from Auxon,[35] and from Perrecy-les-Forges (see map).[36] Sometimes the priors or provosts (*praepositi*) of these places are named as informants and indeed sometimes also as participants in the events surrounding the miraculous occurrences.[37] So we are not dealing merely with the attitudes of the Fleury authors but also with those of people living in a wide area of the middle Loire valley and the lands to the south.

With this in mind, let us now examine what social classes are given most emphasis in the successive books of the miracle-collection and how the functioning of social and political institutions is represented. Book I, when analyzed in this way, seems to display three characteristics. Firstly, peasants figure relatively little except in standard, record-style accounts of cures. The only real exceptions to this are the stories of the saving from fire of a peasant's shack and the recovery of a peasant woman's child from a wolf.[38] A further miracle involving people towards the lower end of the social scale is really concerned with the weekly fair at Fleury, for it deals with a dispute between two traders at this fair over the sharing out of some coins.[39] Secondly, nobles as such scarcely appear. The one exception is a certain Stephen (*haud ignobilis*), who sold a plot of land to a serf attached to Fleury's property at Sacierges and then tried to recover it.[40] Thirdly and most importantly, there is a great emphasis on persons involved at various levels in royal or at least comital government. Stories concerning such persons are not only numerous but also well-developed. At the top of the scale, there are the lengthy accounts already referred to of the wars between Odo, count of Orléans, and his enemies and of the attemped murder of the abbot of Fleury by an earlier count of Orléans, Raho.[41] In additon, we find stories dealing with viscounts, with judges and advocates and with the bishop of Orléans and the count of Meaux acting as *missi dominici*.[42] The army of Louis the Pious makes an appearance, albeit in the role of ravagers of Fleury's

---

[34] *MSB*, II.15–16 (pp. 117–20), III.5–7 (pp. 135–48), III.21 (pp. 170–1), and IV.1–5 (pp. 174–81).

[35] *MSB*, VIII.17–18 (pp. 300–3).

[36] *MSB*, III.15–18 (pp. 161–6), and VIII.38–48 (pp. 340–56). Dyé also features: see *MSB*, II.3 (pp. 99–100), VI.1–2 (pp. 217–19) and VIII.22 (pp. 310–12).

[37] These include: Otherius at Saint-Benoît-du-Sault (III.5 and 7, pp. 136–9 and 147); Theodoric at Vilabbé (III.8, pp. 148–50); Robert at Perrecy-les-Forges (III.16, pp. 162–5); Hisembertus (IV.1, p. 175) and Elisiernus (IV.5, p. 180) at Saint-Benoît-du-Sault; William at Châtillon-sur-Loire (V.5, p. 199); William at St Gondon (V.7, p. 204); Dodo at Dyé (VI.2, p. 219); Isaac at Auxon (VIII.17–18, pp. 300–3); Aimericus at Châtillon-sur-Loire (VIII.36, pp. 337–9); and Odo at *Sulmeriacus* (VIII.48, pp. 355–6).

[38] *MSB*, I.37 (pp. 79–80) and 39 (pp. 82–3).

[39] *MSB*, I.35 (pp. 77–8).

[40] *MSB*, I.38 (pp. 81–2).

[41] *MSB*, I.20–1 (pp. 47–50) and I.18 (pp. 42–6).

[42] *MSB*, I.24–5 (pp. 55–7) and I.32 (p. 69).

lands,[43] and the various officials responsible for royal toll-collection appear, as we have seen, in the story about the salt ship.[44] We must, I suggest, conclude that the Fleury monks in the late ninth century were still pre-occupied with their place in a governmental structure which was at least nominally royal. The monks' attitude towards it was certainly ambivalent. We have already noted Adrevald's hostility to Count Odo.[45] We may further observe that willingness to acquiesce in the judgments of royal officials seemed to hinge on how favourable the judgments were to Fleury. Thus a long passage deals with how a dispute over serfs (*mancipia*) had to be moved to Orléans so that it could be heard under Roman rather than Salic law. When agreement was not reached, trial by battle was proposed and favoured by the Fleury advocate – but an objection raised by one of the opposing party on the grounds that it was an unsuitable method of resolving a dispute concerning Church property was upheld. St Benedict, we are told, struck him dumb.[46]

If we now turn to the eleventh- and twelfth- century books, especially Books II-VIII, we seem to enter a quite different world. Royal officials as such scarcely appear in the stories – the account of Robert, count of Troyes, hearing the case of the runaway serf Stabilis is highly exceptional.[47] Instead the nobles in their own right, and often acting quite in their own interests, appear very frequently. Moreover, some of the most developed and circumstantial stories are devoted to them – elaborate accounts of the seizing of the castle of La Brosse and its aftermath and of the role of Hugh of Gargilissa in the war between Hildebert (*recte* Aldebert), count of Périgueux and the March, and William, count of Poitiers, for example.[48] We should of course bear in mind that Fleury was in all probability a fairly aristocratic community. Andrew himself was the son of a not inconsiderable noble and Abbot Gauzlin was probably an illegitimate son of Hugh Capet.[49] But the pre-occupation with nobles displayed in these miracle-stories is nonetheless striking and deserves further attention. It is important to note how the stories distinguish between, and place different emphases on, the various levels of nobility, especially as they span a period often regarded as vital for the evolution of the feudal nobility and for the

---

[43] *MSB*, I.27 (pp. 61–3).
[44] *MSB*, I.19 (pp. 46–7).
[45] See above, p. 77.
[46] *MSB*, I.25 (pp. 56–7), on which see R. Sohm, *Die fränkische Reichs- und Gerichtsverfassung* (Weimar, 1871), pp. 501–2, and *idem*, 'Die geistliche Gerichtsbarkeit im fränkischen Reich', *Zeitschrift für Kirchenrecht*, ix (1870), 206.
[47] *MSB*, II.6 (p. 219).
[48] *MSB*, III.5–7 (pp. 135–48).
[49] *Vie de Gauzlin*, ed. Bautier and Labory, pp. 7–8; *Adémar de Chabannes, Chronique*, ed. J. Chavanon (Paris, 1897), p. 161, on which see *Vie de Gauzlin*, pp. 18–20 and Devailly, pp. 138–9.

emergence of the knights (*milites*).[50] If we begin at the top of the scale of nobility, we observe that the miracle-stories, as distinct from the passages of historical background, are very little concerned with kings and their families.[51] There are exceptions to this. King Ralph, for example, is represented as pursuing and killing a knight who had usurped Fleury's estate at Dyé,[52] and Queen Gerberga appears because her knight was divinely punished for placing his sword on an altar.[53] In one case only, a member of the royal family is supposed to have been the recipient of divine punishment. Odo, King Henry's brother, is said to have misused the food of the poor and the paschal candles while at Germigny-des-Prés and to have been afflicted with a mortal illness as a result.[54] The upper nobility appear rather more frequently but they are rarely the main subject of the stories as distinct from the historical passages. Thus we hear of how Elias, son of Boso, count of the March, because of the enmity between his father and Gerald, viscount of Limoges, persuaded William, count of Poitiers, to attack the castle of La Brosse. The heroes of the story, however, are not these great nobles but the men of Argenton-sur-Creuse who assisted in breaking the siege and thereby saved the lands of Saint-Benoît-du-Sault from further plundering.[55] The son of a viscount of Limoges appears in a later story as having successfully seized La Brosse and also Saint-Benoît-du-Sault itself. He was killed and his father and uncle divinely punished, the latter being bitten by a ferocious horse.[56] Landry, count of Nevers, also plays an important role in the stories telling of his defeat by Geilo, lord of Sully, and of the unconsummated marriage of his son Gimo.[57] Other examples could be cited but it is nonetheless broadly true that in the majority of stories the upper nobility either do not appear or play subsidiary roles. By contrast, the stories are very much concerned with men who appear to be knights and are almost invariably represented as agents of violence. Thus we read of three separate *milites* described as being of 'perfidious mind', while the perpetrator of the brutal rape of a divorcee and her daughter is also described as a *miles*.[58] In other stories,

---

[50] See, for example: Devailly, pp. 187–96; G. Duby, *La société aux XIe et XIIe siècles dans la région mâconnaise* (Paris, 1971), pp. 191–201; A. Chédeville, *Chartres et ses campagnes (XIe–XIIIe s.)* (Paris, 1973), pp. 306–24; and, for a recent summary, Duby, *Three Orders*, pp. 147–66.

[51] In *MSB*, III.8 (p. 148), King Robert the Pious appears because the story is set in the context of his journey to Arles to collect his new wife Constance, but his appearance is scarcely more than a piece of historical background.

[52] *MSB*, II.3 (pp. 99–100).
[53] *MSB*, II.6 (pp. 105–7).
[54] *MSB*, VIII.1 (pp. 277–8).
[55] *MSB*, III.16 (pp. 118–20).
[56] *MSB*, III.5 (pp. 135–42).
[57] *MSB*, V.15–16 (pp. 212–14).
[58] *MSB*, II.3 (p. 99), III.8 (p. 149), VI.4 (p. 223), VII.7 (p. 259), VII.8 (p. 264), and VIII.18 (p. 302).

the terminology applied is notably vague, which tends perhaps to confirm the notion that we are dealing with an age of transition. Thus we hear of a 'vir saecularis militiae clarus stipendiis', an 'eques', 'unus militaribus deditus stipendiis' and 'unus de familia, equestri ordinis vir'.[59] Some persons are so vaguely described as to make it difficult to decide on their status, although we must assume that 'quidam Walterius jure beneficii sortitus' may well have been a noble.[60] The various advocates mentioned were probably all nobles, although only some are explicitly described as such.[61] What is beyond doubt, however, is the emphasis in the stories on castellans and on the men of castles as perpetrators of violence and rapine. The lords of Sully figure in various stories,[62] as also do Bernard, lord of Uzon,[63] Gaufredus, lord of Sémur,[64] Hugh, lord of *Huben*,[65] and the lords of La Brosse,[66] Gargilissa,[67] Déols,[68] Belabre[69] and Saint-Brice.[70] The story of Seguin and his tower has already been noted. His brother Alberic is the subject of another miracle-story. He is described as 'unus ex primoribus castri Castellionis' and so may have been a 'knight of the castle' rather than a castellan.[71]

The contexts in which these nobles figure are themselves striking. In a few cases the stories represent encounters between St Benedict's power and the nobles as beneficial to the latter. Thus we find a handful of cures and escapes granted to nobles through the saint's intercession.[72] But in the overwhelming majority of cases the nobles are represented as usurping Fleury's lands, ravaging, cattle-rustling, stealing, raping, mismanaging the church's affairs, violating sanctuary, molesting the poor or, at the least, mocking St Benedict.[73] The image of society

[59] *MSB*, II.4 (p. 104), II.14 (p. 116), III.5 (p. 141), and VIII.31 (p. 328).
[60] *MSB*, III.10 (p. 153).
[61] *MSB*, III.13 (p. 159), VI.3 (p. 222), VIII.6 (p. 283) and VIII.17 (p. 301).
[62] *MSB*, II.7 (pp. 107–9), V.15 (pp. 212–13), VI.16 (pp. 242–3), IX.1 (p. 359). Alberic and Achedeus are nobles described as being 'of Sully' and they too may have been lords of the castle (*MSB*, V.4, p. 198, and VI.9, pp. 230–2).
[63] *MSB*, III.16 (p. 163).
[64] *MSB*, VIII.42 (pp. 346–7).
[65] *MSB*, VIII.35 (p. 334).
[66] *MSB*, III.5 and 6 (pp. 136–45).
[67] *Ibid.*, (pp. 140 and 147).
[68] *MSB*, V.2 and 4 (pp. 194 and 196–8).
[69] *MSB*, IV.4 (p. 179).
[70] *MSB*, VIII.35 (pp. 334–5).
[71] *MSB*, VIII.15 (p. 296), and Devailly, pp. 190–1.
[72] See, for example, *MSB*, III.20 (pp. 169–70), VII.8 (pp. 264–5) and VIII.42 (pp. 346–7).
[73] See, for example, *MSB*, II.3 (pp. 99–100), II.7 (pp. 107–8), II.14–15 (pp. 116–18), III.5 (pp. 135–42), III.8 (pp. 148–50), III.10 (pp. 153–4), III.13 (pp. 158–9), III.16 (pp. 163–4), IV.2 (pp. 177–8), IV.4–6 (pp. 179–82), V.5 (pp. 201–2), V.10 (pp. 207–9), VI.3–4 (pp. 221–5), VI.16 (pp. 242–3), VII.7 (pp. 259–64), VIII.6 (pp. 282–4), VIII.15–18 (pp. 296–303), VIII.35 (pp. 334–6), VIII.42 (pp. 346–7), and VIII.48 (pp. 355–6).

projected through these stories is precisely that of the chronic instability and endemic violence so vividly evoked by Marc Bloch.[74] Moreover, the stories show no awareness of even a residual royal or public authority, except on occasions as an object of despair. The monks appealed to King Lothar – or rather to Duke Hugh – concerning the ravages of Herbert of Sully, runs a story told by Aimoin, but they got nowhere.[75] In such a society, men took the law into their own hands, even a bishop, and there are several stories which represent Fleury and its dependencies as caught in the cross-fire of private warfare between nobles.[76] What is perhaps noteworthy is that the monks seem to perceive the situation as deteriorating between the early eleventh and early twelfth centuries. The problem of castles seems, to judge from the stories, to have worsened. In Book II, Aimoin tells of how armed men poured out of the castles around Argenton-sur-Creuse to ravage the surrounding lands and notes that castles were at that time especially numerous in that area of Aquitaine.[77] In the early twelfth century, however, the stories in Book VIII seem to envisage castles to be as much of a threat in the Loire valley itself and it is in that area and period that the story of Seguin's tower is set.[78] The stories also give the impression that the problem of disorder was increasing, for some of the worst cases of ravaging by nobles occur in Book VIII. These include a story of how cattle-rustling by nobles led to private war; and an extraordinary story of how a party of Burgundians crossed the Loire to rustle cattle, led by a minstrel (*scurra*) singing songs of their former achievements.[79] Nothing could be more in tune with the notion of the rise of the *juvenes*, that group of nobles disinherited by primogeniture whom Duby has called 'l'organe d'aggression et de tumulte' of feudal society.[80]

It is against this background that we need to assess the indications in some of the stories told by Aimoin and Andrew of a growing conception of holy war involving St Benedict. On one occasion Fleury's lands around Saint-Benoît-du-Sault were attacked by armed men from the castles around Argenton-sur-Creuse. Forty men opposed this incursion by greatly superior numbers and triumphed because they had had the foresight to obtain from the priory the banner of St Benedict. The passage further suggests, as Carl Erdmann has noted, that the right to carry this banner normally belonged to the advocate of the priory, for the men of Argenton-sur-Creuse justified their request

---

[74] *La société féodale*, 2 vols. (1939–40), ii, 194–201.
[75] *MSB*, II.7 (p. 107).
[76] See, for example, *MSB*, VIII.24 (pp. 315–16) and III.16 (p. 163).
[77] *MSB*, II.15 (p. 117).
[78] *MSB*, VIII.16 (pp. 298–300).
[79] *MSB*, VIII.36 (pp. 336–9); cf. VIII.35 (pp. 334–6).
[80] G. Duby, *Hommes et structures du moyen âge* (Paris, 1973), p. 216.

for it on the grounds that the advocate was their master.[81] The subsequent story has, as Aimoin notes, a similar theme. The men of Argenton-sur-Creuse, we are told, were fighting in alliance with Guy, son of Gerald, viscount of Limoges, against the forces of Boso, count of the March. They rendered themselves immune from death and invincible in battle by securing from Saint-Benoît-du-Sault consecrated bread and wine. No-one who consumed this died.[82] A third story related by Aimoin concerns a campaign led by Hugh of La Brosse, encouraged by Otherius, prior of Saint-Benoît-du-Sault, to recapture the priory from its enemies. In this campaign, we are told, divine intervention also played a part. A dream granted to a *miles* before the crucial battle foretold victory for the Fleury party; and the enemy reported after their defeat that they 'had no help from their missiles'.[83] A final story of this type related by Aimoin concerns Hugh of Gargilissa who, in a war between Hildebert (*recte* Aldebert), count of Périgueux, and William, count of Poitiers, won victory after distributing to his army consecrated bread from the priory of Saint-Benoît-du-Sault. None of the men who had consumed it received a lethal wound.[84] Another developed story involving such elements of holy war is told by Andrew and concerns the aftermath of attacks made on Châtillon-sur-Loire by the men of the castle of Saint-Satur. They, together with Landry, count of Nevers, were defeated by Geilo of Sully who, we are told, triumphed by using St Benedict's name as a war-cry and thus invoking the aid of a saint who was, as Andrew bluntly put it, the 'leader of battle' (*certaminis primicerium*). The enemy suffered heavy losses and were forced to 'drink to the dregs the cup of the Lord's wrath'.[85] These passages have been discussed by Carl Erdmann in connection with the rise of the concept of holy war in the eleventh century and the origins of the idea of Crusade.[86] We should perhaps ponder further their origins. It is striking that Aimoin's stories are the most numerous and all derive from the area around Poitiers and Limoges, from the area in other words where the Peace of God with all its overtones of holy war took root at an early stage. On the other hand, Andrew, whose implied criticism of the Peace of God we have already noted, has a story from the middle Loire a generation later.[87] The evidence is tenuous; but there may be at least a hint here that the concept of holy war, like the Peace of God itself, was in the early

---

[81] *MSB*, II.15 (pp. 117–18), and C. Erdmann, *The Origin of the Idea of Crusade*, translated with additional notes by M. W. Baldwin and W. Goffart (Princeton, 1977), pp. 46–7. Cf. Devailly, pp. 192–3.
[82] *MSB*, II.16 (pp. 118–20).
[83] *MSB*, III.5 (pp. 135–42).
[84] *MSB*, III.7 (pp. 147–8).
[85] *MSB*, V.15 (p. 212–13).
[86] Erdmann, pp. 90–93.
[87] See above, pp. 77–78.

eleventh century most precociously developed in the South. It should be noted in this connection that Andrew relates two further stories involving holy war which he learned from nobles who came to Fleury from Spain.[88] In one the Saracens were divinely prevented from plundering a monastery near Barcelona when, among other things, the wine in the casks froze.[89] In another the Christians won a great victory over the Saracens through saintly intervention. The account of this battle, as Erdmann remarked, 'transports us right into the crusading age'.[90]

Alongside this preoccupation with the nobles and with warfare, there are other perceptions of society revealed in these eleventh- and twelfth-century stories. Peasants, as we have noted, play little part in the developed stories found in Book I and they are not prominent in Books II and III, nor indeed in Book IV, the first by Andrew. But from Book V onwards there is a clear trend to devote more developed stories to the lower orders of society, a trend which is further accentuated in the early twelfth-century stories in Book VIII. Thus in Books V–VIII we find not only the story of Stabilis the runaway serf described above but also an account of another serf, Alberic, who merely contemplated seeking his freedom and had his hand crippled for this presumption.[91] There are also stories of an equally developed nature concerning the fate of those who worked on the saint's feast-days. Although on one occasion it was the rich man who ordered the serfs to work who was struck down, Andrew at least regarded the peasants as especially prone to infringe feast-day prohibitions on work.[92] Less developed but nonetheless containing some circumstantial detail is Andrew's story of a potter called William who swore by St Benedict and had his arm crippled as a result.[93] But it is in Book VIII that developed stories about peasants and others lower in the social scale than the nobles really come to prominence. Four stories concern bailiffs (*villici*). Such men may possibly have been relatively wealthy but they would almost certainly have been servile.[94] We read that Vivian, the bailiff of Germigny-des-Prés, treated the church with disrespect and allowed his dogs and his pigs to enter it: the dogs died after licking up the holy oil, the pigs went mad.[95] Another bailiff, Rainerius, blinded himself in one eye after he had stolen a widow's pig and a fourth, Joscelin, lost his beard for swearing falsely.[96] Further stories concern, like some of those in Books

---

[88] *MSB*, IV.7 (p. 183).
[89] *MSB*, IV.9 (pp. 185–7).
[90] *MSB*, IV.10 (pp. 187–90), and Erdmann, pp. 99–100.
[91] *MSB*, VI.2 (pp. 218–21) and V.8 (pp. 205–7).
[92] *MSB*, V.12 (p. 210). See also *MSB*, VI.10 (pp. 232–3).
[93] *MSB*, VII.6 (p. 258).
[94] Duby, *La société aux XIe et XIIe siècles*, pp. 297–307.
[95] *MSB*, VIII.2–3, (pp. 278–80).
[96] *MSB*, VIII.7 (pp. 284–5) and VIII.22 (pp. 311–12).

V–VII, the fate of peasants and others who worked on the feast-days. A weaver called Tescelina found that her carding-comb stuck to her hand when she committed this offence; tooth-ache seized a girl who was spinning on the feast-day; and a free woman who wove on the feast-day was smitten as also was her employer, a Breton called Ralph.[97] The most developed of all these stories is that concerning a man who ploughed on the feast-day. It is full of agricultural details and describes how a monk appeared to him and bound his hands to an iron component of his plough.[98] There are, however, positive elements in some of these stories. about the lower orders. In addition to accounts of cures and escapes, which are predominant in Book IX, we learn of the son of a widow who, unable to maintain her by work, resorted to theft with a companion. Both were apprehended and hanged but the widow's son, through St Benedict's intercession, remained alive on the gallows and he was released.[99] In a different vein is the story of Robert, whose father had been a serf of St Benedict but had been alienated together with his land to a layman. Discovering this Robert sought to establish his right to be a serf of St Benedict and went to the extent of waging judicial combat, in which his success was procured by the saint's intervention.[100] As Marcel Prou showed, there might well have been practical and spiritual advantages in being an ecclesiastical serf of St Benedict.[101] Some of these stories seem concerned to demonstrate that there were great supernatural advantages in belonging to the *familia* of St Benedict and indeed in making oneself a serf of St Benedict especially as a means of guaranteeing a cure. Many of St Benedict's intercessions for the lower orders are represented to us as especial favours bestowed on the saint's *familia*. Hugh Bidulf, we are told, broke the arm of a peasant who had been born into the *familia*. The peasant accused St Benedict of not protecting him and the saint responded by smiting Hugh's arm and paralysing his whole body, a condition which proved fatal.[102]

In our consideration of these attitudes to society reflected in the Miracles of St Benedict we have noted three trends: the decline in preoccupation with royal government and the upper nobility; the rise in concern with the turbulence of the knights and the castellans from the early eleventh century onwards; and, from the mid-eleventh century and especially in the early twelfth, an increasing concern to portray more fully the lower orders of society. We need now to enquire into the

[97] *MSB*, VIII.10 (pp. 286–7) and VIII.32–3 (pp. 329–33).
[98] *MSB*, VIII.12 (pp. 291–2).
[99] *MSB*, VIII.44 (pp. 349–51). For cures and escapes, see, for example, *MSB*, VIII.8 (pp. 285–6), VIII.13 (p. 293), VIII.38 (pp. 340–2), VIII.39 (pp. 342–4) and VIII.47 (pp. 354–5).
[100] *MSB*, VIII.11 (pp. 287–90). Cf. Devailly, pp. 200–1.
[101] 'Les serfs de Saint-Benoît-sur-Loire', *Bulletin de la Société Nationale des Antiquaires de France*, sixth ser., iv (1893) 216–20.
[102] *MSB*, VIII.46 (pp. 352–4).

function of the miracle-collection and the stories which are contained in it. Why were they written down? Why were they remembered and told? In its finished, literary form, the collection no doubt served as a sort of monastic chronicle, but this cannot account for the genesis and transmission of the stories themselves. The stock accounts of cures and escapes, drawn perhaps from shrine-keepers' registers, were evidently intended to support the shrines' claims to be thaumaturgic centres – no doubt they were of use for proving to pilgrims that the relics in question worked. A few of the stories had a message for the monks themselves. The story of the monk who was nearly carried off by demons before he would confess was presumably an object-lesson in regular confession;[103] and the sad fate of the monk who altered the clause in the Rule of St Benedict stating that monks' goods should be sold more cheaply than others by substituting 'dearly' for 'cheaply' was no doubt a much needed lesson in the curbing of avarice.[104] But by and large the most developed stories concern the laity and deal above all with the retribution wrought by St Benedict on those who attacked Fleury's interests. Such stories no doubt reassured the monks that St Benedict was working for them; but it is difficult to escape the conclusion that they were envisaged also as material suitable for preaching to the laity who frequented the shrines, not only that of St Benedict at Fleury but also subsidiary relic-shrines, notably at Châtillon-sur-Loire, Saint-Benoît-du-Sault and Perrecy-les-Forges.[105] Such shrines were foci for lay as well as monastic piety and we find accounts in Book I as well as in subsequent books of the crowds of laymen coming to the shrines, making offerings, keeping vigils and so on. When new relics from Soissons arrived at Fleury in the reign of Louis the Pious, Adrevald tells us, they had to be placed in a marquee outside the church so that the laity, including women who were not usually allowed inside the church, could approach them.[106] Study of a wider range of miracle-collections suggests that the practice of frequenting shrines became more prevalent among the laity from the late tenth century onwards;[107] and it is certainly possible, as Benedicta Ward has shown, to perceive in the Miracles of St Benedict an organisation for

[103] *MSB*, VI.8 (pp. 229–30).
[104] *MSB*, VIII.14 (pp. 293–6).
[105] See above, pp. 80–81. Châtillon-sur-Loire possessed the relics of St Posennus: see *MSB*, V.6 (pp. 202–3), and B. Gitton, 'Châtillon-sur-Loire, saint Posen et les moines de Fleury du Xe au XIIe siècles, d'après les *Miracula Sancti Benedicti*', *Etudes ligériennes*, ed. Louis, pp. 195–202. Saint-Benoît-du-Sault possessed relics of St Benedict (*MSB*, IV.1 p. 175), and a relic-procession is mentioned in connection with Perrècy-les-Forges (*MSB*, III.16, p. 162). On preaching, see B. de Gaiffier, 'L'hagiographie et son public au XIe siècle', in his *Etudes critiques d'hagiographie et d'iconologie*, Subsidia Hagiographica, 43 (Brussels, 1967), pp. 489–99.
[106] *MSB*, I.28 (pp. 63–5). See also *MSB*, III.2 (p. 128), and VII.14 (p. 272).
[107] B. Toepfer, 'Reliquienkult und Pilgerbewegung zur Zeit der Kloster-Reform in Burgunden-Aquitanischen Gebiet', *Vom Mittelalter zur Neuzeit: Zum 65. Geburtstag Heinrich Sproembergs*, ed. H. Kretzschmar (Berlin, 1956), pp. 420–39.

pilgrims which was increasing in sophistication through the eleventh century.[108] The Church may have been using the appeal of the relic-cults to reach ever deeper into lay society and this may explain among other things the increasing concern with the peasantry manifested in the Miracles of St Benedict from the mid-eleventh century onwards. The miracle-stories may in short have constituted a form of propaganda, seeking to influence the behaviour of the laity by highlighting the fate awaiting those who went against Fleury's wishes and, less often, the rewards of those who respected the Church. As Andrew optimistically remarked of a story in which the wife of a usurper was paralysed, 'When news of this matter reached the ears of all, it filled with terror those plunderers who, following his example, had laid hands with rash presumption on other property of the abbey.'[109]

It would be wrong to claim too much for the Miracles of St Benedict, especially studied in isolation as they have been here. But they do seem to offer us a window on early medieval France: on the provincial historical viewpoints of the writers themselves, on the attitudes to society held at Fleury and its dependencies from the ninth to the twelfh centuries, and, perhaps, on the pressures which the monks felt from and tried to bring to bear on that society.

---

[108] Ward, pp. 48–50.
[109] *MSB*, V.16 (p. 216). In general see Toepfer, *Volk und Kirche*, pp. 38–56, especially p. 56; and B. de Gaiffier, 'Les revendications des biens dans quelques documents hagiographiques du XIe siècle', *Analecta Bollandiana*, 1 (1932), 123–38.

7

Towns and Cottages in Eleventh-Century England

Christopher Dyer

Domesday Book provides us with a marvellous opportunity to explore the early history of towns. As Domesday describes both town and country, we ought to be able to investigate the proportion of town dwellers, and the interactions between urban and rural society. The source can also throw light on the extent to which the *burhs* set up by pre-Conquest rulers had become by the eleventh century true towns, that is settlements which contained concentrations of population and which had a wide range of non-agricultural occupations, especially those deriving from participation in trade and industry.[1]

The potential of Domesday has not been fully realised because of its many inadequacies as a source for the history of towns. It omits London and Winchester. Bristol's great wealth is indicated, but no hint is given of its size.[2] Coventry, as Professor Davis has shown in a characteristically lucid argument, counted as an important town in 1102 when it was chosen to be an episcopal city, and is likely to have had urban characteristics sixteen years earlier, yet Domesday describes it as a rural manor.[3] When Domesday does provide us with more detail, for example in its accounts of Gloucester and Winchcomb, almost contemporary surveys compiled independently show that it grossly understates the number of houses and burgesses.[4] Domesday's inconsistent terminology baffles modern interpretation; in one place we are told of houses, in

---

I am grateful to Mr R. Meeson, who commented on the place-name Coton in a seminar discussion and began the train of thought that led to this essay. References to Domesday Book are to the Farley edition of 1783. *P. N. Berks.* etc. refers to the appropriate volume published by the English Place-Name Society.

[1] This definition resolutely avoids institutional criteria, as in S. Reynolds, *An Introduction to the History of English Medieval Towns* (Oxford, 1977), pp. ix–x; R. H. Hilton, 'Towns in English Feudal Society', *Review (Journal of the Fernard Braudel Center for the Study of Economies, Historical Systems and Civilizations)*, iii (1979), 4–5. Cf. M. Biddle, 'Towns', in D. M. Wilson (ed.), *The Archaeology of Anglo-Saxon England* (London, 1976), p. 100; E. Ennen, *The Medieval Town* (Amsterdam, 1979), pp. 1–3.

[2] *Bristol Charters, 1378–1499*, ed. H. A. Cronne, Bristol Record Soc., xi (1946), 20–22.

[3] R. H. C. Davis, *The Early History of Coventry* (Dugdale Soc. Occasional Paper, 24, 1976), pp. 16–19.

[4] H. B. Clarke, 'Domesday Slavery (Adjusted for Slaves)', *Midland Hist.*, i (1972), pp. 38–9.

another burgesses, in a third, 'men', in a fourth 'enclosures' (*hagae*). Often the terms are mingled. There are good administrative explanations for these problems: the commissioners were not issued with instructions for dealing with towns. The main purposes of the *descriptio*, to investigate the resources of tenants-in-chief, and to provide for reassessment of geld, both led to a focus on rural manors, hides and ploughlands. The king's resources, which included many of the boroughs, received unsystematic coverage.[5]

We must not be demoralised by its omissions and confusions, because Domesday can be made to yield much useful information. One obvious question concerns the proportion of the population who lived in towns. Less than 3 per cent of the people recorded were described as burgesses, but if we calculate the total of burgesses, houses, *hagae* and 'men' in the 112 boroughs, we arrive at a total of a little more than 20,000. As the recorded rural population was 269,000, the proportion of families or households living in towns can be estimated at 7 per cent of the total.[6] The inclusion of conservative estimates for the obvious omissions (London, Winchester and Bristol) would raise the number of urban households to more than 23,000, or 8 per cent of the total.[7] Already these calculations have entered dangerous waters: for example, should the slaves (*servi*) be counted as being the heads of households on a par with villeins (*villani*) or burgesses? Surely they should not because slaves were treated as individuals, so the rural total is an overstatement. Allowance could be made for further omissions, like those already mentioned for the Gloucestershire boroughs, but the calculation would require more guesswork. We would need to estimate also the omitted households in rural society, and we cannot be certain (though we may suspect it) that the surveys of the boroughs were more prone to underassessment than those of the manors. So, although greater precision is impossible, we have good cause to assume that about one in every twelve Englishmen in 1086 lived in a town, making a total urban population (allowing 4.5 to each household) in excess of 100,000.

Domesday contains a great deal of evidence for an association between towns and people called bordars (*bordarii*), cottars (*cotarii*) and coscets (*coscez*), all terms implying tenants with only small holdings of

---

[5] V. H. Galbraith, *Domesday Book: its place in Administrative History* (Oxford, 1974), pp. 147–60; S. P. J. Harvey, 'Domesday Book and Anglo-Norman Governance', *T[ransactions of the] R[oyal] H[istorical] S[ociety]* fifth ser., xxv (1975), 175–93; Davis, pp. 17–18.

[6] These calculations are based on figures given in H. C. Darby, *Domesday England* (Cambridge, 1977), pp. 337, 364–8; for a calculation using different methods but arriving at a similar conclusion see J. C. Russell, *British Medieval Population* (Albuquerque, 1948), pp. 45–54.

[7] M. Biddle (ed.), *Winchester in the Early Middle Ages* (Oxford, 1976), p. 440 suggests 1100 houses for Winchester in 1148. London and Bristol must have had well in excess of 2,000 between them.

land. In some counties the bordars were much superior to the cottars in the size of their holdings, even having as much as fifteen acres (a half-virgate), but often the two terms seem to have been interchangeable. At the lower end of the social and economic ladder, such tenants had no more than a house and garden.[8] These smallholders occur everywhere in Domesday. They account for about a third of the recorded rural population, and in one county, Essex, half of the people were called bordars. There has been much discussion of their origin and function. No doubt some of them were colonizers, who had brought a relatively small amount of land under the plough, and relied for much of their living on the pastures and other resources of the woodlands and wastes.[9] Others originated as *servi casati*, slaves settled on holdings by lords who expected to call on their labour on the demesne.[10] Many of the smallholders must have earned wages by working either on the demesne or on the larger peasant holdings; the latter assumption is supported by the fact that the great majority of manors and vills contained a mixture of villeins and smallholders.[11] Some may have made a living as craftsmen. Here we are concerned with that small section of this large and disparate social group who lived in or near boroughs.

Some smallholders are simply listed in Domesday as part of a borough's population. The small borough of Ashwell (Herts.) is said to have had fourteen burgesses and nine cottars, described in a way that clearly distinguishes them from the tenants of Westminster Abbey's manor there (I, fo. 135b). At St Albans (Herts.) twelve cottars are said to be 'in the same vill', which probably means the borough with its forty-six burgesses (I, fo. 135b). The Yorkshire borough of Tanshelf was populated with sixty 'small burgesses' and sixteen *coteros* (I, fo. 316b). Much larger places than these counted cottars and bordars among their inhabitants. A hundred bordars made up almost a third of Huntingdon's recorded population, though they are said to be 'under' the burgesses (I, fo. 203). At Norwich also 480 out of a total of at least 1300 recorded people were called bordars (II, fos. 116–18). There were eight bordars at Nottingham, and fourteen at Hastings (Sussex), linked with four burgesses of the abbot of Fécamp (I, fos. 280, 17). In the very

---

[8] R. Lennard, *Rural England, 1086–1135* (Oxford, 1959), pp. 340–64; idem, 'The Economic Position of the Bordars and Cottars of Domesday Book', *Economic Journal*, lxi (1951), 342–71.

[9] S. P. J. Harvey, 'Evidence for settlement study: Domesday Book', in P. H., Sawyer (ed.), *Medieval Settlement* (London, 1976), pp. 197–9.

[10] M. M. Postan, *The Famulus* (Economic Hist. Review Supplement, no. 2, 1954), pp. 5–14; this seems to be implicit in J. D. Hamshere, 'A Computer-assisted Study of Domesday Worcestershire', in T. R. Slater and P. J. Jarvis (eds.), *Field and Forest. An Historical Geography of Warwickshire and Worcestershire* (Norwich, 1982), p. 108.

[11] R. H. Hilton, 'Reasons for Inequality among Medieval Peasants', *Journal of Peasant Studies*, v (1978), 271–84; Lennard, *ubi supra*, pp. 362–3.

confusing entry for Bury St Edmunds (Suffolk), fifty-two bordars and probably another forty-three were listed among the population at the time of King Edward, apparently in a subordinate position 'under' other tenants. In 1086 twenty-seven bordars were said to be 'now' living at Bury, again 'under' reeves and knights (II, fo. 372).

The existence of such people and tenements in towns later in the middle ages is well recorded. The Winchester survey of c. 1110 shows groups of *bordelli* (a word translated as 'shacks' by the editor), which presumably were inhabited by bordars, in the western suburbs of the city. Cottages are known at Winchester in the later middle ages, both from documents and excavations.[12] A glance at the surveys in the 1280 Hundred Rolls reveals the presence of numerous cottages in towns as diverse as Coventry (Warw.) and Woodstock (Oxon.). In the rental of Gloucester of 1455 a tenth of the properties were called cottages, and they were also prominent in the 1454 terrier of Southampton.[13] Late medieval urban cottages were smaller than full burgages, and carried a lower rent charge. The buildings themselves could be very small, having a floor area in some cases of five metres by five metres. Their tenants naturally came from the lower ranks of urban society, which would include widows, journeymen, labourers and other wage-earners, and they often held their cottages as subtenancies of burgages. They are found most commonly in the poorer districts of the towns, and especially in the suburbs. Domesday's brief and enigmatic entries do not allow us to make generalisations about urban cottars and bordars in the eleventh century with the same certainty, but it is possible to see some similarities. The Domesday bordars were inferior in status and wealth to the burgesses, as the reference to their poverty at Norwich suggests. The entries for Bury and Huntingdon imply that they were either sub-tenants or servants, or indeed both. As will appear, cottars and bordars were often located in suburbs.

If we turn from the boroughs themselves to the manors and vills in their vicinity, we discover large numbers of cottars and bordars. Occasionally Domesday describes extra-mural smallholders in the main borough entry, giving an impression of a suburb that is part of the borough in terms of tenure. At Lincoln, for example, in 1066, there were twelve tofts and four crofts, terms implying minor tenements, 'outside the city', belonging to the church of All Saints, and therefore probably lying outside the walls of the upper town where the church stood (I, fo. 336). The burgesses of Nottingham themselves had

[12] Biddle (ed.), pp. 48–9, 381, 441; M. Biddle, 'Excavations at Winchester, 1967. Sixth Interim Report', *Antiquaries Journal*, xlviii (1968), 261, 265–6.

[13] *Rotuli Hundredorum* (Record Commission, 1812–18), ii. 839–42; R. H. Hilton, *A Medieval Society*, second edn. (Cambridge, 1983), p. 185; J. Langton, 'Late Medieval Gloucester: some data from a Rental of 1455', *Transactions, Institute of British Geographers*, new ser., ii (1977), 259–77; C. Platt, *Medieval Southampton* (London, 1973), pp. 265–6.

agricultural land outside the borough, and twenty bordars as tenants (I, fo. 280). The location of the seventy-two bordars of Grantham (Lincs.) is not clear. They are not mentioned alongside the burgesses, and they are linked with a plough-team suggesting that they were tenants of the manor rather than the borough (I, fo. 337b). More often Domesday makes plain that there were manors closely linked to boroughs, whose tenants were mainly bordars and cottars. The bishop of Lincoln's manor at Leicester consisted of property both inside and outside the borough.[14] Within the walls were seventeen burgesses; outside there were three villeins and twelve bordars (I, fo. 230b). An analagous manor at Thetford (Norfolk) belonged to Roger Bigot, with thirty-three men in the borough, and a manor outside, which appears to have been normal in its possession of a demesne, a mill, and two slaves, but unusual in its population of twenty bordars and no other type of tenants (II, fo. 173). Beccles in Suffolk is described as a complex estate combining borough and manor. Twenty-six burgesses formed the borough tenants, and the manor contained a predominance of smallholders, including forty-six bordars, and thirty sokemen who had insufficient land – one-and-a-half ploughlands – for us to regard them as anything more than smallholders (II, fos. 369b, 370). The royal demesne of Colchester (Essex) had a tenant population of ten bordars only, and there were four bordars and two slaves on another small manor held by the church of St Peter of Colchester (II, fos. 107, 107b). A comparable pair of manors at Ipswich (Suffolk) held by the Queen and Count Alan contained in the first case twelve freemen sharing eighty acres, and ten bordars with 'no land of their own', but living on eighty-six acres; and in the second simply seven bordars (II, fos. 290, 294).[15] Perhaps the largest concentration of suburban smallholders lay around the city of Canterbury, where St Augustine's Abbey, the archbishop and other lords held manors called Northgate, *Estursete* and St Martins which contained a total of 194 bordars, compared with only thirty-seven villeins, so that smallholders amounted to 84 per cent of the tenant population, whereas in Kent as a whole they were in a minority of 29 per cent (I, fos. 3b, 4, 5, 12).[16]

As we learn more about urban topography, it may be possible to demonstrate that some of the smallholders in manors called 'Grantham' or 'Colchester' in fact lived in separate settlements. Usually it is only possible to show this conclusively from Domesday when a village or hamlet lay in a manor distinct in its lordship and location from the

[14] *V.C.H. Leicestershire*, iv. 350–61.
[15] L. J. Redstone, *Ipswich Through the Ages* (Ipswich, 1948), p. 28 identifies these manors with the later Wicks Ufford and Wicks Bishop.
[16] T. Tatton-Brown, 'The Towns of Kent', in J. Haslam (ed.), *Anglo-Saxon Towns in Southern England* (Chichester, 1984), pp. 10–11; H. C. Darby and E. M. J. Campbell, *Domesday Geography of South-East England* (Cambridge, 1962), p. 617.

borough. So Roger of Iveri's manor of Walton just to the north of Oxford, with its one slave and thirteen bordars, must be regarded as containing a village separate from Oxford, but in its social and economic life overshadowed by that large town (I, fo. 159). In the vicinity of London lay the manor of Bishopsgate, where ten cottars were recorded, and among nearby Stepney's large and varied peasant population were forty-six cottars, crowded into a compact hamlet if we are to accept literally the statement that they together occupied one hide. The mysterious royal manor of 'No man's land' (Middlesex) which probably also lay near London had thirty cottar tenants (I, fos. 127, 128). Other examples from relatively small western boroughs are Allington, next to Bridport (Dorset), where the only recorded tenants were twelve bordars and nine rent-paying tenants (*censores*), and the manor with eighteen cottars as its sole tenants at Ditchampton near Wilton (Wilts.) (I, fos. 80b, 66).

The peculiar social structure and economy of these bordar/cottar settlements are brought home to us most forcefully when the compilers of Domesday, perhaps themselves aware of the distinctive character of some of the places they were describing, sometimes relaxed their usual reticence and revealed the nature of the tenant holdings. A vill on the northern edge of Warwick. *Cotes*, contained a hundred bordars 'with their gardens' (I, fo. 238). Such garden plots (in Latin *horti* or *hortuli*) are mentioned as the tenements of forty-one cottars at Westminster, eight cottars at nearby Fulham, and twenty-three men of Holywell, just to the east of Oxford (I, fo. 128, 127b, 158b). Seven gardens are also mentioned at Grantham, under the jurisdiction of Grantham, but belonging tenurially to the manor of Gonerby, which might point to a suburban location (I, fo. 377).

The Westminster gardens hint at another urban context for smallholders. While the cottars may have been living in a western suburb of London, they are more likely to represent the beginnings of the borough of Westminster. This identification is strengthened by the appearance of communities of bordars at a number of nascent or newly-founded towns. The 'small borough named Seasalter' that appears to have been a relatively recent growth on the lands of the church of Canterbury on the north Kent coast had a recorded population of forty-eight bordars, without any other tenant being mentioned (I, fo. 5). Evesham (Worcs.), which had acquired market rights by 1055, and was developing urban characteristics in the late eleventh century, was said to have a population of twenty-seven bordars (I, fo. 175b).[17] There were twenty-one bordars in the new borough outside the gates of Battle Abbey in Sussex (I, fo. 17b). Sixteen bordars lived 'around the hall' of Tewkesbury (Glos.), physically separate from the thirteen

[17] R. H. Hilton, 'The Small Town and Urbanisation – Evesham in the Middle Ages', *Midland Hist.*, vii (1982), 1–2.

burgesses of the apparently recently founded borough, but perhaps connected to them in their economic activities (I, fo. 163–163b).[18] Cookham (Berks.) also looks like a newly developed borough, though it lay near to the ninth-century *burh* on Sashes island in the Thames. There was a new market, and two submanors held by clergy had as their tenants a total of ten cottars (I, fo. 56b).[19]

Finally, Domesday records bordar/cottar settlements which were not immediately adjacent to a borough, but which were still very near. There must be elements of uncertainty in the topographical interpretation of the written record. For example, the manor of Witton, south of Droitwich (Worcs.) included parts of the main street and the salt-making heart of Droitwich within its complex boundaries, though it also contained presumed settlements as much as a mile from the town centre.[20] So we cannot know whether to count the twenty bordars of the manor as belonging to the town, its suburbs, or some nearby separate settlement; they probably were spread over all three locations (I, fo. 177b). Chesterton, to the north of Cambridge with its two villeins, sixteen bordars and six cottars included both the fringes of the north-western trans-pontine extension of Cambridge, and a more distant settlement to the east (I, fo. 189b). In other cases the settlement of bordars and cottars lay well apart from the town. Whitwell, two-and-a-half miles from Cambridge, had a very unusual social structure, as ten of its eleven tenants were bordars and cottars (I, fos. 194b, 198b, 200b). Good examples of similar cases are Walditch, a mile east of Bridport, Whittington almost two miles south-east of Worcester, and Headbourne Worthy which lay nearly two miles north of Winchester (I, fos. 85, 173b, 46b). Such villages seem to occur too frequently to be coincidences, but there are obvious dangers as we leave the immediate vicinity of towns that we are encountering places where the social and land-holding structure had been influenced by such factors as seignorial policy or colonization. A scatter of manors of which the tenants were wholly or predominantly cottars or bordars can be found in a variety of locations, not just near boroughs.

Further evidence for the link between towns and smallholdings comes from place-names. *Cot* is one of the more common place-name elements, and refers to a cottage or cottages; *cot* names are found in a wide variety of locations, among which a noticeable minority are close

---

[18] For two possible sites of the hall, see *Victoria County History, Gloucestershire*, viii. 125; *Medieval Archaeology*, xx (1976), 160.

[19] N. Brooks, 'The Unidentified Forts of the Burghal Hidage', *Medieval Archaeology*, viii (1964), 79–81; G. Astill, 'The Towns of Berkshire', in Haslam (ed.), pp. 63–4; *idem*, *Historic Towns in Berkshire, an Archaeological Appraisal* (Reading, 1978), pp. 23–7.

[20] Information from Mr S. R. Bassett.

TABLE 1 Place-names incorporating *cot* near early boroughs

County	Modern Name	Borough	Distance from borough centre	Earliest form; Domesday population	Reference
Berkshire	CALDECOTT	Abingdon*	½ mile	CALDECOTE EXTRA ABBINGDON 1261–6	*P.N. Berks.*, ii. 437–8
Berkshire	CLAPCOT	Wallingford	Adjacent	CLOPECOTE 1086 9 villeins, 8 cottars (I, fo. 6lb)	*P.N. Berks.*, ii. 536–7
Berkshire	NORCOT	Reading	2 miles	NORTHCOT 1327	*P.N. Berks.*, ii. 177
Berkshire	NORTHCOURT	Abingdon*	1 mile	NORTHCOTE c.1180	*P.N. Berks.*, ii. 438
Berkshire	SOUTHCOTE	Reading	1½ miles	SUDCOTE 1086 5 villeins, 8 bordars (I, fo. 61)	*P.N. Berks.*, i 177
Buckinghamshire	CALDECOTE	Newport Pagnell	1 mile	CALDECOTE 1086 1 knight, 2 vavassors, 2 villeins, 7 bordars 1 slave, (I, fo. 146b, 148b, 153)	*P.N. Bucks.*, p.21
Buckinghamshire	GAWCOTT	Buckingham	1½ miles	CHAUESCOTE 1086 2 bordars, 1 slave (I, fo. 144)	*P.N. Bucks.*, pp.60–1
Buckinghamshire	FOSCOTT	Buckingham	1½ miles	FOXESCOTE 1086 1 villein, 2 bordars, 1 slave (I, fo. 144b)	*P.N. Bucks.*, p.43
Cambridgeshire	COTON	Cambridge	2½ miles	COTIS 1086 (In D.B. as Whitwell) 1 villein, 1 bordar, 9 cottars (I, fo. 194b, 198b, 200b)	*P.N. Cambs.*, pp.74–5
Cumberland	CALDECOTES	Carlisle*	Adjacent	CALDECOTE 1253	*P.N. Cumb.*, i. 42
Gloucestershire	COATES	Winchcomb	Adjacent	CHOTES and COTA 12th C.	*P.N. Glos.*, ii. 32
Herefordshire	BURCOT	Hereford	1½ miles	BURCOTA before 1172	A. T. Bannister, *The Place-Names of Herefordshire* (Cambridge, 1916), p.34
Kent	CALDECOTE	Canterbury	1 mile	CALDICOT 1326 (in D.B. as *Estursete*), 25 villeins, 114 bordars, 1 slave (I, fo. 3b)	R. A. L. Smith, *Canterbury Cathedral Priory* (Cambridge 1943), p.46
Northamptonshire	COTTON END	Northampton	Adjacent	COTES 1199	*P.N. Northants.*, p.147
Shropshire	COTON	Shrewsbury	½ mile	COTA c.1160	M. O. H. Carver, 'Early Shrewsbury', *Trans. Shropshire Arch. Soc.* lix (1973–4) fig. 27, facing p.237

Somerset	WALCOT	Bath	Adjacent	WALCOT 1260		*Two Cartularies the Priory of... Bath, Somerset Record Soc.,* vii (1893), pt. 2, no. 249
Staffordshire	COTON	Stafford	Adjacent	COTE 1086 1 villein, 1 slave (I, fo. 248)		—
Staffordshire	COTON	Tamworth	1½ miles	COTON 1309		H. Wood, *Medieval Tamworth* (Tamworth, 1972), p. 101
Warwickshire	COTEN END	Warwick	Adjacent	COTES 1086 100 bordars (I, fo. 238)		*P.N. Warw.*, p. 264
Warwickshire	GLASCOTE	Tamworth	1 mile	GLASCOTE t. Henry II		*P.N. Warw.*, p. 26
Wiltshire	CALCUTT	Cricklade	1 mile	COLECOTE 1086 1 villein, 4 bordars, 1 slave (I, fo. 73b)		*P.N. Wilts.*, pp. 42–3

*Not recorded as boroughs in 1086. Show urban characteristics in twelfth century.

TABLE 2 Money rents paid by bordars, cottars, etc.

County	Manor	Borough	Type of tenant	Number	Rent *per annum*	Rent *per capita per annum*	D.B. reference
Dorset	Allington	Bridport	*censores*	9	11s. 0d.	14.7d.	I, fo. 80b
Middlesex	'No man's land'	London	cottars	30	14s. 10½d.	6d.	I, fo. 127
Middlesex	Holborn	London	cottars	2	20d.	10d.	I, fo. 127
Middlesex	Stepney	London	cottars	46	30s. 0d.	7.8d.	I, fo. 127
Middlesex	Bishopsgate	London	cottars	10	18s. 6d.	22.2d.	I, fo. 128
Middlesex	Westminster	London	cottars	41	40s. 0d.	11.7d.	I, fo. 128
Sussex	—	Hastings	bordars	14	63s. 0d.	(rent total includes payments by 4 burgesses)	I, fo. 17
Warwickshire	Coten	Warwick	bordars	100	50s. 0d.	6d.	I, fo. 238
Worcestershire	—	Evesham	bordars	27	20s. 0d.	8.9d.	I, fo. 175b

to towns.[21] *Cotes* near Warwick, now Coten End, has already been mentioned, as also has the Domesday manor of Whitwell near Cambridge, in which a settlement in 1086 was known as *Cotis*, which later became Coton. Table 1 gives twenty-one examples. Nine of the names are mentioned in Domesday or in a Domesday satellite, and seven of them show the predominance of small-holders that we would expect. Another twelve names are not recorded until the twelfth, thirteenth or early fourteenth centuries, though this should not be taken to mean that the settlements did not exist in 1086. As the example of Whitwell/Coton shows, the name by which a manor or village was known could vary, and two names could have co-existed at the same time. Many of these small places were not mentioned earlier than the twelfth century merely because they tended not to be the chief settlement of a manor and so would not appear in early charters or Domesday, and it is likely that all of them originated before the Conquest. Indeed, they may be much earlier, because although it was once believed that the formation of these names came in the late Anglo-Saxon period, it is now thought that some *cots* could belong to the period before 850. This means that the settlements, and the distinctive social structure which gave rise to their names, might belong to the formative stages of the boroughs near which they lay. The development of the manorial centre of Caldecote (Bucks.) is likely to have pre-dated the late borough of Newport Pagnell.[22] The majority of the settlements with *cot* names look like small subsidiary places, notably the Northcots and Southcote in Berkshire which were named in relation to the boroughs of Abingdon and Reading, or at least with reference to the estates, settlements or churches that acted as 'pre-urban nucleii' at these places.[23]

Having established the existence of numerous cottars and bordars, and cottage settlements, in and around more than forty early boroughs, we can begin to examine their significance. Who were the bordars and cottars? How did they live? The size of the woodland smallholdings can be taken to reflect the relatively minor contribution of arable farming to their economies. The urban or suburban cottars and bordars also had holdings of arable land too small to feed themselves and their families. The better-off, such as those at Ipswich, had as much as 8.6 acres each, but the forty-six Stepney cottars who lived on one hide must have

---

[21] It might be alleged that *cot* is such a common place-name that a random distribution would result in a number of such names lying near towns. However, *cots* are not very numerous in Berkshire, for example, yet five of them lie near towns.

[22] *P. N. Berks*, iii. 924–5; M. Gelling, 'On Looking into Smith's Elements', *Nomina*, v (1981), 42–3.

[23] Astill, *loc. cit.*, pp. 57–61; M. Biddle *et al.*, 'The Early History of Abingdon, Berkshire, and its Abbey', *Medieval Archaeology*, xii (1968), 26–69.

averaged only a few acres each, and the Bishopsgate cottars each had less than an acre. These smallholdings could have been cultivated intensively under stimulus of the demand from the nearby market. Like later urban gardens, they may have been planted with such saleable crops as vegetables and fruit, or with industrial crops like flax and hemp.[24] The tenants no doubt supplemented their income from agriculture or horticulture with wages or other profits gained from trading and industrial activity in the borough. That some of their income came in the form of cash is implied by the money rents recorded sporadically in Domesday (see Table 2). Others are known to have paid rents or taxes, but the exact amount is not recorded: nine coscets outside the borough of Malmesbury 'geld with the burgesses', and the origin of the name of Gawcott near Buckingham, which means 'gafol-cot', refers to the bordars' predecessors' obligation to pay rent, perhaps to the reeve of the borough of Buckingham (I, fols. 64b, 144).[25] The bordars on the Bigot manor near Thetford paid head-money (*scotum de suo capite*) to the king, again acknowledging their connections with the royal borough.

The smallholders were expected to produce sums of money in rent comparable with, or sometimes in excess of, those paid by the burgesses, which tended to be standard sums of between 6d. and 1s. 0d. *per annum*.[26] Indeed some of the rents listed in Table 2, such as those at Westminster and Evesham, may represent embryonic burgage rents. Evidently the lords of the bordars and cottars, observing the profits that they could make from the sale of produce, wage-earning and petty trading, fixed rents in cash that would enable them to reap a share of the benefits of urban growth. The exact nature of the smallholders' participation in the urban economy must remain hidden from us. In the case of a town with a prominent industry, like Droitwich, it seems reasonable to guess that the bordars of Witton cut and loaded fire wood and manned the boiling houses of the salt works. Elsewhere they could have been involved in a wide range of crafts and trades, judging from later evidence, especially those regarded as too noxious or dangerous to be practised in the town centre, and perhaps even at this early date the suburbs contained the criminals and prostitutes who gave an unsavoury reputation to such late

---

[24] On the viability of small-holdings, see e.g. J. Z. Titow, *English Rural Society* (London, 1969), pp. 89–90; on urban gardens in the fifteenth century, *Ministers' Accounts of the Collegiate Church of St Mary, Warwick, 1432–85*, ed. D. Styles, Dugdale Soc., xxvi, 1969, 125–7, and for earlier crops grown near towns, H. K. Kenward et al., 'The Environment of Anglo-Scandinavian York', in R. A. Hall (ed.), *Viking Age York and the North* (C.B.A. Research Report, 27, 1978), p. 61.

[25] *P. N. Bucks*, p. 60.

[26] A. Ballard, *The Domesday Boroughs* (Oxford, 1904), pp. 71–2; M. de W. Hemmeon, *Burgage Tenure in Mediaeval England* (Cambridge, Mass., 1914), pp. 61–77; on bordar rents in general, see Lennard, *ubi supra*, pp. 359–60.

medieval extramural enclaves as Southwark in London or the Tithing at Worcester.[27] It is no accident that the word *bordellus* has two meanings, of a small cottage and a brothel.

The importance of the bordars and cottars for our understanding of towns is twofold. They help indicate the scale and intensity of urban development by 1086; and they contribute to our knowledge of urban origins. The inclusion of the bordars and cottars in our view of eleventh-century society dispels any lingering doubts that the boroughs were really towns. A small place like St Albans looks more convincing as a significant concentration of population when the cottars are added to the burgesses, giving a total of more than 250 people (using a multiplier of 4.5). Middle-sized towns like Warwick gain in our estimation when the hundred bordars of *Cotes* (and their dependents and families) are added to the 244 burgesses and houses of the borough, to suggest a population of more than 1,500. The inclusion of the urban and suburban bordars and cottars with the burgesses and houses for the whole country would help to push the number of town-dwellers of Domesday nearer to 10 per cent of the total population. Their land-holdings should present no obstacle to regarding the bordars and cottars as part of the urban economy, as burgesses often had some land, yet still gained their main income from non-agricultural pursuits.[28] The cottars could only have made a living if the boroughs were generating wealth and employment. Places like Buckingham, Grantham, and Warwick, which were not to become very large or thriving towns in the later middle ages or in modern times, must have had relatively healthy economies in the eleventh century to maintain the large numbers of bordars and cottars settled on their peripheries. In this respect the towns of the eleventh century resemble those of the later middle ages, on whose outskirts concentrations of smallholdings are also found.[29]

Not all of these groups of smallholders can be regarded as part of the urban population. Those who lived in a separate settlement a mile or two from the town were still under its influence, judging from their ability to make a living in spite of the small size of their holdings. The interaction between town and country can be seen as falling within a series of zones, of which Domesday allows us to observe an outer and an inner. In a large outer area, up to a radius of ten or twenty miles, lay manors which held burgesses or houses in the town, indicating long-distance connections with the urban market, where rural produce was

---

[27] D. J. Keene, 'Suburban Growth', in M. W. Barley (ed.), *The Plans and Topography of Medieval Towns in England and Wales* (C. B. A. Research Report, 14, 1975), pp. 71–82.

[28] J. Tait, *The Medieval English Borough* (Manchester, 1936), pp. 68–75.

[29] e.g. D. Greenblatt, 'The Suburban Manors of Coventry, 1279–1411', Univ. of Cornell Ph.D. thesis, 1967, pp. 27–30.

sold, and manufactured or traded goods purchased.[30] In a much smaller penumbra lay the villages under more intense influence, where the town stimulated the countryside into fulfilling its needs for commodities and labour. The outlying villages had only occasional contact with the town; those in the inner ring would have participated frequently, even continuously, in the intercourse between town and country.

In the late eleventh century we can observe both well-established royal boroughs, mostly developed over the previous two centuries, and a recent generation of small boroughs on the estates of churchmen and lay magnates. In the latter the bordars and cottars represented the new townsmen, who appear to have begun as servants and dependents, with the function of supplying goods and services to their lords. This is especially clear at Evesham, where the twenty-seven bordars were called 'servants of the court'. The inhabitants of Battle were described in Domesday as bordars, and a list compiled twenty years later shows the town containing abbey servants living alongside artisans and traders; a comparable case is Seasalter, where the bordars apparently belonged to the archbishop or the monks of Christ Church, Canterbury, to provide those lords with salt and fish.[31] Townsmen seem to have originated as servants or minor tenants at Tewkesbury, Bury St Edmunds, and Westminster. Those who held manors on the edge of royal boroughs, like the pre-Conquest lords of Holywell and Walton near Oxford, could also have deliberately settled dependents in the suburbs in order to gain some profit from the town.

All of this might seem to strengthen the arguments of those who see pre-Conquest towns as deliberate and conscious creations by rulers.[32] This is not the whole story of urban development, and the presence of the bordars and cottars indicates the various paths that led to the emergence of towns. The gatherings of relatively poor people around centres of economic activity suggest the results of migration. A specific example of this might be Clare (Suffolk), a developing borough on an aristocratic estate, where the numbers of bordars on the manor between 1066 and 1086 increased threefold from ten to thirty, while the numbers of villeins dwindled (II, fo. 389b).[33] Possible sources of newcomers would include the pedlars, settling in or near a town in accordance with the classic Pirenne model, but a more plausible recruiting ground would be the peasantry, especially their younger sons, gravitating towards the town from an already crowded countryside. Settlements

[30] Darby, *Domesday England*, pp. 309–13.
[31] *The Chronicle of Battle Abbey*, ed. E. Scarle (Oxford 1980), pp. 50–59; Tatton-Brown, *loc.cit.*, pp. 32–34.
[32] e.g. M. Biddle and D. Hill, 'Late Saxon planned towns', *Antiquaries Journal*, li (1971), 70–85; R. Hodges, *Dark Age Economics* (London, 1982), pp. 153–98.
[33] G. A. Thornton, 'A Study in the History of Clare, Suffolk, with special reference to its Development as a Borough', *T.R.H.S.* fourth ser., xi (1928), 87.

near towns and suburbs could have served as staging posts for such migrants who could not immediately become burgesses. Another explanation of the role of smallholders in the growth of towns would be to link them with those theories of origin, as proposed for such places as Cambridge, Lincoln and Norwich, which portray the town emerging from the coalescence of a number of nucleii (some or all of which would have had a semi-rural character before the tenth century), or expanding to swallow a nearby rural settlement.[34] In such a model the smallholders would represent an intermediate stage in the social mobility of people en route from the peasantry to full integration into urban society. Under the stimulus of the trade and industry of nearby growing towns large villein holdings would have been fragmented, because lords would have seen the advantages of increasing the number of tenants, and because the tenants would have been tempted to divide their inheritance in view of the chances of their heirs making a good living out of smaller holdings. Some holdings could have broken up under the pressures of the land market.[35] So even if the evidence from such places as Evesham points to the originating urban nucleus being organised by a higher authority (and this does not need to be true in every case), in their expansion towns took in peasants, whether because they happened to be living nearby, or because they were attracted as migrants. In other words, in seeking the origins of urban populations we must allow for evolutionary and spontaneous elements as well as direction from above.

In the same way the development of towns must have taken place in a favourable rural environment, one in which exchanges of goods and services were growing. The existence of large numbers of smallholders is in itself evidence of the penetration of small-scale exchange throughout English society by the eleventh century, because such people needed to buy foodstuffs to supplement the produce of their holdings, and they had surplus labour to sell. In such a context, especially when at a higher social level lords were anxious to sell demesne produce, and to squeeze more cash in rents from their tenants, towns in the tenth and eleventh centuries look more like natural growths and less like alien implants.[36]

Finally the urban and suburban bordars and cottars of Domesday

---

[34] M. D. Lobel, 'Cambridge', in *The Atlas of Historic Towns*, ii (London, 1975), pp. 3–5, D. Perring, *Early Medieval Occupation at Flaxengate, Lincoln* (The Archaeology of Lincoln, ix, pt. 1, C.B.A., London, 1981), pp. 44–5; A Carter, 'The Anglo-Saxon Origins of Norwich: the Problems and Approaches', in P. Clemoes (ed.), *A[nglo]-S[axon] E[ngland]*, vii (Cambridge, 1978), 175–204.

[35] W. G. Runciman, 'Accelerating Social Mobility: the Case of Anglo-Saxon England', *P[ast and] P[resent]*, 104 (1984), 19–21.

[36] G. Duby, *Early Growth of the European Economy* (London, 1974), pp. 221–48; J. Merrington, 'Town and Country in the Transition to Capitalism', in R. H. Hilton (ed.), *The Transition from Feudalism to Capitalism* (London, 1976), pp. 170–95.

draw attention to the role of the lower ranks of society in medieval towns. The written sources leave no doubt of the sharply differentiated social hierarchy, even in early towns, and the excavation of urban sites indicates great inequalities in housing conditions.[37] Various historians have attempted to assert the importance of craftsmen rather than merchants in the early stages of urban growth.[38] Towns in Poland, for example, seem to have begun as small industrial communities established at the gates of aristocratic residences.[39] One of the achievements of recent archaeological research in England has been to show the wide range of industries practised both in an early emporium like *Hamwih* and in a city like York which flourished in the tenth and eleventh centuries.[40] A feature of the economic history of late Saxon England was the growing concentration of certain industries in towns, most easily demonstrated in the case of pottery manufacture, but also evidently in cloth-making.[41] No doubt the economy of the larger towns depended a good deal on long-distance and inter-regional trade, but they supported large populations within their walls, in their suburbs, and beyond, through the flourishing of labour-intensive industries and crafts. The urban economy, especially in the smaller towns, must have also provided many roles for the petty trader, like the one-eyed garlic (or onion) seller who appears in an Old English riddle. Small towns, when they are better documented in the thirteenth century, were full of people who traded on a small scale over short distances in cheap commodities, mostly food-stuffs.[42] This must have been the economic basis for eleventh-century towns like Ashwell and Evesham, and for the cottars and bordars who lived in such places.

The association between cottages and towns can be traced at all stages of medieval urban development. Cottager communities might

---

[37] Russell, p. 46; B. K. Davison, 'The Late Saxon Town of Thetford', *Medieval Archaeology*, xi (1967), 189–208.

[38] E. V. Gutnova, 'Levitsky's Artisanal Theory in England', in J. F. Benton (ed), *Town Originis* (Boston, Mass., 1968), pp. 37–41; C. Verlinden, 'Marchands ou Tisserands? À propos des origines urbaines', *Annales E.S.C.*, xxvii (1972), 396–406.

[39] P. Francastel (ed), *Les Origines des Villes Polonaises* (Paris 1960), pp. 20–4.

[40] P. Holdsworth, 'Saxon Southampton: a New Review', *Medieval Archaeology*, xx (1976), pp. 26–61; A. MacGregor, 'Industry and Commerce in Anglo-Scandinavian York', in Hall (ed.), 37–57.

[41] J. G. Hurst, 'The Pottery', in Wilson (ed.), pp. 314, 323, 326–34. E. Crowfoot, 'Textiles', in M. O. H. Carver, 'Three Saxo-Norman Tenements in Durham City', and J. W. Hedges, 'Textiles', in C. M. Heighway *et al.*, 'Excavations at 1 Westgate Street, Gloucester, 1975', *Medieval Archaeology*, xxiii (1979), 36–9, 190–3.

[42] R. H. Hilton, 'Lords, Burgesses and Hucksters', *P.P.*, 97 (1982) 3–15.

form proto-urban settlements. Cottages could become part of the fabric of urban society, within the town centre and especially in its suburbs. Cottar settlements on the edge of the towns might be deliberately created by lords, or gather more spontaneously. Urban growth exerted an influence on the countryside, by engulfing peasant settlements, attracting migrants, and transforming the economy and landholding structures of nearby villages, in all cases providing an environment in which cottars could live. If we focus our attentions too narrowly on the burgesses and the town centres, we are in danger of minimising the extent and the influence of early medieval urbanization.

8

Guibert of Nogent and his World

R. I. Moore

Guibert of Nogent is no longer admired as a precocious rationalist. His mockery of the claims of the Holy Tooth of Soissons was inspired by institutional rivalry rather than intuitive scepticism, to defend the interests of the Virgin of Laon; his treatment of relics in general was dictated by the canons of twelfth-century biblical scholarship, not those of nineteenth-century positivism.[1] Nowadays Guibert seems more interesting as a pioneer of the irrational. The lively interest he displays in magical activity of all kinds, including sorcery and divination, and in the intervention of the devil in human affairs, especially when conjured up by those who had made pacts with him, foreshadows a preoccupation which became increasingly widespread and increasingly intense in the next two centuries.[2] We need not assume that he took it all equally seriously. Many of the stories which enliven his narratives, and especially those collected in the last part of each book of the *Monodiae* (the so-called memoirs[3]) belong to the rhetorical tradition well established among monastic writers, of presenting bizarre and lurid stories of the supernatural in the most circumstantial fashion, to add colour and force

---

[1] M. Bloch, *Les rois thaumaturges* (Strasbourg, 1924, new edn. Paris, 1961), pp. 29–32; J. Chaurand, 'La conception de l'histoire de Guibert de Nogent', *Cahiers de Civilisation Médiévale*, 8 (1965), 395–6. For the positivist view, B. Monod, *Le moine Guibert et son temps, 1053–1124* (Paris, 1905).

[2] See particularly N. Cohn, *Europe's Inner Demons* (London, 1975), pp. 16–74.

[3] Guibert mentions the work only once, referring to the 'Manichees' of Soissons 'super quibus in libris monodiarum mearum laciniosus dixi', *De pignoribus sanctorum* I, iii, Migne, *Patrologia Latina* 256, col. 622. The use of his phrase, whose aptness is commended in the final paragraph of this paper, avoids the misleading connotations of such titles as 'autobiography', 'memoirs' and even the seemingly neutral 'de vita sua'. It is cited here, by Book, chapter and page reference alone, in the edition of E. R. Labande, *Guibert de Nogent: Autobiographie (Les classiques de l'histoire de France au moyen-âge*, (Paris, 1981), which at last provides a sound translation into a modern language. The notoriously inaccurate version of C. C. Swinton Bland (London, 1925) was based on D'Achery's text instead of G. Bourgin's, in *Guibert de Nogent: Histoire de sa vie* (Paris, 1907); nevertheless I owe an enduring interest in Guibert to the copy which Ralph Davis lent me as a freshman. That of J. F. Benton, *Self and Society in Medieval France: The Memoirs of Abbot Guibert of Nogent* (New York, 1970), is too heavily based on Bland to provide a reliable text, despite extensive revision, though its notes and appendices remain indispensable.

to their moral purpose.[4] Thus the tale of the monk who called on the devil to turn his mistress into a dog so that she would escape detection on leaving his cell casts no light on Guibert's own convictions.[5] But some of his expressions of belief in magic and sorcery occupy a much more central place in his exposition, and occur in contexts of personal importance to him. He is quite explicit in endorsing the plausibility of the story that his mother's virginity was preserved for a number of years by a magical ligature – *satis credibile est* – and that of the incubus who assailed her in bed.[6] Such beliefs were not generally approved among the literate of the eleventh century; Burchard of Worms had condemned many of them, including specifically belief in incubi, as revivals of pagan superstition for which penance should be imposed on those who confessed to entertaining them.[7]

To the extent that the belief which he expressed in such things was real, therefore, Guibert may be thought to anticipate a credulity which became more evident after his time. More sure is his place among those writers whom Edward Peters has identified as having 'created a distinctive form of invective (which) – having part of its roots in Roman invective against magicians, objects of satire, Jews and deviant Christians – was applied to both heretics and magicians in the twelfth century'.[8] Thus when Guibert interrogated Clement of Bucy and his associates he relied upon assumptions about their beliefs and behaviour drawn from Augustine's account of the Manichees much more heavily and much more systematically than those who encountered heretics in the eleventh century had done, and very much as the inquisitors would do in the future.[9] And his satisfaction at the burning of these heretics by the people of Soissons contrasts sharply with Archbishop Aribert's attempt to restrain the *majores* of Milan from burning those discovered at Monforte in 1028, or Wazo of Liége's firm advice against the physical coercion of heretics, and his disciple Anselm's outright condemnation of the hanging of heretics by Henry III at Goslar, in 1053.[10] Again in his intense hatred of Jews, and his readiness to associate them with black magic, poisoning and the summoning of the devil, as well as the more mundane offences of usury and procuring, Guibert exhibits not the relatively detached and even on occasion sympathetic interest of Gilbert Crispin or Abelard, but the long and depressingly familiar tradition of

---

[4] Edward Peters, *The Magician, the Witch and the Law* (Philadelphia, 1978), pp. 24–5, 39–45.

[5] [*Monodiae*] I, xxvi [(ed. Labande, *Autobiographie*)] pp. 202–4.

[6] I, xii, p. 84; xiii, p. 90.

[7] Burchard, *Decretum*, xix (the *Corrector*), Migne, *Patrologia Latina*, 140, vol. 973; H. C. Lea, *Materials Toward a History of Witchcraft*, I (New York, 1957), pp. 126–37, 147–51, 182–7.

[8] Peters, *op. cit.* p. 42.

[9] R. I. Moore, *The Origins of European Dissent* (London, 1977), pp. 67, 243–6.

[10] *ibid.* pp. 35, 39.

rhetorical anti-semitism which developed so rapidly during the twelfth century, and to which he himself contributed the first western stories of Jewish magicians operating as agents of the devil, and binding themselves to him by the libation of sperm.[11]

In these respects, in short, Guibert was particularly prone to pollution fears. As we might expect they are especially evident in his attitudes to sex and women, and it is in what those attitudes reveal about his social rather than his psychological situation that their interest lies.[12] Women are regularly associated with the agents of evil, as when the mother of John of Soissons hired a Jew to poison her brother; Guibert knew far more stories about their sleeping with the devil than decency allowed him to repeat.[13] Decency did not prevent him, however, from attributing to the unsatisfied lusts of Sybil of Coucy direct and indirect responsibility for the savage and destructive warfare between Godfrey of Namur and Enguerrand of Boves (who 'hardly did anything except at the dictation of women's impudence'[14]), the murder of Gerald of Quierzy which inaugurated the whole disastrous train of events that included the communal rising at Laon in 1112 and the assassination of Bishop Gaudry, and the dreadful atrocities committed by Thomas of Marle when 'by her woman's cunning she kept him from his right . . . and "drove him from folly to insanity".'[15] Sybil was only the most shameless exponent of the force which Guibert, passionately eloquent in the best moralist tradition, saw as the great scourge of his time. 'In this and similar ways this modern age is corrupt and corrupting, distributing evil ideas to some while their filth spreads to others and continues to increase unceasingly.'[16]

We have learned to associate the currency of ideas like these with the fear of social change, and so it is with Guibert. He is, of course, firmly attached to the established social order – or to what he found it necessary to proclaim as the established order – and deeply hostile to change. Serfs, as Archbishop Ralph of Reims preached at Gaudry's funeral, must heed the injunction of St Peter, and 'be subject to your masters with all fear, and not only to the good and gentle, but also to

---

[11] J. Trachtenberg, *The Devil and the Jews* (New Haven, 1943), pp. 66, 213.

[12] Guibert is subjected to psychiatric analysis by J. F. Benton, *Self and Society*, pp. 21–27 and 'The Personality of Guibert of Nogent', *Psychoanalytic Review*, 57 (1970–71), 563–86, and J. Kantor, 'A psycho-historical source: the *Memoirs* of Abbot Guibert of Nogent', *Journal of Medieval History*, 2 (1976), 281–304, and to spiritual examination by M. D. Coupe, 'The Personality of Guibert of Nogent Reconsidered', *ibid.*, 9 (1983), 317–30.

[13] III, xvi, p. 422; xix, p. 456.

[14] III, iii, p. 274.

[15] III, xiv, p. 398. The quotation is from Terence, *The Eunuch*.

[16] I, xii, pp. 80–2.

the froward'.[17] The harshness of their masters was no excuse. Guibert is famous for his hostility to the commune and his portrayal of the wickedness of the people of Laon, and he gives occasional hints that the docility of serfs in the countryside might not always be relied upon. The peasants whom Bishop Gaudry brought from his manors to guard against a rising in the city 'hated him almost as much (as the townsmen), since they knew that the pile of money which he had promised the king must be drained from their own purses'.[18] When Thomas of Marle later left Laon unguarded it was occuped by *pagenses*, also described as a *rustica manus et suburbani*; and that two years previously he had found it necessary to go to Soissons *contra quosdam rusticos opem cuidam laturus* implies a revolt or rising of some kind.[19]

For all his fear and dislike of the peasantry, however, Guibert did not hold them principally to blame for the troubles he describes. If his sense of corruption is commonplace enough, though often strikingly expressed, it informs his view of people and events with great consistency. The cast of characters assembled in the *Monodiae* is as unregenerate a crew as the grimmest of realist novelists could devise, sunk almost to a man, or woman, in every combination of the deadly sins. Among all those whom Guibert knew personally, apart from the ambivalent cases of his mother and his tutor, only Anselm of Bec and Anselm of Laon emerge with their characters intact. And time and again Guibert shows how the vanity, greed, lechery and weakness of the rest is the root cause of the upheavals which he describes so graphically. The weakness began at the top. 'Since ancient times it had been the misfortune of the city of Laon that . . . the public authority was involved in rapine and murder. To begin with the source of the plague, whenever the king, who ought to have exacted respect for himself with royal severity, happened to visit the city, he was shamefully fined on his own property . . .'[20] Royal weakness and venality (abetted by the same qualities at the papal court) had secured the bishopric of Laon for Gaudri in the first place, and then precipitated the events of 1112 by first granting the commune and then, after a competition in bribery, withdrawing it. The breaking of their oaths by bishop and nobles 'without regard for honour or the holy season' was the direct cause of the catastrophe which followed.[21]

---

[17] III, x, p. 360. For a convenient summary of the progress of serfdom in northern France at the beginning of the twelfth century, see J. P. Poly and E. Bournazel, *Le mutation féodale, x–xii siècles* (Paris, 1980), pp. 312–19, and for a brilliant sketch of Guibert's world R. Fossier, *Histoire de la Picardie* (Collection Univers de la France, ed. Ph. Wolff, Toulouse 1974), pp. 135–75.

[18] III, viii, p. 334.

[19] III, xi, pp. 366–8, 364.

[20] III, vii, pp. 316–8.

[21] III, vii, p. 330.

In this as in most things Guibert was more picturesque than original: he was hardly alone in seeing 'rebel lords and unworthy clerks' at the root of violence and disorder.[22] But once again his response points more to the future than to the past. His admiration is reserved for those who contrast most strongly with the agents of evil, the 'clean' men who renounced office, power and connections in the pursuit of holiness, like Everard of Breteuil or Bruno of Reims. Yet if the best renounce power someone must remain to exercise it, and Guibert is clear what their qualifications should be. In characterising successive bishops of Laon as lacking trustworthiness (Adalbero), family and education (Helinand), strength and piety (Enguerrand), humility, compassion and self-denial (Gaudry), Guibert in effect enumerates the qualities of the ideal bishop.[23] One of them was particularly important to him: 'he who does not know the sacraments of the church' he said in the sermon he preached on his installation as abbot of Nogent, which is, as we shall see, the pivot upon which the *Monodiae* turns, 'is unworthy of its administration'.[24] At the personal level that view was strikingly at variance with, might almost have been designed to answer, the assertion of Guibert's mother that his inexperience of worldly business unfitted him for the office of abbot.[25] But in public terms it has wider significance. The identification of education as the key to legitimate power is also central to the argument of Guibert's *de pignoribus sanctorum*, where it is not superstition that is condemned as such, but the designation of sanctity by popular acclaim rather than clerical authority.[26] This is the claim to power of the clerks, which Dr. Murray has described so compellingly and associated so firmly with the growth of a spirit of contempt for the illiterate. I shall argue elsewhere that the development during the twelfth century of a rhetoric of contamination against dissidents and minority groups – especially heretics and Jews – to which we have seen Guibert contribute was part of the same process. In his personal attitudes as in his public opinions Guibert was not only a man of his time, but one who represented the wave of the future – and especially those clerks whom Murray, like Duby, portrays as representing, in association with renewed royal authority founded on their skills, the basis of a new social order.[27] Guibert's personal development, therefore, is of more than personal interest; to the extent

---

[22] The phrase is borrowed from J. P. Poly, 'La Provence et la société féodale', (Paris, 1976), pp. 205–6; closer to home, Guibert's nostalgia for royal authority leads him to see the root of the events of 1112 in Adalbero's desertion of the Carolingian line (III. i, p. 268).

[23] III, i–iii, pp. 268–80; Chaurand, *ubi supra* n. 1, p. 389n.

[24] II, iii, p. 238.

[25] I, xix, p. 166.

[26] B. Stock, *The Implications of Literacy* (Princeton, 1983), pp. 244–52.

[27] A. Murray, *Reason and Society in the Middle Ages* (Oxford, 1978), especially pp. 121–37, 213–51; G. Duby, *The Three Orders*, (London, 1980), pp. 257–353.

that his idiosyncracies can be illuminated by the circumstances of the world in which he lived they may offer some clues to the development of the one which lay ahead.

'Confiteor amplitudini tuae, Deus, infinitorum errorum meorum decursus . . .': the intention of the *Monodiae* to invite comparison with Augustine's *Confessions* is obvious from the beginning. Guibert's general disposition to present his life and circumstances in a fashion which recalls Augustine's has often been noticed – most obviously and immediately in the dominant role of his mother in family life and his spiritual development, which his father's chief function is to threaten, and in the delineation of Guibert's own precocious intellectual development and his indefatigable love for his books in spite of brutal, Quintilianesque floggings. The more the two books are compared the more clear it becomes how well Guibert knew Augustine. The *Confessions* is his most quoted work, and Augustine his most quoted author outside the scriptures, but beyond the direct quotations are constant echoes of phrase and anecdote. The resemblance between Guibert's mother and Monica, for instance, extends to their both having had difficulties as young wives with, respectively, a jealous stepmother and mother-in-law, and with gossiping servants; the young Guibert was seduced from serious study by the pagan poets as Augustine was by the theatre; like Augustine Guibert produced a brother otherwise unmentioned to attend – or in his case fail to attend – his mother's deathbed.[28] Guibert does not sustain the imitation of the *Confessions* in the structure of his book, but he does, perhaps more significantly, follow Augustine in focussing attention at critical points less on the externals of people and events than on the operation of the will, or heart, which is the real theme of the *Confessions*: the terms in which he describes the onset of adolescence, for instance, are clearly inspired by the first two chapters of Augustine's second book.[29]

The point is worth making because the differences between Guibert and Augustine are so much greater than the resemblance. Guibert was conscious of them even in small things: he remembers how he was kept from the childhood games in which Augustine excelled, and paints his mother's jealous fury at his promotion to Nogent in colours which contrast sharply with the maternal affection that made Monica resist her

---

[28] Compare respectively I, xii, p. 78 with *Confessions*, IX, ix; I, xvii, p. 134, with III, ii; II, iv, p. 242 with IX, xi.

[29] Guibert's I, xvi, p. 122, begins 'Cum ergo, paulatim succrescente corpusculo, etiam animam in concupiscentiis pro suo modulo et cupiditatibus prurientem saecularis vita titillaret . . . '; Augustine's II, i (ed. M. Skutella, Stuttgart, 1969, p. 25), 'Recordari volo transactas foeditates meas et carnales corruptionem animae meae . . . ' Guibert's interest in the workings of the *anima* is discussed by C. Morris, *The Discovery of the Individual* (London, 1972), pp. 65–7; cf. Peter Brown, *Augustine of Hippo* (London, 1967), pp. 28–9, 168–73.

son's departure for Rome.³⁰ And if Guibert was deeply enough soaked in Augustine for points like those to emerge so obviously – whether always deliberately or not – from his narrative he can hardly have been quite insensitive to the larger differences between them. As both of those examples recall, Augustine's account of his upbringing, however sternly overlaid by the adult's sense of sin, describes a happy and gregarious childhood. The threat which Patricius represented to his son's salvation is more than balanced by the picture, in the pages following the death of Monica (whom Patricius 'loved, respected and admired', to whom he was remarkably kind, and whom he did not beat), of a united and harmonious family life.³¹ At every stage of his life Augustine was popular and successful, surrounded by friends with whom he shared his sins and spiritual crises alike. Even his account of the wanton destruction of the pear tree, most powerful symbol of youthful sinfulness, is essentially a comment on the strength of the ties of friendship; the nearest Guibert got to that companionship in wrongdoing was in reciting to his fellow novices obscene verses whose authorship he dared not acknowledge.³² In childhood Guibert had no society but that of his mother and his tutor – neither, by his account, an easy companion – and got no closer to other boys than to sit 'dressed as a clerk, watching the crowd at play as though I were an intelligent animal'.³³ It is an image that persisted for life, capturing not only Guibert's loneliness but his inability to communicate with other men, whose doings he observed with contempt indeed, but contempt often tinged with envy. The image is reversed, with the same effect, when he refers to the rest of his *genus* (except his mother) as *animales Dei ignaros*:³⁴ there are passing references to several of its members in the *Monodiae* but nothing to imply that he was close to any of them. It is clear too that he had difficulties with both of the communities to which he belonged, though he insisted that he did not reciprocate the hatred of the monks of St Germer, which caused him much distress (and which, characteristically, he attributed to their envy of his superior abilities), or of those of Nogent, who seem to have rebelled against his abbacy.³⁵

This points clearly to an equally profound and even more obvious contrast between Guibert and Augustine. Augustine was not only the greatest of the fathers but a bishop for thirty-five years, and a leader of standing and influence in the African church. For a man of Guibert's abilities, especially on his own estimate of them, the abbacy of the insignificant house of Nogent-sous-Coucy was a modest position in

---

³⁰ I, v, p. 30 and *Confessions* I, xix, p. 166 and *Confessions* V, viii.
³¹ *Confessions* IX. 9, ed. Skutella pp. 196–7.
³² *Confessions* II, iv–vi; Guibert, I, xvii, p. 138.
³³ I, v, p. 30.
³⁴ I, ii, p. 14.
³⁵ I, xvi, pp. 82–4; and below n. 44.

which to complete a career that was obviously in its evening as he wrote, in his fifties at least.[36] The young Guibert was no stranger to ambition. In adolescence he had resented his vows, 'dwelling repeatedly on what and how great I might have been in the world', and exemplifying for Duby the resentment and rationalisation of the younger son deprived of marriage and glory for the preservation of patrimony.[37] Later, considering himself possessed of 'a person well fitted for the world, and no mean birth', he longed for advancement in the church, and urged his family to get it for him.[38] He mastered ambition only with great difficulty, and only shortly before his election to the abbacy of Nogent in 1104, when he was forty, if not fifty years old. Even then his strictures upon the integrity and competence of every office-holder he knew cannot but suggest personal disappointment. It is especially noticeable that his comments on his predecessor as abbot, Godfrey of Namur, who had left for the bishopric of Amiens, are particularly feline, and by comparison with other accounts clearly unfair. Indeed the coolness of his reference to the election of Barthélemy de Jur to succeed Gaudry at Laon – *iste legitime et invitus eligitur* is all he has to say[39] – almost invites speculation whether Guibert might not have hoped for the job himself. The part he had played in the events surrounding Gaudry's murder, when Guibert showed courage (by his own account) both in standing up to the bishop beforehand and in denouncing the assassins afterwards, might easily have suggested that he was a possible successor.

Augustine's *Confessions* are perfectly clear about the key (beyond his character and abilities) to his success. At every stage he frankly acknowledged the advancement he received from influential patrons and the good offices of his friends. For Guibert it was not so

---

[36] The clearest indications that the *Monodiae* was written during 1115 are that the account of the Carthusians in I, xi seems to be based on information from a monk who accompanied Godfrey of Amiens on the journey to La Chartreuse from which he returned in April of that year, and that Guibert writes of Godfrey, who died on 8th November 1115, as though he were still alive (III, xiv, pp. 414–6; Benton, *Self and Society*, p. 237). Benton's case for dating Guibert's birth to 1064 instead of the traditional 1053 or 1055 (*ibid.* pp. 229–33) has been taken less seriously than it deserves. Guibert's statements that he was born *vigilia paschalis* and *iduato ferme aprili* (I, iii, 18) limit the possible years to 1053, 1055, 1064 and 1066. Granted that Guibert's various protestations about his youth should not be taken literally, and that the sacraments he received from Guy, bishop of Beauvais from 1063–4, need not have included baptism (I, xiv, p. 100, and Labande's n. 2), it remains true that if, with Mabillon, we construe Guibert's reference to his father's capture at the battle of Mortemer 'necdum enim natus eram, nec longo post tempore fui' (I, xiii, p. 88) as 'I was not born then, nor for a long time afterwards' there is no reason to prefer the earlier dates, while the later make much better sense of the other stages of Guibert's life; that Guibert's novitiate began some time before Anselm became abbot of Bec, c. August 1078, points towards 1064.

[37] I, xvi, p. 122; G. Duby, *Le chevalier, la femme et le prêtre* (Paris, 1981), pp. 155–8.

[38] I, xix, p. 158.

[39] III, xiv, p. 396.

straightforward. The patronage he had sought through family connection in his youth was not only ineffectual but morally unacceptable in his maturity. Before he took his vows he had tried with his mother's help to secure a canonry of Beauvais from the lord of Clermont, in payment of a debt which the latter owed to Guibert's brother, by exploiting popular hostility against the married incumbent.[40] Success would have placed Guibert himself firmly among the corrupt clergy whom he excoriates with such savagery. Nor did his vows by any means resolve the problem. The renunciation of ambition which is one of the less obvious themes of the first book of the *Monodiae* is therefore directly interwoven with the drawing away from family which is one of the most obvious. Both involve, in turn, abandonment of his inheritance with the vow of dedication to the monastic life at birth, which Guibert believed his father would have broken, if he had lived, by making him a knight;[41] the renunciation of secular preferment after the affair of the canonry of Beauvais; of the world, when he entered St Germer de Fly as a novice; and of ambition itself as he matured and abjured the influence of his family on his behalf; and lastly, of his home at St Germer and his native region when renunciation was rewarded by the call to Nogent. In a similar, though less systematic fashion, the third book recounts Guibert's involvement in public affairs in a manner which distances him from the holders both of secular and ecclesiastical authority by his account of the ways in which they both acquired and exercised it.

In these ways Guibert's life exemplifies the processes which underlay the rise of the clerks in the twelfth century, and his attitudes the development which accompanied it of an ideology in which learning and attainment displaced kinship as an acceptable claim to office and status – irrespective of the actual role which birth and connection may have continued to play in the careers of many who disowned them. Hence, as we have noticed, Guibert's general admiration of those who renounced worldly position, while reserving his approval as holders of office for men like Anselm of Bec, Anselm of Laon and Bruno of Reims who combined freedom from corrupting ties with intellectual distinction.

These values, however, do not help to account for Guibert's own lack of success. On the face of it he could scarcely have been blamed for feeling that his own name would have sat among those without incongruity. It is easy for a modern reader to see why Guibert was a poor abbot. His sharp tongue and ready sneer, his over-valuing of his own talents and under-valuing of everybody else's, his readiness to attribute the behaviour of those around him always to the lowest of motives, and in particular disagreement with, or dislike of, himself to

[40] I, vii, pp. 42–8.
[41] I, iv, p. 24.

envy and malice, his authoritarian attitudes and weakness in the exercise of authority, as when, in the election of Gaudri, 'wrongly afraid of others who outranked us we followed their lead' instead of joining Master Anselm in dissent[42] – all these qualities contribute to a comprehensive portrait of a man unfit for office. But though it is drawn by Guibert's own hand, and not always unwittingly, it remains a generalised portrait; direct accounts of his dealings with others are relatively few and formal in nature. At one point, though rather evasively, Guibert invites us closer, when he touches on his relationship with the monks of Nogent. 'What would they have thought' he remarks of his election, 'if they had known what sort of head over them I would be?'[43] That it is not simply a rhetorical question is confirmed by the mysterious references to an occasion when he left Nogent and returned to Fly. It followed some sort of quarrel, or even revolt, for Bishop Gaudry accused one of his archdeacons of 'publicly taking your side but secretly stirring me up against you'.[44] Indeed it is not difficult to read the *Monodiae* as offering Guibert's account of himself to his monks, in which the first book describes his life before his election and the third his public activity as abbot, while the second discusses his life at Nogent itself and, as directly as he can bring himself to do, his relations with its community.

This is why Guibert's account of his installation as abbot and the sermon which he preached on the occasion is central not only to the structure of the *Monodiae* but to understanding both his public view of office and authority and his private experience of it. All the main themes of the book are to be found here, in the third chapter of Book Two. It opens with a declaration of purity: 'I do not know whether God disapproved or accepted the choice; but this one thing I can say with confidence, that the nomination was made without any intrigue or knowledge on my part or that of anyone among my kin'.[45] He adds immediately that their mutual ignorance of one another may have been the reason why he and his monks failed to get on, characteristically feeling himself punished even for his virtue. He repeats in some detail how one of the monks attempted to divine the omens for his reign by the verse of the Gospel upon which his eye fell as he opened the book, showing, we need hardly add, none of the disapproval of such practices that was evinced by Gratian.[46] The sermon, on Isaiah 3, 6–8, deals with rulership: it is here that Guibert observes that 'he who does not know the sacraments of the church is unworthy of its administration', but the burden of the sermon, at least as he now recounted it, was the rightness

---

[42] III, iv, p. 284.
[43] I, xix, p. 166.
[44] II, iv, p. 242; III, vii, p. 322.
[45] II, iii, p. 234.
[46] *Decretum*, C. 26 q. 2 c. 1.

of refusing a position of authority for which one is externally qualified but spiritually unfit. The whole chapter is deeply Augustinian. In his only direct statement about his purpose in writing the *Monodiae* he echoes the *Confessions* very directly: 'Thou knowest, most merciful God, that I began this work not in the spirit of pride but wishing to confess my wickedness . . .',[47] and inner motive, the operation of the hearts of Guibert and his monks in their relations with each other and of the protagonists in his sermon, is central. So is the theme of confession itself. He emphasises that the monks inaugurated their relations with him in admirable fashion because 'by faithful confession they revealed their hearts to me to such a degree that I, who thought I knew something of monks elsewhere, knew none to compare with them in this respect'. He returns to confession at the end of his sermon. 'When confession of sins which puts an end to all evil is wanting through any kind of despair, there is a proper reason for refusing the office of pastor. When a mind which is disquieted by burgeoning vice and obscured by evil cannot dispel them through confession it cannot rule itself, and is justly prevented by others, and more justly prevents itself, from exercising authority.'

There is Guibert's own confession. His inability to reveal his heart as his monks had done unfitted him for office. He was by the best values of the age eminently fitted for it by education, and free of disabling bonds and affiliations; he had obtained it legitimately, and on merit – or, as he put it more bitterly, because the electors were blinded by his literary reputation.[48] Yet it was vitiated by his inability to communicate with those over whom he was placed. It was, at a personal level, very much the condition of his class over the next two or three centuries. But for Guibert it was more. His spiritual heroes were men who by renunciation had voluntarily made themselves outsiders. Guibert was an involuntary outsider, who tried, and failed, to make the best of it. Confession was the sacrament of reconciliation with the community To fail in it was to remain, like the heretics and Jews whom he feared and detested so much, the animal set apart of his childhood memory. All that remained was to make the confession which he could not speak in its proper place here, in his monody – the song for a single voice, as Isidore defined it,[49] sung in Greek tragedy by an actor who remains outside the chorus.

---

[47] II, iii, p. 234; *Confessions*, II, 1.
[48] I, xix, p. 166.
[49] Isidore, *Etymologiae*, VI, xix, 6, ed. W. M. Lindsay (Oxford, 1911).

9

Henry I and the Invisible Transformation of Medieval England

C. Warren Hollister

Historians in the present century have tended to view the reign of Henry I as an historical turning point. Albert Brackmann credits Henry with developing a new type of political organization that set European civilization on a new course.[1] Richardson and Sayles ascribe to Henry's reign the genesis of 'a carefully articulated machine of government' unparalleled in the West since the fall of Rome.[2] 'Looking to the future', Sir Richard Southern writes, 'it is here, we feel, that the history of England begins – a history which is neither that of the Norman conquerors, nor of the Anglo-Saxons, but that of the English crown and aristocracy'.[3]

Southern evaluated Henry's reign by looking to the future, but contemporaries necessarily did so by looking to the past. Like modern historians they regarded his reign as noteworthy, but for altogether different reasons. They cast him in the age-old role of the model king who, with wise, seasoned advisers, restored the good, ancient laws, kept the peace throughout his dominions, and protected the church, the impoverished and the helpless by chastising evildoers. These medieval clichés, echoing well-known passages from Scripture, shaped even the most sophisticated contemporary perceptions of the reign. Henry was praised as a great king, and great precisely because he played the ancient role so well. His royal virtues were old, hallowed virtues. His seldom-mentioned vices – avarice, lust – were older still. How is it that contemporary writers could have missed the big story, overlooking the innovations that contributed to what we now regard as a fundamental reorientation of medieval governance?

Let me be more concrete on the matter of contemporary perceptions. Henry I was viewed, above all, as the embodiment of the *rex pacificus* – an

---

[1] A. Brackmann, 'The Beginnings of the National State in Mediaeval Germany and the Norman Monarchies', in *Medieval Germany, 911–1250: Essays by German Historians*, ed. Geoffrey Barraclough (Oxford, 1948), pp. 287–88.
[2] H. G. Richardson and G. O. Sayles, *The Governance of Mediaeval England from the Conquest to Magna Carta* (Edinburgh, 1963), pp. 159, 172.
[3] R. W. Southern, *Medieval Humanism and Other Studies* (Oxford, 1970), p. 207.

ancient ideal that all kings pursued but few attained.[4] The Anglo-Saxon chronicler praised Henry for having given England 'peace for man and beast'. William of Malmesbury lauded him for 'having established such peace in Normandy as had never before been known, such as even his father . . . had never been able to effect'.[5] 'God grant him peace', wrote Hugh, archbishop of Rouen, on Henry's death, 'for peace he loved'.[6]

In the conventional wisdom of the time, peacekeeping required the king to act severely toward violent subjects – rebels, rapists, arsonists, violators of churches, exploiters of widows and orphans. Accordingly, contemporaries stress that Henry punished such people with exile, forfeiture, death, or mutilation. It is hard for us to read accounts of some of these punishments without concluding that their authors were condemning Henry I for acts of unspeakable cruelty. Yet a careful reading of such passages makes it clear that in nearly all of them he is being applauded for fulfilling the responsibilities of Christian kingship.[7] Isaiah had prophesied the coming of the virtuous king, a ruler both compassionate and stern, whose word is a rod that strikes the ruthless, whose judgements bring death to the wicked (XI, iv). Echoing the old tradition, St Anselm urged the king of Scots to 'behave in such a way that the bad shall fear you and the good shall love you'.[8] Only in this context can one comprehend the passage in which Eadmer of Canterbury, St Anselm's companion and panegyrist, reporting that Henry I reestablished the ancient practice of mutilating false minters, proudly explains that he did so 'on the advice of Anselm and the nobles of the realm . . . to alleviate the kingdom's suffering', and that 'great good immediately resulted'.[9] All contemporaries would have agreed, except of course the minters.

Eadmer's statement displays still another traditional royal virtue: the good king will consult on important matters with his magnates and

---

[4] See, for example, William A. Chaney, *The Cult of Kingship in Anglo-Saxon England* (Berkeley, 1970), pp. 90–94.

[5] *Anglo-Saxon Chronicle*, A.D. 1135; William of Malmesbury, *Gesta Regum Anglorum*, ed. William Stubbs (1887–89), 2: 476; cf. Orderic Vitalis, *Ecclesiastical History*, ed. Marjorie Chibnall (Oxford, 1969–80), 6:472; Suger, *Vie de Louis VI le Gros*, ed. Henri Waquet (Paris, 1964), p. 186.

[6] William of Malmesbury, *Historia Novella*, ed. K. R. Potter (London, 1955), p. 14.

[7] C. W. Hollister, 'Royal Acts of Mutilation: The Case against Henry I', *Albion*, 10 (1978), 330–40. Only rarely did a contemporary criticize Henry for his punishments: *Anglo-Saxon Chronicle*, A.D. 1124; Henry of Huntingdon, *Historia Anglorum*, ed. Thomas Arnold (1879), pp. 255–6.

[8] *Sancti Anselmi Cantuariensis Archiepiscopi Opera Omnia*, ed. F. S. Schmitt (Edinburgh, 1946–61), 5, Ep. 413.

[9] Eadmer, *Historia Novorum in Anglia*, ed. Martin Rule (1884), pp. 192–93, echoed by Florence of Worcester, *Chronicon ex Chronicis*, ed. Benjamin Thorpe (London, 1848–49), 2:57.

prelates.[10] The fact that Henry I regularly did so is made clear by repeated and pointed statements in the narrative sources of his reign. But the conventional good king was further expected to select as his closest counselors men of widsom and experience. Thus, Orderic Vitalis assures us that 'King Henry did not follow the advice of rash young men as did Rehoboam' – the son of Solomon whose rash advisers and resulting calamities are chronicled in the book of Kings. To the contrary, Henry 'prudently took to heart the experience and advice of wise and older men'.[11] Employing the same topos, William of Malmesbury speaks of Henry's closest adviser, Robert count of Meulan, as being deservedly a member of the king's inner circle 'because he was of ripe age to counsel'.[12] Other princes were less judicious in choosing their advisers. King Eadwig is said to have been renounced by the Mercians and Northumbrians in 957 because he was misled by foolish counselors.[13] Stephen of Blois, Orderic explains, 'was guided, like Rehoboam, by the fawning of flatterers, not the counsel of older men', and Robert Curthose duke of Normandy was urged by his father William the Conqueror to choose better counselors: 'Have the good sense to mistrust those rash spirits who have shamelessly goaded you on to lawless deeds'.[14] Unlike Stephen and Robert, Henry deferred to men of experience and therefore 'deservedly governed many provinces and peoples.'[15]

Contemporary writers, in short, laud Henry not as a new monarch but as a good monarch of the old school. Orderic sums up Henry's policies in these familiar terms: 'He always devoted himself, until the end of his life, to preserving peace . . . . He shrewdly kept down illustrious counts and castellans and bold tyrants to prevent seditious uprisings, but always cared for and protected men of peace and monks and humble people'.[16] To William of Malmesbury, 'He was venerated by the nobility, loved by the common folk. If it happened that important men, forgetting their sworn oath, drifted from their fidelity, he promptly recalled them to the straight way . . . bringing back the

---

[10] See, for example, Éric Bournazel, *Le gouvernement capétien au XIIe siècle, 1108–1180* (Paris, 1975), pp. 152–54, and, if you can find it, Paul Ward's unpublished and undated paper, 'On the King's Taking Counsel'.

[11] Orderic, 5:299.

[12] *Gesta Regum*, 2:483. Conversely, at the height of the English investiture dispute, Anselm and Paschal II regarded Robert of Meulan as a kind of Wormtongue. Adopting the conventional ecclesiastical fiction of the well-meaning king led astray by wicked advisers, Paschal warned Robert against giving evil counsel and eventually excommunicated him: *Anselmi Opera*, Ep. 353–4, 361, 364, 388.

[13] Vita Dunstani auctore B. in *Memorials of St Dunstan*, ed. William Stubbs (1874), p. 36.

[14] Orderic, 6:207; 3:99.

[15] *Ibid.*, 5:299.

[16] *Ibid.*, 6:99.

recalcitrant to soundness of mind by inflicting bodily wounds'.[17] Suger of St Denis observes that Henry I, with the counsel of wise and skilful men, gave the kingdom of England good order through the law of its ancient kings. He brought order to Normandy, too, imposing peace by force on its ferocious inhabitants, promising nothing less than blinding to thieves or robbers'.[18] Here again, Henry is being pictured not as cruel and savage but as exemplifying the conventional royal virtues, rooted in Scripture.[19] Indeed, all these passages pile topos on topos to such a point that the real, living, breathing Henry I is scarcely visible at all.

When we do catch glimpses of him, we find him playing unquestioningly the role in which contemporaries cast him. Their thought world was also his. He did prefer wise counselors, did avoid rash actions, did inflict severe punishments on traitors, thieves and counterfeiters, did pursue peace and did achieve it to a remarkable degree. 'I establish peace throughout all my kingdom', Henry said in a prophetic and singularly unoriginal clause in his coronation charter, 'and I order that this peace shall henceforth be maintained'.[20]

Was there nothing new in this man? Was he simply a crowned cliché? There is of course his coronation oath from which I have just quoted, and which later served as a precedent for Magna Carta. But as Mlle. Raymonde Foreville has reminded us, similar coronation oaths had been taken, and broken, by Henry's predecessors.[21] William the Conqueror had sworn before the altar of Westminster Abbey, in the presence of the clergy and people, to defend the holy churches of God, to rule his kingdom with justice, to make and uphold just laws, and rigorously to prohibit every sort of rapine and unjust judgement.[22] Henry's only original contributions to the tradition were to make the oath more explicit, and to put it in writing.

Henry I has likewise been credited with raising up new men 'from the dust' through an elaborate system of patronage involving gifts of land, wardships, administrative offices, marriages to aristocratic heiress and the like. But in essence such a policy can scarcely be regarded as innovative. Orderic described the Conqueror as having

---

[17] *Gesta Regum*, 2:487.

[18] *Vie de Louis VI*, p. 100.

[19] Suger frequently applauds his hero, Louis VI, for inflicting far more bloodcurdling punishments on evildoers: see Hollister, 'Royal Acts of Mutilation', *passim*.

[20] *Select Charters*, ed. William Stubbs (ninth ed., Oxford, 1913), p. 119, cl. 12. Cf. the Coronation Oath of King Edgar: *Die Gesetze der Angelsachsen*, ed. Felix Liebermann (Halle, 1903–16), 1:214–15.

[21] Foreville, 'Le sacre des rois anglo-normands et angevins et le serment du sacre (XI – XII siècles), *Proceedings of the Battle Conference on Anglo-Norman Studies*, 1:1978, ed. R. Allen Brown (Ipswich, 1979), pp. 52–62.

[22] Florence, 1:229.

endowed his closest followers with riches 'that raised them above the station to which they were born'; William Rufus, Orderic tells us, raised up 'underlings whom he exalted by the grant of vast honours as a reward for their flattery'.[23] Indeed, new men are essential to any stable regime, and complaints about them constitute still another medieval topos. A contemporary of Harun-al-Rashid's grumbled about base-born men rising to wealth in the caliph's service: 'Sons of concubines have become too numerous among us; lead me to a land, O God, where I shall see no bastards'.[24] Leopold Genicot reminds us that medieval rulers rewarded their *fideles* with lands, offices, and rich heiresses, 'whether in sixth-century England, eleventh- and twelfth-century Poland, thirteenth-century Hungary or fourteenth-century Castile'.[25]

Nevertheless, the impression lingers that Henry I raised up new men on a scale larger than before, and in an atmosphere of administrative bustle and menaces that contrasted sharply with the quieter, more genial, and more aristocratic environment of Louis VI's France.[26] I myself find Henry's England, with its thirty-three years of unbroken peace, a good deal quieter and more genial than contemporary France with its incessant warfare, urban riots and mass suffering, chronicled in grisly detail in the pages of Suger, Clarius, Guibert of Nogent, Galbert of Bruges, and the chronicler of Morigny. But perhaps more to the point, recent research on royal patronage and charter attestations suggests that Henry's regime included the established aristocracy to a far greater degree than did Louis VI's. Henry favoured and consorted with men new and old,[27] including representatives of such Conquest families as the Beaumonts, Bigods, Warennes, d'Avranches, and Clares. Conversely, as the researches of Éric Bournazel have demonstrated, Louis VI's regime consisted chiefly of ordinary *milites*. It excluded by and large not only the great princes and prelates but even, well into the twelfth century, the castellans of the Ile de France.[28] Henry I,

---

[23] Orderic, 2:190; 5:202.
[24] Philip K. Hitti, *The History of the Arabs,* sixth ed. (London, 1956), p. 333.
[25] Génicot, 'Recent Research on the Medieval Nobility', in *The Medieval Nobility,* ed. Timothy Reuter (Amsterdam, 1978), p. 20; cf. *ibid.,* p. 33 n.38; Franz Irsigler, 'On the Aristocratic Character of Early Frankish Society', *ibid.,* p. 124; Karl F. Werner, 'Important Noble Families in the Kingdom of Charlemagne, *ibid.,* p. 177. Karl Schmid, 'The Structure of the Nobility in the Earlier Middle Ages', *ibid.,* p. 53: 'The first rulers of the Saxon royal house showed their strength by surrounding themselves, as their powerful predecessors had done, with noble families which they themselves had raised up.'
[26] E.g. Southern, *Medieval Humanism*, p. 153.
[27] C. W. Hollister, 'Henry I and the Anglo-Norman Magnates', *Proceedings of the Battle Conference on Anglo-Norman Studies,* 2, 1979, ed. R. Allen Brown (Ipswich, 1980), pp. 93–107, 184–7; cf. Barbara M. Walker, 'King Henry I's Old Men', *Journal of British Studies,* 8, no. 1 (1968), 1–21.
[28] Bournazel, *Le gouvernement capétien,* pp. 26–53, 57, 90–91, 94–102, 175–77.

in short, resembles the ideal medieval king surrounded by his great nobles much more closely than does Louis VI.

The community of interests between king and nobility in Henry's England is further suggested by the fact that the tenurial insecurity which had characterized English society since the Norman Conquest came to an end as early as 1113.[29] Baronial honours were remarkably stable throughout the last two decades of Henry's reign, during which the configuration of royal and baronial holdings, with the greatest honours in the hands of royal kinsmen, closely paralleled the configuration disclosed by the Domesday survey at the close of the Conqueror's reign.[30]

Henry I thus had no novel political philosophy but only a cluster of old assumptions drawn from French, Norman and Anglo-Saxon traditions and from the more recent 'tradition' of the Anglo-Norman monarchy. The political abstractions of the so-called Anglo-Norman Anonymous penetrated neither the royal *curia* nor the minds of contemporary historians. Professor Sally Vaughn has shown that Henry's adviser, Robert of Meulan, articulated an early version of *raison d'état*, but we hear of it only once.[31] Much more typically, Henry saw himself as the good steward of his inherited dominions and privileges, responsible to God for preserving them all and passing them on intact to his heirs.

This conception of stewardship was very old. It was shared by contemporary prelates and magnates with respect to their lands and privileges. It governed Archbishop Anselm's views on the lands and primacy of Canterbury.[32] Anselm had gone into exile under Rufus because of having been denied the full restoration of Canterbury's estates along with such traditional archiepiscopal privileges as the right to call synods and to participate in the inner circle of royal advisers.[33] The newly-crowned Henry I summoned Anselm home with the honest intention, so it seems, of conceding everything that the archbishop had formerly demanded of Rufus. Henry must have been flabbergasted when Anselm, on returning, refused to render him the customary

---

[29] RaGena DeAragon, 'The Growth of Secure Inheritance in Norman England, *Journal of Medieval History*, 8(1982), 381–91. Cf. Southern, *Medieval Humanism*, p. 233.

[30] Hollister, 'Henry I and the Anglo-Norman Magnates', pp. 105–6.

[31] Sally N. Vaughn, 'Robert of Meulan and Raison d'État in the Anglo-Norman State, 1093–1118'. *Albion*, 10 (1978), 352–73. Although the statement occurs in a 'quotation' attributed to Robert by Orderic writing many years later, there is reason to suppose that it represents Robert's view rather than Orderic's. Richard of Leicester, a monk of Orderic's abbey of St Évroult at the time Orderic was writing the passage, had earlier served Robert of Meulan as an intimate counselor and major administrator and would thus have been able to provide Orderic with reasonably accurate information on Robert's thinking: Orderic, 5:314–16; 6: 488.

[32] R. W. Southern, *St. Anselm and his Biographer* (Cambridge, 1963), p. 127–8; *Anselmi Opera*, Ep. 452.

[33] *Ibid.*, Ep. 212; Eadmer, *Historia Novorum*, p. 119.

homage and to receive the archbishopric from the royal hands on the grounds that the homage of clerics and lay investiture had been banned at a papal synod that Anselm had attended the previous year.[34] In a letter to Pope Paschal, Henry based his case squarely on custom and the responsibilities of royal stewardship. Echoing an oft-quoted letter of William I to Gregory VII, Henry agreed to pay Peter's Pence 'which blessed Peter had from my predecessors' and to render 'that obedience which your predecessors had in the kingdom of England in my father's time', but only on condition that traditional royal customs remain inviolate. 'So long as I live', Henry wrote, 'the dignities and usages of the English realm shall not be diminished'.[35] These are brave words but scarcely original, and they express a rigidly conservative viewpoint unbefitting a king about to set European civilization on a new course.

The novelty of Henry's reign is to be found neither in his goals nor in his political assumptions, but in the development of new, highly effective means to conventional ends. Focusing on ends, contemporaries seem unconscious of the great administrative innovations of the reign: exchequer, central treasury, systematic judicial eyres, specialized viceregencies. The exchequer system, as we know it from the Pipe Roll of 1130, may well have been developed to assist the collection of an aid in 1110 on the betrothal of Henry's daughter Maud to the emperor Henry V.[36] Contemporary Anglo-Normans saw it as a brilliant stroke of policy that the granddaughter of a bastard duke should marry an emperor; the auditing improvement passed unnoticed. Thereafter the exchequer continued to function, always backstage, as a means of enhancing the collection of revenues to be used for traditional and newsworthy purposes: fortifications, hired knights, diplomatic bribes and the like. Its value is suggested by the fact that whereas Henry seems to have run short of money during his Norman campaign of 1105, he had a substantial treasure in 1120 at the conclusion of three years of heavy warfare, and again in 1135 after having completed a military campaign along the Norman frontier.[37] Predictably, contemporary writers concentrated on the warfare and diplomacy. Their occasional allusions to the royal revenues are limited to complaints about taxes. Similarly, Henry's creation of a central

---

[34] *Ibid.*, pp. 119–20.

[35] *Anselmi Opera,* Ep. 215; cf. *Beati Lanfranci archiepiscopi Cantuariensis opera omnia,* ed. J. A. Giles (Oxford, 1844), p. 32.

[36] *Regesta Regum Anglo-Normannorum,* ed. H. W. C. Davis and others (Oxford, 1913–69), 2, No. 963. The problem of the origin of the exchequer defies precise solution: see *Dialogus de Scaccario,* ed. Charles Johnson (London, 1950), pp. xxii–xxiii; Richardson and Sayles, *Governance,* pp. 157–67.

[37] *Anglo-Saxon Chronicle,* A.D. 1105; Eadmer, *Historia Novorum,* pp. 171–5; Orderic, 6: 306, 448; Malmesbury, *Historia Novella,* pp. 14, 17; Robert of Torigny, *Chronicle,* in *Chronicles of the Reigns of Stephen, Henry II, and Richard I,* ed. Richard Howlett (1884–89), 4: 129.

treasury and viceregency courts were inconspicuous accommodations to the problem of ruling England and Normandy jointly, and his system of judicial eyres constituted a gradual, scarcely visible extension of curial control over the local courts.[38]

The secondary importance of such procedures and institutions to contemporary minds has been obscured by a certain misconception of the role in Henry's regime of Roger bishop of Salisbury, the creator and manager of much of the new machinery. William of Malmesbury and Henry archdeacon of Huntingdon both assert that Roger was Henry I's right-hand man – *secundus a rege* – but both had reason to exaggerate.[39] Malmesbury Abbey was under Roger's jurisdiction and rejoiced in his gifts, while Henry of Huntingdon's archdeaconry pertained to the see of Lincoln whose bishop, Alexander, was at once Henry of Huntingdon's patron and Roger of Salisbury's nephew. There can be no doubt that the king relied heavily on Roger for the administration of England and even for advice on episcopal appointments. But Roger was not a major advisor on matters of high policy – war and diplomacy – as should be clear from the fact that he rarely accompanied the king to Normandy.[40] We have explicit evidence, for example, that he was not consulted on the vital matter of the Empress Maud's marriage to Geoffrey of Anjou.[41] Roger was a brilliant, powerful, indispensable functionary, as was his Norman administrative counterpart, John bishop of Lisieux, who seldom went to England. Roger became the sole regent of England when Henry crossed to Normandy in 1123, but only because Henry, desperate for an heir, wanted his new queen, Adeliza of Louvain, at his side at all times and, presumably, in his bed as often as possible. Henry's advisers on matters of major importance to him were magnates such as Robert of Meulan, William of Tancarville, and, later, Robert earl of Gloucester, Brian fitz Count and Humphrey of Bohun,[42] all of them wise old men – regardless of age.

Yet for all my reservations, these useful administrative mechanisms, these means to ends, betoken a fundamental shift in the style of governance. Sir Richard Southern caught the significance of Henry's reign when he observed that 'these years when nothing happened –

---

[38] On these matters see C. W. Hollister and John W. Baldwin, 'The Rise of Administrative Kingship: Henry I and Philip Augustus', *American Historical Review*, 83 (1978), 870-91. Cf. Karl Leyser, 'Ottonian Government', *English Historical Review*, 91, (1981), 722: 'The Ottonian writers dwell on the ideals of Ottonian governance. About its means and methods they kept almost total silence. They were not interested in administration and the *munera sordida*.'

[39] Malmesbury, *Gesta Regum*, 2: 483–4; Huntingdon, *Historia Anglorum*, p. 245.

[40] Hollister and Baldwin, 'Rise of Administrative Kingship', p. 888, Table 4; Edward J. Kealey, *Roger of Salisbury* (Berkeley, 1972), pp. 150–51, n. 11.

[41] Malmesbury, *Historia Novella*, p. 5.

[42] *Ibid.*; Vaughn, 'Robert of Meulan'; Hollister and Baldwin, 'Rise of Adminstrative Kingship', p. 888, Table 4.

largely because nothing happened – were decisive in the development of English society'.[43]

Let me review some of the half-hidden factors that may provide clues to the decisive yet elusive shift in orientation. Henry's regime marked a drift toward systematization, explicitness, not only in the major administrative innovations already discussed, but as well in such matters as the standardization of measures and coins, the establishment of regulations governing the conduct, wages and perquisites of the royal household, the granting of fixed stipends for barons attending court, the common use of royal writs purged of superfluous verbiage, cast in the most starkly economical style.[44] Royal patronage, while an age-old practice, was now systematized as never before. Writs granting lands and privileges were copied and preserved in the treasury at Winchester. Recent research by Stephanie Mooers has clarified the ways in which Henry's annual Pipe Roll recorded not only income but patronage as well; exemptions from danegeld, *auxilium civitatis* and *murdrum*; pardons or non-collections of debts; wardships, beneficial marriages, and the granting of royal ministries – for a price.[45] Under Henry I the expansion of the Anglo-Norman regnum ceased and, with it, the opportunity to expand the royal estates through conquest and win new lands to bestow on *fideles*. The Anglo-Norman monarchy survived this lowering of expectations by tightening its judicial and fiscal procedures.[46]

The trend toward systematization was accompanied, appropriately, by growing literacy and mastery of Latin among Henry's magnates and administrators, and by a substantial increase in written records.[47] Memory was giving way more and more to documentation, and an illiterate sheriff or royal justice could find himself as incapacitated as a handless minter. Henry's own literacy may have been rudimentary: recalling that William the Conqueror was both illiterate and short tempered, historians have doubted Malmesbury's account of young, bookish Henry remarking in his father's presence that an illiterate king

---

[43] *Medieval Humanism*, p. 233.

[44] E.g., R. C. Van Caenegem, *Royal Writs from the Conquest to Glanvill* (Selden Society, London, 1959), pp. 252–53; Edward J. Kealey, 'Anglo-Norman Policy and the Public Welfare', *Albion*, 10 (1978), 343; Constitutio Domus Regis, in *Dialogus de Scaccario*, pp. 129–35; Hollister and Baldwin, 'Rise of Administrative Kingship', pp. 870–71.

[45] Stephanie Mooers, 'Patronage in the Pipe Roll of 1130', *Speculum*, 59 (1984) 282–307, and, by the same author, 'Familial Clout and Financial Gain in Henry I's Later Reign', *Albion*, 14 (1982), 268–91.

[46] See Judith Green, 'William Rufus, Henry I and the Royal Demesne', *History*, 64 (1979), 337–52.

[47] Richardson and Sayles, *Governance*, pp. 269–84; Ralph V. Turner, 'The *Miles Literatus* in Twelfth- and Thirteenth-Century England: How Rare a Phenomenon?' *American Historical Review*, 83 (1978), 928–45.

is a crowned ass.[48] But whatever the case, Henry saw to it that his sons were well educated. His chief adviser Robert of Meulan is described as a man of extraordinary intelligence, and Robert's sons, Waleran of Meulan and Robert earl of Leicester, while still in their mid-teens, are alleged to have overcome a group of cardinals at the papal curia in a debate on logic[49] – a debate that must surely have been waged in Latin. Robert of Leicester, and perhaps Waleran as well, had been educated at Abingdon under its learned Italian abbot, Faritius, and Richard fitz Neal would later describe Robert as well educated and practised in legal affairs.[50] Another of Henry's rising stars, Othuer, bastard son of Hugh earl of Chester and castellan of the Tower of London, was sufficiently well educated to serve as tutor of Henry's own sons, one of whom, Robert earl of Gloucester, was described by William of Malmesbury as a man of great learning, a book lover.[51] Robert of Gloucester became one of Henry I's wealthiest magnates and most active *curiales*. The Pipe Roll of 1130 shows him conducting an audit of the Winchester treasury along with another of Henry's new magnate-*curiales*, Brian fitz Count, who would later demonstrate his learning by writing letters supporting the Empress Maud's claim to the English throne.[52] The sons and nephews of several of Henry's key administrators were students at the school of Laon.[53] Roger of Salisbury sent his nephews Alexander and Nigel to study there, and both subsequently became bishops and *curiales* of Henry I. Nigel became royal treasurer in the mid-1120's and would later be called upon by Henry II to restore the exchequer system after its deterioration in Stephen's reign. It is suggestive that one of the Laon masters, Ralph, wrote a treatise on the abacus, as did Adelard of Bath, who also taught at Laon and may later have served in Henry's administration.[54]

The pursuit of traditional ends through novel means characterized not only the reign of Henry I but many other facets of twelfth-century

---

[48] C. W. David, 'The Claim of King Henry I to be Called Learned', in *Anniversary Essays in Mediaeval History by Students of Charles Homer Haskins* (Boston, 1929), pp. 45–56; V. H. Galbraith, 'The Literacy of the Medieval English Kings', *Proceedings of the British Academy*, 21 (1935), 211–21.

[49] Malmesbury, *Gesta Regum*, 2: 482.

[50] *Dialogus de Scaccario*, pp. 57–58; *Chronicon Monasterii de Abingdon*, ed. Joseph Stevenson (London R.S., 1858), 2: 229: Robert's education is misdated back to the reign of King William (I or II).

[51] *Gesta Regum*, 2: 518–21.

[52] *Pipe Roll 31 Henry I*, ed. Joseph Hunter (London, 1833), pp. 129–31; Richardson and Sayles, *Governance*, p. 273.

[53] On the connections between Laon and Henry's court, see *Patrologia Latina*, 156: 961 ff.; R. L. Poole, *The Exchequer in the Twelfth Century* (London, 1912), pp. 53–56; Richardson and Sayles, *Governance*, pp. 270–1; Kealey, *Roger of Salisbury*, pp. 48–50. On the school at Laon, Valerie I. J. Flint, 'The "School of Laon": A reconsideration', *Recherches de Théologie ancienne et médiévale* 43 (1976), 89–110.

[54] *Pipe Roll 31 Henry I*, p. 22; Poole, *Exchequer*, pp. 56–57.

civilization as well. In theology, law, monastic life, music and art, no less than in political organization, the twelfth century witnessed a heightened creativity devoted to the service of older ideologies. As Frank Barlow recently expressed it, the new rationalism was neither secularist nor, in the modern sense, sceptical; it implied no criticism or hostility toward the church and its beliefs; logic was applied to theology 'in order better to understand, and display, the teachings of the church',[55] just as a radically new architecture was developed, I would add, to provide a more capacious and appropriate setting for the ancient liturgy (which was itself being developed and systematized). Many historians would agree that during the twelfth century European civilization underwent a change of the most fundamental significance, but the nature and degree of the change is too often obscured by the fact of ideological continuity. Far more visible are the changes that occurred in that allegedly pivotal century between 1450 and 1550, where so many courses and textbooks in European civilization wrongheadedly commence. The cultural transformation of the twelfth century was surely the more fundamental one, but it is marked by no such headline events as the voyages of discovery, the invention of printing, the Protestant Reformation, or Copernican astronomy. Henry I, although a much abler king, will never enjoy the glamour of Henry VIII. In contrast to the revolutionary century of Columbus and Luther, the twelfth century reorientation was subtle, elusive, and imperfectly understood by contemporaries.

Undaunted, medievalists continue to seek the key to what Charles Homer Haskins called 'the renaissance of the twelfth century'. M. T. Clanchy sees it as a vital period in the evolution from memory to written record; Alexander Murray stresses that a major increase in the circulation of money shifted political and economic power into the hands of men trained in reasoning and reckoning.[56] Peter Brown describes the change as a shift from consensus to authority – 'perhaps the greatest single precondition for the growth of rationality'.[57] M.-D. Chenu emphasizes the realization among twelfth-century thinkers that the physical world functioned on natural rather than supernatural principles.[58] Similarly, Charles M. Radding, adopting a biological analogy, sees the century as marking childhood's end: the primitive notion of imminent justice gave way to the adult concept of a natural order – a gradual demystification of

---

[55] Frank Barlow, *The English Church, 1066–1154*, (London, 1979), p. 4, n. 21.
[56] M. T. Clanchy, *From Memory to Written Record: England, 1066–1307*, (Cambridge, Mass., 1979); Alexander Murray, *Reason and Society in the Middle Ages* (Oxford, 1978).
[57] Peter Brown, 'Society and the Supernatural: A Medieval Change', *Daedalus*, 104, no. 2 (1975), 143.
[58] Chenu, *Nature, Man, and Society in the Twelfth Century*, ed. Jerome Taylor and Lester K. Little (Chicago, 1968), p. 6.

what Carolly Erickson has called 'the enchanted world'.[59] Colin Morris credits the twelfth century with the discovery of the individual, Caroline Bynum with the discovery of self through new religious communities.[60]

All these efforts at explanation involve subtle if pervasive changes, many of which are exemplified by the increased systematization of governance that occurred under Henry I: written records, reasoning and reckoning, experimentation, a clear shift, using Peter Brown's terminology, from local consensus toward central authority, more royal administration and less royal charisma in a world of diminishing enchantment. I have little to add to these hypotheses, expect to suggest that we may possess a clue to the twelfth-century puzzle in the character of Henry I himself. Henry's contemporary, the scientist Adelard of Bath, once remarked testily that a person who made no effort to appreciate the rational plan of the universe was as contemptible as one who lived in a house but knew not how it was built.[61] Unlike most of his royal and aristocratic contemporaries, Henry I knew how his house was built. It was an old house, just as Henry wished it to be, but it had new plumbing, the workings of which Henry seems to have understood perfectly. For all his traditional attitudes, Henry was a man of intense curiosity. 'He inquired into everything', Orderic declares, 'and retained all that he heard in his tenacious memory. He wished to know all the business of his officials and dignitaries, and . . . . kept his eye on the many happenings in England and Normandy.'[62] In 1101 we find him personally showing his English foot soldiers how to oppose cavalry charges with their shields and how to return stroke for stroke.[63] At the siege of Pont-Audemer in 1123 he instructed his carpenters on the building of a siege tower.[64] At Woodstock, his favourite hunting park, he displayed his interest in animals not only by pursuing them but also by collecting them: his Woodstock zoo is said to have included lions, leopards, lynxes, camels, and a porcupine.[65]

I shall now hazard the modest proposal that the great mental shift of the twelfth century is epitomized in Henry's approach to hunting. As we all know, hunting was the favoured sport of the medieval

[59] Charles M. Radding, 'Superstition to Science: Nature, Fortune, and the Passing of the Medieval Ordeal', *American Historical Review*, 84 (1979), 945–69; cf., by the same author, 'Evolution of Medieval Mentalities: A Cognative-Structural Approach', *American Historical Review*, 83 (1978), 577–97; Carolly Erickson, *The Medieval Vision* (New York, 1976), pp. 3–28.

[60] Morris, *The Discovery of the Individual, 1050–1200* (New York, 1972); Caroline Walker Bynum, *Jesus as Mother: Studies in the Spirituality of the High Middle Ages* (Berkeley, 1982), pp. 82–109.

[61] Chenu, *Nature, Man, and Society*, pp. 11–12, 57; Radding, 'Superstition to Science', p. 966.

[62] Orderic, 6: 100.

[63] Malmesbury, *Gesta Regum*, 2: 472.

[64] Orderic, 6: 342.

[65] Malmesbury, *Gesta Regum*, 2: 485.

aristocracy. In keeping with the grand old tradition, Henry loved to hunt. Embedded among the concessions in his coronation charter is the stubborn assertion, '. . . I have retained the forests in my own hands as my father did before me'.[66] But Henry seems to have approached the chase in a novel way. Master Wace describes William of Warenne, earl of Surrey, as ridiculing Henry some years before his accession for having studied hunting so thoroughly that he could tell the number of tines in a stag's antlers simply by examining his footprint.[67] Earl William mockingly refers to Henry as 'Stagfoot' for having turned a joyous, mindlessly athletic pastime into a science.

Once again a traditional goal, the stag in this case, is pursued by novel means. In a sense, as in the entire reign of Henry I, as in the whole unfolding of twelfth-century culture, nothing had happened. But the new approach transformed European civilization – not to mention hunting.

---

[66] *Select Charters*, ed. Stubbs, p. 119, cl. 10.
[67] *Le Roman de Rou de Wace*, ed. A. J. Holden, 3 vols. (Paris, 1970–73), 2: 275–76.

Map 5. Wales at the time of Henry I.

10

Henry I and Wales

R. R. Davies

Henry I left a deeper imprint on the affairs of medieval Wales than any king of England other than Edward I. The contemporary Welsh chronicler stood in awe of his stature and achievement: to him alone among English kings did he accord the title 'the Great'; he was 'the man who had subdued under his authority all the island of Britain and its mighty ones'.[1] English chroniclers also soon looked back nostalgically to Henry I's reign as a period when Wales had been brought firmly under control, its inhabitants subdued, its people civilized, new laws imposed upon it and the country blessed with fertility and prosperity. In short, as the author of the *Gesta Stephani* put it smugly, 'it might very easily have been thought' by 1135 that parts of Wales were 'a second England'.[2] Gerald of Wales, from a much closer personal knowledge of Wales and with the benefit of a much longer chronological hindsight, came to the same conclusion. It was in Henry I's reign, as he saw it, that Wales had been finally subjugated and that the power of the English (*sic*) prevailed throughout the country; as a result Wales enjoyed an unparalleled period of peace, plenty and prosperity.[3]

The magnitude of Henry I's achievement in Wales, as elsewhere, was doubtless exaggerated in retrospect, if only to highlight the calamity that overwhelmed the Anglo-Normans there in Stephen's reign. Yet that achievement is not to be gainsaid; it emerges as clearly from the cool light of the historical records as it does from the rhetoric of the chroniclers. By 1135 most of the southern half of the country – broadly south of a line from the estuary of the river Dyfi to the valley of the river Teme – had been brought, in greater or lesser measure, under Anglo-Norman

---

[1] T. Jones (ed. and trans.), *Brut y Tywysogyon or The Chronicle of the Princes. Peniarth Ms. 20 version* (Cardiff, 1952), pp. 59, 42. This version of the native chronicle will henceforth be cited as *Brut*.

[2] K. R. Potter and R. H. C. Davis (eds.), *Gesta Stephani* (Oxford, 1976), pp. 15–17.

[3] Gerald of Wales, *Opera*, ed. J. S. Brewer *et al.* (Rolls Series, 1861–91), iii, 152–3; vi, 79, 103, 106, 121; 'Invectiones', ed. W. S. Davies, *Y Cymmrodor*, xxx (1920), 137, 162–4. It was also in Henry I's reign that the story of Edgar being rowed on the Dee at Chester by Welsh kings was being elaborated: M. Brett, 'John of Worcester and his contemporaries', in R. H. C. Davis and J. M. Wallace-Hadrill (eds.), *The Writing of History in the Middles Ages. Essays presented to R. W. Southern* (Oxford, 1981), p. 115, n. 4.

control, while the remaining princelings of native Wales acknowledged their client status *vis à vis* the king of England, visiting his court, surrendering hostages to him, paying tribute to him and even acknowledging that they held their land of him. Parts of lowland south Wales had been intensively colonized by Anglo-Norman knights, burgesses and peasants; Henry I himself was responsible for establishing the single most significant alien colony in the country – that of the Flemings in the *cantrefi* of Rhos and Daugleddau in western Dyfed.[4] It was during his reign that some of the great marcher families of the future (notably the Clares and the Fitzalans) made their first appearance in Wales or on its borders and that the lineaments of civilian organisation began to emerge in some of the great lordships of southern Wales (notably Glamorgan and Brecon). It was under Henry I that a Welsh county under direct royal control (Pembroke) first presented its account at the exchequer and that royal justices first held their pleas in Wales.[5] The reign was equally momentous in church affairs. Henry foisted his own nominees on the sees of Llandaff in 1107 and St David's in 1115 and exacted from both of them, as from the bishop of Bangor on his elevation in 1120, a formal profession of canonical obedience to the archbishop of Canterbury. Norman abbeys and priories sprouted in the southern half of Wales as the monastic adjuncts of Norman domination: whereas only five had been founded before 1100 a further eighteen were added during Henry's reign. Contemporaries were well aware that ecclesiastical subordination was but the spiritual arm of secular conquest. Gerald of Wales made the point with characteristic forthrightness: Henry I 'conquering Wales with a strong hand, ordained that the Welsh church, which he found free should be placed under the church of his own realm, just as he subdued the country to his kingdom'.[6]

The outlines of the story of Anglo-Norman advance in Wales in these years – as with so much else in the history of medieval Wales – were definitively pieced together, from fragmentary and often cryptic evidence, by Sir John Edward Lloyd in his *History of Wales from the Earliest Times to the Edwardian Conquest* (1911). One may take issue with Lloyd in the construction he placed on the exiguous evidence – notably his tendency to pre-date and over-estimate the recovery of Gwynedd[7] – and one may also have reservations regarding the national and nationalist assumptions which underlie his account; but in its outline his

[4] The main sources for this plantation and for Henry I's role in it are *Brut*, pp. 27–28; William of Malmesbury, *Gesta Regum*, ed. W. Stubbs (Rolls Series, 1887–9), ii, 365, 477; Florence of Worcester, *Chronicon ex Chronicis*, ed. B. Thorpe (English Historical Society, 1848–9), ii, 64; R. R. Darlington (ed.), *The Worcester Cartulary* (Pipe Roll Society, new series, vol. 38), pp. 134–5.

[5] *Pipe Roll 31 Henry I*, ed. J. Hunter (Record Commission, 1833), pp. 136–7.

[6] Quoted in R. Bartlett, *Gerald of Wales 1146–1223* (Oxford, 1982), p. 53.

[7] J. E. Lloyd, *A History of Wales from the Earliest Times to the Edwardian Conquest* (3rd edn. 1939), ii, 416, n. 56, 464, 466, n. 15, 467.

narrative remains convincing. No major sources of evidence relating to the period have come to light since his day; and the most promising line for future advances in the subject would seem to lie in detailed studies of the local patterns of conquest and settlement, drawing fully on topographical, onomastic and genealogical evidence, such as have proved so richly rewarding in Scotland.[8] Yet there would also appear to be room for a less ambitious enterprise – to try to locate Henry I's activities in Wales within the general context of his concerns and policies; in other words, to look at the issues not from the perspective of 'the history of Wales' or of 'the development of the march of Wales' but from that of the Norman 'empire' and in particular of its king.

It needs to be emphasized at the outset that Henry I, in common with the other Norman kings, regarded Wales as part of his dominions. It was part of the bundle of lordships and overlordships which he had inherited and over which he claimed authority. Walter Map made the point crisply: Henry I, he remarked 'reigned long and happily over England, Wales, Normandy and Brittany'.[9] Henry himself made the same point, not by assuming flamboyant titles or by propounding grand claims, but by taking it for granted in his written commands that his authority extended over Wales. He addressed his writs 'to all faithful French and English and all the Welsh of the whole of England and Wales';[10] he confirmed the gifts of his barons in Wales;[11] he granted liberties and exemptions throughout Wales as well as England;[12] he directed his letters, where appropriate, to embrace Wales as well as England and occasionally addressed them specifically 'to all in Wales'.[13] His coinage, and his alone, circulated in the Norman lordships there[14] and, since there was no native coinage, was doubtless already penetrating into areas under native control. He asserted his control over the church in Wales and in particular over the southern bishoprics; and,

---

[8] Much the most important recent contribution is the fine study by I. W. Rowlands, 'The Making of the March: Aspects of the Norman Settlement of Dyfed', *Proceedings of the Battle Conference on Anglo-Norman Studies*, iii, 1980, ed. R. A. Brown (Woodbridge, 1981), pp. 142–57.

[9] Walter Map, *De Nugis Curialium* ed. M. R. James, J. E. Lloyd, E. S. Hartland (Cymmrodorion Record Series, ix), p. 241.

[10] C. Johnson and H. A. Cronne (eds.), *Regesta [Regum Anglo-Normannorum]*, ii, no. 846, p. 368 (no. 1646).

[11] *Regesta*, ii, nos. 800, 847, 1490, 1874 etc.

[12] *Regesta*, ii, nos. 1014, 1263, 1646.

[13] *Regesta*, ii, nos. 1187, 1490, 1552, 1646, 1725; *Worcester Cartulary*, p. 28. For a writ of Henry I addressed to 'all his faithful French and English, Flemings and Welsh of Wales (de Walis)', see T. Phillips (ed.), *Cartularium Prioratus S. Johannis Baptiste de Carmarthen* (Cheltenham, 1865), no. 33.

[14] During Stephen's reign Henry of Neuborg issued coins in his own name at Swansea and Robert of Gloucester minted coins in Matilda's name at Cardiff: G. C. Boon, 'Treasure Trove from Angevin Wales, *Seaby's Coin and Metal Bulletin*, 1981, pp. 194–6.

like his father before him, he insisted that episcopal lands were held directly of him and came under his protection. He exercised his power over Welsh princelings and Norman magnates in Wales as magisterially as in any part of his dominions. His position in Wales, it is true, differed from that which he held in England and there were serious practical limits on his authority, especially his direct authority, there. Yet Wales, though it posed its own problems, was not unique in this respect. The nature of Henry's authority differed in the various parts of his 'dominions', in Britain and on the continent, and indeed within them.[15] What needs to be examined is what form or forms that authority assumed in Wales and how it changed over time.

Strategically, Wales was bound to command Henry's attention. It did not do so solely or even mainly because of the actions of the Welsh as such. Their incursions no longer posed a direct threat to the western counties of England as they had done in the 1050s and late 1060s. The dynastic ambitions and quarrels of the native Welsh dynasties could likewise for the most part be ignored or indeed even encouraged, for as Henry I's deputy in Shropshire had observed wryly, 'they were all killing one another'.[16] Rather was it that instability in any part of the Norman dominions, Wales included, could easily threaten the security of the whole. Henry I had been taught that lesson clearly in 1102, when the revolt of the house of Montgomery centred on Shrewsbury and Bridgnorth. In that revolt Earl Robert of Shrewsbury conspired with the native Welsh dynasty of Powys and sent his Welsh allies to foray in Staffordshire, while his brother, Arnulf of Montgomery, used his base at Pembroke to forge an Irish marriage and alliance in order to promote his ambitions. That revolt alone would have diverted Henry's attention firmly to Wales and to the English border counties; indeed it was by exploiting divisions within the Powys dynasty and by bribing a member of that dynasty to defect to him that he was able to suppress the revolt quickly. The territorial ambitions of the Norman barons in Wales also attracted his attention. Wherever the acquisitiveness of the Normans led them, there the king's attention was immediately engaged – keeping a watchful eye on what was happening and exploiting every opportunity to assert his control and to exercise his overlordship to his own ends. Brecon and Glamorgan, Ceredigion and Pembroke were counters on the chessboard of territorial politics and patronage as much as any lordship or honour in England or Normandy; Henry I would forego no occasion to demonstrate that he was in control of the game. In that game 'national' boundaries counted for little: just as aristocratic estates straddled the English channel and just as feudal honours in Wales – such as Chepstow, Brecon or Montgomery – encompassed lands in England, so the king's supervisory control and interest extended to the limits, potential and

[15] J. Le Patourel, *The Norman Empire* (Oxford, 1976), chap. 6.
[16] *Brut*, p. 36.

actual, of his dominions. What Henry wanted to achieve in Wales, as elsewhere, was mastery; but the nature of that mastery and the means to achieve it differed from one part of the Norman 'empire' to another; indeed it differed from one part of Wales to another. It is to north and mid-Wales and to Henry's attitude toward the native rulers there that we turn first.

Henry I's accession coincided broadly with a major change of direction and tempo in Norman enterprise in Wales. The rapid Norman advance in north Wales in the 1080s and 1090s suddenly faltered. In 1098 Earl Hugh of Shrewsbury was killed in Anglesey – not by the Welsh but by Magnus Barefoot of Norway; in 1101 Earl Hugh of Chester died, leaving a young son of seven as his heir; in 1102 the forfeiture of the house of Montgomery broke the chain of command and penetration which had once reached from Shrewsbury through mid-Wales to Ceredigion and thence to Pembroke. The vacuum of authority and leadership that was thus created presented Henry I with an opportunity – especially given the frailty of the dynasty of Gwynedd and the frictions within that of Powys – to undertake the conquest of north Wales himself. Yet he did not do so. Why?

Much of the answer, doubtless, lies in his preoccupations elsewhere; part in the military problems that such a campaign of conquest would pose; part in the small returns that such a conquest offered. But other considerations need also to be borne in mind. The Normans, the king included, had no mission to conquer the Welsh because they were Welsh. Such ideas might occasionally surface in the thirteenth century – as racial distinctions became sharper and more abrasive and as notions of governmental and judicial dependence and of legal and even moral uniformity became more common[17] – but they were alien to the Norman *conquistadores* of the early twelfth century. They were motivated by greed and power, not by racial or 'national' animus. They took their pickings where they could find and hold them without undue effort; they were easily diverted elsewhere if the effort proved disproportionate to the results or if more tempting and easy pickings were to be spotted elsewhere (as in Ireland after 1170). Above all, military conquest and direct lordship were only one way in which Norman kings could exercise domination; overlordship was another. The form of domination that was appropriate and feasible depended on circumstances – on the pre-existing pattern of authority and relationships, on the military and strategic centrality or otherwise of the area, on the attractiveness of the district to Norman barons and settlers. In much of lowland south Wales circumstances showed that direct domination was feasible; in mid- and north Wales, however, Henry I decided that his strategic needs were generally satisfied by

[17] Cf. R. R. Davies, 'Lordship or Colony?' in J. F. Lydon (ed.)., *The English in Medieval Ireland* (Dublin, 1984), pp. 142–60.

overlordship. The decision seems to have been a conscious one: in Gwynedd Gruffudd ap Cynan was specifically allowed to recover his patrimony with Henry's support;[18] in Powys the native dynasty and that of neighbouring Arwystli were allowed to fight out their internecine quarrels with no more than an occasional nudge and threat from the king;[19] even in Deheubarth, members of the local dynasty were granted land and offered a role in the governance of the area. Overlordship could achieve its ends without too great an investment of effort, men or money, especially in areas where the existing patterns of authority were fluid and which were geographically distant from the primary concerns of the Norman kings. Therein lay part of its attractiveness.

Overlordship was an elastic concept. It could mean as much or as little as the relative power of suzerain and dependant warranted; it could expand and contract in response to the changing fortunes and circumstances of both parties; it could, where appropriate, pave the way for the imposition of a more direct lordship, but equally it could be diluted to the point – as in the relationship between the king of France and the duke of Normandy – where it was little more than a loose and occasional relationship, if that, between two virtually independent princes. The overlordship that the kings of Wessex had exercised *vis à vis* the Welsh princes in the last centuries of Anglo-Saxon England had ranged over the whole gamut of the relationship – the giving of hostages, visits to the king's court, witnessing his charters as underkings (*sub-reguli*), payment of tribute, formal oaths of fealty and submission, and open-ended promises of service. The Norman kings inherited this tradition of overlordship and used it, along with the campaigns and conquests of their barons, to bring Wales into their 'domain' or 'power'.[20] Thus William the Conqueror almost certainly used the occasion of his visit to St David's in 1081 – much the farthest that any king of England had penetrated into Wales – to exact fealty from the ruler of Deheubarth and to impose an annual tribute of £40 on him. It was into a tradition of overlordship that was already being intensified that Henry I entered.

It is in his reign that we can study for the first time in some detail how the mechanics of Norman overlordship operated in native Wales and how effective a strategy of domination it could prove. This may possibly be the result of more abundant sources – notably the remarkably expansive and revealing narrative of the native Welsh annals for the period 1102–21; but it also surely reflects a conscious effort on Henry I's

---

[18] D. Simon Evans (ed.), *Historia Gruffud vab Kenan* (Cardiff, 1977), p. 28; Arthur Jones (ed. and trans.), *The history of Gruffydd ap Cynan* (Manchester, 1910), p. 151.

[19] D. J. Cathcart King has observed how very few castles were built on either side of the border in northern Powys: *Castellarium Anglicanum* (1983) i, p. xxxviii.

[20] The phrase is used in the *Anglo Saxon Chronicle*, E. *sub anno* 1087 (1086).

part to weave the web of suzerainty more closely and to give a more regular and demeaning content to the concept of overlordship. The Welsh themselves were under no illusion: when Gruffudd ap Rhys, the heir to the native kingdom of Deheubarth, sought to assert his independence in 1115 his action was immediately construed as an attempt 'to leave the overlordship (*arglwyddiaeth*) of the king'. Such an act of bravado was a hopeless gamble; his misguided supporters were dismissed by the native chronicler as 'imbeciles' and 'hotheads'.[21] No one, it seemed, could withstand Henry's overlordship. It operated at several levels. Welsh princelings were invited or summoned – the distinction was academic – to court: Gruffudd ap Cynan of Gwynedd probably before 1109 and again in 1115; Cadwgan of Powys in 1110 and his son Owain in 1111, 1114 and 1116; Gruffudd ap Rhys of Deheubarth at least once.[22] Such visits were in part social and doubtless flattered the ego of the guests, as they were plied with gifts, pensions, feasts and other signs of attention. But their political intention was also evident – to display the dependence of the Welsh princelings and to do so publicly and to begin the process of integrating them into the court life of the Norman dominions. The king gradually bound them in a nexus of obligation, patronage and reward: he cajoled them with gifts (as he did Iorwerth ap Bleddyn of Powys in 1102); he flattered them with attention and honours (as in his promise to Owain ap Cadwgan of Powys in 1114 to make him a knight); he bribed them with offers, 'as it was the custom of the French to deceive men with promises' (as he did Gruffudd ap Cynan of Gwynedd in 1115); and enticed them with the prospect of exalting them 'over and above their kinsmen' (as he did with the sons of Rhirid ap Bleddyn in 1109 and with Owain ap Cadwgan in 1114).[23] Henry I was wily enough to realise that there was more to overlordship than bluster and threat; flattery and reward also had their place. So also had cunning. Henry proved an adept master at exploiting the fissures and tensions of Welsh 'political' life, taking advantage of family divisions to his own ends (as he did in Powys in 1109–10 and in Deheubarth in 1116) and fomenting inter-dynastic rivalries (such as those between the dynasties of Gwynedd, Powys and Deheubarth) to serve his own purposes.[24] Overlordship worked most cheaply and often most effectively by setting dependants at each other's throats, by destabilising dynasties, by hoodwinking client princelings to act on the king's behalf while at the same time persuading them that they were acting in their own interests.

[21] *Brut*, 39–41. For a variant version of the first passage quoted see T. Jones (ed.), *Brut y Tywysogyon or The Chronicle of the Princes. Red Book of Hergest Version* (henceforth *Brut, R.B.H. Version*) (Cardiff, 1953), p. 83.
[22] *Historia Gruffud vab Kenan*, p. 28; *Brut, R.B.H. Version*, p. 85 (Gruffudd ap Cynan); *Brut*, pp. 34, 36, 38, 44 (Cadwgan ap Bleddyn and Owain ap Cadwgan); Gerald of Wales, *Opera*, vi, 34 (Gruffudd ap Rhys).
[23] *Brut*, pp. 24, 38, 39, 29, 38.
[24] *Brut*, pp. 29, 32, 40–41 (family quarrels); pp. 39, 44 (inter-dynastic rivalries).

Personal control and manipulation were important facets of the exercise of overlordship; they could be complemented and reinforced by an increasing measure of territorial dependence. Welsh princelings did not formally hold their lands of the king of England; their dependence upon him was personal rather than territorial. Yet Henry I seized every opportunity to make their territorial lordship contingent on his grant and munificence and thereby to create a sense of indebtedness and indeed of precariousness in their territorial status. The process is particularly well exemplified in Powys: in 1102 Iorwerth ap Bleddyn, in return for his support during the Montgomery revolt, was granted a large tract of south-west Wales by the king 'for his lifetime, so long as the king lived, quit of rent and tribute' – a munificent grant, but a grant nonetheless and a conditional one; in 1109 Henry stripped Cadwgan ap Bleddyn of almost all his lands and then allowed him – as if he were an English baron – to redeem Ceredigion for £100 and under strict conditions; when those conditions were subsequently broken Henry had no hesitation in resuming the grant and reallocating Ceredigion to Gilbert fitz Richard of Clare; in 1111, when Iorwerth ap Cadwgan was murdered, the king 'gave Powys to Cadwgan ap Bleddyn' and when Cadwgan in turn was slain Henry in effect partitioned Powys between the squabbling members of the princely dynasty and exacted hostages and 'much money' from them; and, finally, in 1114 he enticed Owain ap Cadwgan with the promise, 'I will *give* thee thy land free'.[25] Powys in these years was clearly a client state; its territorial expansion and contraction and even its internal territorial politics were subject to the ultimate control and good will of the king. Much the same was true of such of south Wales as was allowed to remain under native control. Henry established his own native nominee in Ystrad Tywi, Cydweli and Gower in 1102 and his failure to support him was the cause of the downfall of this puppet ruler in 1106; he 'gave' a portion of Cantref Mawr to a member of the native dynasty and allowed the direct claimant, Gruffudd ap Rhys, to hold one commote there.[26] The king's power even extended to north Wales, for the biographer of Gruffudd ap Cynan of Gwynedd acknowledged that it was Henry I who had granted (*y rhoddes*) him most of his patrimony west of the river Conwy.[27] Henry I had given overlordship a much more precise and demanding territorial dimension in native Wales; thereby the dependence of client princes was made more secure from the king's point of view, more precarious from theirs.

There were other ways in which overlordship could be intensified. Hostages were demanded and held as securities for compliant

---

[25] *Brut*, pp. 24, 31, 34, 35–36, 38.

[26] *Brut*, pp. 25–26 (note the phrases 'gave', 'entrusted'), p. 40; Gerald of Wales, *Opera*, vi, 34.

[27] *Historia Gruffud vab Kenan*, p. 28. (Also *History of Gruffudd ap Cynan*, p. 151).

behaviour; princelings were detained in honourable custody or required to accompany the king on foreign expeditions; massive tributes and gifts could be exacted.[28] Even more suggestive of future developments was the way in which vassal princes were regarded as judicially answerable to their suzerain. Thus in 1103 the most powerful of the Powys princelings, Iorwerth ap Bleddyn, was summoned to appear before a royal tribunal at Shrewsbury, charged with various offences, convicted and thrown into prison (where he was to remain until 1110).[29] Formal submissions were now exacted from Welsh princes which must have been construed in Norman eyes as having the solemnity and force of feudal bonds: thus in 1114, according to the Anglo-Saxon chronicle, 'the Welsh kings came to him [Henry] and became his vassals and swore oaths of allegiance to him'.[30] Such bonds could indeed be brittle, especially among the Welsh who were notorious for their perfidy; yet there is no doubt that cumulatively Henry's overlordship in Wales was approximating more closely to his lordship elsewhere. 'The fear of King Henry'[31] was the overriding emotion in the political life of the country.

Contemporary Welshmen had no illusions about their predicament. 'God', said one of them, 'has placed . . . us in the hands of our enemies and has brought us so low that we cannot do anything according to our will'.[32] His outburst may have been unduly hysterical, but it is a reminder that to contemporaries Henry I's overlordship was in its way as effective as his direct lordship. The mechanics of control he deployed in native Wales were different from those which operated in England and the character and intensity of lordship were thereby different. Power flowed along different channels; but it flowed nevertheless. The king could tighten the screw of his authority as occasion required and as his commitments allowed; and in the last resort – as in 1114 and 1121 – he could lead expeditions to reassert his overlordship, to punish errant vassals and to extract new concessions from them. In spite of the hysterical fears of the native chronicler that the king was intent on 'exterminating all the Britons (i.e. Welsh)',[33] Henry's campaigns into Wales were not national crusades nor were they undertaken to effect the conquest of the country; rather were they the ultimate weapon in the assertion and reassertion of overlordship. As such they fulfilled their

---

[28] *Brut*, pp. 30, 32; William of Malmesbury, *Gesta Regum*, p. 478; J. R. H. Weaver (ed.), *The Chronicle of John of Worcester* (Oxford, 1908), p. 16 (hostages); *Brut*, pp. 34, 38 (custody of prince; accompanying king on expedition. Cf. the way Henry took Alexander of Scotland with him on his Welsh expedition of 1114); *Brut*, pp. 32, 38, 48 (tributes).
[29] *Brut*, p. 26; cf. the slightly different account in *Brut, R.B.H. Version*, p. 49.
[30] D. Whitelock (ed.), *The Anglo-Saxon Chronicle* (1961), p. 183 (Version H).
[31] *Brut*, p. 29.
[32] *Brut*, p. 32.
[33] *Brut*, p. 37.

purpose admirably; they brought the native princes quickly to heel.

In southern Wales the situation was different. There direct Norman lordship made striking advances in the early twelfth century: much of the country was militarily subjugated; castles were built; knights' fees were created; boroughs and priories were founded; settlers and colonists migrated in large numbers; and native princelings, where they survived, were reduced to the status of distressed gentlefolk. It is customary to regard this rapid Norman advance as essentially a baronial enterprise and one which led to the establishment of important 'private' lordships which were largely independent of effective royal control. Such an interpretation tallies well with the distinction that was drawn in the thirteenth century between the march of Wales (*marchia Wallie*) and native Wales (*pura Wallia*) and with marcher liberties as they were articulated and vigorously defended in that period. Viewed from the vantage-point of the early twelfth century, however, such an interpretation exaggerates the distinctiveness of Norman Wales – both in the character of its conquest and in the nature of its institutions. It also pre-dates the appearance of marcher liberties: as yet the march of Wales was a geographical description, not a constitutional or legal category.[34] Above all, from the point of view of the present argument, it underestimates the formative and directive role of the king in the making of Norman Wales. None more so than Henry I.

His opportunities to play such a rôle were many; he grasped each of them purposefully. At the outset of his reign the post-Hastings dispensation along the Welsh border collapsed. By 1102 the three great border earldoms were under his control – two through forfeiture (Hereford, 1075; Shrewsbury, 1102), and the third through custody (Chester, 1101). His power in south-eastern Wales had been further enhanced by other recent forfeitures – notably those of William count of Eu and Roger Lacy in 1096, both of whom had hitherto filled some of the vacuum in the area created by the earlier proscription (1075) of Roger of Breteuil. Failure of families in the direct male line also provided an opportunity to introduce new men into the area: thus Thurstin fitz Rou's lands in Lower Gwent were given as a reward to one of the Ballon brothers from Maine while Alfred de Hispannia's land in Caerleon passed, with his daughter, into the hands of a close confidant of the king, Robert de Chandos.[35] All in all, Henry I was

---

[34] These arguments are elaborated in D. G. Walker, 'The Norman settlement in Wales', *Proceedings of the Battle Conference*, i, ed. R. A. Brown (Woodbridge, 1978), 131–143, esp. pp. 139–40; R. R. Davies, 'Kings, Lords and Liberties in the March of Wales, 1066–1272', *Transactions of the Royal Historical Society*, fifth ser., xxix (1979), 41–61. Parallels with the Norman penetration of northern England and southern Scotland may be followed in G. W. S. Barrow, 'The pattern of lordship and feudal settlement in Cumbria', *Journal of Medieval History*, i (1975), 117–139; W. E. Kapelle. *The Norman Conquest of the North* (1979, esp. chaps. 5–7.

[35] For Thurstin fitz Rou and the Ballons see J. H. Round in *V[ictoria] C[ounty]*

given a free hand to shape a new dispensation along the Welsh border; he used the occasion, as his father had done before him, to create a pattern of authority which, in its organisation and personnel, remained firmly under his control.

The earldom of Shrewsbury was not revived. Instead Shropshire was placed under the control of Richard of Beaumais, a former servant of the Montgomeries and, in Eadmer's words, 'a most able man in secular affairs' and an exceptionally loyal servant of the king. He remained in charge of the county as virtual royal governor for over twenty years, combining his rôle there from 1108 with that of bishop of London.[36] Henry I reinforced his grip on the county by installing other followers in key positions along the western border of the shire: the Breton newcomer, Alan fitz Flaad (ancestor of the Fitzalans) at Oswestry and probably as deputy to Bishop Richard; the Lestranges, quite possibly associated with Alan fitz Flaad and Henry I in the Cotentin before 1100, at Knockin; the Peverels at Ellesmere, Overton and Whittington; Baldwin de Bollers, married to one of Henry's nieces, in the new honour of Montgomery; and William Pantulf in his formerly forfeited estate at Wem.[37] On Bishop Richard's death in the mid-1120s, his position in Shropshire was taken over by one of the key household servants of Henry, Payn fitz John. Payn had already established himself as the premier baron in Herefordshire through his marriage to Sybil de Lacy and appears to have acted as virtual governor of the county.[38] Gloucestershire was likewise firmly under the control of another experienced royal servant, Walter of Gloucester, sheriff of the county for over thirty years to *c.* 1128 and a constable of the royal household. Walter was in his turn succeeded by his son, Miles, who rose to be earl of Hereford.[39] The border shires of western England in the second half of Henry's reign lay securely under the control of Payn and Miles, 'the king's secret and special councillors', as Gerald of Wales aptly termed

H[istory], Herefordshire (1905), p. 280 and in 'The Family of Ballon and the Conquest of South Wales', *Studies in Peerage and Family History* (1901), pp. 181–215. For Robert de Chandos, I. J. Sanders, *English Baronies* (Oxford, 1960), pp. 67, 79 and Orderic Vitalis, *Ecclesiastical History*, ed. M. Chibnall (Oxford, 1969–80), vi, 342 and n.3.

[36] For Bishop Richard's career see [R. W.] Eyton, *[Antiquities of] Shropshire* (1854–60), ii, and *V. C. H. Shropshire*, iii (1979), 10. The quotation from Eadmer is in *Historia Novorum*, ed. M. Rule (Rolls Series, 1884), p. 197.

[37] J. H. Round, *Studies in Peerage and Family History*, pp. 120 sqq.; *V. C. H. Shropshire*, iii, 10, 35 (Fitzalan and Lestrange); Eyton, *Shropshire*, x, 232–3, xi, 30; Orderic Vitalis, *Ecclesiastical History*, vi, 519 (Peverel); Eyton, *Shropshire*, xi, 120 (Bollers); ix, 159–61 (Pantulf). The Crown appears to have retained control of its powers over hundreds in the western counties of England much more firmly than elsewhere: *V. C. H. Shropshire*, iii, 43.

[38] W. E. Wightman, *The Lacy Family in England and Normandy 1066–1194* (Oxford, 1966), pp. 175–182; *V. C. H. Shropshire*, iii, 10–11.

[39] D. G. Walker, 'Miles of Gloucester, Earl of Hereford', *Trans. Bristol and Gloucestershire Archaeological Society*, lxxvii (1959), 66–84; idem, 'The "Honours" of the Earls of Hereford in the Twelfth Century', *ibid.*, lxxix (1960) 174–211.

them; their overweening power extended 'from the Severn (at Shrewsbury) to the sea (the Bristol Channel)'.[40] It also extended deep into Wales.

Henry I ensconced himself equally firmly in Wales. His direct territorial stake in the country was greater than that of his brother or father. In the south-east he retained the forfeited estates of Roger of Breteuil and William of Eu in Chepstow and Usk in his own hands until he bestowed them on Walter fitz Richard of Clare; in the march adjoining Shropshire he took over the forfeited estates and claims of the house of Montgomery, refashioned them into baronies and honours for his own followers,[41] and gave his justiciar a watching brief over the turbulent politics of the neighbouring principality of Powys. But it was in the south-west above all that Henry I showed his determination to maintain a major Crown interest in Norman expansion in Wales. He did not allow Carmarthen to become a private lordship for the Devon branch of the Clare family. Instead he converted it into the *caput* of a royal honour in eastern Dyfed from which royal authority radiated outwards over Norman and Welsh districts alike; he endowed a priory there; he introduced the habits of feudal governance – such as reliefs and military aid – to the area; and he sent his son and key household officials, such as Walter of Gloucester, thither on missions. His choice of Carmarthen showed singular judgement: it became in the thirteenth century the key centre from which English authority was imposed in Deheubarth.[42] In western Dyfed Henry I went event further: he retained the lordship of Pembroke, confiscated from Arnulf of Montgomery in 1102, in his own hands; he converted it into a shire whose sheriff was directly accountable to the exchequer in England; he sent his justices to hold pleas there; he brought contiguous lordships into dependence on it; he caused his own illegitimate son (Henry, by Nesta daughter of Rhys ap Tewdwr) to be appointed steward of the neighbouring estates of the bishop of St David's; he introduced Flemish settlers into the dependent lordships of Rhos and Daugleddau.[43] Southwest Wales bade fair to become a major enclave of direct royal power in Wales. It was a measure of the difference between Henry I and Stephen that early in the new reign all this was lost: Carmarthen was captured

---

[40] Gerald of Wales, *Opera*, vi, p. 34; *Gesta Stephani*, p. 25.

[41] It was in his reign, out of the debris of the Montgomery estates, that the honour of Montgomery and the barony of Caus were created: Eyton, *Shropshire*, xi, 120–147; *V. C. H. Shropshire*, viii (1968), 310.

[42] *Pipe Roll, 31 Henry I*, pp. 89–90; *Brut*, pp. 29, 44; J. E. Lloyd, 'Carmarthen in Early Norman Times', *Archaeologia Cambrensis*, sixth ser., vii (1907), 281–92; J. G. Edwards, 'The Early History of the counties of Carmarthen and Cardigan', *English Historical Review*, xxxi (1916), 90–98.

[43] *Pipe Roll, 31 Henry I*, pp. 136–7; *Regesta*, ii, nos. 1611, 1754–5; J. Conway Davies (ed.)., *Episcopal Acts Relating to Welsh Dioceses* (Historical Society of the Church of Wales, 1946–8), i, 297 (D. 263).

by the Welsh in 1137 and in the following year Stephen surrendered the county of Pembroke, along with the title of earl, to Gilbert fitz Gilbert of Clare.[44]

Henry's power in Wales was not confined to the areas he held himself, for he also used the full range of royal authority, patronage and feudal control to set his own stamp on the distribution of territorial power in southern Wales generally. Indeed nowhere was his masterfulness demonstrated to better effect than in south Wales: forfeitures, failure in the direct male line and custody gave him a particularly free hand to operate; the counters on the board of territorial politics were here so much larger and more compact than in much of England; and munificence in Wales cost him little or nothing, for the responsibility and cost of conquest and control devolved on the beneficiaries. He disposed of lordships, conquered or unconquered, by his fiat: the vast district of Usk and Chepstow to Walter fitz Richard of Clare;[45] Cantref Bychan to Richard fitz Pons;[46] Ceredigion to Gilbert fitz Richard of Clare.[47] But what he could grant he could also resume: Richard fitz Baldwin was granted half of Dyfed in 1102 but lost it soon after and, likewise, Saer was placed in charge at Pembroke in 1102 only to be dismissed three years later.[48] He exploited the incidents of feudal tenure to the full to extend his control and to provide openings for his own men. Rights of custody gave him control of the county of Chester and adjacent parts of north Wales for fourteen years after 1101, while in south Wales Glamorgan and Gwynllwg were likewise in his control after the death of Robert fitz Hamon in 1107. Rights of marriage were used to even more spectacular effect. Three marriages in particular stand out: those of Mabel, daughter and heiress of Robert fitz Hamon (Glamorgan and Gwynllwg) to Robert of Gloucester; of Sybil, the daughter and heiress of Hugh de Lacy (Ewyas and extensive estates in Herefordshire) to Payn fitz John; and of Sybil, daughter and heiress of Bernard of Neufmarché (Brecon, Hay, Talgarth) to Miles of Gloucester. Between them these marriages transformed the map of territorial power in south-east Wales: the king's illegitimate son and two of his closest confidants had assumed the premier lordships in the area and that at no cost to the king himself. It was an exercise in which the king – as the marriage agreement of Miles of Gloucester and Sibyl

---

[44] For Gilbert, see R. H. C. Davis, *King Stephen* (1967), p. 136.

[45] The date of the grant to Walter fitz Richard is unknown but he was probably in possession by c. 1119; J. C. Davies, *Episcopal Acts*, ii, 616 (L. 30). The honour of Chepstow at this stage was taken to comprehend the later lordship of Usk; A. J. Taylor, 'Usk Castle and the Pipe Roll of 1185', *Archaeologia Cambrensis*, xcix (1947), 249–56.

[46] *Brut*, p. 40.

[47] *Brut*, p. 34. His son was paying relief for his lands in Wales in 1130, *Pipe Roll, 31 Henry I*, p. 53.

[48] *Brut*, pp. 24–26, 29.

of Neufmarché makes abundantly clear[49] – played the directive and determining role. He also intervened in other ways to determine the descent of estates, especially where the ill-defined customs of inheritance allowed him an opportunity. Thus Payn fitz John, though a favoured servant, was not allowed to secure the whole of the Lacy patrimony on his marriage to Sibyl.[50] Likewise when Hamelin de Ballon, lord of the honour of Abergavenny died, his daughter was not allowed to succeed to his lands in Wales (and her descendants nursed a sense of grievance accordingly); rather were they used to reward another leading member of Henry I's household and one of his most devoted protegés, Brian fitz Count, the natural son of Count Alan of Brittany.[51]

Henry I's genius, it has been observed, was that 'he created men'.[52] Nowhere did he do so to better effect than in Wales. Some of them were drawn from aristocratic families, whose acquisitiveness was further satisfied by lands in Wales and whose indebtedness to the king was thereby increased – notably the brothers Gilbert and Walter fitz Richard of Clare (Ceredigion, Chepstow and Usk) and Henry de Beaumont (Gower). Others were clerical servants – notably Richard of Beaumais (Shropshire), Roger of Salisbury (Cydweli) or Bernard, the queen's chancellor installed as bishop of St David's. Most, however, were men who owed much, if not all, of their territorial eminence to his service and to the rewards it brought: Miles of Gloucester (Brecon), Payn fitz John (Ewyas), Brian fitz Count (Abergavenny), Alan fitz Flaad (Oswestry), Baldwin de Bollars (Montgomery).[53] Whatever their origins, he had created in south Wales a baronage which, in its higher echelons, was almost entirely beholden to his generosity. They, in return, showed him a deference which manifested his authority more effectively than any institutional control – issuing their charters by consent of their lord, King Henry; making important agreements 'in the presence of King Henry', and turning to him for help and military aid when they were in trouble.[54] In these circumstances how lordships were governed, what liberties their lords claimed or exercised, how far there was a pattern of institutional answerability and judicial control

[49] J. H. Round (ed.), *Ancient Charters prior to A.D. 1200* (Pipe Roll Society, vol. x), no. 6.

[50] W. E. Wightman, *The Lacy Family*, pp. 175–6.

[51] J. H. Round, *Studies in Peerage and Family History*, p. 199; idem (ed.), *Ancient Charters prior to A.D. 1200*, no. 26.

[52] R. W. Southern, 'King Henry I', *Medieval Humanism and Other Essays*, p. 211.

[53] J. O. Prestwich has brilliantly located the careers of such men in the military household of Henry: 'The military household of the Norman kings', *English Historical Review*, xcvi (1981), 1–35. Cf. the way in which Richard II placed some of his chamber knights in key positions in Wales: K. B. McFarlane, *Lancastrian Kings and Lollard Knights* (Oxford, 1972), pp. 188–9.

[54] 'Cartularium Prioratus S. Johannis de Brecon', *Archaeologia Cambrensis*, fourth ser., xiv (1883), 141–2; *Episcopal Acts*, ii, 620–1 (L. 45); *Brut*, p. 37.

were secondary issues. Henry I controlled the men themselves. He had made them; he could break them.

It is in the context of the Norman 'empire' as a whole and in terms of the practice of authority and the realities of power in the early twelfth century that Henry I's actions and policies in Wales must be viewed. The Normans and their king lived for the present rather than planned for the future. Viewed in those terms, Henry I's achievement in Wales was indeed notable. He had secured a mastery there that was commensurate with his needs. Norman power in general and royal authority in particular in Wales in 1135 were arguably more extensive than they were to be again until 1277. Suzerainty over native dynasties had been intensified and their client status clearly confirmed; while the conquest and control of south Wales had been effected under ultimate royal supervision and to the advantage of the king's servants and dependants. Such an achievement fell well short of conquest and dominion as Edward I understood those terms: but to contemporaries, viewing events without the hindsight of knowing what happened after 1135, Henry's mastery was self-evident. He had 'subjugated the whole of Wales' was John of Worcester's comment. The Welsh chronicler was even more flattering – and despairing: Henry was 'the man against whom none can contend save God himself'.[55]

---

[55] *Brut*, p. 42.

Plate 1(a). David I for Robert de Brus (B. L. Cotton chr. xviii, 45).

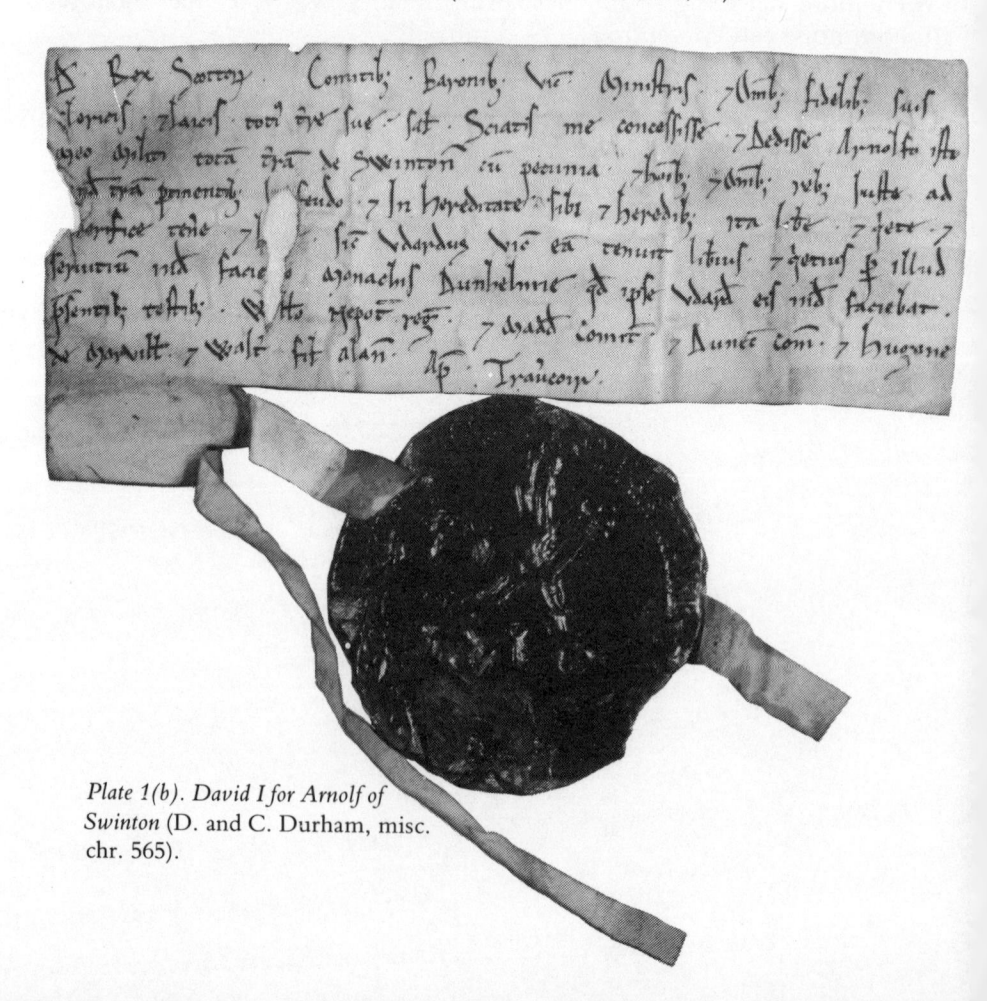

Plate 1(b). David I for Arnolf of Swinton (D. and C. Durham, misc. chr. 565).

11

The Scots Charter

G. W. S. Barrow

In the classical age of the feudal lawyers, Craig, Stair and Mackenzie, the Scots charter had become merely a part, already indeed a subordinate part, of an established system of conveyancing little regulated by legislation and almost exclusively directed by expert notaries, the rise of whose class to a monopolistic position in the legal landscape has recently been traced, with matchless erudition, by Dr John Durkan.[1] It has to be admitted that at the hands of these notaries the charter became the perfect exemplification of all that is driest and dustiest in the work of Dr Dryasdust. The charters they composed could be and often were lengthy, verbose and repetitive. They were not so much essays in Latin prose as concatenations of obligatory formulae permitting scarcely any variation save, naturally, in the proper nouns and in certain technicalities. Queen Mary's charter for the burgesses of Jedburgh, which passed the seals in 1556, runs to some 860 words.[2] It tells us that Jedburgh had enjoyed burghal status from ancient times but that being situated close to the border had suffered severely from incursions of our old enemies of England and had consequently lost its 'evidents and infeftments'. The charter confirms to Jedburgh its immemorial status as a royal burgh with all customary rights of trade, markets and fairs, and goes out of its way to empower the burgh magistrates to put to the assize those caught thieving within the burgh, to drown, hang and justify them, to administer justice to them for their crimes to the point of death, and to build and maintain gallows for this purpose. Otherwise the charter is replete with phrases of common form. In September 1559 Patrick Hepburn bishop of Moray issued a feu-ferme charter, in his capacity as commendator of Scone Abbey, granting to William Chalmer the lands of Netherton of Cloquhat in Alyth in return for a down

This paper was first delivered as the Edwards Lecture in the University of Glasgow on 16 February 1984.

[1] J. Durkan, 'The early Scottish notary', in *The Renaissance and Reformation in Scotland: essays in honour of Gordon Donaldson*, ed. Ian B. Cowan and Duncan Shaw (Edinburgh, 1983), 22–40.
[2] *R[egistrum] M[agni] S[igilli] Regum Scotorum], 1546–80*, ed. J. Maitland Thomson (Edinburgh, 1886), no. 1119; transcript of full text *penes* Department of Scottish History, University of Edinburgh.

payment of 500 merks, an annual rent of 6 lib. 13s. 4d. (10 merks) and a quinquennial gressum of 26s. 8d (2 merks), together with certain other payments.[3] The document recording the transfer of this modest estate comprises some 1100 words, few of which convey any original information. It took John Murray laird of Black Barony about 500 words to convey the lands of Westloch in Peeblesshire in 1497 in conjunct fee to his daughter Gelis (Egidia) Murray and her husband William Duddingston of Southouse, for a blench ferme rent of ½ merk payable half yearly in the parish kirk of Eddleston.[4] His notary drafted a *tenendas* clause which broadly resembles the example given by Stair, omitting bloodwites, heriots and merchet but including springs, lochs and charcoal.[5] Bishop Hepburn's notary evidently used a formulary practically identical to Stair's, but he too preferred charcoal, iron and lead to bloodwites. These charters have been chosen almost at random and could easily be replicated a thousand times. Two of them, in effect all three of them, are what Stair would call 'original infeftments, by which the fee was first constituted and therefore are most plain and simple'.[6] To be fair to the notaries, it seems that the most powerful single factor including longwindedness in charters was the fourteeth-century device of the 'inspection' or 'confirmation in the larger form', in which the full texts of earlier charters were recited *seriatim*.[7] For this practice, however, the historian must be grateful, for it has often preserved the contents, inducing longwindedness in charters was the fourteenth-century device perished.[8]

We should not expect classical Latin – there can be no more striking contrast in sixteenth-century Scotland than the scholar's love of Cicero and Tacitus and the lawyer's addiction to jingle – but it is at times hard to forgive the prolix style, the wearisome repetition, the labouring of synonyms, especially if we are reading an unprinted document and the handwriting happens also to be as execrable as the humanity. Our lack of enthusiasm for the classical feu-charter or the charter of lands in ward

---

[3] Transcript *penes* Department of Scottish History, University of Edinburgh.

[4] Transcript *penes* Department of Scottish History, University of Edinburgh.

[5] James, Viscount of Stair, *The Institutions of the Law of Scotland*, ed. D.M. Walker (Edinburgh and Glasgow, 1981), 340 (Tit. 3, 15).

[6] *Ibid.*, 338.

[7] R[egesta] R[egum] S[cottorum], vi, *The Acts of David II, king of Scots, 1329–71*, ed. B. Webster (Edinburgh, 1982), 19, 23–4. The practice of incorporating the full texts of earlier documents in an instrument designed to confirm them seems to have developed from the device of the *inspeximus*, or certified copy, towards the end of the thirteenth century.

[8] E.g., *RMS, 1424–1513*, ed. J. B. Paul (Edinburgh 1882), no. 3136, a charter of James IV incorporating important thirteenth-century charters relating to Argyll, published in full in *Proceedings of the Society of Antiquaries of Scotland*, xc (1956–7), 218–9. In Skene of Pitlour Muniments, c/o Messers. Pagan, Osborne & Grace, W.S., Cupar, Fife, there is a charter of 1359 x 72 by Isabel countess of Fife incorporating a charter of her father Earl Duncan IV, 1315 x 53.

or burgage or blench-ferme may be given added point if we read the presumably magisterial passage in which Stair deals with the process and procedure of infeftment. 'Any disposition', he tells us, *per verba de praesenti* in fee, is valid as to that part of the infeftment, and although the disposition contained an obligement to grant charters, yet the not granting thereof does not prejudice'.[9] And again, 'Precepts of *clare constat* . . . and other precepts of seasin not relating to particular charters or seasins, but either simple or bearing *secundum chartam conficiendam* ('according to a charter to be composed') are sufficient, although these charters be never granted'.[10] The *coup de grace* was administered by the instrument of sasine. 'After instruments of seasin became in use, they were not only sustained as the mean of probation, that possession or seasin was given or taken, but they were the necessary solemnities to accomplish the right, which could not be supplied by any other mean of probation; though the superior with a thousand witnesses, should subscribe all the contents of a seasin, it would be of no effect to make a real right without the attest of a notary.'[11]

The charter thus dwindled in legal and social significance as it grew in length and prolixity. Yet symbolically it remained immensely powerful. Earls and barons, bishops and abbots possessed their charter rooms and charter chests. The king's Great Seal was affixed only to charters and letters patent and a handful of other types of document;[12] the Register of the Great Seal took pride of place among the official records of the Crown. George Martine of Claremont, secretary to Archbishops Sharp and Burnet in the reign of Charles II, treasured as the palladium of archiepiscopal rights and liberties the 'Golden Charter' given to Bishop Kennedy by James II in 1452,[13] and confirmed to Archbishop Scheves by James III twenty-seven years later.[14] As printed by Martine's editor at the end of the eighteenth century, the charter, 'a famous evident' as Martine calls it admiringly,[15] occupies five and a half large quarto pages.[16]

The Scots charter on which I prefer to dwell in this Edwards Lecture is the charter, more especially the royal charter, before the notaries, almost before the lawyers, got hold of it and went to work on it. For much of the twelfth century the charter is not to be seen in terms of Erskine's definition,[17] as a writing containing the grant or transmission

[9] Stair, *Institutions*, 337.
[10] *Ibid.*, 338.
[11] *Ibid.*, 342.
[12] J. Maitland Thomson, *The Public Records of Scotland* (Glasgow, 1922), 70–71.
[13] *RMS, 1424–1513*, no. 1444.
[14] *Ibid.*
[15] G. Martine, *Reliquiae Divi Andreae* (St Andrews, 1797), 96.
[16] *Ibid.*, 97–102.
[17] J. Erskine, *An Institute of the Law of Scotland* (8th edn, 1871), II, iii, 19 (ii, 310).

of a feudal right, but rather as a letter conveying information, commands or prohibitions. Considered as a corpus of letters, the charters of twelfth-century Scotland are rightly to be viewed as part of the country's surviving literature, narrative, dispositive and descriptive. What is more, and yet at the same time surprisingly overlooked, the surviving original charters of this period form a collection of contemporary artefacts which possess unique characteristics – datability within very narrow limits, a high degree of individuality, a combination of creative art and business functionalism. Texts as a whole and originals in particular take us more immediately into the heart of twelfth-century Scotland, or at least of its *classe dirigeante*, than any other group of artefacts still preserved to us from that now rather distant epoch.

Contemporaries did not call our letter an *epistola* or *litterae*; they preferred the terms *breve* or *carta*. The doctrine on which we were all brought up is that the charter was not itself dispositive, but evidentiary.[18] It narrated or recorded, but did not actually effect or constitute, a grant. The grant was effected by a solemn, public and partly physical ceremony involving the handing over of materials such as earth and stone or symbolic objects such as knives or horse trappings. The charter might follow some time later, in leisurely fashion, telling the story of how the gift was made, perhaps also explaining why it was made. It would conclude with a selective list of names chosen from among those who were present when the gift was made and would bear witness to it. It would be authenticated by the donor's seal attached as permanently as possible to the main body of the document.

When King David I brought the first Scottish colony of Cistercian monks from Rievaulx to Melrose in June 1136 his grant of their earliest endowments – Melrose itself, Eildon and Darnick – was consented to immediately and confirmed by his son Earl Henry. The earl headed the list of eighteen witnesses who, however important, might be thought to be in some manner 'outsiders', Anglo-Norman barons or knights for the most part but including John bishop of Glasgow, William son of King Duncan II and Earl Madeth of Atholl. In addition to these eighteen there were 'the men of that land', fourteen of them, mostly belonging to Lothian, Tweeddale or Teviotdale such as Earl Cospatric or Ulfkil son of Æthelstan but including, surprisingly, Robert de Brus the younger, Raoul son of Thurstan and Roger nephew of the bishop of St Andrews. Whether, as seems possible, this initial grant and list of witnesses were set down in writing there and then, or not, we cannot be certain, for no such document survives. But a few years later, on

---

[18] V. H. Galbraith, *Studies in the Public Records* (1948), 64–5; W. Holdsworth, *A History of English Law* (third edn, 1944), ix, 164–5; F. Pollock and F. W. Maitland, *History of English Law* (second edn. 1911), ii, 82–90.

Friday 29th May 1142,[19] the king and his son perambulated the lands of Gatton Haugh and Gattonside before bestowing them on the abbey in augmentation of their original gift. On this occasion, or perhaps a little while afterwards, the complete tally of royal benefaction was recounted in two charters of closely similar wording.[20] Only six magnates were named as witnesses to what was called 'this present gift', all of them among the witnesses to the earlier grant.

Each one of this pair of charters refers to the king's gift being confirmed by the king's son and heir. The verb *confirmare* is perhaps better translated 'establish' rather than 'confirm'. Thus in King David's words Earl Henry assents to his father's grant, grants it himself, and *establishes* it by his charter;[21] in the earl's own words 'I have given, and by this my charter *established*, the gift of my father King David'.[22] It was in fact comparatively rare for David I or Earl Henry to employ the formula *hac mea carta confirmare*, rare enough to suggest that until *c.* 1140 their acts were thought to be sufficiently established in themselves.[23] Does that mean that all their charters were no more than casual notifications to bishops, earls, justiciars, sheriffs and the rest that such and such a monastery had been piously founded, such and such a bundle of privileges bestowed upon a favoured subject, such and such an estate alienated in fee and heritage? I am inclined to believe that almost the opposite was true. 'Earl David greets John the bishop and Colban and Cospatric and all his lieges. May you yourselves know that it was adjudged before me between the monks of St Cuthbert and my drengs of the land of Horndean that if the monks had lawful witnesses or the charter (*breve*) of my brother that land would remain to them quit; and for this reason I wish you to know that I myself have seen the charter and gift of my brother King Edgar *which I have sent to you*, and whatever that charter attests to them I will and grant they shall have, freely and quit.'[24] King Edgar's deed of giving and the *breve* or brief charter by which his deed was announced to all his lieges throughout his realm, both Scots and English, were apparently one and the same thing. Conversely, though the earliest references to this come from a considerably later period, a gift was not cancelled or revoked without the relevant charters being cancelled or surrendered. Whoever

---

[19] *RRS*, i, 157, n.l.
[20] *Ibid.*, no. 41; [Sir Archibald] Lawrie [ed., *Early Scottish*] *Charters* (Glasgow, 1905), no. 141.
[21] *Ibid.*, 107; 'annuente et concedente Henrico filio meo et herede et per cartam suam confirmante.'
[22] *RRS*, i, no. 41 (p. 157).
[23] In *RRS*, i, nos. 7–46 (omitting no. 19 as spurious) the phrase occurs four times, perhaps signficantly all towards the end of the series. In Lawrie, *Charters*, nos. 54–267 *passim* there are twenty-one occurrences, mostly belonging to the later years of David I's reign.
[24] Lawrie, *Charters*, no. 32.

possessed the charter duly sealed and witnessed possessed – or could confidently lay claim to – the property.[25]

If the charter could give and be a gift, it could also restore. 'David, by God's grace king of Scots to the bishops, abbots, earls, sheriffs, barons, *prepositi*, officers and all his responsible men of his whole land, French, English and Scots, greeting. May you know that I have given and restored (*reddidisse*) to God and the church of the Holy Trinity of Dunfermline and the abbot and monks serving God there the whole shire of Kirkcaldy which Earl Constantine withheld from them by force.'[26] In the reign of William I the verb *reddere*, to restore, might be used in the case of heritable fiefs where there had been, as far as we can tell, a normal break in tenancy and a son and heir received from the crown the land which his father had peacefully held and had not forfeited. In this way the king 'restored' Annandale to the younger Robert de Brus,[27], Benvie and Panmure to William de Valognes[28] and Benholm in Kincardineshire to Hugh of Benholm.[29] In all three cases the father of the recipient had held the restored land of the king peacefully and lawfully. Likewise, King William's father Henry earl of Northumberland 'restored' the land of Dilston in Corbridge to William son of Alfric in succession to his brother Richard.[30]

Such caution, though not very commonly displayed, suggests that the feudalists were anxious to hold back the tide which was rapidly turning 'in fee and heritage' into 'for ever'. Charters in the twelfth century were far too flexible to be confined to perpetuities. David I's gift of Athelstaneford to Alexander of St Martin was indefinitely, if not perpetually, 'in fee and heritage', but we cannot say the same of the king's promise, contained as an integral part of his charter, to pay Alexander 10 merks a year until he has made up the estate to a full knight's fee.[31] The Augustinian canons of Nostell in the West Riding took care to retain the charter by which King David granted them three merks a year from his silver mine at Alston until he should have restored to them an exchange for this rent elsewhere.[32] Admittedly it was usual for grants to the church, both of land and of regular money rents,

---

[25] For charters and other instruments being declared null and void because they might threaten a new proprietor see, e.g., *Registrum de Dunfermelyn* (Bannatyne Club, 1842) no. 87 (1278); for charters being regarded as cancelled by a former proprietor on resignation, see ibid., no. 156; for charters being surrendered, see *ibid.*, no. 169 ('all the old charters of the land of "Keith Siwin" speaking for the abbot and convent of Dunfermline to be restored and given up as faithfully as possible').

[26] Lawrie, *Charters*, no. 94.
[27] *RRS*, ii, no. 80.
[28] *Ibid.*, no. 405.
[29] *Ibid.*, no. 428.
[30] *RRS*, i, no. 22.
[31] Lawrie, *Charters*, no. 186.
[32] *RRS*, i, no. 39.

to be made in perpetuity, whether it was the land of Selkirk for the monks of Tiron (though they soon afterwards moved to Kelso)[33] or one hundred shillings a year from Hardingstone by Northampton for the building and repair (*restauratio*) of Glasgow Cathedral.[34] But most of the grants embodied in charters are best seen as indefinite, effective until such time as the terms and conditions ceased to be appropriate or enforceable.

As the distinction grew sharper between what was intended to endure for ever, or at least for a very long time, and what was indefinite or merely ephemeral, the structure of the document dealing with the former class began to diverge from that of documents used for the latter. Moreover, the term *carta* (*charta*), 'charter', became more and more restricted to the perpetual or the long term. In the earlier decades of the twelfth century the words *breve*, a 'brief' or 'brieve', *anglicé* a 'writ', and *carta* or *cartula*, a parchment containing formal business writing, seem to have been practically synonymous. Gradually the words *breve* and *litterae* came to be supplied to the ephemeral documents, commands, interdictions or simple notifications. By *c.* 1200, the *carta* was well on its way to becoming the solemn charter of later medieval and earlier modern times.

The clerks who composed and produced the written acts of the earlier twelfth-century kings, Edgar, Alexander I and David I, seem to have been chiefly concerned, not to draw a distinction between documents as acts of state and documents as oil in the wheels of government, but to convey their masters' will unambiguously and inexorably. The device which they employed to achieve this was almost invariably – the exceptions are so few as to be insignificant[35] – the verb *sciatis*, 'may you know'. They performed remarkable things with the help of this simple verb. 'May you know that I have given to Almighty God and to his holy confessor Cuthbert and to his monks, for the souls of my father and mother, and for the souls' weal of myself and my brothers and sisters, Coldingham and all those lands they have in Lothian as I had them in my hand.'[36] 'May you know that I have given and granted to Robert de Brus Annandale and all the land from the march of Dunegal of Strathnith to the march of Ranulf le Meschin.'[37] 'May you know that I will and firmly command that you see that the monks of Dunfermline have all the teinds and dues and services as fully as I gave these to them most fully.'[38] 'May you know

---

[33] Lawrie, *Charters*, no. 35.
[34] Ibid., no. 46.
[35] This may be verified by reference to Lawrie, *Charters*, and *RRS*, i, *passim*, but see separately ibid. 75–6.
[36] Lawrie, *Charters*, no. 18.
[37] Ibid., no. 54.
[38] Ibid., no. 61.

that I will and firmly command that no poind shall ever be seized in the lands belonging to the church of St Andrews for an offence or for debts committed or incurred by those unconnected with St Andrews.'[39] 'May you know that I have given Ragewin and Gillepatric and Ulchil *for ever* to the church of the Holy Trinity of Dunfermline as my own men.'[40] 'May you know that I have given and granted to God and to the church of the Holy Trinity of Dunfermline and the abbot and monks serving God that their men shall be free of all labour service on castles and bridges.'[41] 'May you know that I have exempted the abbot of Dunfermline's ship and everything within it from all customs belonging to me.'[42] 'May you know that I have granted and confirmed the marches between Coldingham and Bunkle which I caused to be perambulated with my responsible men.'[43] 'May you know that I have given and granted to the church of St Kentigern of Glasgow and to the bishopric of that church Govan with its marches to be possessed for ever in charitable tenure.'[44] 'May you know that I have given and granted to Andrew bishop of Caithness, "Hoctor comon" free and quit from every service save common army.'[45]

It is not really practicable to attribute to the royal clerks a nice distinction between notifications and mandates and precepts and prohibitions, as though the verbal formulae had all been carefully worked out and assigned to their respective functions. Among direct injunctions without any notification, we have the following variations: 'I command', 'I command and firmly order', 'I command and request', 'I forbid'.[46] But we also have injunctions (including prohibitions) introduced by a notification – 'May you know that I command (forbid, etc).[47] – and conversely we have verbs of commanding and forbidding used to introduce a narrative of gift or disposition, all as though it made little or no difference. Finally and familiarly we have the notification and dispositive or narrative text followed by *quare volo et (firmiter) precipio, volo itaque et firmiter precipio, ideo mando (volo), quare prohibeo (defendo)* etc., etc.[48]

Chancery clerks of a later age would have made the king issue a formal charter, addressed generally, granting Kirkham and Bispham to the monks of Shrewsbury, and then drafted a brieve to enforce this,

[39] *Ibid.*, no. 67.
[40] *Ibid.*, no. 68.
[41] *Ibid.*, no. 84.
[42] *Ibid.*, no. 88.
[43] *Ibid.*, no. 90.
[44] *Ibid.*, no. 104.
[45] *Ibid.*, no. 221.
[46] *Ibid.*, nos. 58, 60, 66, 70, 85, etc. ('I command'); 130, 202 ('I command and firmly order'); 174 ('I command and request'); 96 ('I forbid').
[47] *Ibid.*, nos. 61, 67; and cp. *ibid.*, no. 57.
[48] *Ibid.*, nos. 32, 56, 69, 84, 86, 89, 94, 118, 119, 124, 126, 134, 135, 156, 199, 267 (and others, *passim*).

The Scots Charter 157

addressed to the relevant officials. But in fact David I issued two documents both addressed to his justiciars, barons, sheriffs and all responsible men of the Honour of Lancaster, one beginning 'May you know that I will and firmly order that the monks of Shrewsbury shall have Bispham etc.', the other beginning 'I order that the abbot and monks of Shrewsbury shall have Kirkham church and Bispham etc.'[49]

To classify in such circumstances is to chase a will o' the wisp. I believe the clerks were not categorizing but luxuriating among a large (but not infinite) range of variations in verbal formulae, very much as they luxuriated among an even larger (but still not infinite) range of variations in the caroline minuscule which was the received official handwriting of the period. And for the same reason: possessing a minority skill held to be of special value, they also enjoyed the freedom of practitioners in a completely new technique. But I do not see them as patient experimenters systematically trying now one method and now another until they obtained a result already envisaged; rather were they pioneers blazing trails across virgin prairie, only some of which proved passable in the long run or were found to be leading to some place to which people actually wanted to go. One example of a false trail is provided by the attempt to give a date of time to royal acts. It is noticeable that those documents which are written in a thoroughly professional cursive hand bear no such dating, merely the place of issue or sealing in the familiar form *apud Sconam, apud Castellum puellarum* etc.[50] But an appreciable number of David I's charters have the time date, whether the rather vague 'at Yardley [Hastings] on the day of the dedication of the church of St Andrew at Yardley',[51] 'at the siege of Norham in June' (though that is linked to St Barnabas' day, A.D. 1138 in the body of the charter)[52] or, more commonly, the precise: 'at Roxburgh, the 17th of the Kalends of September in the year 1139'[53] or 'this my charter was established in the year of the Lord's Incarnation 1144, in the 20th year of my reign',[54] or 'at Coldingham on the day of the Invention of the Holy Cross in the year of the Lord's Incarnation 1147, that is the year in which the king of France and many Christians reached Jersualem'.[55]

This practice was continued sporadically into the reign of Malcolm IV, at the close of a few of whose acts we find 'this charter was established in the year of the Lord's Incarnation 1159'[56] or 'in the year of

---

[49] *Ibid.*, no. 138, 139.
[50] *Ibid.*, nos. 54, 160
[51] *Ibid.*, no. 59.
[52] *Ibid.*, no. 119.
[53] *Ibid.*, no. 121.
[54] *Ibid.*, no. 172.
[55] *Ibid.*, no. 178.
[56] *RRS*, i, no. 131.

the Lord's Incarnation 1160 at St Andrews'[57] or 'at Perth at Christmas next after the peace between the king and Somerled [of Argyll]',[58] or 'in the eleventh year of King Malcolm's reign, at Stirling'.[59] On the whole these constructions have an ecclesiastical flavour and their use tended to reflect the practices familiar to the beneficiaries' own scribes and clerks. The custom, if it can be given so strong a description, was abandoned under William the Lion. Only from 1195, possibly at the instigation of William del Bois, afterwards chancellor, was a time-date regularly put at the end of royal acts, in the day-of-the-month form also found in the contemporary English royal chancery.[60] In course of time, by c.1222, this practice led to the adoption of the full dating clause by place, day of the month and regnal year familiar to students of later medieval royal documents.[61]

We cannot seriously doubt that the clerks who created the Scots charter of the twelfth century performed a notable service to the monarchy by giving it, in a form which could be stored permanently and seen regularly, the stamp of a particular style. It is they more than the moneyers or seal-makers, very much more than the chroniclers, who ensured that the rulers of Scotland were kings of Scots; they who fixed the rule faithfully observed till the eighteenth century that the king's lieges were 'his responsible men' (*probi homines*); they who set a standard of terse, businesslike clarity in royal utterances which was maintained until well into the fourteenth century.

We may now turn to the visual aspect of the work of these royal clerks and scribes. If I am right in believing that they were animated by self-confidence, possibly even by a measure of self-satisfaction, these feelings would surely not have been misplaced. It is clear that much discretion was given to them by the country's potentates, that they bore a good deal of responsibility for the way in which royal authority was communicated and for the language which formed the continuous framework of governmental and legal tradition. It is also clear that their willingness to use discretion and take responsibility was duly rewarded in the only manner practicable in the twelfth and thirteenth century, namely by ecclesiastical preferment, and that of the highest kind.

The crown was relatively slow to develop a professional writing office. Nevertheless, it is possible to discern professionalism at work on behalf of King Edgar, King Alexander and their younger brother

---

[57] *Ibid.*, no. 174.
[58] *Ibid.*, no. 175.
[59] *Ibid.*, no. 243.
[60] *RRS*, ii, 82.
[61] Cf. *Handlist of the Acts of Alexander II*, ed. J. Scoular (Regesta Regum Scottorum Committee, 1959), 17ff.

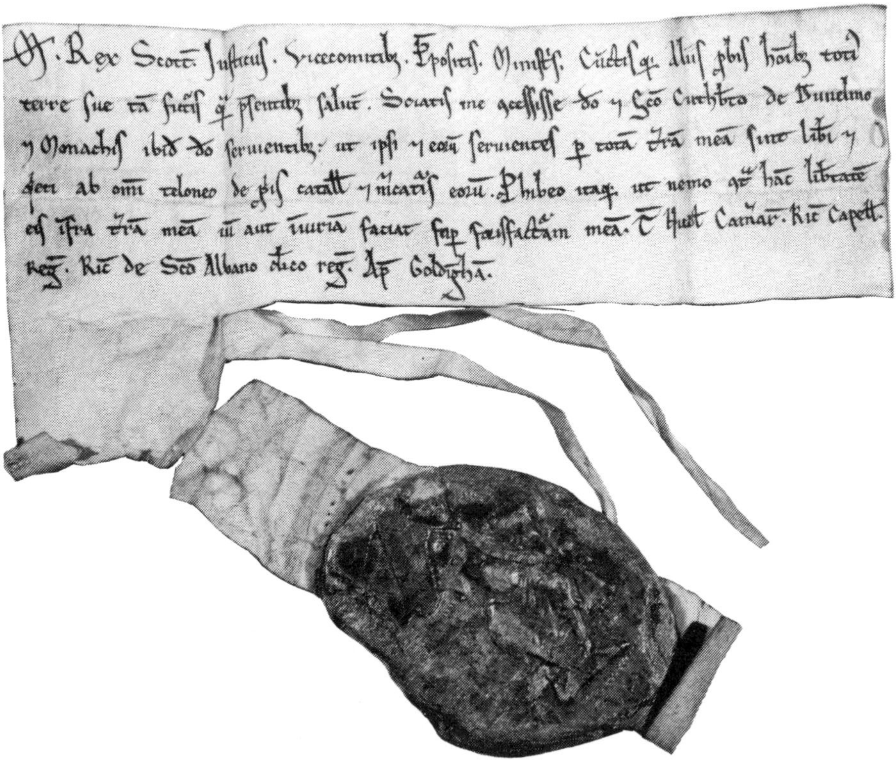

Plate 2. Malcolm IV for Durham Cathedral Priory (D. and C. Durham, Misc. chr. 580).

David, later David I.[62] The relevant documents were all produced for the benefit of Durham Cathedral priory, and since those of Alexander I and Earl David are in the handwriting of the same scribe it seems reasonable to locate him at Durham rather than in two different royal households, existing simultaneously but presumably in different places. The hand is cursive but not highly so; the documents are well produced but lack the unmistakably telegraphic quality of the little writs emanating from the writing office of Willaim Rufus and Henry I. The question we are bound to ask but cannot answer is to what models could this scribe and his fellows have had recourse, and how did he or they become familiar with them? There were no Scottish precedents and the English precedents, though followed in a general way, were not followed slavishly but in some respects ignored or rejected

With the accession of David I there appears to be, not a leap, but a cautious movement forward. His Annandale charter and one of his Swinton charters are evidently in the same hand, unquestionably a 'chancery' cursive of Anglo-Norman type.[63] William Cumin, who served as King David's chancellor from c.1136–1141, is known to have belonged to the household of Geoffrey Rufus who had worked in Henry I's writing office before his elevation to the see of Durham.[64] If the scribe of these charters, dated 1124 x 1135, was not Cumin himself he seems nevertheless to belong to the Anglo-Norman royal tradition rather than to, say, the Honour of Huntingdon or the church of Durham. Taking the surviving written acts of David I as a whole, we must be surprised by the relative lack of authentic 'chancery' hands although there are plenty of good professional ones. No doubt the picture would be very different if the originals survived of the little brieves issued for such establishments as Glasgow Cathedral, Dunfermline Abbey and the cathedral priory of St Andrews.

Professionalism in the service of Malcolm IV – perhaps inherited from the court of his father Earl Henry as much as from that of his grandfather – is typified, indeed dominated, by the highly distinctive, and to my mind highly attractive, hand of an anonymous scribe whom in *RRS*, vol. I, I called 'A'.[65] He was conceivably one of the royal clerks named Richard, just possibly Richard of St Albans, who figures last among the witnesses to a Coldingham brieve one version of which is

---

[62] Dean and Chapter, Durham, Muniments Misc. ch., nos. 557, 558, 561, 562, 759 760, 762. The last five are in the hand responsible for four writs for Durham issued by Henry I of England, D. and C. Durham, 2.1 Reg. 11, 14, 17 and 3.1. Reg. 6 (see P. Chaplais, in *English Historical Review*, lxxv (1960), 262–3). The texts of the seven Scottish royal acts listed above are in Lawrie, *Charters*, nos. 21, 22, 26, 29, 30, 31, 32 (D. and C. Durham numerical order differs from that in Lawrie).

[63] See plates 1(a) and 1(b). (Texts in Lawrie, *Charters*, nos. 54, 101.)

[64] Alan Young, *William Cumin: Border Politics and the Bishopric of Durham 1141–44* (York, Borthwick Papers no. 54, n.d.).

[65] See plate 2.

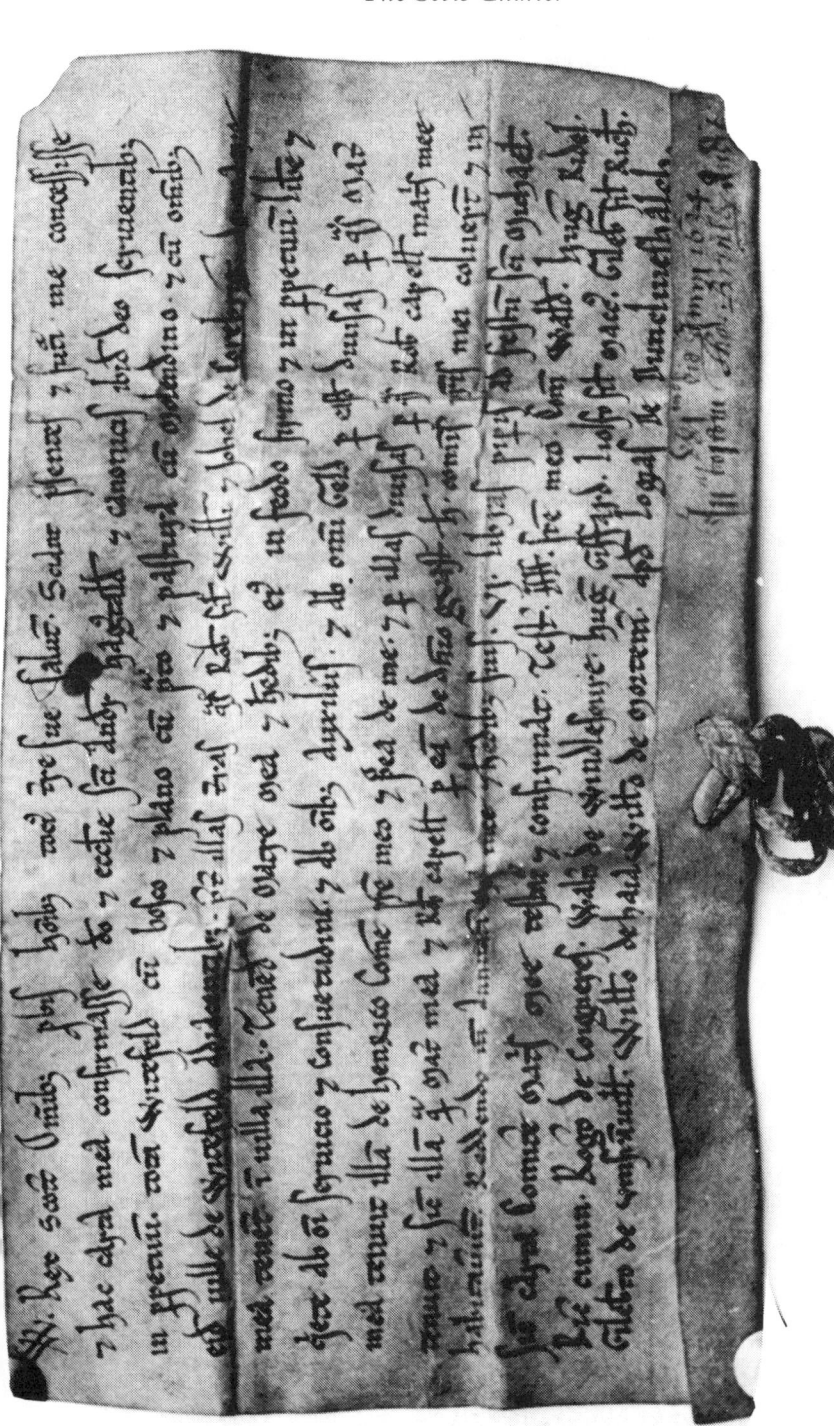

Plate 3. William I for Hexham Priory (J. C. Blackett Ord, Whitfield Hall, Northumberland).

written in this hand.[66] The close Scottish connexions with the Honour of Huntingdon made links between Scotland and the vast diocese of Lincoln easy and inevitable. It is at least worth mentioning that a certain Richard 'of Scotland' appears last among the Lincoln church sureties or witnesses in an agreement made by Alexander the Magnificent, bishop of Lincoln, dating perhaps as late as 1147.[67]

More clerical Richards emerge in the reign of William I and the work of one of them, Richard of Lincoln, may be studied in originals.[68] His career as scribe was relatively long (c.1166–c.1182) and we can hardly fail to be impressed by his high degree of skill and professionalism. It seems to me, I hope not fancifully, that his hand reveals also a strength and consistency of character. Although the point cannot, on present evidence, be proved, it would surely be darkening counsel to ignore the probability that the scribe Richard of Lincoln was the royal clerk named Richard whom the king appointed to the see of Moray in 1187 and who died in 1203.[69] A Lincoln connexion in the diocese is traceable from the time of Richard's successor Brice (1203–22)[70] and seems to have continued in the episcopate of Brice's successor Master Andrew de Moravia (1222–42).[71] Possibly the connexion went back to Bishop Richard's time, although I have not been able to discover any reference to Bishop Richard in the Lincoln records, nor any sign among Lincoln muniments of his strong, simple and unadorned handwriting. Nevertheless, it may be mentioned that Richard brother of 'A. of Lincoln' witnesses his brother's gift of a town house in Lincoln and an oxgate of land to the cathedral, c.1150–60.[72]

The surviving original royal charters of King William's reign (150 all told) show us the work of some eight professional scribes who, like Richard of Lincoln, may be said to have set the standard of Scottish chancery practice.[73] It is surely remarkable that we can fairly confidently put names to five of these scribes and make an educated guess about a sixth. Besides Richard of Lincoln there were Berenger, active from 1173 to 1196,[74] Gervase (1177–1203), who seems to have

---

[66] *RRS*, i, no. 201.

[67] *English Episcopal Acta I, Lincoln 1067–1185*, ed. D. M. Smith (1980), 14 (no. 18).

[68] See plate 3.

[69] *RRS*, ii, 32.

[70] *Registrum Episcopatus Moraviensis*, nos. 45–49.

[71] *Ibid.*, nos. 81 (p. 93), 93; and for the Lincolnshire retainers of Bishop Andrew, Simon of Orby and Simon of Gunby, see G. W. S. Barrow, *The Anglo-Norman Era in Scottish History* (1980), 28.

[72] *Registrum Antiquissimum of the Cathedral Church of Lincoln*, ed. C. W. Foster, ii (Lincoln Record Society, 1933), 20.

[73] *RRS*, ii, 85 ff., scribes Aj, Ba, Bb, Da, Db, Dd, De, Df.

[74] *Ibid.*, 87, scribe Bb. This hand is to be found in a private document witnessed by Berenger 'clerk of the lord king', printed with a facsimile in Historical Manuscripts Commission, *Report on the MSS. of Milne Home of Wedderburn* (1902), 223–4. (The copy in St John's House Library, University of St Andrews has a facsimile of this document).

Plate 4. William I for Kelso and Melrose Abbeys (B. L. Cotton chr. xviii, 17).

transferred to the royal service from the household of Bishop Jocelin of Glasgow,[75] possibly Hugh *de sigillo* (1189–1211),[76] William del Bois [*de Bosco*] (1189–1203), who became chancellor in 1211,[77] and finally and, in terms of output and length of service, most impressively, Gilbert of Stirling (1189–1225).[78] It is noteworthy that of these responsible and senior clerks three – Richard of Lincoln, Hugh *de sigillo* and Gilbert of Stirling – became bishops, and one – William del Bois – became chancellor and archdeacon of Lothian.

In later centuries writing became the ordinary medium of government. The personal written output of kings such as Philip II and James VI, to say nothing of the great ministers of the European states, Matéo Vázquez, the Cecils, Mazarin, Colbert, the duke of Newcastle and so on, was large, in some cases prodigious, yet at the same time taken for granted. We are still a long way from that state of affairs in twelfth-century Scotland. Kings did not put pen to parchment, and even at the close of the century we are only just beginning to see the production of routine governmental documents. Nevertheless we may safely deduce from the surviving corpus of Scottish charters that the principle of government by writing was established by 1214, if not (as I would be prepared to argue) by 1153. By that time, a sealed parchment letter had become the normal device for conveying the king's will in acts intended to have permanent effect, or to be in force for an appreciable period, or to be transmitted over an appreciable distance. Moreover, most of the norms for this letter had been established in the course of the century. These norms stood the test of time, surviving the vicissitudes of wars of independence, prolonged royal minorities and foreign captivities, a reformation of religion, the union of the Crowns of Scotland and England in 1603 and foreign conquest and occupation from 1651 to 1660. In the last decades of the seventeenth century, James VII and William and Mary, by now disguised as sovereigns of Great Britain, France and Ireland by God's grace, nevertheless still addressed the lieges of their 'ancient realm of Scotland' by the time-honoured formula *omnibus probis hominibus totius terre sue*[79] just as David I began to do in the 1120s or '30s.[80]

---

[75] *RRS*, ii, 88–9, scribe Da.
[76] *Ibid.*, 89, scribe Dd.
[77] *Ibia.*, 89–90, scribe De.
[78] *Ibid.*, 90, scribe DF. See Plate 4.
[79] See, e.g., *Charters and other Documents Relating to the City of Glasgow*, ii (1649–1707), ed. J. D. Marwick and R. Renwick (Glasgow: Scottish Burgh Record Society, 1906), 229, no. CLIV (James VII, 1687); 236, no. CLVIII (William and Mary, 1690).
[80] Lawrie, *Charters* nos. 59, 67, 68, 72, 84, 87, 90.

12

The First English Pilgrims to Santiago de Compostela

D. W. Lomax

From the eleventh to the thirteenth century, three historical processes dominated the development of Christian Spain: the Reconquest; the acquisition of Arabic learning and its transmission to the rest of Western Europe; and Europeanisation, that is, the introduction of those ideas and institutions which had developed elsewhere in Christendom during the previous three centuries. Englishmen played a significant role in all three processes, and especially in a major channel of communication between Spain and other Christian countries, that is, the pilgrimages to Santiago de Compostela.

This shrine first seems to have attracted attention when a tomb believed to be that of St James the Greater was discovered in the diocese of Iria Flavia at some date between 818 and 842. Over the tomb was built a succession of ever more splendid churches, to which the headquarters of the diocese were soon transferred although its title was officially changed only in 1095; and pilgrims began to come from elsewhere in Spain and then from other countries. Their numbers grew continually, except for a temporary drop during the Reformation, until the Napoleonic invasions after which the pilgrimages almost came to an end, to be revived on a smaller scale in the twentieth century.[1]

The role of English pilgrims in the middle ages is of unique importance because of the nature of the surviving evidence. Scholars investigating which pilgrims went to Santiago from each country and the circumstances of their visits have to rely mainly on scanty references in chronicles and charters; but thousands of English pilgrims are mentioned in safe-conducts, letters of protection, ships' licences, confirmations of wills, payments of civil servants' salaries, *inquisitiones post mortem* and other documents enrolled in the great series of the Public Records Office. It is to be hoped that the results of Mrs Storrs's exhaustive search for such mentions will eventually be published, as its

---

[1] A. López Ferreiro, *Historia de la Santa Apostólica Metropolitana Iglesia de Santiago de Compostela*, 13 vols. (Santiago de Compostela, 1898–1911); J. Guerra Campos, article 'Santiago' in *Diccionario de historia eclesiástica de España*, 4 vols. (Madrid 1975), iv, 2183–2191; L. Vázquez de Parga, J. M. Lacarra & J. Uría Riu, *Las peregrinaciones a Santiago de Compostela*, 3 vols. (Madrid, 1945–49); R. A. Fletcher *Saint James's Catapult* (Oxford 1984), pp. 53–101; J. Sumption, *Pilgrimage* (London, 1975).

statistical analyses will undoubtedly make a unique contribution to our knowledge of the pilgrimage after 1201.[2]

Before this date, however, it is to the same types of narrative and charter evidence as are available in France or the Empire that we must turn if we are to discover who the first English pilgrims to Santiago were.

Given the enthusiasm of the Anglo-Saxons for pilgrimages to Rome and elsewhere, it is of course likely that many also visited Santiago before 1066 and that some, at least, went by sea. Ever since the Phoenicians the Bay of Biscay had linked Britain and the Iberian Peninsula as much as it had separated them, and despite its storms the sea-route to Santiago was probably safer than the overland routes infested by Moslem slavers and Christian robbers. For the English, Galicia was not the *finis terrae* which it was for Franks or Italians, but simply one of many points on the Continental coast where a skilful captain might land. It is thus likely that many English pilgrims of whom we know nothing visited St James's tomb in the early centuries after its discovery; but who was the first of whom any evidence survives?

A claim can be made for Walter Giffard, lord of Longueville in Normandy, who fought in the great 'crusading' expedition which in August 1064 captured Barbastro from al-Muqtadir, emir of Saragossa. According to Wace, he also visited Santiago and brought back to Normandy a Spanish war-horse on which William the Conqueror rode at Hastings; the horse was a gift to William from a Spanish king, possibly Sancho Ramírez of Aragón (1063–94), for whom the crusaders had conquered Barbastro and who pursued a lifelong policy of making friends and recruiting warriors in Northern France. As one of the victors of Hastings, Giffard was rewarded with many estates, especially in Buckinghamshire, and, if not the first Anglo-Norman known to have made the pilgrimage to Santiago, he was probably the first known pilgrim to have settled in England.[3]

More genuinely English was St Godric of Finchale. Born of a poor Norfolk family soon after Hastings, he became a pedlar, sailor and merchant, sailing round the North Sea and then the Mediterranean. He nurtured his piety on constant reading of the Psalter, his only book, and began to combine his merchant voyages with visits to shrines such as St Andrews, Rome and Jerusalem, until his journeys became purely

---

[2] Constance M. Storrs, 'Jacobean Pilgrims from England from the Early Twelfth to the Late Fifteenth Century' (unpublished M.A. thesis, London, 1964); C. Storrs & F. R. Cordero Carrete, 'Peregrinos ingleses a Santiago en el siglo XIV', *Cuadernos de Estudios Gallegos*, xx, (1965), 193–224; F. R. Cordero Carrete, 'Embarques de peregrinos ingleses a Compostela en los siglos XIV y XV', *ibid.* xvii, (1962), 348–357; G. Hartwell Jones, 'Celtic Britain and the Pilgrim Movement', *Y Cymmrodor*, xxiii, (1912), 1–581, esp. pp. 244–274.

[3] T. A. Archer, 'Giffard of Barbastre', *E.H.R.*, xviii, (1903), 303–305.

religious in nature. Eventually he settled as a hermit at Finchale, near Durham, and lived there for sixty years until his death in 1170. One of his pilgrimages included both Jerusalem and Santiago, and is described by his contemporary biographer as 'Dominicae vexillum crucis in humeris deferens, primo Ierosolimam profectus est, atque in regrediendo Beati Jacobi Apostoli limina adiit'. It clearly occurred before 1110, and probably in 1102, if Godric is to be identified with the 'Gudericus, pirata de regno Angliae' who transported King Baldwin I of Jerusalem from Arsuf to Jaffa on 29 May 1102. It is perhaps appropriate that the first Anglo-Saxon whose pilgrimage to Santiago can be dated should have combined the characteristics of pilgrim, merchant, musician, pirate and saint, and that he should have gone to the shrine not by the land-route frequented by the Anglo-Norman aristocracy but by the sea-ways of his forgotten predecessors. His journey was recorded because he afterwards became a miracle-working hermit, but there must have been many similar pilgrims in an age which saw other Englishmen journeying to the Holy Sepulchre or to Byzantium.[4]

Documentary evidence survives, of course, not of such pilgrims but of wealthy landowners who travelled overland, received hospitality in French religious houses and repaid it with gifts of property in England, which often provided the nuclei of alien priories. Charters recording such gifts occasionally survive in French archives, where a thorough search would no doubt produce a good harvest of names; but from the earliest days only a few are known.

Possibly the earliest was Richard Mauleverer, a Yorkshire landowner who gave a chapel with one carucate of land in Allerton Mauleverer to the Holy Trinity convent in York, itself a priory of Marmoutier near Tours. Then Richard went to Santiago, and on his return stopped at Marmoutier where, in the presence of its abbot, Hulgod (c.1100–1104), he placed the charter of his gift on St Martin's altar. Richard then offered more property; monks were installed in Allerton; and Allerton chapel was turned into a parish church by Archbishop Thomas of York (1109–14).[5]

A Lincolnshire contemporary of Richard was Ansgot de la Haye, who appears in the Lincolnshire Domesday owning the churches of Burwell

---

[4] J. Stevenson ed., *Libellus de vita et miraculis S. Godrici, heremitae de Finchale, auctore Reginaldo monacho Dunelmensi*, Surtees Society 20 (1847), 34; *Alberici Aquensis Historia Hierosolymitana, Liber IX*, cap. ix, in *Recueil des historiens des croisades. Historiens occidentaux, Tome IV*, (Paris, 1879), pp. 595–597.

[5] I am grateful to my good friend, Professor Michel Garcia, for sending me a xerox copy of the original charter, document H 363 in the archives départementales of Indre-et-Loire; this confirms the accuracy of the text printed from a later copy by W. Farrer, ed. *Early Yorkshire Charters*, (Edinburgh, 1915), vol. II, doc. 729. See also *V.C.H. York* III, (London, 1913), pp. 387, 389; and J. H. Round, *Calendar of Documents Preserved in France, 918–1206*, (London 1899), no. 1233.

and Muckton and various properties in nearby villages. He too visited Santiago, and on his return enjoyed exceptional hospitality at Sainte-Marie de la Sauve-Majeure, a monastery founded near Bordeaux about 1077 by St Gerard of Corbie. In return, Ansgot endowed La Sauve with the churches of Burwell, Carleton, Muckton and Walmsgate, a chapel at Authorpe and a bovate of land with a toft in Carleton. Burwell became a priory of La Sauve and remained so until the remarkably late date of 1439. Ansgot's charter, preserved in La Sauve's Great Cartulary, is undated but addressed to Robert Bloët, Bishop of Lincoln (1094–1123), and his pilgrimage may have occurred, therefore, in the late eleventh rather than the early twelfth century.

Ansgot himself lost his lands probably about 1120, but they passed to a relation, Robert de la Haye, and then to Robert's son Ralph, who similarly went to Santiago and enjoyed the hospitality of La Sauve on his way there, being received formally into the benefits of the monastery (presumably prayers and spiritual privileges) by the seventh abbot, Pierre ($c.1126–c.1150$). Ralph's charter, rewarding La Sauve with two bovates of land and other property, is undated, and his pilgrimage can only be assigned, tentatively, to the first decade of Pierre's abbacy.[6]

Burwell may not, however, have been La Sauve's first English property. Hugh of Montgomery, earl of Shrewsbury (1094–1098), and his brother Arnulf gave to La Sauve Quatford church in Shropshire; and Arnulf, alone, gave it the churches of Bytham and Barrow-on-Humber, to pay for woollen shirts for the monks. Lastly, Earl Hugh's seneschal, Gual, granted the church of his Shropshire manor of Worfield, with various tithes, fisheries and other rights, to La Sauve and its second abbot, Achelme-Sanche (1095–1102). These gifts, of which the first two were confirmed by William Rufus, were perhaps the first to be received by La Sauve in England and must presumably have been made in La Sauve itself rather than to any of its monks astray in Shropshire. Although the surviving charters do not mention Santiago, the parallels with those of Ansgot, Ralph and Richard suggest that the most likely reason for the Montgomery brothers to be in La Sauve was that it lay on

---

[6] J. P. Trabut-Cussac, 'Les possessions anglaises de l'abbaye de la Sauve-Majeure: le prieuré de Burwell (Lincolnshire)', *Bulletin philologique-historique du Comité Travaux historiques et scientifiques*, (1957), 137–183, (for a copy of which I thank Dr. G. R. West); C. W. Foster & T. Longley, *The Lincolnshire Domesday and the Lindsey Survey*, (Lincoln, 1924), pp. 175–176. The charters of Ansgot and Ralph survive in the Bibliothèque municipale de Bordeaux, Grand Cartulaire de la Sauve, pp. 298, 462, and are printed, with many mistakes, in E. Martène & U. Durand, *Thesaurus novus anecdotorum*, 5 vols. (Paris, 1717), i, columns 247 and 371.

the main road to Santiago, and that they, and Gual, may have been among the earliest pilgrims from England.[7]

Indisputably a pilgrim was Oliver of Merlimond, chief steward of Hugh de Mortimer, lord of Wigmore. On his return from Santiago in the 1130s, he stayed with the canons of St Victor at Paris, to whom he offered a church which he was building at Shobdon and which was eventually dedicated by Robert de Béthune, Bishop of Hereford (1131–43). Shobdon church is now ruined, but some of its surviving sculptures, like the nearby churches of Kilpeck, Brinsop and Stretton Sugwas, seem to show strong artistic influence from Santiago cathedral and from other churches along the pilgrim roads, such as Parthenay-le-Vieux; and it seems possible that Oliver was accompanied on his pilgrimage by a sculptor who drew various sculptures in the churches which they visited on the way, and then copied them in stone, on their return, for the Herefordshire churches.[8]

About 1145, Waleran de Beaumont, count of Meulan and earl of Worcester (c.1138–66), gave property to Bec Abbey while visiting it on his way to Santiago. No doubt later pilgrims also left charter evidence of their gratitude for hospitality, in the archives of French churches; but almost nothing similar happened in Spain. After emerging from the terrifying gorges where Roland had been slain, relief at entering the hospital of Santa María de Roncesvalles encouraged some pilgrims to endow it with property in their homelands; and perhaps this is how it acquired Charing Cross hospital and St Mary Aylward's church in London. However, though the remainder of the road from Roncesvalles to Santiago was dotted with pilgrim-hostels, monasteries and other churches, an examination of the records of a score of these shows that none seems to have obtained property in England or anywhere else outside Spain, except Santiago cathedral itself, which acquired some hospitals in Italy and Southern France.[9]

---

[7] These charters, except for that of Hugh and Arnulf, which is lost, are in the Grand Cartulaire de la Sauve, pp.460–462, and cited by Round, *op. cit.*, nos. 1234–1236, 1238. The royal charters are listed in *Regesta* i, nos. 410 and 483. The former, Rufus's confirmation of the gift of Quatford, is printed by Martène and Durand, *op. cit.*, i, 260; but its addressee, 'R. episcopo', is presumably not R. Bloët of Lincoln, as all commentators state, but the diocesan of Quatford, Robert de Limesey, bishop of Chester (1086–1117): J. F. A. Mason, 'The Norman earls of Shrewsbury', *Trans. Shropshire Arch. Soc.*, 57 (1961–64), 152–161, and P. A. Barker, 'The Norman castle at Quatford', *ibid.* 37–62.

[8] W. Dugdale, *Monasticon Anglicanum*, 8 vols. (London, 1817–1830), vi, 345; G. Zarnecki, *Later English Romanesque Sculpture, 1140–1210*, (London, 1953), pp. 9–15.

[9] G. H. White, 'The career of Waleran, Count of Meulan and Earl of Worcester (1104–1166)'; *T.R.H.S.*, fourth ser. xvii (1934), 19–48, and L. Delisle, *Recueil des Actes de Henri II* (Paris 1916–17, 3 vols.), Introduction, p. 466. M. I. Ostolaza, *Colección diplomática de Santa María de Roncesvalles*, 1127–1300, (Pamplona, 1978), esp. pp. 36–39. For Santiago's property in France see Ostolaza, doc. 130; López Ferreiro, *op. cit.*, vol. IV, *Apéndice*, doc. LII.

English charters, indeed, are more informative than Spanish ones, which never seem to mention any English pilgrims by name. Robert II, earl of Derby, (c.1139–1159), promised to hand over four bovates of land in Abbot's Bromley to Burton Abbey within fifteen days of returning from Santiago; Emery, son of Audin de Hunmanby, gave three perches of land in Hunmanby to Bardney Abbey, which he visited on his way to Santiago at some date between 1173 and 1184; and William de Roumare, earl of Lincoln (c.1141–1161), returned from Santiago to receive a fief from his brother, Ranulf de Gernons, earl of Chester (1129–1153), presumably sometime between 1141 and 1153. No doubt a systematic search of English cartularies would produce several more early examples.[10]

Chroniclers, too, mention English pilgrims, if of high social status: Hugh of Cyveiliog, son of Ranulf de Gernons and earl of Chester (1162–1174, 1177–1181), returned from Santiago just in time to join the unsuccessful general rebellion of 1173 against Henry II, and to lose, temporarily, his earldom; Patrick, earl of Salisbury, was returning in 1168 from Santiago when he was killed in Poitou by Guy de Lusignan, whose consequent exile led him eventually to become king of Jerusalem; and Henry of Blois, the great bishop of Winchester, visited Rome in 1151 and, fearful of being attacked on his return by Tuscans, Lombards or Burgundians, came back by sea, visiting Santiago on the way.[11] It was an unusual decision, but the voyage occurred precisely after the collapse of the Almoravide empire and before the rise of Almohade sea-power, when most of the Peninsular coast-line was controlled by either Christian monarchs or their Moslem clients, such as Mohammed ibn Mardanish, emir of Murcia and Valencia.

It was this situation of Moslem weakness that gave a great victory to the biggest band of English pilgrims yet to visit Santiago. In May 1147, a fleet of 164 ships left Dartmouth carrying about 13,000 crusaders, mainly English but with strong German and Flemish contingents, with the intention of sailing round Spain to join Louis VII and Conrad III in the Holy Land. They made landfall in Asturias, probably at Gozón, after a difficult crossing of eight days, then sailed round to the Tambre estuary, where they disembarked, to celebrate Whitsunday, on 8 June, at Santiago. From there they went via Oporto to Lisbon, which was still in Moslem hands; but, at the invitation of King Alfonso I, they helped him

[10] M. Jones, 'The charters of Robert II de Ferrers', *Nottingham Medieval Studies*, xxiv (1980), 7–26; G. Wrottesley, 'An Abstract of the Contents of the Burton Cartulary in possession of the Marquis of Anglesey at Beaudesert', *Collections for a History of Staffordshire edited by the William Salt Archaeological Society*, vol. V, part i, (1884), p. 50; Farrer, *op. cit.*, doc. 1192; G. Ormerod, *The History of the County Palatine and City of Chester*, (London, 1819), Vol. I, p. 25.

[11] R. Howlett, ed. *Chronica Roberti de Torigneio*, in *Chronicles of the Reigns of Stephen, Henry II and Richard I*, Vol. IV (London R.S., 1889), pp. 256, 236; M. Chibnall, ed. *The Historia Pontificalis of John of Salisbury*, (London, 1956), pp. 80, 91–94.

to besiege it and to capture it on 24 October. Its capture was immeasurably assisted by the Moroccan civil war, and by the simultaneously Christian attack on Almería; nevertheless, it was a deservedly famous victory, the prototype of the Anglo-Portuguese alliance, and many of the English pilgrim-crusaders forgot Jerusalem and settled at once in Lisbon, where one of their chaplains, Gilbert of Hastings, became the first bishop.[12]

Most of them, of course, were humble seamen like St Godric and their names are unknown to us. Yet similar pilgrims appear as distinguishable, and occasionally named, individuals in the twelfth century, in another type of source, the collections of stories of saints' miracles such as those of St James's hand at Reading Abbey, which mention that Richard de Leurs, a knight of *Wavercurt* near Banbury, twice visited Santiago, the second time with his young son Peter, before 1127. In the miracle collection of St Godric, there is the man from Chester-le-Street, who did not return from Santiago when expected, so that his father assumed that he had died and asked St Godric to pray for his soul; but the saint assured him that his son was even now crossing the Humber and would be home within eight days. In fact, the son covered the distance in seven days, showing that his average walking speed was about twelve miles a day along a good highway. Another pilgrim was the cleric who on 21 March 1170 asked the saint's permission to go to Santiago and suggested, rather callously, that Godric was looking so ill that he was likely to be dead and buried before the pilgrim had returned; but Godric's answer, that he himself was dying but that the cleric would also die on his return journey, came true for he died in Paris on his way back from Santiago. A third northern pilgrim was Eda, daughter of Salerno, a citizen of Durham; she suffered daily attacks of fever for seven years and twice visited Santiago in the hope of cure, but only recovered her health on coming to St Godric's tomb. Finally, a noble lady from the northernmost part of England set out for Santiago with her son, but on arriving at the English coast she became very ill, with all her body swelling, and it was only after she bent a penny and swore immediately to visit St Godric's tomb that she recovered.

These stories show that, as one would expect, some pilgrims went to Santiago specifically seeking a cure for sickness, that they used the normal pilgrim customs such as bending a penny as a sign of a vow, and, above all, that Santiago could be used as an accepted standard of comparison for the powers of other saints. This is true also of stories in other miracle-collections. Ralph of Attenborough suffered from insanity and constant rolling of his head for most of 1200, but seemed

[12] C. W. David, ed. *De expugnatione Lyxbonensi*, (New York, 1936); H. A. R. Gibb, 'English Crusaders in Portugal', in E. Prestage, ed. *Chapters in Anglo-Portuguese Relations*, (Watford, 1935), 1–23.

to recover on setting out for Santiago about 2 February 1201. He was still well on his return, about 12 May, but suffered a relapse in early August and was only finally cured after spending the night of 28 September in vigil by the tomb of the not-yet-canonized Gilbert of Sempringham, in whose canonisation dossier the story survives. Particularly interesting are the phrase for setting out for Santiago, 'accepit baculum ad Sanctum Jacobum', and the hundred days which the pilgrimage lasted. Since the overland distance was at least 1,200 miles in either direction, Ralph must have kept up a pace of twenty-four miles a day, or taken ship to a half-way point such as Bordeaux and walked from there, or, just possibly, walked to Santiago and then sailed back directly from Galicia to England.

In his collection of St Thomas Becket's miracles, Benedict of Peterborough relates how a prophecy was fulfilled that eventually pilgrims would flock to Canterbury as they already did to Santiago, Jerusalem, Rome and Saint-Gilles; and tells how pilgrims crossing the Channel on their way to Santiago prayed for deliverance from storms not to St James but, successfully, to St Thomas. On reaching Sandwich harbour safely, they went to St Thomas's tomb, where many of them offered 'the crosses which, in the English manner, they had intended for St James' – a curious comment which suggests that making *ex-voto* offerings of crosses (but of what material?) at Santiago was a peculiarly English custom, though it seems to have left no trace there. Other stories of St Thomas include that of the Armenian bishop, released miraculously from Moslem captivity, who tried to visit Rome, Cologne and Santiago seeking the appropriate saint to thank, until he found his true goal in Canterbury, and the account of the woman from Cologne, cured of diabolical possession by St Thomas, but instructed to go as a penance for her sins to either Santiago or Rome, a quite early example of Santiago's being the goal of a penitential pilgrimage.[13]

Another Channel storm is to be found among the miracles of St William of Norwich, written about 1172. At some time in the previous quarter of a century, Botilda, wife of Gerard the cook of Norwich cathedral chapter, was crossing the Channel, or 'Norman Sea', on her way back from a pilgrimage to Santiago and Saint-Gilles. St William warned her in a dream that a storm was coming and urged her to persuade all those on board to call on him so that the storm might abate and the sun return; and, of course, everything happened as he had prophesied. Botilda's fellow-pilgrims are not named, but had

---

[13] B. Kemp (see note 18), pp. 18–19; Stevenson, *op. cit.*, pp. 268, 298, 374, 443; R. Foreville, *Un procès de canonisation à l'aube du XIII*ᵉ *siècle (1201–1202). Le livre de saint Gilbert de Sempringham*, (Paris, 1943), pp. 65–67; J. C. Robertson, ed. *Miracula sancti Thomae Cantuariensis, auctore Benedicto, abbate Petriburgensi*, in *Materials for the History of Thomas Becket, Archbishop of Canterbury*, vol. II, (London R.S., 1876), pp. 35–36, 112–113, 273–279, 208–209.

presumably also combined Santiago with Saint-Gilles; and Gerard does not seem to have accompanied his wife, whom other stories depict as a particularly forceful woman and, in that respect at least, no unworthy predecessor of a later Santiago pilgrim, Dame Alison of Bath.

In striking contrast is the vulnerability of another pilgrim, a young man of Gloucester, who set out for Santiago with only five shillings in his purse, and entered St Frideswide's church in Oxford only to have his purse stolen in the crowd of worshippers. He went up to her tomb to make a small offering, discovered his loss, begged St Frideswide for help and at once began to shout aloud that he had lost his purse and to ask everyone if they had seen it. The thief, meanwhile was deprived of his wits, could not find the way out and began to run into the church's walls; eventually he handed over the purse and fled, leaving the young pilgrim earnestly thanking St Frideswide, in whose miracle-collection the story was recorded shortly after 1180.[14]

At the very end of the century, three pilgrims appear in judicial records. Because his brother Walter had killed a man named William, Osmund of Etchilhampton was imprisoned in Salisbury jail, but escaped when the future King John broke into the jail, and went off to Santiago. In Staffordshire, a certain Matilda claimed one third of Wolseley village on the grounds that her husband, William of Wolseley, had died whilst going to Santiago on pilgrimage, and won her case when Reginald de Morton and Ulric de Scopton stated that they had seen his tomb, in late 1200. Finally, there was one Philip Durill, in 1199. However, all three appear in the first series of judicial records which begin at the end of the century and issue in a new age of detailed documentary evidence, into which we shall not enter here.[15]

Looking back on the twelfth century, as well as the pilgrims whom we have seen set out for, even if they did not always reach, Santiago, there were also some who proposed to go, but never did. Henry 'the young king', son of Henry II, asked his father for permission to go on pilgrimage to Santiago in 1176, during one of their frequent quarrels; and, after trying to dissuade him, his father agreed. However, the young king was held up at Porchester by contrary winds and then persuaded by his father to postpone the pilgrimage indefinitely. In the following year, Henry II sent three envoys to Alfonso VIII of Castile and Sancho VI of Navarre to discover their response to the decision he had given, as arbitrator, in their boundary-dispute; but the envoys were also to ask Fernando II of León – 'King of Santiago' as some English

[14] A. Jessop & M. R. James, *The Life and Miracles of St William of Norwich by Thomas of Monmouth*, (Cambridge, 1896), p. 178; *Miracula Sanctae Frideswidae*, in *Acta Sanctorum. Octobris . . . Tomus VIII*, (Brussels, 1853), p. 579.

[15] Record Commission, *Placitorum in domo capitulari Westmonasterii asservatorum abbreviatio. Richard I – Edward II*, (London, 1811), p. 18; *Curia Regis Rolls, Richard I – 2 John*, (London, 1922), p. 151. I take both references from Storrs, *op. cit.*, pp. 54, 82, who also cites Philip Durill as a pilgrim in 1199.

chroniclers call him – to grant Henry letters of safe-conduct for the pilgrimage to Santiago which, he said, he had long proposed to make. However, no trace of this correspondence seems to survive in León, and Henry's motive was perhaps less devotion to St James than a desire, now that he had ventured into the complex world of Iberian politics, to make contact with the one Christian king there with whom he had so far apparently had no relations.[16]

More fruitful was the desire to reach Santiago of Anselm of St Saba, nephew of St Anselm and abbot of Bury St Edmund's (1121–48), who was dissuaded from making the pilgrimage by his monks, perhaps with the help of a letter of Henry I, but who built a church dedicated to St James instead – perhaps the first English example of the commutation of the pilgrimage into some other good work. Moreover, it seems to have been Anselm who first heard from St Hugh of Cluny the story of the pilgrim who castrated himself and was restored to life by Our Lady, and then launched it on its European popularity in the collections of miracles, both of Our Lady and of St James.[17]

In contrast, various authors have claimed that the Empress Matilda did make the pilgrimage to Santiago after her husband, Henry V, died, bringing back a hand of St James which her father, Henry I, then gave to Reading Abbey; and J. S. Stone even gives a detailed description of her entry into Compostela. However, they cite no sources, and the pilgrimage almost certainly never occurred. The hand of St James at Reading Abbey, to which many miracles were ascribed, was certainly given by Henry I, but its previous history has now been traced by Professor Leyser: from Torcello, near Venice, where it had been preserved since about the sixth century, it passed through the hands of Bishop Vitalis of Torcello, Archbishop Adalbert of Hamburg-Bremen (who died in 1072), the Emperors Henry IV and Henry V and the latter's widow Matilda, who brought it to England in 1125 with other imperial treasures. Presumably the story of her pilgrimage to Santiago arose from the assumption that only there could she have obtained a hand of St James, but the assumption was baseless. Even the New Testament lists several disciples named James; and the multiplications, division and subtraction of relics, authentic, dubious and forged, during the early middle ages are sufficient to account for the further confusions.[18]

---

[16] 'John of Brompton', *Chronicon*, in R. Twysden, *Historiae Anglicanae scriptores decem*, (London, 1652), col. 1110; W. Stubbs, ed. *Chronica magistri Rogeri de Houedene*, vol. II, (London R.S., 1869), p. 33.

[17] T. Arnold, ed. *Memorials of the Abbey of St. Edmund at Bury*, (London R.S., 1890–1896), vol. I, p. vii, vol. II, p. 289; R. H. C. Davis, 'The Monks of St. Edmund 1021–1148', *History*, xl (1955), 227–39; E. W. Williamson, *Letters of Osbert of Clare*, (Oxford, 1929), pp. 191–200; *Regesta ii*, 1340.

[18] G. G. King, *The Way of St James*, (New York, 1920), vol. I, p. 108; J. S. Stone, *The Cult of Santiago*, (London, 1927), p. 250–253; L. Vázquez de Parga, *op. cit.*, vol. I,

Yet the significance of Matilda's relic, the miracle-collection to which it gave rise and the Anglo-German argument over its ownership presumably owed something to the popular devotion to St James which the Compostellan pilgrimages encouraged and expressed. This brief examination of some early English pilgrims suggests that that devotion was strong in all social classes (though our sources give the names mainly of aristocrats) and all regions, though with a certain concentration in the midlands and the north-east; but this distribution may merely reflect the documentation so far examined, for it is likely that a further examination of English and French sources, charter, chronicle and hagiographic, would produce more information. This is not, unfortunately, true of Peninsular sources. Yet it is clear that Christian Spain was by no means unknown territory for the English in an age when they provided a queen in Burgos, canons in Salamanca, students in Toledo and, in Pamplona, an archdeacon busily translating the Koran into Latin. In following the pilgrim road to Santiago, as in encouraging Peninsular scholarship, Englishmen of the period to which Ralph Davis has devoted his life's work were laying a sound basis for traditions which would survive until the present day and to which our *homenajeado* would contribute some of his own wide-ranging sympathy, enthusiasm and energy.

p. 59; B. Kemp, 'The Miracles of the Hand of St James', *Berkshire Archaeological Journal*, lxv, (1970), 1–19; K. J. Leyser, 'Frederick Barbarossa, Henry II and the Hand of St James', *English Historical Review*, xc, (1975), 481–506. Stone also mentions (p. 249), a pilgrim in the late twelfth century named Maurice of Barsham, though again without citing any evidence.

13

Prester John and the Three Kings of Cologne

Bernard Hamilton

In the centuries between the rise of the Arab empire and the Mongol invasions people in the Christian West had virtually no contact with Asia beyond Islam. The detailed geographical knowledge of the ancient world was not available to them because Ptolemey's *Geography* was not translated into Latin until 1406,[1] while contemporary arabic works, which were well-informed about further Asia, were not read in the West.[2] Scholars there knew only that beyond Islam lay the vast region of the three Indies.[3]

For more detailed information about these regions they relied on the Latin translation of the pseudo-Callisthenes, the *Alexander Romance*, which gave a fanciful account of Alexander's Indian campaigns,[4] and on the misleading fables of writers like Solinus. Biblical commentators, following Josephus, frequently identified the Phison, one of the four rivers of Paradise, with the Ganges[5] and this led men to associate the East with fabulous wealth, for Genesis records that the Phison 'compasseth the whole land of Havilah, where there is gold: and the gold of that land is good: there is bdellium and the onyx stone'.[6] The Indies were therefore thought of as lands of uncertain location and extent, containing a strange variety of flora and fauna and possessing great natural wealth.

It was also believed that Christians lived there, communities founded by the apostles, who had obeyed the Lord's command and preached the Gospel to every creature. This was known from the apocryphal *Apostolic History* which related that St Bartholomew had evangelized upper India,

---

I am indebted to Professor Giles Constable for allowing me to consult a photocopy of A. A. Vasiliev's unpublished manuscript, 'Prester John. Legend and History', deposited in the Dumbarton Oaks Library, Washington, D.C.

[1] J. H. Parry, *The Age of Reconnaissance* (1963), pp. 9–13.
[2] This was even true of Idrisi's treatise, commissioned by Roger II of Sicily. J. K. Wright, *The Geographical Lore of the Time of the Crusades* (second edn, 1965), pp. 80–2.
[3] *Ibid.*, pp. 272–4.
[4] G. Carey, ed. D. J. A. Ross, *The Medieval Alexander* (1956).
[5] Flavius Josephus, *The Jewish Antiquities*, i, 3, ed. with English trans., H. St.J. Thackeray (Loeb, 1930), *Josephus*, iv, p. 19. The *Glossa Ordinaria* identified Havilah as a region of India, ed *P. L.*, cxiii, 87.
[6] Gen. ii, 11–12. All Biblical quotations are from the A.V.

St Thomas lower India and St Matthew the third India.[7] St Thomas's adventures in particular caught the popular imagination,[8] for they told how, when commissioned by King Gundophorus to build a palace, the apostle had given the money to the poor and had only been saved from execution for misappropriating funds by the timely appearance of the king's dead brother, who complained that whereas he had no palace in Paradise, a splendid one awaited Gundophorus, whereupon the king and many of his subjects were baptised.[9]

Jews were also reputed to live in further Asia, descendants of the Ten Lost Tribes, last recorded as living in 'Halah and Habar by the river of Gozan'.[10] In the late ninth century a certain Eldad ha-Dani, claiming to belong to the lost tribe of Dan, visited the Jews of Kairouan and gave them news of their compatriots. They were, he said, settled in various parts of Asia, some in independent states, but the Levites were cut off from the rest by the river Sambatyon, which was unnavigable, being composed not of water, but of sand and stones. In obedience to the Torah it ceased to flow on the sabbath day, but that was no help to Jews who wished to cross it since they were similarly immobilised by the precepts of the law.[11] In this way the Ten Lost Tribes were added to the list of the marvels of Asia.

Both Jewish and Christian beliefs about Asia were partly true. There was a large Jewish dispersion there, including the state of Khazaria, whose rulers professed Judaism.[12] There was also a huge Nestorian church, whose patriarch lived in Baghdad and numbered among his flock some of the nomad tribes of central Asia,[13] and who also had jurisdiction over the Christians of the Malabar coast of India.[14] Nestorians from Iraq and the Malabar lived in crusader Jerusalem in the twelfth century and the West knew about them from pilgrims who

---

[7] Attributed to the mythical Abdias, bishop of Babylon, but compiled in Gaul in the sixth or seventh century. Ed. J. A. Fabricius, *Acta Apostolorum Apocrypha, Codex Apocryphus Novi Testamenti* (Second edn, 1719), ii, 402–742. Partial translation in M. R. James, *The Apocryphal New Testament* (1924), pp. 462–9.

[8] It remained a favourite subject in medieval art. E.g. G. Kaftal, *Saints in Italian Art. Iconography of the Saints in Tuscan Painting* (1952), cols 970–8.

[9] *Acta Apostolorum Apocrypha, Liber Nonus, De rebus beati Thomae*, ed. Fabricius, *op. cit.*, ii, 687–701.

[10] 2 Kgs., xvii, 6.

[11] A. Neubauer, 'Where are the Ten Tribes?', *Jewish Quarterly Review*, i (1889), 95–114.

[12] A. Koestler, *The Thirteenth Tribe* (1976), pp. 13–121.

[13] E. Tisserant, E. Amann, 'Nestorius. 2. L'Église nestorienne', *D[ictionnaire de] T[hólogie] C[atholique]*, XI, i, 187–218.

[14] L. Brown, *The Indian Christians of St Thomas* (2nd edn, 1982), pp. 65–91; E. Tisserant, *Eastern Christianity in India* (1957), pp. 11–18.

visited the Holy Land,[15] yet no Christian from the Indies is known to have visited the medieval West before 1122.

Odo, abbot of St Rémi at Rheims, was in Rome that year when an Indian archbishop with a Byzantine escort had audience of Pope Calixtus II. The archbishop had first gone to Constantinople to seek help for his church from the Emperor John Comnenus, who sent an ambassador back with him to India; but the ambassador died on the journey, as did the replacement whom John appointed, and so when the archbishop returned to Constantinople for the third time the emperor passed the problem to the pope and sent the archbishop to old Rome. Speaking through an interpreter, the archbishop told the papal court that his people had been converted by St Thomas, whose body was preserved incorrupt in the cathedral. Each year, at his patronal feast, the dead apostle presided at the liturgy, opening his hand to receive the offerings of the faithful, but closing it firmly if a heretic approached him. When the pope forbade the archbishop to tell such lies he solemnly swore that every word of his story was true.[16]

This visit is also recorded in an independent, anonymous source, which, while varying in detail, gives broadly the same account as Abbot Odo. It names the archbishop as John, patriarch of the Indies, and includes a more detailed description of the thaumaturgic shrine of St Thomas. It also relates how through the capital city flow 'the pure waters of the Physon, one of the rivers of Paradise, which gives to the world outside most precious gold and jewels, whence the regions of India are extremely rich. The whole interior of that land is thickly inhabited by devout Christians'. It is possible that the anonymous author invented these picturesque details, but more likely that the archbishop himself, who seems from Odo's more sober account to have had an extravagant turn of phrase, told them in order to enhance the importance of his own people. Misunderstandings were, in any case, likely to have arisen because the archbishop relied on an interpreter, and his interlocutors may well have learned what they wished to know.[17]

John, Patriarch of the Indies, may have been an impostor, or a genuine Nestorian bishop from the Malabar, for if Indian Christians could reach crusader Jerusalem there is no reason why one of them should not have travelled to Constantinople and Rome. Yet, whoever he was, the bishop had given the West a completely unrealistic picture of the size and wealth of the church of the Malabar. His story roused

---

[15] John of Würzburg, *Description of the Holy Land, A.D. 1160–70*, trans. C. W. Wilson, P[alestine] P[ilgrims] T[exts] S[ociety] (1890), p. 69; B. Hamilton, *The Latin Church in the Crusader States. The Secular Church* (1980), pp. 209–10.

[16] Ed. F. Zarncke, 'Der Priester Johannes', *Abh[andlungen der philologisch-historischen Classe der k.] sächs[ische]n [Gesellschaft der Wissenschaften]*, vii (1879), 843–6.

[17] *Ibid.*, pp. 837–43.

great interest, for the fuller, anonymous, account of his visit survives in eleven manuscripts.[18] Like Eldad ha-Dani, he had spoken to the condition of his fellow-believers in the West, telling them that there were powerful Christian communities to the east of Islam, and confirming them in their opinion that the Indies were a land of marvels.

Some twenty years later, in 1145, Otto of Freising, who was collecting materials for a universal history, heard the following story from Hugh, bishop of Jabala in the crusader principality of Antioch. A few years before 'a certain John, king and priest, who lived in the extreme east beyond Armenia and Persia', had captured Ecbatana, capital of the Persian kings called Samiards. He intended to march to Jerusalem, but was prevented by the freezing of the Tigris. John was immensely rich, had a sceptre made from a single emerald, and was said to be of the race of the Magi who had come to worship the infant Christ.[19] This was the first report that the West received of Prester John.

This extraordinary story was based partly on fact. In 1141 the Kara-Khitai, or Black Cathayans, a people subject to the Chinese empire, had attacked the dominions of the Seljuk Sultan Sinjar (the *Samiardi* of Otto), which lay beyond the Oxus, had defeated his army and overrun the country.[20] The ruler of the Kara-Khitai was a pagan, but some of his subjects were Nestorians.

The story of Prester John's emerald sceptre, however, is derived from the Sixth Voyage of Sinbad in the *Arabian Nights* where it forms part of the regalia of the King of Ceylon,[21] but Hugh of Jabala had probably been told the whole story by arabic-speaking merchants who had come to Frankish Antioch to trade, and such details would have formed part of their folklore.

Scholars have long been divided about the origins of Prester John's name. Oppert believed that John was a mistranslation into Syriac of Gur-Khan, title of the ruler of the Kara-Khitai,[22] but this is untenable for Syriac was a written, not a spoken language in the twelfth century, whereas Hugh of Jabala's source was almost certainly oral, so that that particular mistake could not have been made. Vasiliev suggested that the name was chosen as a reference to the Apostle John, who used this

---

[18] *Ibid.*, pp. 831–3.
[19] Otto of Freising, *Chronica, sive historia de duabus civitatibus*, vii, 33, ed. A. Hofmeister, *M.G.H. Scriptores (SS) rerum Germanicarum in usum scholarum* (1912), pp. 365–7.
[20] Abu l-Fida, *Annals*, A. H. 536, extracts ed. with French trans., *R[ecueil des] H[istoriens des] C[roisades], H[istoriens] Or[ientaux]*, i, 25.
[21] E. W. Lane, trans., *The Thousand and One Nights* (1877), iii, 68.
[22] G. Oppert, *Der Presbyter Johannes in Sage und Geschichte* (1864), pp. 134–5.

title in his Epistles,[23] and who was sometimes credited with being deathless.[24] Though attractive, this hypothesis is unsubstantiated, and it seems more probable that Otto of Freising was influenced in his choice of a name for this unknown ruler by memories of Archbishop John of India. Otto connects Prester John with the Magi, who were linked in the minds of some western churchmen with the Apostle Thomas, and Archbishop John was the custodian of St Thomas's shrine.[25]

The connection between St Thomas and the Magi had been formed over the centuries by Biblical commentators. St Matthew's Gospel gives little information about the Magi: 'Behold, there came Wise Men from the East to Jerusalem'.[26] It is not said that there were three of them: commentators inferred this from the gifts which they brought; nor is it said that they were kings, but Tertullian commented that they had fulfilled the prophecy of Psalm 72, 'The kings of Arabia and Saba shall bring gifts to him',[27] an interpretation which he justified on the specious grounds that 'almost the entire east has kings who are Magi'.[28] The Magi thus became the Three Holy Kings and they were later associated with St Thomas. During the Middle Ages a Latin commentary on St Matthew's Gospel was read quite widely in the western church, perhaps because it was ascribed to St John Chrysostom. This related that St Thomas had found the Magi still alive when he came to India and had baptised them.[29] This story may have led Otto of Freising to associate the unknown ruler of the Indies with the Magi and also with the last-known custodian of St Thomas's shrine, Archbishop John.

Otto completed his *History* in 1157.[30] At that time no church in western Europe claimed to have the relics of the Magi and they enjoyed no special cult there, although they were widely represented in the iconography of the Nativity and were liturgically commemorated at Epiphany.[31] But in the following year the Milanese, who were demolishing buildings in the suburbs in readiness for a siege by the forces of Frederick Barbarossa, found, as they were dismantling the

---

[23] Vasiliev, *op. cit.*, p. 114. Although the Greek texts of 2, 3 Jn. begin 'The presbyter to the Elect Lady/Gaius', St Jerome, with whose text Otto would have been familiar, translates these passages 'Senior Electae Dominae/Gaio'.

[24] Cf. Jn. xxi, 22.

[25] Melchizedek, the most famous priest-king in the Christian tradition, is never mentioned in the Prester John sources and seems to have had no influence on the development of the legend.

[26] Mt. ii, 1.

[27] Pss. lxxii, 10; Vulgate, lxxi, 10.

[28] Tertullian, *Adversus Judaeos*, ix, 12, ed. A. Kroymann, *Corpus Christianorum, Series latina*, II, ii (1954), 1367–8.

[29] *Opus Imperfectum in Matthaeum*, ed. [Migne], P[atrologia] G[raeca], lxiii, 638. This cites as its source a *Book of Seth*.

[30] Otto of Freising, *op. cit.*, p.1.

[31] P. Kehrer, *Die heilige drei Könige in Literatur und Kunst* (1908–9), 2 vols.

church of St Eustorgius, three bodies which they recognised 'by manifest signs' to be those of the Magi. This came as a surprise to the priests who served the church and the people of Milan evinced so little interest that the discovery receives no mention in their annals.[32]

Frederick I's attack on Milan marked the beginning of a twenty-year struggle between papacy and empire, and those years saw a growth both in the Prester John legend and in the cult of the Three Kings. Those developments were shaped by the political context in which they occurred, which must therefore be briefly described. Otto of Freising's nephew, Frederick I Barbarossa, had become western emperor in 1152. He had a high conception of his office, based on the revived study of Roman law, and held that imperial authority derived directly from God and that the emperor was the divinely appointed guardian of right secular order in a Christian society. He sought to make his authority a reality in the imperial lands of Germany and Italy. His attempts to control the church there brought him into conflict with the holy see, which had fought strenuously for almost a century to free senior church appointments from lay control; while his attempts to rule Lombardy were resisted by the cities which had become virtually self-governing under his predecessors. When Frederick prepared to invade Italy in 1158 Pope Hadrian IV co-ordinated opposition to him among the Lombard cities, led by Milan, and also allied with the Byzantine Emperor, Manuel Comnenus, and William I of Sicily, both of whom feared an overmighty western empire and were prepared to subsidise the Lombards in their wars against Frederick.

Hadrian IV's death in 1159 led to a papal schism. The pro-imperial cardinals elected Victor IV, while the anti-imperial cardinals elected Alexander III. Since the Election Decree of 1059 provided only for a unanimous choice, it was unclear which of the two candidates was lawful pope. Barbarossa claimed the right to adjudicate, and summoned a synod which endorsed the election of Victor IV, but most of the rest of Europe acknowledged Alexander III. When Victor IV died in 1164 Alexander III was still master-minding the opposition to Frederick, so that no accommodation was possible, and Frederick's chancellor, Rainald of Dassel, archbishop-elect of Cologne, supervised a conclave of the pro-imperial cardinals, which met at Lucca and elected Paschal III as successor to Victor.[33] Yet whereas Victor IV had had some claim to be regarded as legitimate pope, Paschal III was clearly an imperial puppet, whose elevation was an assertion by Frederick and his advisers that the holy see was subordinate to the empire.

Immediately after the election Rainald of Dassel visited Milan, which

[32] William of Newburgh, *Historia rerum Anglicarum*, ii, 8; *The Chronicle of Robert of Torigni*, ed. R. Howlett, *Chronicles of the Reigns of Stephen, Henry II and Richard I*, R.S., 82 (1889), i, 115–6, iv, 199.

[33] P. Munz, *Frederick Barbarossa: a Study in Medieval Politics* (1969), p. 236.

Prester John and the Three Kings of Cologne 183

had submitted to Frederick, where, with the emperor's permission,[34] he impounded certain relics, including 'three bodies which were found in a box in the church of St Eustorgius and which were said to be those of the three Magi'.[35] These relics were solemnly translated to Cologne cathedral on 24 July 1164.[36] This was not primarily intended to increase the prestige of the cathedral, in which Rainald of Dassel customarily showed very little interest,[37] nor was it inspired by reverence for the relics themselves, for they had enjoyed no special cult at Milan: it was a piece of propaganda. The shrine of the Three Holy Kings was intended to become the centre of a cult of Christian kingship, and its establishment in Germany should be seen as part of a conscious design by the emperor and his chancellor to assert the rightful place of kings in the Christian community, a more exalted place than that assigned to them by the emperor's chief opponent, Alexander III. It was not an isolated act: in 1165, when Frederick was keeping Christmas at Aachen, the antipope Paschal III canonized Charlemagne, founder of the western empire.[38] Thus within eighteen months the empire acquired its own pope, subservient to the emperor, and two royal shrines, one in honour of oriental kings, at Cologne, the other in honour of a western ruler, at Aachen.

At about this time the Latin version of a letter written by Prester John to Manuel, ruler of the Romans, began to circulate in western Europe. The addressee was Manuel Comnenus, the Byzantine emperor, and some of the earliest manuscripts include a rubric stating that he had sent a copy of the letter to Frederick I.[39] The letter is not dated, but Alberic of Trois-Fontaines, writing 1232–52, says that it was received in 1165.[40] It was certainly written before 1177[41] and Alberic's date is generally accepted as approximately correct. There are over 100 manuscripts of the Latin version and Zarncke, who produced the standard edition, established the primitive text and identified five later redactions, each incorporating additional material.[42]

The earliest form of the letter gives a description of Prester John's kingdom. He rules over the three Indies, from the far south, where St Thomas is buried, to the Tower of Babel in the desert of Babylon; seventy-two kings are subject to him and when he goes to war 10,000 knights and 100,000 foot march behind each of his twelve jewelled

---

[34] [G.D.] Mansi, [*Sacrorum Conciliorum nova et amplissima collectio*], xxi, 865–6.
[35] *Annales Mediolanenses*, ed. G. H. Pertz, *MGH SS*, xviii, 375.
[36] *Annales Colonienses Maximi*, ad. an. 1164, ed. G. H. Pertz, *MGH SS*, xvii, 779.
[37] Munz, *op. cit.*, p. 239, n. 3.
[38] D[ictionnaire d'] A[rchéologie] C[hrétienne et de] L[iturgie], iii 656–825.
[39] Zarncke, *op. cit., Abh. sächsn.*, vii, 878.
[40] Alberic of Trois Fontaines, *Chronica*, ed. P. Scheffer-Boichorst, *MGH SS*, xxiii, 848–9.
[41] When the pope answered it.
[42] Zarncke, *op. cit., Abh. sächsn.*, vii, pp. 872–908.

crosses. Among his subjects are the Amazons, the Pygmies and the Ten Lost Tribes, all of whom are shut off by the stony river Sambatyon, which was presumably not a barrier to a Christian king who was not sabbath-observant. Through his kingdom flows one of the rivers of Paradise, bringing with it gold and jewels, while among the fauna of the realm are elephants, camels, gryphons and the phoenix. Prester John's palace is an earthly replica of that which St Thomas had built in Paradise for King Gundophorus, and every day 30,000 guests dine at a table made of emerald. The show-piece of the court is a magic mirror, balanced on a series of platforms which would pose considerable construction problems to advanced modern technology. Prester John's subjects are free from vice: not merely do they refrain from adultery and theft, they also abhor avarice and never tell lies. None of his subjects is poor, while even the wild beasts in his kingdom refrain from harming men. The letter ends with a description of the relation between secular and ecclesiastical authority:

Do not be surprised that . . . we do not allow ourselves to be called by a more exalted name than that of Priest. For we have many servants at our court who hold greater offices than we do in the ecclesiastical hierarchy and even higher orders in the sacred ministry. For our steward is a primate and king, our butler an archbishop and king, our chamberlain a bishop and king, our marshal a king and archimandrite, our chief cook a king and an abbot. And therefore we have not allowed ourselves to be called by the same names or to receive the same holy orders as those with whom our court is filled.[43]

All scholars agree that there are sound philological grounds for accepting that the letter has not been translated from an oriental language,[44] but Vasiliev maintained that the Latin text had been translated from a Greek original.[45] This view has received little support since, although the letter is addressed to Manuel Comnenus, no Greek text of it has ever been found. Moreover, Slessarev has pointed out that even the Russian and South Slavonic versions were translated from Latin, although it would have been more natural for Slav scholars to translate a Greek examplar if one had existed.[46] The Greek words found in the Latin text do not weaken this hypothesis, since they are either loan words, or official titles, familiar to western chancery clerks in the twelfth century.[47] Prester John's comment

---

[43] *Ibid.*, pp. 909–24.
[44] R. Hennig, *Terrae Incognitae* (1937), ii, 371.
[45] Vasiliev, *op. cit.*, pp. 90–100.
[46] V. Slessarev, *Prester John, the Letter and the Legend* (1959), pp. 42, 107, n. 28.
[47] *Ibid.*, p. 47.

For although we know that we are mortal, you little Greeks think you are God, but we know that you are only mortal and subject to decay[48]

strongly suggests a western rather than a Byzantine authorship. Finally, the letter appeared at a time when Manuel Comnenus was financing the Lombard communes to fight Frederick I,[49] so that a friendly exchange of letters between the two courts seems unlikely.

Malcolm Letts has shown that almost all the sources used by the author of the letter were available in the west in the 1160s.[50] The most important were the Alexander Romance, the apocryphal Acts of St Thomas, the anonymous account of John of India's visit, Otto of Freising's *Chronicle*, the Vulgate and standard Latin commentaries on it, the works of Solinus and Latin bestiaries and lapidaries. The author also used some Jewish sources, either oral or written, as is seen from his account of the Ten Lost Tribes and from his use of the name Samarkand for the city which classical writers had called Macaranda.[51] Only one phrase in the letter has no known western source: Prester John complains 'we have few horses and they are wretched',[52] which apparently was the only defect in his otherwise perfect kingdom. It was indeed difficult to rear horses in medieval south India[53] and no western European could have had direct knowledge of this in 1165, but Slessarev has pointed out that western merchants trading in the Crusader States could have picked up this information from Muslim contacts.[54]

Yet although there is general agreement that the letter was written in western Europe, the author's motive has not been satisfactorily explained. Olschki maintained that the letter was intended as a criticism of contemporary western society, torn apart by internecine wars, which the author implicitly contrasts with the realm of Prester John where war between Christians does not exist and where, as a result, the people live peaceful and virtuous lives, while the military power of the state can be deployed exclusively against unbelievers.[55] This view has gained wide acceptance and is true in part, but it fails to take account of

---

[48] Zarncke, *op. cit.*, Abh. sächsn., vii, 910.

[49] P. Lamma, *Comneni e Staufer: ricerche sui rapporti fra Bizanzio e l'Occidente nel secolo xii* (1957), ii, 1–161.

[50] M. Letts, 'Prester John: sources and illustrations', *Notes and Queries*, clxxxviii (1945), 178–80, 204–7, 246–8, 266–8; clxxxix (1945), 4–7.

[51] The earliest western writer to use the form Samarkand is Benjamin of Tudela, *Itinerary*, ed. and trans. M. N. Adler (1907), pp. 57, 62, 82. E. Ullendorff, C. F. Beckingham, *The Hebrew Letters of Prester John* (1982), pp. 15–17.

[52] Zarncke, *op. cit.*, Abh. sächsn., vii, 915.

[53] E.g. Marco Polo, *The Description of the World*, trans. A. C. Moule, P. Pelliot (1938), i, 386.

[54] Slessarev, *op. cit.*, pp. 48–9.

[55] L. Olschki, 'Der Brief des Presbyters Johannes', H[istorische] Z[eitschrift], cxliv (1931), 1–14.

the central difference between the world of Prester John and that of Frederick Barbarossa: the Emperor Frederick's wars were fought against the pope and his allies who sought to keep the church free from lay control, whereas in the utopian world of the Indies supreme power in both church and state was vested in the Priest King.

Prester John's kingdom mirrored the kind of empire which Barbarossa was trying to establish. The antipope Paschal III dined at Frederick's table, just as the patriarch of St Thomas did at that of Prester John,[56] while in both empires prelates who held higher offices in the ecclesiastical hierarchy than their respective rulers were subordinate to their authority. Prester John, who was only a priest, had servants who were bishops and abbots, just as Frederick I, who by virtue of his anointing ranked as a deacon,[57] commanded the obedience of the prelates in his empire.

The aim of the author of this letter is to show that Frederick's concept of church-state relations, unlike that of Alexander III, produced harmony in the Christian world, and enabled Christians to unite against the enemies of the faith. It was a subtle piece of propaganda. No educated person had any reason to doubt that Prester John existed, since he is named in Otto of Freising's *Chronicle*: and it therefore followed that if the emperor of the Indies and the emperor of the West shared a common view of the nature of Christian society even though their empires had developed in isolation from each other, this represented an authentic tradition, while Alexander III's assertion that the pope was superior to lay authority was made to appear both eccentric and innovatory.

The pretence that the letter had been sent to Manuel Comnenus was a literary device to explain how it had reached Frederick at a time when no oriental envoys had visited his court. It would seem to have been written in Germany, since the earliest manuscripts are all German,[58] and although the author is unknown there is strong presumptive evidence that Rainald of Dassel commissioned it. He was a noted patron of scholars.[59] As imperial chancellor he played a prominent part in Frederick's struggle against Alexander III. He also supervised the election of the antipope and was responsible for promoting the religious cult of kingship through his translation of the Magi to Cologne. I would suggest that the Prester John letter was a by-product of the need

---

[56] Zarncke, *op. cit.*, *Abh. sächsn.*, vii, 920.

[57] The emperor had never been regarded as a bishop or a priest since he could not celebrate Mass. The theology of his sacred character was formulated in the thirteenth century, but was justified by reference to the *Decretum* of Gratian. In thirteenth-century coronation *ordines* the emperor is regarded as a deacon or sub-deacon, M. Bloch, *The Royal Touch*, trans. J. E. Anderson (1973), p. 117.

[58] Zarncke, *op. cit.*, *Abh. sächsn.*, vii, 947.

[59] F. J. E. Raby, *A History of Secular Latin Poetry in the Middle Ages* (Second edn., 1957), ii, 180–9.

Prester John and the Three Kings of Cologne 187

which Rainald experienced to provide the Three Holy Kings with suitable *Acta*.

Official lives of saints form an integral part in the promotion of any successful cult, but no lives of the Magi existed in the western church before 1164. Under Rainald's patronage they were speedily written, for when Abbot Isingrim visited Cologne four years later he reported that 'the histories relate that [the relics of the Magi] were brought from the east to Constantinople by the Empress Helena'.[60] More details are given by the chronicler of Afflighem, writing before 1189:

> Whoever wishes to know how [the bodies of the Three Kings] were translated from their own country to Constantinople and from Constantinople to Milan will find this in the church of St Peter at Cologne.[61]

By the end of the twelfth century a collection of written legends about the Magi existed in Cologne cathedral[62] which formed the basis for the fullest account of their activities, the *Historia Trium Regum*, written by John of Hildesheim in the early fourteenth century.[63] This gives an explanation of the connection between the Magi and Prester John. John of Hildesheim relates that the Apostle Thomas, when working in India, baptised the Three Kings and subsequently consecrated them all archbishops. They then chose priests and bishops from among their subjects and ordained them and when St Thomas died they appointed a patriarch of the Indies to succeed him. As none of them had a son, they designated a joint-heir and required that he and his successors should be called 'the priest John'.[64] Subsequently the relics of the Kings were found by St Helena while travelling in the east and taken to Constantinople, whence they were translated to Milan by Bishop Eustorgius.[65]

Although the primitive *acta* composed for Rainald of Dassel are no longer extant, the information which John of Hildesheim incorporated in his *History* formed part of the Cologne legend by 1200 and had probably done so from the start. For most of this information was already available in Rainald's lifetime. John of Hildesheim's account of the early life of the Kings is based on the Gospels and on the pseudo-

---

[60] *Annales Isingrimi maiores*, ed. G. H. Pertz, *MGH SS*, xvii, 314.
[61] *Auctarium Affligemense*, ed. G. H. Pertz, *MGH SS*, vi, 405.
[62] Part of this collection is preserved in a manuscript written by a native of Cologne in c. 1200, The Hague, Bibliothèque royale, MS 269, ed. H. J. Floss, *Dreikönigenbuch* (1864), pp. 116–22.
[63] John of Hildesheim claimed to have based his work on French translations made at Acre of books 'caldayce et hebrayce scriptos' brought there from India. See the Latin text ed. C. Horstmann, *The Three Kings of Cologne*, E[arly] E[nglish] T[ext] S[ociety], o.s., 85 (1886), 206–312. The passage about sources is p. 215. An Old French version of this work has been edited by M. Elissagaray, *La Légende des Rois Mages* (1965).
[64] Horstmann, *op. cit.*, cc. 31–4, pp. 255–9.
[65] *Ibid.*, cc. 40–1, pp. 270–5.

Chrysostom commentary on St Matthew,[66] while his description of the subsequent translations of the relics is substantially the same as that which Abbot Isingrim was told in 1168.[67] The connection between Prester John and the Magi had already been made by Otto of Freising, who would have been an obvious source for any German scholar writing about the Kings in the 1160s. This certainly seems to have been an important part of the early version of the legend and one which impressed itself on the minds of western people, for when the Mongols invaded in the thirteenth century not only did some people suppose that they were the forces of Prester John, but some writers imagined that their chief purpose in moving west was to recover the bones of the Three Kings from Cologne.[68]

It therefore seems possible that the scholar whom Rainald of Dassel engaged to write the Life of the Magi also wrote the letter of Prester John. According to the *Life* Prester John traced his origin to the Magi, and the same kinds of information about the Indies were needed for both works. Moreover, both the letter and the *Life* present the same picture of an ideal Christian society in which the church hierarchy is subordinate to the secular ruler.

A memory of Rainald's involvement may be preserved in the colophon found in some thirteenth-century manuscripts of the Prester John letter:

Here ends the book of . . . Prester John that was translated from Greek into Latin by Archbishop Christian of Mainz.[69]

Hennig has shown conclusively that Christian of Mainz had no connection with the letter,[70] but he succeeded Rainald as Frederick I's chancellor, and the colophon may indicate that some people remembered that the letter was associated with an imperial chancellor, even though the wrong one is named.

That Alexander III took the letter seriously is evident from the reply which he wrote to it from Venice on 27 September 1177.[71] Significantly he omits the title 'Priest' and addresses John as 'illustrious and magificent king of the Indies'. Alexander states uncompromisingly that he is the head of the church on earth, and then explains his reasons for writing. Philip, his physician, had been sent on a mission to John and had met some of his subjects who, he discovered, held heretical opinions about some points of doctrine. They had asked to be given a church in Rome and an altar at the Holy Sepulchre in Jerusalem, to

[66] *Ibid.*, cc. 10–31, pp. 226–55.
[67] *Ibid.*, c. 40, pp. 270–3.
[68] *Annales Marbacenses*, ed. R. Wilmans, *MGH SS*, xvii, 174–5.
[69] Zarncke, *op. cit., Abh. sächsn.*, vii, 924.
[70] R. Hennig, 'Neue Forschungen zur Sage des Priester Königs', *Universitas*, (1949).
[71] Zarncke, *op. cit., Abh. sächsn.*, vii, 941–4.

which their clergy might come to be instructed in the Catholic faith. The pope is therefore sending Philip back to John to give him Catholic instruction and to discover what his true wishes are. The pope ends with a veiled reference to Prester John's own letter:

the less you, who are considered to be exalted and great, seem to be puffed up by your riches and power, the more willing we shall be . . . to grant your petitions.

It is often supposed that this letter gives a factual account of Alexander III's attempts to make contact with Prester John. It has been suggested that Philip, the pope's representative, met Nestorian or Ethiopian Christians, perhaps in Jerusalem, and mistook them for subjects of Prester John, thereby inaugurating the negotiations of which this letter forms part.[72] This interpretation is not without difficulties, the chief of which is the total absence of corroborative detail in the pope's letter. It does not say when or where Philip had met Prester John's subjects, nor does it give any details about their doctrinal errors. In this regard the letter differs markedly from other letters written by twelfth-century popes to eastern-rite, Christian rulers in which such information is usually given in considerable detail.[73] It is, moreover, astonishing that a religious mission of this kind should have been entrusted to the pope's physician, who was presumably a layman. Normally such negotiations would have been conducted by a papal legate skilled in theology. The choice of a lay physician for such a purpose is unique in the history of the medieval papacy. It is also worthy of note that no mention is made in any source of the progress of this mission.[74]

It is, however, possible that the pope's letter was written for a quite different reason. When Prester John's letter began to circulate Alexander III was on excellent terms with Manuel Comnenus and would have been able to verify that he had not sent the letter to Frederick I.[75] He may therefore have inferred, just as modern scholars have done, that it was a western forgery. It clearly originated in Barbarossa's circle and implicitly defended the kind of Christian society

---

[72] E. Denison Ross, 'Prester John and the Empire of Ethiopia', in A. P. Newton, ed., *Travel and Travellers in the Middle Ages* (1926), pp. 179–80.

[73] E.g. papal correspondence with the rulers of Cilicia, B. Hamilton, 'The Armenian Church and the Papacy at the Time of the Crusades', *Eastern Churches Review*, x (1978) 61–87.

[74] Nothing is known about Philip the physician apart from this letter, Zarncke, *op. cit.*, *Abh. sächsn.*, vii, 945–6. Alberic of Trois Fontaines, writing in the thirteenth century, tried to regularize Philip's position by stating that the pope had consecrated him a bishop, *op. cit., MGH SS*, xxiii, 853–4, but this receives no support from Alexander's letter.

[75] Lamma, *op. cit.*, ii, 123–43.

which the emperor was trying to implement. The timing of the pope's reply is significant: he waited for twelve years after the publication of the letter until the Peace of Venice had been concluded. On 24 July 1177 Alexander had the satisfaction of seeing the Emperor Frederick prostrate himself before him, disown the antipope and restore the western empire to Alexander's obedience.[76] On 27 September, after the practical details of the Peace had been arranged, Alexander wrote to Prester John, emphasising that the emperor of the Indies, who had shown caesaro-papist tendencies in his letter, had now agreed to be instructed in the truths of the Catholic religion by the only competent authority, St Peter's vicar. Arguably this letter was not written to an eastern Christian prince whom the pope had wrongly identified as Prester John, but to the faithful of the west who had read and been misled by Prester John's letter. Alexander certainly arranged for his own letter to be widely distributed for it survives in a considerable number of copies.[77]

Although the cult of the Three Holy Kings and belief in Prester John may have been deliberately promoted by Rainald of Dassel as propoganda devices to aid Frederick Barbarossa in his struggle against Alexander III, they did not lose their popularity after that conflict had been resolved. Rainald's successor, Archbishop Philip of Cologne, commissioned a shrine for the Kings which is one of the glories of German medieval art[78] and within fifty years of the translation of the relics Cologne vied with Rome, Compostella and Canterbury as one of the principal pilgrimage centres of Western Europe.[79] But the pilgrims who flocked there did not, as Rainald of Dassel had intended they should, see in the Magi exemplars of Christian kingship, but saints versed in occult learning who could protect them against the malefic influences of witchcraft and sorcery, and amulets to defend men against the black arts were blessed at their shrine.[80]

Prester John's fame likewise continued to grow. His popularity was in no way diminished when, in the wake of the Mongol invasions, western missionaries and merchants gained direct access to further Asia

---

[76] M. Pacaut, *Alexandre III. Étude sur la conception du pouvoir pontifical dans sa pensée et dans son oeuvre* (1956), pp. 179–81.

[77] Zarncke, *op. cit., Abh. sächsn.*, vii, 935–8.

[78] H. Schnitzler, P. Bloch, 'Der Meister des Dreikönigschreins, Ausstellungskatalog', in *Achthundert Jahre Verehrung der Heiligen Drei Könige in Köln, 1164–1964* (1964), pp. 413–516.

[79] In the thirteenth century the Inquisition imposed visits to Rome, Compostella, Canterbury and Cologne as a penance for serious offences.

[80] Elissagaray, *op. cit.*, p. 53,

and failed to find the Priest King.[81] Some men supposed that he had withdrawn from the Mongol fury to the unknown land of Ethiopia[82] but that too proved a disappointment when western travellers finally reached it, for although that empire was indeed Christian, its people were backward and barbaric and showed few signs of the wealth and marvels associated with Prester John.[83] Prester John remained popular because he had become part of western mythology, and his letter continued to circulate in increasingly elaborate versions. It was translated into most European languages and also into Hebrew, for the benefit of Jews who wanted to know more about the Ten Lost Tribes and less about Christian Asia.[84]

The Prester John letter and the Life of the Three Holy Kings are like the Fourth Eclogue of Virgil: they may all have been written as imperial propaganda, but they continued to shape the imagination of the western world long after their original purpose had been forgotten.[85]

---

[81] E.g. William of Rubruck identified him with the khan of the Keraits and thought that his fame had been much exaggerated, *The Journey of William of Rubruck to the Eastern Parts of the World, 1253–55*, trans. W. W. Rockhill (Hakluyt Society, 1900), p. 110.

[82] Jordanus Catalani of Sévérac, *Mirabilia Descripta*, ed. with French trans., H. Cordier (1925), pp. 85–6, 119.

[83] C. F. Beckingham, 'The Quest for Prester John', *Bulletin of the John Rylands Library*, lxii (1980), 291–310.

[84] Ullendorff and Beckingham, *op. cit.*

[85] V. Langlois, *La vie en France au moyen âge. III. La connaissance de la nature et du monde* (1927), pp. 44–70.

14

Functions of a Twelfth-Century Shrine: The Miracles of St Frideswide

Henry Mayr-Harting

Large numbers of twelfth-century English men and women visited the burial places of saints, in search of healing or other kinds of help. From some of these places there survive collections of narratives recounting miracles worked at, or in connection with, the shrine; particularly from those of St Ithamar at Rochester, little St William at Norwich, St James the Great (the relic of his hand) at Reading; St Godric at Finchale near Durham, St Frideswide at Oxford, and above all St Thomas Becket at Canterbury.[1] These saints were of various periods and various conditions within the church. What mattered was that in one way or another the body of each (or the formerly imperial relic of the apostle's hand) had become the prize possession of a monastery (in the cases of Rochester, Norwich and Durham a cathedral monastery) which created, publicized and managed the shrine. There were other important shrines, St Albans may serve as an example, which were certainly visited, but from which we lack any miracle collection. In recent years important studies have been made of the surviving collections, especially of the typology of the miracles, the geographical and social catchment areas of their clients, and the attitudes to the supernatural which they evince.[2] But there is still a rich harvest of social history to be reaped from them. It will be impossible, for instance, to write an adequate history of the parish

I should like to thank Paul Hyams and Eric Southworth for some helpful discussion of this paper.

[1] Miracles of St Frideswide, *Acta Sanctorum*, October viii, 568–89 = MF (I have used the printed text, but checked it at certain points against the manuscript, Bodleian Library, MS Digby 177); Denis Bethell, 'The Miracles of St Ithamar', *Analecta Bollandiana*, 89 (1971), 421–37; *Life and Miracles of St William of Norwich*, ed. A. Jessopp and M. R. James (1896) = Jessopp & James; Brian Kemp, 'The Miracles of the Hand of St James', *Berks. Archaeol. Journ.*, 65 (1970), 1–19 = Kemp; *De Vita et Miraculis S. Godrici*, auct. Reginaldo monacho Dunelmensi, ed. J. Stevenson, Surtees Soc., 20 (1845) = M. Godric; *Materials for the History of Thomas Beckett*, ed. J. C. Robertson, (R[olls] S[eries]) vol. 1 (1875, William of Canterbury), vol. 2 (1876) Benedict = MTB.

[2] R. C. Finucane, *Miracles and Pilgrims* (1977), and Benedicta Ward, *Miracles and the Medieval Mind* (1982). For an important study of Norman miracles, see D. Gonthier & Cl. Le Bas, 'Analyse socio-economique de quelques recueils de miracles dans la Normandie du XIe siècle', *Annales de Normandie*, 24 (1974), 3–36.

clergy without extensive use of them, so frequent, interesting and varied are their appearances in such sources. There are overtones, too, in these narratives of the competitiveness which one might associate with expanding economic opportunities: the punishment of a cutler for working on a feast day, or supernatural assistance in the fermentation of beer.[3] Again, even in simple matters of local history and topography they can often be helpful but have sometimes been ignored. No use was made of the Miracles of St Frideswide for the history of Eddington mill in the Berkshire VCH (1924), nor for the history of Binsey in that of Oxfordshire (1979).[4]

In a paper written to honour Professor R. H. C. Davis it seems appropriate to use the Miracles of St Frideswide as an examplar of what can be learned from such narratives about twelfth-century England, considering the light which he has shed on this period; and particularly appropriate to use an Oxford source in view of his own notable contributions to twelfth-century Oxford history. St Frideswide was an eighth-century royal Mercian lady, if she was anyone. It is said that Canon Jenkins preached a sermon on St Frideswide in the 1930s, in the very church where all our miracles occurred, consisting of only four words: 'Saint Frideswide – never existed.' The balance of probability is actually that she did, otherwise it would be difficult to explain how her cult and the richly endowed priory of St Frideswide were already well established in Oxford during Anglo-Saxon times. But William of Malmesbury, around 1120, some four centuries after she was supposed to have lived, was the first to record her legend. It was the legend of a princess and avowed virgin, who, pursued by a royal suitor, struck him blind, took refuge in Oxford, and founded the monastery where she spent the rest of her life.[5] It may be added in parentheses that the later elaboration of this legend which connected the saint with the holy well at Binsey is first found in a mid twelfth-century manuscript *Life* of St Frideswide.[6] It must surely be a response to the one and only challenge which St Frideswide's Priory ever faced to its ownership of Binsey, in 1139, when the townsmen of Oxford claimed it as theirs, probably because they thought it part of Port Meadow.[7]

If one has to admit that St Frideswide left no single reliable fact of her earthly life, she nonetheless made up for it handsomely afterwards. And the decade 1180 to 1190, indeed probably the single year 1180, was

---

[3] MTB, ii, 240, 253.

[4] *V[ictoria] C[ounty] H[istory]*, Berkshire, iv, 193; Oxfordshire iv, 268–71. The holy well features interestingly in MF, 48. My numbers are of paragraphs in the Acta Sanctorum edition.

[5] Sir Frank Stenton, 'St Frideswide and her Times', in his *Preparatory to Anglo-Saxon England*, (1970), pp. 225–28.

[6] Bodleian Library, MS Laud. Misc. 114, fos. 135^v, 136^v, 137^r, a Pershore MS with a collection of saints' *vitae*.

[7] Oxfordshire VCH, iv, 269.

easily the busiest, the most spectacular and the best documented of her whole *posthumous* career. Early in 1180, Prior Philip of the Augustinian Canons of St Frideswide's Priory, translated the putative relics of the saint to a new shrine, or feretory, behind the high altar of his church (now Oxford Cathedral). In the following years, or perhaps months, this galvanized her into many miracles of healing. The prior himself acted as registrar and recorded them in a collection of narratives. He was certainly influenced in all this, if not obsessively as was the author of the Miracles of St Godric, by the shrine of Thomas Becket at Canterbury. His predecessor as prior, the Parisian scholar Master Robert of Cricklade, had taken more than a passing interest in Becket's shrine during the 1170s,[8] and Prior Philip himself, like the monks William and Benedict at Canterbury, drew up his collection with prophecies of the development of the shrine first, followed by miracles of healing.

It is easy to brand, or applaud, the translation as an act of financial entrepreneurship. But lucrative to its owners as was any shrine which drew pilgrims, it also offered a service of cure and comfort in cases of misfortune and sickness. Moreover, alongside the supernatural element perceived in the alleviations and cures reported at these shrines, one should not overlook an important element of practical care for the sick by the custodian communities. There was indeed every inducement to such care, given the element of competition between shrines for clientele and for successful cures. At Reading, as at Oxford, sufferers often remained for some days in the church awaiting a cure or they stayed after it to convalesce.[9] The hospital of St Mary Magdalen at Reading may well have had a function here. Some sufferers would arrive at the church in the crisis of their illness, writhing on the floor, coughing up blood, vomiting all night.[10] The monks of Reading, or the canons of St Frideswide, or their servants, could have spent a great deal of time mopping up after miracles.

Overwhelmingly, the clientele at both Oxford and Reading, mostly drawn from within a radius of forty miles of the shrine, seems to have been composed of knights, townsmen, upper peasants, and their womenfolk. This was a sector of society whose members were especially benefitting from the rising economic prosperity of the mid to late twelfth century.[11] We are told by Donald Sutherland that from this social group came many of the plaintiffs in the early legal assizes of novel disseisin, rank-and-file freemen, some of them, claiming against

---

[8] MTB, ii, 96–101.
[9] MF, 13, 31, 49, 66; Kemp, no. 8.
[10] E.g. MF, 35, 66, 67, 88, 89, 93; Kemp, nos. 2, 20, 24.
[11] See E. Miller, 'England in the twelfth and thirteenth centuries: an economic contrast?', *Econ. Hist. Rev.*, second ser., 24 (1971), 1–14.

their lords.[12] One might see novel disseisin as satisfying the aspirations of freemen and knights to keep their landed property together, and saints' shrines as playing a part in fulfilling the aspirations of similar people to better health.

Health care was a matter of widespread concern in twelfth-century English society, and it is not against this generalization that supernatural and more scientific methods were very closely intertwined with each other. The twelfth century marked an important early stage in the development of a modern positivist approach to medicine, albeit the supernatural or popular approaches by no means collapsed. Twelfth-century men and women could move with fluidity between them. This was a great age for the founding of hospitals. True, twelfth-century hospitals had much broader charitable purposes than simply to care for the sick, as is illustrated by the foundation of St Bartholomew's, Smithfield, which made special provision for the care of children whose mothers had died in childbirth.[13] But there is much evidence that a primary concern of hospitals was to look after the sick. The twelfth century also saw growing numbers of men described in the documentary sources as *medicus*, so much so that it has been seen as the first age of an English medical profession. There may be exaggeration here. It is quite uncertain what this term meant in the twelfth century; probably it had different meanings in different contexts. Most often it must have meant no more than a wise and unscientific village healer.[14] Even when it indicated some knowledge of practical surgery or of medical textbooks, a *medicus*, so designated, was not necessarily a full-time doctor, any more than the Magister Willelmus Poeta who appears in the 1199 Curia Regis Roll is likely to have spent his time doing nothing but writing poetry.[15] Nonetheless, when every salutary caution is borne in mind, we do appear to have the embryonic beginnings of a medical profession in England during the second half of the twelfth century. Talbot and Hammond list 98 doctors for this half century and the number could almost certainly be considerably raised by an exhaustive search amongst charter witness-lists. Most of the 98 seem to be men of substance (three, at least, in Oxford), some are known to have owned medical books, 31 are given the title *magister*

---

[12] D. W. Sutherland, *The Assize of Novel Disseisin*, (1973), pp. 47–50.
[13] E. A. Webb, *The Records of St Bartholomew's Priory (1928)*, i, 385–92.
[14] See Peregrine Horden's salutary but strict review of E. J. Kealey, *Medieval Medicus: a Social History of Anglo-Norman Medicine* (Baltimore, 1981), which in fact has much useful and interesting evidence up to 1154, in EHR, 99 (1984), 411, for cautions about *medici* and hospitals. For village healers still in the seventeenth century, see the penetrating chapters 7 and 8, in Keith Thomas, *Religion and the Decline of Magic* (1971).
[15] *Rotuli Curiae Regis*, ed. F. Palgrave, ii (1835), 89, particularly if he were William of Blois, who became bishop of Lincoln in 1203 (see F. J. E. Raby, *Secular Latin Poetry in the Middle Ages*, ii (1967), 61–63).

(which was not always recorded when it might have been).[16] A *magister* was a person of education and trained intellect, whose medicine, even if secondary in his professional life, was unlikely to have been mere folk healing.

When we read in the miracles, therefore, as we often do, that before visiting a shrine the sufferer had tried every remedy of the doctors, or spent all his money on doctors, to no avail, the kinds of doctor involved might have varied very much from one case to the next. But in general the shrines had their place, now as an alternative, now as an extension, in a pursuit of mental and physical health, whose possibilities were altogether expanding around the year 1180.[17] Many sufferers in their search for health were like those litigants of Henry II's reign who appealed to every possible court, sometimes simultaneously, in the hope of advancing their suit. The legal analogy has much to commend it. The period of the St Frideswide and the Becket miracles is also the high period of Henry II's legal reforms. In some of Becket's miracles, appeal was actually made to the saint, as if to yet another court, during litigation, for example by the horse dealer accused at Richmond-on-Thames of having stolen a horse, who won his case in a judicial duel after praying to the martyr.[18] It is not easy to tell how many of the persons who figure in St Frideswide's miracles were themselves at another time also litigants, partly because of the scarcity of sources until a little later, partly because of the difficulties of identification across the sources, especially in the case of women with common christian names. But Roger Fitz Ralph of Stratton (Wilts.) who fined for a virgate of land in 1199, seems likely to be the knight of that name whose daughter was cured of scrofula at St Frideswide's.[19] While Emma of 'Piritona' (Purton, Wilts.) who suffered from swellings and mental derangement, took fifteen days to reach Oxford, pernoctated for three weeks in the church, vomited, and was cured, may well have been the Emma 'de Peri' who was seeking to recover her chattels from a royal official in 1199.[20]

In one respect St Frideswide's was unusual: females outnumbered males in the recorded cures there by two to one. According to my

[16] C. H. Talbot and E. A. Hammond, *The Medical Practitioners in Medieval England: a Biographical Register* (1965).
[17] In addition to other considerations, the earliest reception of Salernitan medicine into England is now dated to before 1200; see Rodney M. Thomson, 'Liber Marii de Elementis', *Viator*, 3 (1972), 179–89, and B. Lawn, *The Salernitan Questions* (1963), pp. 58–66. This cannot have been a factor in medical care around 1180, therefore, but its reception may be taken as a sign of the times and of a positivist mentality of the last quarter of the twelfth century.
[18] MTB, i, 295; e.g. also i, 276–77.
[19] *Feet of Fines 10 Richard I*, Pipe Roll Soc. 24, no. 198 cf. MF 37.
[20] As at note 15 above, p. 138. 'Piritona' is said in MF, 66 to be not far from the shire of Oxford and must be Purton, Wilts. Emma de Peri appears in the Wiltshire section of the 1199 Curia Regis Roll.

count, out of 99 miracles all of healing, 67 concerned females as against only 32 concerning males. The Miracles of St Godric alone show a similar proportion, but Reginald of Durham knew less or was much less interested in the social and psychological background of his women, at least outside the Durham clientele at Finchale, than was Prior Philip, and so Prior Philip's Miracles have the greater interest for the historian. When we look at these miracles of healing as historians, it is worth putting out of our minds the question of what physically happened; we are too dependent on the perceptions of contemporaries who were only interested in this question at a superficial level to make it a fruitful one for us . My question, as the title of the paper signifies, concerns rather the social function of the shrine and its miracles.

It was natural enough, perhaps, that women should resort to the shrine of a female saint. But equally one could say that there were characteristically female problems, and a shrine with which women felt a particular *rapport* could perform a useful function in society. The most obviously physical problems of women do not, for some reason, figure in the Miracles of St Frideswide. None of the miracles refers to difficulties in childbirth, unlike both the Canterbury and Reading narratives. Perhaps Prior Philip was personally reticent to write about childbirth or menstruation, the details of which certainly did not inhibit Benedict of Canterbury in his generally less female orientated Miracles.[21] But it is a different matter with the psychological difficulties. One sees, for instance, in the Miracles of St Frideswide the perennial dislocations and illnesses caused by sexual problems, compounded for women by their being regarded in that society as inferior to men and having far fewer alternative outlets for their energies and emotions. Amongst those who were cured at St Frideswide's was a woman called Alveva, who had had sexual intercourse and had then gone mad for three years, so that she became an object of horror to her husband and to her neighbours, and, developing homicidal tendencies, was kept in chains until released at her own prayer in order to be taken to St Frideswide's; or another woman called Beatrix (of Elingdon, Wilts.) who had sexual intercourse with her husband and promptly got a headache which lasted for two years; or Helen (of Ludgershall, Wilts.) who had been the concubine of a priest for three months, who was then repudiated by the priest because she ceased to be attractive to him, who suffered horrible internal pains and insomnia, and who came to the shrine contrite and humble; or Cecily, a wife of Chadlington (Oxon.), whose stomach grew immense and who was in great pain, but whom nobody believed to be pregnant until she received a reassuring vision from St Frideswide, and who went afterwards to give thanks and proclaim her debt to the saint at the

[21] *MTB.* i, 226–28, 264–65; ii, 48–49, 136, 143–44, 196, 222–23.

shrine.²² Prior Philip was not intending to write a tract on sexual psychology, but the strains arising in these cases from sexual fear or rebuff are nonetheless obvious.

Several of the disorders cured by St Frideswide were of girls who seem to have been about the age of puberty. The onset of puberty is no doubt always an uneasy time, but in an age when women were socially disparaged by purchase of marriage rights, and when stories were probably legion of girls who fled into vows of virginity to avoid arranged marriages (like that of St Frideswide herself),²³ puberty must have been for many girls a time of almost unbearable anxiety. Some of the stories of these girls show a need for attention and acceptance, very like the *cris de coeur* of attempted suicides. A girl called Mathilda from near Northampton, some 17 years of age, had for six years lost the sight of both eyes and had been spurned by relatives and friends. She came to Oxford, and as the procession for mass in St Frideswide's church on the feast of Pentecost passed her, she wept tears of blood all over her face as if her eyes had been pierced. This happened again during mass (in case anyone had failed to notice it the first time), and yet again at Vespers, after which she could see.²⁴ Here was the playing out of a drama between saint, sufferer and crowd. Mathilda's cure, and the awareness of her cure by the gasping onlookers, were certainly not two separate issues, least of all in the case of a girl who had obviously had difficulty to gain any kind of social acceptance from the time of her puberty.

What part fear of marriage or adult life played in the psychological disturbances, the neuroses, and the sometimes humiliating physical disorders of the St Frideswide female teenagers it is impossible to say in detail for lack of precise evidence on the point; though it occasionally seems fairly explicit, as with the daughter of a clerk of Collingbourne whose father arranged a marriage with a Burghfield man, whereupon she contracted spleen trouble for over two years so that she could hardly work.²⁵ But it is possible to suggest a general reason why the anxieties of marriageable girls should have been intensified in the second half of the twelfth century. On the one hand there was a barrage of literature and sermons increasingly stressing the right of men and women to enter freely into marriage and the necessity to have love within it, thereby raising the level of human and emotional satisfaction

---

[22] MF, 81, 36, 97, 41.

[23] See, for example, *The Life of Christina of Markyate*, ed. C. H. Talbot (1960); or the young woman of Dunwich described by Thomas of Monmouth, Jessopp & James, pp. 79–80; or J. Leclercq, *Monks on Marriage: a Twelfth-century View*, (1982), pp. 41–42, on the French nun Oda of Bonne Espérance (such stories as hers could well have been known and told in England).

[24] MF, 45. Cf. M.E. Hume-Griffiths, *Behind the Veil in Persia and Turkish Arabia*, (1909), p. 162, for the cure of hysterical blindness of a Persian woman. I owe this reference to Patricia Morison.

[25] MF, 76,

expected from marriage.²⁶ The canonists developed (apparently under Pope Alexander III, 1159–81) the possibility of annulling coerced marriages.²⁷ Preachers exhorted husbands and wives to tender affection and to agreement in everything good 'like a pair of eyes'.²⁸ Ailred of Rievaulx (ob. 1167) wrote movingly about friendship in marriage, in his treatise on Spiritual Friendship,²⁹ and it may be supposed that his ideas gained a wide currency since the English Cistercians of the Angevin period had manifold connections with the knightly classes.³⁰ His ideas have an earlier background and also a continuation in the late twelfth-century treatise on Friendship by Peter of Blois.³¹ On the other hand coercion of girls into marriage continued unabated; if anything it was exacerbated by the Angevin system of government as the twelfth century wore on. This is apparent from Magna Carta. Clause 6 is against coercion and social disparagement in marriage, clause 8 against the forcing of widows to remarry. Other evidence points in the same direction as Magna Carta. The citizens of Bristol in 1189–91, for instance, felt it necessary to seek, and they obtained, the liberty for themselves, their sons (this was mainly, but not exclusively a female problem) and daughters and widows to remarry without the licences of their lords.³² Hugh de Plugenet, actually mentioned in the Miracles of St Frideswide, had a niece whose custodian, a royal official called Thomas Fitz Bernard, married her to a certain freeman (cuidam libero homini) of her father's fief.³³ In the *Rotuli de Dominabus* (1185), records of women who could not be married without royal licence, we find the widow of a king's falconer paying to be allowed to marry whom she would.³⁴ The evidence for coercion of widows reflects badly on the attitudes of administrators, custodians, landlords and parents to first marriages; because in most societies where there is marital constraint, choice is freer for a second marriage.³⁵ In the peasant classes there are

²⁶ J. Leclercq, pp. 26–30, 43–45, 58–59. Rosalind and Christopher Brooke, *Popular Religion in the Middle Ages* (1984), pp. 113–14.
²⁷ J. Noonan, 'Marriage in the Middle Ages: power to choose', *Viator*, 4 (1973), 419–43, esp. 432.
²⁸ D. L. d'Avray and M. Tausche, 'Marriage sermons in *ad status* collections of the central Middle Ages', *Archives d'Hist. Doct. et Litt. du Moyen Age*, 47 (1980), 77–80.
²⁹ *Ailredi Rievallensis Opera Omnia*, ed. A. Hoste and C. H. Talbot, Corpus Christianorum, Continuatio Medievalis i (Turnhout, 1971), 298–99.
³⁰ Bennett D. Hill, *English Cistercian Monasteries and their Patrons in the Twelfth Century* (Illinois, 1968), pp. 64–70.
³¹ J. Leclercq, pp. 44–45, and Peter of Blois in *Patrologia Latina* 207, col. 878C, Bk, I, 8.
³² *Earldom of Gloucester Charters*, ed. R. B. Patterson (1973), no. 10, p. 37. Paul Hyams drew my attention to this charter.
³³ *Rotuli de Dominabus*, ed. J. H. Round, *Pipe Roll Society* 35 (1913), p. 29, Cf. MF, 12.
³⁴ Ibid., p. 9.
³⁵ Lucy Mair, *Marriage* (Penguin, 1971), pp. 44–45, 79.

indications that marriage was becoming more subject to formal control by the church courts and no less subject to constraint in the choice of partner, not by lords who merely pocketed their licence money (merchet), but by parents.[36] Indeed, while some canonists were emphasizing free consent in marriage, Vacarius, writing his *Summa de Matrimonio* in England (perhaps in the late 1150s), was emphasizing the contractual character of marriage in which parents and guardians had their proper role.[37]

Here, therefore, lies the problem for England's twelfth-century teenagers, especially the girls: a widening gap between true love as they were led to expect it, and the harsh realities of actual marriage.

The torments of adolescence are perhaps too perennially of the same character to be in themselves of much interest to the historian as a student of change. But when there arises a new means of social control and adaptation, by which these torments may be alleviated or through which they may be refracted, they become of far greater interest. The reader may jib at the word 'new', thinking that recourse to saints' shrines was no new phenomenon around 1180. Around 1180, however, there was something new about the *awareness* in England of the functions which saints' shrines might altogether serve; it is reflected in the fact that the miracle collections of Canterbury, Norwich, Reading, Oxford and Durham/Finchale were all written up in the last three decades of the twelfth century. There is little to match this earlier.

Yet one should not expect miracle collections of the same period to be a historical litmus paper showing up exactly the same social ills and aspirations as each other. There is a characteristic strain of female social misfits in the Miracles of St Frideswide. This strain is not wholly lacking in the Miracles of St William of Norwich, for instance, where poor women also figure. But characteristic of the latter, in so far as the miracles relate to women, is the release from physical suffering of respectable Norwich and East Anglian matrons, women of known family or women married to prosperous citizens: Botilda wife of the monks' cook, from the labours of childbirth; Ida, wife of Eustace, the Norwich moneyer, from knee and shoulder trouble; Alditha, wife of a Norwich chandler, from what looks like arthritis and later from deafness.[38] These miracles were a kind of support system for the Norwich and East Anglian non-Jewish economic establishment. One may doubt whether the different emphases of the miracle collections are

---

[36] Jean Scammell, 'Freedom and Marriage in Medieval England', *Econ. Hist. Rev.* second ser., (1974), 523–37; and Paul Hyams and Paul Brand, 'Seigneurial control of women's marriage', *Past and Present*, 99 (1983), 132.

[37] F. M. Maitland, *Collected Papers*, iii (1911), 101–02, 96.

[38] Jessopp & James, pp. 78–79, 154–55, 147, 217–18, for the examples mentioned. For the economic history of Norwich at this period, James Campbell, *Norwich*, in *Historic Towns*, ed. M. D. Lobel (1975), pp. 9–10 (incidentally showing the desirability of a post as cook).

the result of selection by the registrars, who, it is to be feared, pressed every scrap of 'evidence' into service. It is more likely that they were caused by the known sympathies of the custodian communities attracting various kinds of clientele, rather in the way that the various gifts of different confessors may attract their own kinds of penitent. It should not be supposed that every shrine was an equally satisfactory recipe for all social problems in its region.

One tormented adolescent (puella aetate adulta) of the St Frideswide miracles was Emelina of Eddington (opposite Hungerford on the river Kennet and a St Frideswide's manor). She stole out of her parents' house one night in the autumn of 1179, while the balance of her mind was affected (mentis alienatione percussa), recited an Ave Maria, and threw herself into the river. The current carried her under the wheel of the mill whence she was rescued by the miller (warned in his sleep), who returned her, protesting, to her mother. Gradually she lapsed into a state of hysterical dumbness, and in May 1180 she was brought to the shrine of St Frideswide by her mother and brother. Here she pernoctated for several nights without effect, and she was cured only at the point where her mother lost patience, the cure being achieved in histrionic style with gasping, trembling and stuttering. The bishop of Norwich, who was present at the time, interested himself in her case, and she became a servant of St Frideswide's Priory, 'adhering in body and devotion to the service of her curer.'[39] There are several features of interest in this story: the sympathetic attitude (whatever the official teaching) to attempted suicide, paralleled in the Becket miracles,[40] the impatience of the mother, the outcome for the girl. For Emelina, St Frideswide's shrine offered an alternative authority to the parental. Her cure, moreover, provided her with a secure niche in society at St Frideswide's, where on eleventh-century French analogies revealed by the work of Patricia Morison, the canons might have been glad to show her off.[41] And in decades of marked urban growth, it enabled her to exchange the constraints of the country for the freedoms of town life.

The late twelfth and early thirteenth centuries in England were a period of almost frenetic seeking after liberties, freedoms, privileges; urban liberties, like those of Bristol cited above, freedom from the forest laws, suits of villenage in which men tried to establish that they

---

[39] MF, 31. Cf. Victor Turner and Edith Turner, *Image and Pilgrimage in Christian Culture: Anthropological Perspectives* (1978), p. 30: 'Pilgrimage provides a carefully structured, highly valued route to a liminal world where the ideal is felt to be real, where the tainted social persona may be cleansed and renewed.'

[40] MTB, i, 524.

[41] Patricia Morison, *The Miraculous and French Society c. 950–1100*, (Unpublished Oxford D. Phil. thesis, 1983), which has been altogether stimulating in my work for this paper. See p. 109 for a jester called Witbert after St Faith had replaced his eyeballs.

were freemen.[42] Many of these liberties had to be purchased, from the arbitrary and authoritarian but at the same time financially straitened crown; individuals and communities, however, with their growing prosperity, were happy to pay the money. It is now a commonplace of historians that all this forms an important background to Magna Carta. To see how a saint's shrine could enlarge the area of freedom, not least for women, in this period, one has only to think of Emelina of Eddington, or the wife of John of Chadlington mentioned earlier, who found understanding with nobody but the saint herself, or the woman who visited St Godric's tomb and who was believed to be deceived by evil spirits because she avoided human company when she could.[43] The same point has been made of late antique saints by Peter Brown with fine insight. 'In a society where the bonds of the kin tended to draw closer around the individual', he writes, 'offering protection and control in a less certain world, the saints, as Ambrose pointed out, were the only in-laws that a woman was free to choose. Their shrines offered to half the inhabitants of every late-Roman town respite and protection which they lacked the freedom to find elsewhere.'[44]

The saints, however, were not only a sanctuary and a retreat; their shrines could also influence the position of women when they returned to their own family or community circle, having experienced a cure. I. M. Lewis has pointed out that Somali women often respond with spirit possession to the abuses of neglect and injury in a conjugal relationship which is heavily biased in favour of men. The voices of these possessing spirits, which are disliked but accepted by the men, make heavy demands of clothes, perfume, and exotic dainties from them. The exorcising treatment consists of costly cathartic dances and also demands highly paid therapists. In all this, says Lewis, 'the sick wife is made to feel the centre of attention and her husband may even be constrained to modify his behaviour towards the spouse.' He adds that possessed wives, overcome by an arbitrary affliction for which they cannot be held accountable, are treated with a deference and respect which they would not otherwise be accorded.[45] One need not suppose that all these Somali women are guilty of malingering in order to manipulate their menfolk in this way, and it would be absurd to suppose it of the St Frideswide's women. But it cannot be denied that the effect of many a pilgrimage must have been to elicit a new attention from the husbands of women or the parents of girls, not least in the expenses and disruptions of the journey itself. The narratives frequently say who brought the sufferer; it was not by any means always a

---

[42] For instance, J. C. Holt, *Magna Carta* (1965), c. 3, and P. R. Hyams, *Kings, Lords and Peasants in Medieval England* (1980), c. 13.
[43] M. Godric, c. 40; p. 383.
[44] Peter Brown, *The Cult of Saints* (Chicago, 1981), p. 44.
[45] I. M. Lewis, *Ecstatic Religion* (Penguin, 1971), pp. 73–88.

husband or the parents, but it often was. And for anyone in the social groups concerned, even a twenty or thirty mile journey conveying a mad, disabled, or paralysed person, and a stay at the shrine, might at this period have involved no small financial undertaking.[46] Margaret, the fourteen-year-old daughter of Roger Fitz Ralph of Stratton St Margaret (Wilts.), was so badly affected by scrofula that she could neither walk nor ride and had to be brought to Oxford in a carriage. Once cured (though lest anyone were to forget her previous debility she continued to breath heavily), she defiantly seized the initiative against her parents which she clearly thought that her cure had given her. 'Far be it from me', she said ingratiatingly, 'to return home by carriage. If you want me back, bring me horses (equos).' Maybe this particular young lady overplayed her hand, for Prior Philip adds mysteriously: 'not long afterwards, lest evil should turn her head or deceit enter her soul, she contracted an illness and died.'[47] Be that as it may, Margaret was surely right to recognize that she had a hand to play.

The crowd scenes, reactions and rejoicings, sometimes in the middle of the monastic services, were an integral element of the Oxford cures.[48] My interest in the miracles of St Frideswide has been sharpened by the fine book of a Cambridge authority on Japan, Carmen Blacker's *The Catalpa Bow*. In her study of the healings and exorcisms of the Nichiren sect of Buddhism in Japan, she observes that women are mainly their subjects. Much of her book is about the acquisition by the priests and spirit mediums of a rigorous asceticism which qualified them to identify and cast out the spirits and malignant creatures which caused mental and physical suffering. Their sacred powers were analogous to those of St Frideswide's relics, the relics of one regarded as having been a high ascetic during her life. Dr Blacker sees the Japanese exorcisms as a dramatic therapy of religion where sufferers are helped to bring what is repressed and neglected into the open, to come to terms with themselves and their social situation.[49] All these features have echoes in St Frideswide's. But the discreet dramas of the Japanese temples are a far cry from the responsive, highly strung, milling crowds of twelfth-century Oxford.

In the later twelfth century Oxford was a populous, prosperous and much visited town. It had a Guild Merchant, and guilds of weavers and shoemakers. Its sixty three leading citizens, listed in a charter of 1191,

[46] Patricia Morison comments on the cost of making a journey to a shrine at p. 128. R. Finucane, 'Posthumous miracles of Godric of Finchale', *Trans. Architect Soc. of Durham and Northumberland*, n.s. 3 (1974), 47–50, has shown that the majority of pilgrims in this case were poor and very local; 68% came from within 20 miles of Finchale. But another 20% came from between 20 and 40 miles away.

[47] MF, 37.

[48] E.g. MF, 24, 37, 43 (a cure while the archbishop of Canterbury was celebrating mass, which also shows the ecclesiastical validation of the new shrine), 45, 48, 49, 91.

[49] Carmen Blacker, *The Catalpa Bow* (Cambridge, 1975), esp. c. 15.

included a shoemaker, two goldsmiths and two wine merchants. It was in the forefront of English towns seeking political and municipal liberties for themselves in the twelfth century.[50] The evidence of the 1170s for its schools, which includes a Yorkshireman studying at Oxford, who is mentioned in the Miracles of St Frideswide, suggests that they were already more important at so early a date than Sir Richard Southern would allow.[51] The miracles of St Frideswide occurred at the very time when, as Professor R. H. C. Davis has shown, Oxford's prosperity derived from its position in the trade and navigation of the Thames, must have been at its height, a decline setting in at the turn of the twelfth and thirteenth centuries.[52] There is no difficulty, therefore, to explain all the visitors and their relatives, the tradesmen, the townsmen whether devout or curious, as well as the canons themselves, who formed the crowd at St Frideswide's. It was their acceptance and acclaim of a cure, and of a whole person, which was often all-important. In the moment at which an impoverished widow was cured of her humped back, all present distinctly heard her back creaking into shape again.[53] One need not deny a religious experience here in order to say that, for a widow reduced to begging alms in a society perhaps hard towards such,[54] her cure needed the crowd. It was a not ineffective way of drawing attention to her plight and of gaining for herself a sort of social recognition. The great St Frideswide herself had audibly noticed her.

We would do well always to bear in mind the wise caution of Peter Brown that it is not why men sought cures but what kind of cure satisfied them which is important. 'The history of what constitutes a cure in a given society', he writes, 'is a history of that society's values.'[55] In late twelfth-century Oxford a high value was set on a ritual therapy which brought St Frideswide, the sufferer and the crowd, in a three-cornered relationship, face to face with each other. The power of this therapy lay not only in its effect on the sufferer, but also in its effect on the crowd, and thence again, through their acceptance of the sufferer, on the sufferer himself or herself. Those who suffered physical as well as mental illness were often the subjects of social repudiation in the twelfth century, as in other ages. A ritual for reversing this

---

[50] R. H. C. Davis, 'An Oxford Charter of 1191 and the beginnings of municipal freedom', *Oxoniensia*, 33 (1968), 53–65.

[51] MF, 51, and R. W. Southern in *The History of the University of Oxford*, i, ed. J. I. Catto (1984), 10–16.

[52] R. H. C. Davis, 'The Ford, the River and the City', *Oxoniensia*, 38 (1973), esp. 262–67.

[53] MF, 30.

[54] *Rotuli de Dominabus*, p. 37, shows an example of this with two widows whose husbands had been on the borders of the freeholder and knightly classes.

[55] P. R. L. Brown, 'The rise and function of the Holy Man in Late Antiquity', *Journal of Roman Studies*, 61 (1971), 96.

repudiation was a vital part of many a cure. Ritual may sometimes allow a reversal of an action or an attitude of an individual or a society where the loss of face would be too great without it;[56] and this could be important in a society very ready to categorize, to accuse and to exclude. To perceive the whole social context of someone suffering from physical or mental illness was an essential precondition of a sufferer's acceptance back into society. This kind of perception needed a quality of mind which Prior Philip himself had in a high degree.

---

[56] I have gained this insight, if insight it is here, from the same point made in a very different context by K. J. Leyser, *Rule and Conflict in an Early Medieval Society: Ottonian Saxony* (1979), p. 95.

15

Peter of Blois and the Third Crusade

Sir Richard Southern

I

Bodleian MS. lat. misc. f. 14 offers a unique and suggestive combination of little-known works of Peter of Blois.[1] These are works which so far as they appear at all in the printed editions are separated into four disjointed and chronologically unattached pieces;[2] but the Bodleian manuscript makes it clear that they were originally two works with the single theme of the need for greater urgency and dedication in coming to the aid of the Holy Land. But, though they have a single general purpose, they are the fruits of two personal experiences of Peter of Blois, which impelled him to write. They therefore give us some insight into the problem, which has been much discussed, of the relationship between the rhetoric of the writer and the circumstances and experiences which unleashed his only too copious flow of words. How genuine were the sentiments he expressed? Were his letters actually sent to those whose names appear at the head of the letters? And, if sent, were their texts the same as those which the manuscript collections preserve? These are complicated questions and the small investigation which is the subject of the present paper cannot throw light on more than a corner of the whole web of problems. But, on the whole it will tend to strengthen the view that, though he was perhaps more than any other twelfth-century author a professional writer engaged in the task of putting other men's thoughts into fine words, the thoughts were also his own and arose from experiences connected with identifiable people, places and events.

In the two works with which we are concerned, the events which moved him to write can easily be identified. The first was the arrival at the papal court in Ferrara in October 1187 of the news of the crushing

---

[1] What follows is a revised version of an unpublished paper written around 1937. I offer it to commemorate a friendship which goes back to that time, though I can scarcely hope that it has worn so well.

[2] Pierre de Goussainville, in his edition of Peter of Blois's works which is still the best (reprinted from the second edition, 1677, in Migne's *Patrologia Latina*, vol. 207) printed only no. 1b of the works discussed below. J. A. Giles found the others in English manuscripts and printed them in his *Patres ecclesiae Anglicanae*, 4 vols. 1846–7, whence they were reprinted by Migne.

defeat of the Christian army at the Battle of Hattin which destroyed the Latin kingdom of Jerusalem. The second was the tragic situation of Henry II in 1189, under the relentless military blows administered by his rebellious sons in alliance with the great enemy of the Angevin dynasty, Philip II of France. Peter of Blois was a spectator of both. They made a profound impression on him, and he saw them both as indications of God's judgement on the indifference of western rulers to the real needs of Christendom. In 1187, they had failed to respond to earlier appeals to send help to Jerusalem before it was too late; and, in 1189, they had failed to send help to the survivors of the Latin kingdom, despite the oaths which they had sworn when the news of the disaster at Hattin was still fresh.

II

It will be convenient if we deal with the two works in the order in which they appear in the Bodleian manuscript. Although this is not the chronological order of events, the arrangement has a sound logical basis and should be preserved.

We begin with a brief account of the manuscript.

It is a small, pocket-size book of the mid-thirteenth century, of uncertain origin. The portion which contains the works of Peter of Blois originally formed a separate volume of 60 folios containing two works which, for ease of reference, I shall distinguish into four parts as they are found in Migne's *Patrologia Latina*, volume 207:

1a. f.1 *Dialogus Petri Blesensis Bathoniensis archidiaconi inter regem Henricum secundum et abbatem Bonnevallensem.* (*P.L.*, cols. 975–988)
1b. f.15^v *Conquestio de dilatione vie Ierosolimitane.* (*P.L.*, cols. 1057–1070)
2a. f.27^v *Idem de passione Reginaldi principis Antiochie.* (*P.L.*, cols. 957–976)
2b. f.53^v This is followed in the manuscript without a break by the fragment which is printed as *Exhortatio ad eos qui nec accipiunt nec predicant crucem* (= Letter No. 232, *P.L.*, cols. 529–534).

1a. As the title announces, it is a dialogue between Henry II and an abbot of Bonneval, a Benedictine abbey about fifty miles east of Le Mans. The name of the abbot is not mentioned and it would be unknown to us, but for a charter of Theobald count of Blois in 1188, which names Christian abbot of Bonneval as one of its witnesses.[3] This is all that we know about him, and the question which must first arise is why Peter of Blois should have chosen such an obscure character for a debate with the

---

[3] See *Gallia Christiana*, viii, 1744, 1243–4; and cf. 1234 for a conjecture that he might be the author of sermons in Paris, Bibl. Nat. MS lat 12413. In support of this conjecture, see *Hist. Littéraire de la France*, XIV, 606–7.

king at the most harrowing moment in his life. The most obvious reason, and the one which I believe to be the right one, is that the conversation actually took place, and that Peter of Blois was either present or at least had immediate knowledge of it. This is by no means improbable. Henry II's headquarters of government from July 1188 till his death a year later was in the border country between Normandy and Anjou, with his main centre from 1 February till 12 June 1189 at Le Mans. During most of this time he had Baldwin archbishop of Canterbury in attendance on him with Peter of Blois as one of the most influential of Baldwin's advisers. We know from Giraldus Cambrensis, who like Peter of Blois was with the archbishop of Canterbury during these months, that Henry spent much time conferring with religious men about the situation in which he found himself; and, as Giraldus further says, he often took their advice rather than that of his military advisers.[4] During the months of which Giraldus speaks, the king's position was gloomy but not yet desperate. The homage of the eldest son to the king of France on 18 November 1188 was indeed an act of almost unimaginable folly and betrayal, which aroused Henry's fierce anger, but he seems to have been unable to grasp the magnitude of the disaster or to make effective plans to meet it. He alternated between moods of utter despair and blasphemy, succeeded by hopes that something would turn up to bring a new dawn. As the spring of 1189 turned into summer, Henry became increasingly a hunted and hopeless fugitive, unable to take any action to avert the final calamity from which he was only released by his death on 6 July 1189. During his last two months he could scarcely have had time for conversations of the kind that Giraldus describes in the early months of the year. The period between February and May, when the king still had a solid base at Le Mans, and was supported by Baldwin archbishop of Canterbury, Hugh bishop of Lincoln, and his faithful supporters like William Marshal, would seem to be the most likely time for a conversation of the kind that Peter of Blois describes.

The mood of the conversation in Peter of Blois's *Dialogus* agrees perfectly with this state of affairs. The king is portrayed as bitter and bewildered, but not as hopeless; and the abbot is still able to sketch a future in which the king will regain all that he has lost by emerging as a leader of a great Crusade. Of course, it is not to be imagined that the words which Peter of Blois attributes to either of them are as close to the original as a *reportatio* of a debate in the schools. What he produces is a highly polished literary performance in which the king's words bear perhaps as little relation to any words he can have spoken as Shakespeare's account of Henry V's words at Harfleur or Archbishop Chichele's in London in the same play. But Shakespeare reproduced in splendid words speeches for which he had a historical source, and Peter

[4] Giraldus Cambrensis, *De Principis Instructione, Opera*, R[olls] S[eries], viii, 255–7, 259–60.

of Blois also reproduced in splendid words a conversation of which he had perhaps been an eye-witness or at least in close touch with the participants. The result is a remarkably vivid picture of the king's state of mind, which we know from other sources.

The work starts sharply, without Introduction or Prologue:

Rex: 'Filios enutrivi et exaltavi; ipsi autem spreverunt me.'

This was the thought uppermost in Henry's mind during these months, expressed in the words of Isaiah (1.2): Richard's treachery was at the bottom of all his calamities. Peter of Blois no doubt embellished the king's words – it was his job to embellish – but the king's thoughts are also described by Giraldus:

'Cur ego Christum venerar? Cur illum honorare dignarer qui mihi honorem in terris aufert et per garcionem quendam (ad Francorum id regem referens) me confundi tam ignominiose permittit?'[5]

Peter of Blois is too conscious of the dignity of his subject to be quite as colloquial as this; but in his own way he presents a convincing portrait of the king's anger and frustration at his humiliation, and his need to relieve his despair by cursing the sons who had brought him to such a pass. The abbot naturally attempts to soften the king's anger and tries to persuade him to seek solace in prayer and good works, and more especially in speeding up the preparation for the Crusade. The king's replies show the ready wit which we know he possessed. For instance, when the abbot produced as an example of David's patience his words when he was cursed by Shimei as he fled from his son Absolom: 'Do not kill him for God has sent him to curse me', Henry turned the tables by maintaining that God had sent *him* to curse his sons. And when the abbot argued that anger was wrong, Henry replied that anger was natural, and therefore could not be wrong.[6] Several other details too present a portrait of the king as he was in real life: his extreme pressure of business, his host of petitioners, his promptness in business that interested him, and his long delays when his interests were not engaged.

In the end, the abbot brings the conversation round to the question of the Crusade: it was here that a full remission of sins was readily available even for those who had delayed or neglected earlier penances. The king professes that his greatest desire is to take part in liberating the Holy Land, and the abbot urges him to seek this way of finding peace which has so far eluded him.[7] He then goes on to deplore the long delay

---

[5] *ibid.*
[6] *P.L.*, 207, 977C, 978D–979A, 982 B–C.
[7] *ibid*, 984A

which has left the Holy Sepulchre too long in the hands of infidels. 'Let me,' the abbot continues, 'turn aside to express my anguish in the words of the Prophet of Lamentations' (i.e. of Jeremiah).

1b. The sequence of ideas here demands a passage from Jeremiah and a further expression of the abbot's anguish. The printed text, however, following the only other known manuscript of the Dialogue, stops at this point. But the Bodleian manuscript continues, 'Quis dabit capiti meo aquam et oculis meis fontem lacrimarum et plorabo interfectos populi mei' (Jeremiah 9.1).

This text is followed by a lament on the fall of Jerusalem and the long delay of the Western leaders in going to its relief. A particular object of the lament is Richard's failure to fulfil his Crusading vow and his becoming the chief obstacle and rock of offence. The Emperor and king of France are also criticised for allowing worldly considerations to deter them from their supreme Crusading duty: if they had set out when they made their vows, their success would have been assured; they should have learned from Lucan that 'dilatio magna ruina est'; and even supposing that they had good reasons for delay, they should have used the time in spying out the land, in arranging their route, in laying up stocks of food and arms.[8] All sensible advice, and consistent only with the date of the Dialogue in the early months of 1189, for by May 1189 the Emperor had assembled his army at Regensburg, whence he finally departed on 11 May.[9]

We may be sure, therefore, that by this date or shortly afterwards the whole work, both Dialogue and the Lament which followed, was complete. Yet the manuscript transmission shows that something went wrong. Only the Bodleian manuscript presents the two parts in their integrity; only one other manuscript has the Dialogue; and several others have the Lament without the Dialogue. What went wrong? I suspect it was the death of Henry II which changed the whole scene. There is some reason to think that Peter of Blois intended to dedicate the whole work to him as a trumpet call for the Crusade and a prelude to a new and more glorious period in his reign.[10] But the moment when Henry had died and Richard reigned in his place was an inauspicious time to dwell on the baseness of the king's sons. And, besides, Richard quickly showed his Crusading zeal; so the call which lay at the heart of Peter's work became otiose.

---

[8] *ibid.* 1061A–1065B, 1069B–1070A.

[9] For the date, see *Hist. de Exped. Frederici Imperatoris*, ed. A. Chroust, *M.G.H.*, Scriptores rerum Germanicarum, 1928, N.S., v.17.

[10] The lack of a preface or dedication is puzzling; a small indication that it was intended for Henry II is found in Peter's own list of his writings where he refers to it as *Dialogus meus ad regem Henricum, P.L.*, 207, 1115.

III

2a. We now turn to the second work in the Bodleian manuscript.

Its theme can be briefly sketched. It also was a call to the Crusade, but it was written earlier, under the immediate impact of the news of the battle of Hattin and the capture of the Holy Sepulchre, which reached the West in October-November 1187. As I have already remarked, Peter of Blois was at the papal court when the first news of the fatal battle was brought in letters from the Templars and Hospitallers and from the Genoese. He was there on the business of Baldwin, archbishop of Canterbury, in his dispute with the monks of Canterbury.[11] He had been at the papal court at Verona since June 1187 and he had not been very successful. Then he had ridden with the pope to Ferrara pressing on him the merits of his old friend of student days, Archbishop Baldwin. The pope was still unimpressed and more than ever determined to undo Baldwin's work. Then came the dreadful news of disaster in the Holy Land, and the pope sank under a complication of physical and mental ills, and died on 20 October. Peter scarcely knew whether to be more relieved at the pope's death or distressed at the fate of Jerusalem. The former promised a better turn in the business which had brought him to the curia; the latter gave him a wonderful subject to think about, feel about, and above all write about. The new pope, Gregory VIII, excepted the Canterbury case from his confirmation of the decisions of his predecessor;[12] and Peter, with renewed hope, followed the papal court from Ferrara to Bologna, to Modena, to Parma, and finally to Pisa, where it arrived on 11 December 1187. Peter was still expecting a final decision which would release him to return to England, when the pope unexpectedly died on 17 December. His successor, Clement III, was an old enemy of the archbishop's cause, and Peter must now have waited despondently for a decision which would bring his mission to an end. On 26 January 1188 the pope finally ordered the archbishop to demolish his new buildings.[13] The curia had by this time reached Siena and Peter probably left it there and returned to report his failure.[14] He would have reached England in March 1188.

---

[11] Peter says that he spent eight months at the papal court on this business (*Epistolae Cantuarienses*, ed. W. Stubbs, R.S. (*Chronicles and Memorials of the Reign of Richard I*, vol. 2), no. CCCLV. His arrival at the papal court at Verona early in June 1187 is reported by Gervase of Canterbury (*Opera Historica*, ed. Stubbs, R.S. i, 366). A full eight months would bring him to about the end of January 1188. For his presence at the papal court when the news of the battle of Hattin and the fall of Jerusalem reached it, see *Gesta Regis Henrici secundi Benedicti abbatis*, ed. Stubbs, R.S., ii, 15.

[12] *Epistolae Cantuarienses*, no. CXXXIX.

[13] *ibid.*, no. CXCIII.

[14] The monks of Canterbury who arrived at the papal court in April 1188 reported that, since Peter of Blois had departed, the archbishop had no adequate representation at the court (*ibid.* no. CCXXVIII).

It is against this background that we must imagine him writing his account of what he had heard most dramatically in October 1187 about affairs in the Holy Land, with supplementary bulletins as fresh news reached the papal court. Peter's work begins as a lament, 'I sigh before I eat, and my groans pour forth like water for the fearful thing that has come upon me' (Job, 3,24). While the West has slept, the kingdom of Jerusalem has been destroyed. But, in the midst of all the torpor of the West and the horror and vileness of events in the East, one man has stood out in all the glory of Christian martyrdom. This man was Reginald of Chatillon, pious, dedicated, heroic; the man whom Saladin atrociously slew with his own hand after the battle. This theme is luxuriantly – and, in view of what we know about Reginald, wildly – elaborated as a passion story.[15] Peter writes as if canonization might be expected to follow. The long highly seasoned and extremely detailed narrative leads to further reflections on the torpor of those who had failed and were still failing, at the risk of final damnation, to answer the call for a Crusade. **2b.** Then the author changes his posture and addresses a single prelate urging on him the duty of preaching the Crusade. The terms which are used show that this prelate must have been an archbishop, for Peter urges his obligation to preach more widely than to a single diocese; and, though he does not name him, he can only have been Baldwin, archbishop of Canterbury, Peter's friend and employer. His words speak for themselves:

Tu vero, venerabilis Pater, vide si tuae famae consulas dum crucem nec accipis nec predicas, et injurias Christi turpi silentio et periculoso neglectu dissimulas. Si nunc molestias et labores saluberrimae peregrinationis evadis, scias quod Dei judicium non evadas ... Noveris, amantissime pater, quod ideo vocavit et elegit te Dominus in sacerdotem sibi, ut sis in populo eius doctor et ductor. ... Dicis autem, 'sufficit mihi illis prodesse quibus voluit dominus me praeesse. Numquid ita alligatum aut potius decurtatum est verbum Domini ut ad unius parochiae limites augustetur?'[16]

On this note after much elaboration the treatise ends.

The date of writing can be fixed within fairly narrow limits. The news of the battle of Hattin and death of Reginald had arrived at the papal court in Ferrara on about 17 October 1187, and this is spoken of as a still recent event. But Peter has clearly spent some time collecting information about other events in the Holy Land, and particularly about the life of Reginald of Chatillon, and his sketch of the situation contains one remark about the siege of Tyre which could scarcely have been written before December 1187. The hero of this siege was Conrad marquis of Montferrat, who arrived at Tyre from Constantinople

---

[15] For a modern assessment of Reginald of Chatillon, see Steven Runciman, *History of the Crusades*, i, 1952, 345–52, 436–9, 450, 459–60.
[16] *P.L.*, 207, 532B

about the end of July 1187.[17] He organised the defences, drove off the first attacks, and sustained the full pressure of the siege. This became really serious in November and was finally broken off at the beginning of January 1188. Peter described the siege as prolonged and critical: 'nobilis ille marchio, longa Tyri obsidione atque continua hostium impugnatione vexatus et fame confectus, diutissime occidentalium principum adventum et auxilium expectavit'.[18] Clearly it was not yet known that the siege had been abandoned; but, equally clearly, Peter was writing when the situation of the city – the last stronghold of the Crusaders – was extremely critical. December 1187, or even January 1188, would best fit this state of affairs.

As we have seen, his business at the papal court was concluded on 26 January 1188, and it would accommodate all the known facts if we imagine that Peter returned to England during the next two months, carrying with him his powerful account of the situation with its final exhortation to Archbishop Baldwin to undertake the preaching of the Crusade.

If so, he can scarcely have been pleased to discover when he reached England that he arrived too late. Baldwin had other advisers at home who were quite as persuasive as Peter of Blois – notably Giraldus Cambrensis. When Peter arrived, Baldwin had already taken the Cross on 11 February;[19] and probably he had already set out on just such a widely ranging preaching campaign as Peter recommended – of all places, to Wales, with Giraldus as his chief mentor.[20] Peter had written in vain, and it was left to Giraldus to seize his opportunity and write a description of this preaching mission which would become much more famous than Peter's exhortation, which virtually disappeared. Just a year later, Peter was to try again to stir up – not now the archbishop but the king and other rulers – to hasten the Crusade; and once more he missed his opportunity, this time as a result of the death of Henry II. So he was left with two works on his hands, written in his best style on a subject which deeply engaged his mind and sympathies, but directed at targets which disappeared as soon as his verbal assault had been launched. What could he do with what he had written? To answer this question we must understand his situation.

---

[17] For Conrad of Montferrat and the siege of Tyre, see Runciman, *op. cit.*, 471–2.
[18] *P.L.*, 207, 958B.
[19] Gervase, *op. cit.*, ii, 410.
[20] Giraldus Cambrensis, *Itinerarium Cambriae*, Opera, R.S. vi, 13–14, says that Baldwin was in Wales at Radnor about the beginning of Lent (2 March) 1188; but this is only approximate and Stubbs, *Epistolae Cantuarienses*, p.lxiv, thinks that the true date would be about a week later.

IV

After the death of Henry II, events moved quickly. On 5 August 1189, the archbishop was back at Canterbury presumably with Peter of Blois. Three days later he was at a great assembly at Winchester to meet the new king, whom he crowned in London on 3 September. On 11 December, the king left England on the first stage of his Crusade, and Peter tells us that he went with him.[21] Three months later, on 6 March 1190, the archbishop sailed from Dover, also on the Crusade.[22] He met the king in France, but left him at Marseilles to go straight to the Holy Land, while the king went to Sicily where he lingered for six months. Meanwhile, Archbishop Baldwin arrived outside the besieged town of Acre on 12 October 1190,[23] with Peter of Blois in his party. The last fact is known to us by a lucky chance, to which we will turn as soon as this brief sketch of his movements is completed. The archbishop took a vigorous part in the defence of Acre, but died on 19 or 20 November, six weeks after his arrival.[24] His household must now have dispersed, the majority no doubt returning home. Peter was back in England before the fall of William Longchamp in October 1191. It is very likely that for part of his journey, he travelled with Eleanor, the Queen Mother, who returned from Sicily after Richard had gone on to the Holy Land.[25] For the next few years, Peter found it difficult to settle. He suffered from much illness after his return, and he worked for a succession of employers, Queen Eleanor, Archbishop Hubert Walter of Canterbury, and Archbishop Geoffrey of York; but he went on writing, revising and promoting the circulation of his works. In all this, what happened to his Crusading treatises?

In the first place he revised them. As always, his revisions took the form of correcting errors, making stylistic improvements, adding new quotations and sometimes new facts. All these types of correction are to be found in his revisions of the Bodleian texts. He corrected inaccurate Biblical references, changing 'Timothy' to 'Hebrews', and 'Jeroboam' to 'Zachariah'. Also he deleted his false attribution of the phrase 'dilatio magna ruina est' to Lucan. But more interesting for us, he added

[21] For the date, see *Gesta Regis Henrici Secundi*, ii, 101. For Peter's statement that he left England with the king, see Ep. 87 (*P.L.*, 207, 273A).

[22] Gervase, *op. cit.*, i, 485. The archbishop joined the king at Vézelay on 4 July and they travelled together to Marseilles, where they parted – the archbishop for Tyre, the king for Sicily. (*Gesta Regis Henrici Secundi*, ii, 101–112).

[23] *Epistolae Cantuarienses*, no. CCCXLV.

[24] *Itinerarium Regis Richardi* (*Chronicles and Memorials of the Reign of Richard I*, vol. i, ed. W. Stubbs, R.S.), p. 116; Gervase, *op. cit.* i, 488.

[25] His letter to Longchamp, no. 87, before October 1191, was written after Peter's return. Longchamp was already in the difficulties which led to his fall, but Peter writes as if he has been back for some time and has now joined, or rejoined, Queen Eleanor in Normandy. For Eleanor's movements, see *Chronica Rogeri de Hoveden*, ed. Stubbs, R.S., iii, 100, 179.

sentences to the *Passio Reginaldi* which proved that he was in Acre with Archbishop Baldwin in October–November 1190. This becomes clear when we compare two passages in the Bodleian text with the later revision. Here are the passages with the later additions in italics. After describing the death of Reginald of Chatillon, he writes:

Circa verba principis nihil prorsus immuto, sed in illa simplicitate qua domino papae et multis qui tunc aderant relata et scripta sunt *tandemque a fratre regis Hierosolymitani, qui ibidem captus est, Cantuarensi archiepiscopo et nobis qui pariter aderamus vivae vocis officio apertius declarata*, eadem memoriae et scripturae commendo.

And in another passage, he records the same facts with a similar later addition:

Referebat nobis frater regis Hierosolymitani qui cum cruce captus est; Referebant *etiam* fratres Hospitalis et Templi . . .[26]

From this it is clear that in the first recension Peter had heard what he recorded from the Hospitallers and Templars in the presence of the pope; and in the second he had also heard the same story from the brother of the king of Jerusalem in the presence of the archbishop of Canterbury.

There is no problem about the first recension. We know all about the reports of the Hospitallers and Templars which reached the papal court when Peter was present in October 1187. But what about the later incident when he heard the brother of the king of Jerusalem tell the same story to the archbishop of Canterbury? For this we have no direct testimony apart from Peter's own addition to his earlier text, but the circumstances can be reconstructed with complete confidence. The brother of Guy king of Jerusalem who is referred to here was Amalric the Constable, who was captured at Hattin. He was held in captivity with his brother the king until June 1188. Then they both went to Antioch, and from Antioch to Tyre. From Tyre, King Guy went to lay siege to Acre in August 1189, and Amalric was a witness of his charters throughout the whole period of this siege.[27] Archbishop Baldwin was present at the siege from October to November 1190. We have only to infer that Peter was with him, as he had been on so many occasions, and the chain of evidence is complete. Having left England with the king, Peter must have joined the archbishop's party in France and sailed with him from Marseilles and so to Acre.

[26] The original version of these two passages is in Bodley MS. lat. misc. f. 14, ff. 43 and 34 verso. The revised version in *P.L.*, 207, 969A, 962C.

[27] For the presence of King Guy of Jerusalem and his two brothers at the siege of Acre, see Radulfus de Diceto, *Opera Historica*, R.S., ii, 80.

V

Although Peter revised the text of his Crusading treatises, the only part of them which he succeeded in putting into circulation was the lament and exhortation which followed the Dialogue between King Henry and the abbot of Bonneval. He must almost at once have separated the two parts of the work, and from about 1189 onwards the final lament and exhortation begins to appear in some copies of his letter collection, either as a letter addressed to two archdeacons or as a treatise without address.[28] The *Passio Reginaldi* followed by its exhortation, which in Giles and in Migne is printed as a separate letter, circulated in a few manuscripts of Peter's works in the late Middle Ages.[29] The Dialogue alone fell into complete neglect: a strange fate for the most interesting of all these works – killed, one may suppose, by the death of the king and the succession of Richard, the main object of his curses. But they were all failures. Peter deserved better success for works on which he had expended much energy, on a subject which for a few years at least lay close to his heart.

I began these remarks by saying that these works had a common theme in advocating the need for a Crusade. It can now be added that the two works had the same structure: in each, a historical incident was elaborately described, and this was followed by a lament on the negligence of the West in failing to go on Crusade, and an exhortation to vigorous effect. They were complementary in the audiences to which they were addressed: the *Dialogue* and its appendix dealt with the disunity of princes, and appealed to them for unity in the great cause; the *Passio Reginaldi* exhibited a martyr-hero in action, and appealed to a prelate to preach to the people. The one is more secular, the other more spiritual. The former was probably intended for Henry II; the latter was certainly intended for Archbishop Baldwin. Indeed it seems quite

---

[28] As a letter it is always addressed to two archdeacons, but not always to the same ones. In MSS. Bodley 759 and B.L. Arundel 227, they are named Savaricus and Gaufridus. In MS. Bodley 570 they are Guido and Gol(fridus). Savaricus is identifiable as archdeacon of Northampton in the diocese of Lincoln *c*. 1175–1192, when he became bishop of Bath and Wells. It is hard to see why a letter should be jointly addressed to two archdeacons unless they were close associates, but there is no archdeacon Geoffrey in the diocese of Lincoln at this time. In other MSS. of the letters it appears without any address; and, with or without the address, its usual title is *Tractatus de Ierosolimitana peregrinatione* or *Conquestio super nimis dilatione Ierosolimitani itineris*. All forms have considerable additions to the primitive form in Bodl. lat. misc. f. 14. But in all forms it shows several signs of uncertainty of purpose towards the end.

[29] It is found in MSS. B.L. Arundel 227, New College, Oxford, 127, and Erfurt, Amplonius F.71 – all of them late manuscripts which show signs of going behind the normal letter collections to some primitive stock of Peter's writings.

possible that Peter looked on them as letters to these patrons.[30] If so, they would have been the most extensive and artistically elaborate of all his letters.

The 'open letter', addressed to a real person on a distinct occasion for a distinct purpose, but with an eye to a wider public, was the literary form for which Peter's special talents were best adapted. He is a king among medieval practitioners of this art: his stylistic accomplishment, his instinctive response to the circumstances in which people found themselves, and his great stock of general images and precepts which he could deploy for every occasion, all helped to give him his renown. All these elements were present in these two works, and they might have been among his greatest successes. Their failure was caused by adverse circumstances. For success they needed to be launched at the right moment; and the moment passed before they could be delivered. When they are put together again in their original context, they gain in stature and show how the embroidery of rhetoric enhanced events which deeply moved him and turned them into works of art with – as he vainly hoped – a practical purpose.

---

[30] Curiously, each, on a single occasion and in a similar context, is called an *epistola*: in the Passio Reginaldi, (col. 966A) 'Saladinus, cuius funesto et damnato nomine invitus et dolens hanc epistolam contamino'; and in the lament which followed the Dialogus (col. 1063C) 'ille filius perditionis (Saladinus), cuius nomine presentem nolo epistolam funestare'.

16

Magna Carta and the Common Pleas

M. T. Clanchy

Clause 17 of Magna Carta rules that 'common pleas shall not follow our court, but shall be held in some certain place (*communia placita non sequantur curiam nostram, set teneantur in aliquo loco certo*)'.[1] What were common pleas? Why, and for how long, had they followed the king's court? Was some action of King John's the cause of this grievance? Did 'some certain place' refer to the court of the Bench at Westminster? In that case why did the drafters of Magna Carta not say so, if not in 1215 at least in the revisions of 1216, 1217, or 1225? What was the relationship of this clause to clause 18, which rules that assizes of novel disseisin, mort d'ancestor and darrein presentment are to be taken in the county courts? Were these assizes included in the category of common pleas? Had they also followed the king's court? Historians' answers to such questions as these have been varied and inconclusive. Indeed, they could not be satisfactorily answered until recently because the whereabouts of court sessions in John's reign had not been pinpointed and the principal judicial institution of Henry III's reign, the eyre for the common pleas, was not understood.

In the seventeenth century, clause 17 was interpreted so narrowly that 'some certain place' was understood to refer to the particular part of Westminster Hall where the justices' bench was placed. This was immediately by the great door. When it was proposed after the Restoration in 1660 to move the bench away from the draught, Orlando Bridgman, Chief Justice of the Common Pleas, objected that it would be contrary to Magna Carta to move it even 'the distance of an inch'.[2] The term 'Court of Common Pleas' is anachronistic. The court was called the 'Bench' in the thirteenth century and thereafter it was known also as the 'Common Place'. The latter description evoked clause 17 in its assonance; in law-French it was *le comen place* where *les communs ples* were pleaded.[3] In their descriptions of England's ancient institutions the Elizabethans,

---

[1] J. C. Holt, *Magna Carta* (Cambridge, 1965), p. 322. Throughout this article I am grateful to Dr Paul Brand for his comments. He is not responsible for the views expressed, nor for any errors which remain.
[2] Roger North, *Lives of the Norths* (London, 1826), i, 199.
[3] Examples of *comen place* in *Cases in the Exchequer Chamber*, ed. M. Hemmant (Selden Society [SS henceforward], li, 1933) indexed at p. 206.

Thomas Smith and William Lambarde, praised this 'standing place' of justice fixed at Westminster by Magna Carta.[4] Clause 17 continued to validate the existence of the court until its jurisdiction in common pleas was amalgamated with that of the new High Court in 1873 and clause 17 was at last repealed in 1879. Nineteenth-century law reform opened the way for Magna Carta to be interpreted as an historical document and no longer as a legally binding statute.

Twentieth-century scholarship has aimed to strip away anachronistic overlays, interesting though they are for later legal history, in order to reveal what the original makers of Magna Carta had in mind. Clause 17 has proved resistant to this treatment. Although D. M. Stenton pointed out in 1953 that 'it was a later generation which equated *in aliquo loco certo* with *apud Westmonasterium*',[5] historians continue to follow Tudor and Stuart tradition, as three books published in 1973 demonstrate. The 'fixed seat at Westminster' of the justices of the Bench 'was one of the stipulations of Magna Carta', writes R. C. van Caenegem in *The Birth of the English Common Law*.[6] In *The Law Courts of Medieval England*, A. Harding cites clause 17 and explains that 'the establishment of the Court of Common Pleas, and of Westminster as the headquarters of the legal profession, answered the interests of the class of greater barons'.[7] In *The Assize of Novel Disseisin*, D. W. Sutherland agrees that 'the Common Bench was missed and King John had to promise in Magna Carta that he would restore this "fixed place"'.[8] In fact, however, in the decades following Magna Carta there was no permanent court at Westminster, nor was the term 'common pleas' applied at first to proceedings there but to the justices' eyres (that is, visitations) in the counties. The makers of Magna Carta did not intend to confine the hearing of common pleas to Westminster but to provide justice throughout the realm. A proper understanding of clause 17 clarifies their intentions as well as showing how the courts worked at the time of Magna Carta.

The Meaning of 'Common Pleas'

The term 'common pleas' rarely occurs before Magna Carta. Glanvill's lawbook divides pleas into criminal and civil, not common and

---

[4] *De Republica Anglorum*, ed. M. Dewar (Cambridge, 1982), ch. 10, p. 91. *Archeion* ed. C. H. McIlwain and P. L. Ward (Cambridge, Mass., 1957), p. 26. For the later history of clause 17 see: W. Blackstone, *Commentaries*, bk. iii, ch. 4, ed. E. Christian, 17th edition (London, 1830), iii, p. 38; F. Thompson, *Magna Carta: its Role in the Making of the Constitution* (Minnesota, 1948), pp. 200–3; A. Pallister, *Magna Carta: the Heritage of Liberty* (Oxford, 1971), p. 97.

[5] *Pleas before the King or his Justices*, i. (SS, lxvii, 1948), p. 3. See also *The Earliest Lincs. Assize Rolls* (Lincoln Record Soc., xxii, 1926), p. xviii.

[6] (Cambridge, 1973), p. 22.

[7] (London, 1973), p. 76.

[8] (Oxford, 1973), p. 60.

uncommon. The pipe rolls, which exist in a continuous series from 1156, refer to many sorts of plea, but only once do they mention 'common' ones: in 1180 the burgesses of Leicester owe 80 marks to be 'quit of murders and common pleas in this justices' eyre'.[9] I have not been able to find any other references to common pleas in the indexes to royal records before 1215. There probably are a few grants of quittance from common pleas recorded in monastic cartularies, but they are scattered and too poorly indexed to search systematically. The *Dictionary of Medieval Latin from British Sources* gives one reference earlier than 1215: a grant by Henry I to Osney priory of quittance from common pleas.[10] By itself this is almost valueless, as it comes from a fourteenth-century confirmation, into which the references to common pleas could have been interpolated after Magna Carta. Nevertheless Henry's grant is undoubtedly genuine, as it is also recorded in three original charters dating from 1129 × 1133.[11] (In the Osney and Leicester instances, the grant of quittance means that the beneficiary will not be fined.) An earlier reference than these explains what a common plea was. The *Leges Henrici Primi*, dating from 1113 × 1118, states:

Default of justice and violent withholding of a right demanded a first, second and third time according to law, is a common plea of the king over and above all persons, whether or not they have their own soke.[12]

The context here is private rights of jurisdiction (the Anglo-Saxon sake and soke) and the author is emphasizing that these rights do not include the most serious cases, such as a repeated miscarriage of justice, because the king's authority overrides all lesser jurisdictions. The practice of proving default by demanding justice three times was Anglo-Saxon. On the fourth occasion, according to the laws of Cnut, the plaintiff was authorized to use self-help.[13] By the time of the *Leges Henrici Primi*, on the other hand, he was aided by royal power because default of justice was 'a common plea of the king'.

From Henry I's reign onwards the power to remedy default of justice was the pivot of the king's disciplinary jurisdiction over feudal lords. The earliest writ in a set form, the writ of right, threatened the

[9] *Pipe Roll 26 Henry II* (Pipe Roll Soc., xxix, 1908), p. 101. The enrolment is repeated until the debt is paid: *Pipe Roll 27 Henry II*, p. 76; *28 Henry II*, p. 94; *29 Henry II*, p. 35.
[10] Fascicule ii (1981), ed. R. E. Latham, p. 400, no. 7b. *Charter Rolls, 1300–26*, p. 418. Mr R. Sharpe of the *Dictionary* tells me he has no further instances before 1215.
[11] *Facsimiles of Early Charters in Oxford Muniment Rooms*, ed. H. E. Salter (Oxford, 1929), nos. 57, 58, 64. *Regesta Regum Anglo-Normannorum*, ii (1956), ed. C. Johnson and H. A. Cronne, nos. 1470, 1468, 1726.
[12] Ed. L. J. Downer (Oxford, 1972), ch. 59, no. 19, p. 188. My translation differs from Downer's.
[13] *Laws*, ed. A. J. Robertson (Cambridge, 1925), II Canute, 19 (1), p. 182.

plaintiff's lord with the sheriff's intervention 'so that I [the king] may hear no further complaint for default of right'.[14] Henry II's writs were even more peremptory and (in the words of the writ *Praecipe*) instructed the sheriff to command that the land in question be rendered up 'justly and without delay'.[15] Actions on such writs were 'common pleas' in the sense that they invoked the king's universal or common jurisdiction 'over and above all persons'. They were not intended to be 'common' in the sense of being routine occurences, since feudal justice was the norm. Still less were they originally so named because they were pleas between 'common persons' or 'commoners'.[16] Royal writs came to be used frequently by tenants against lords, but Sir Edward Coke was right to insist (against Elizabethan interpretations) that 'they are not called *communia placita* in respect of the persons, but in respect of the quality of the pleas'.[17] Nevertheless he did at the same time mislead historians by identifying common pleas with real property in particular, whereas every failure of justice was included.[18] To sum up so far, 'common pleas' was a rare term before 1215, but it nevertheless embraced the wide-ranging principle of royal jurisdiction over default of justice.

Common pleas were not referred to after Magna Carta until, with Henry III's coming of age, the tribunal which followed the king (the court *Coram Rege*) was revived in the 1230s. Clause 17 was invoked by the Earl of Chester in 1236 and the Earl Marshal in 1237 to oppose the hearing of their cases *Coram Rege*. These are the earliest citations of the clause and both involve the greatest men in the land and not commoners. In Chester's case a contrast was made between 'common' pleas and 'singular' ones, and in the Marshal's between 'common' and 'private'.[19] 'Common' therefore signified something 'universal' (in Chester's case) or 'public' (in the Marshal's). In 1245 the chancery clerks first used the term 'common pleas' to describe the jurisdiction of the justices in eyre.[20] For the next twenty years the close and patent rolls abound with references to the 'common pleas being summoned' in specified counties, or to justices being commissioned 'to go on eyre for

---

[14] *Glanvill*, ed. G. D. G. Hall (London, 1965), p. 138. Embryonic writs of right from Henry I's reign are discussed by R. C. van Caenegem, *Royal Writs* (SS, lxxvii, 1959), pp. 206–10. In general, see S. F. C. Milsom, *The Legal Framework of English Feudalism* (Cambridge, 1976).

[15] *Glanvill*, p. 5.

[16] As suggested by G. O. Sayles in *Cases in King's Bench*, iv (SS, lxxiv, 1955), pp. xxix, xxxii, and *Scripta Diversa* (London, 1982), pp. 221, 225.

[17] *Fourth Part of the Institutes* (London, 1797), p. 98.

[18] Mistaken in this respect are the annotated translations of Magna Carta by J. C. Dickinson, *The Great Charter* (Historical Association Pamphlet G. 31, 1955), p. 21, and W. L. Warren, *King John* (Penguin edition, Harmondsworth, 1966), p. 290.

[19] *Curia Regis Rolls*, xv, no. 1958; xvi, no. 8.

[20] *Patent Rolls, 1232–47*, p. 462. *Close Rolls, 1242–47*, p. 356.

the common pleas (*ad itinerandum ad communia placita*)'.[21] Why this usage begins in 1245 is difficult to explain, as the eyre's jurisdiction did not change in that year and neither was Magna Carta cited more often in the 1240s than in the previous or subsequent decade. Nevertheless it seems to have been this change in chancery usage which first associated 'common pleas' with a particular jurisdiction, and that jurisdiction was not the central court at Westminster but the justices in eyre.

The term 'common pleas' may have first been applied to the eyre courts in the counties, rather than to Westminster, because the eyre embraced the king's universal jurisdiction, whereas the authority of the Bench at Westminster was narrower and of more recent origin. Common pleas had originated from royal commands to sheriffs in the county courts, which the justices reinforced in their eyres. 'It is important to emphasize', S. F. C. Milsom points out, 'that it was in the eyre that such pleas could first come to royal justice as a matter of routine. It was the central court that was at first the exceptional thing'.[22] As far as eyres were concerned, therefore, the chancery clerks used 'common pleas' as a synonym for 'all pleas'.[23] In an enrolment in 1253 'common pleas' were described as 'pertaining to lands and tenements as well as to the crown'.[24] When the eyre's jurisdiction became a matter for dispute in the baronial struggle of 1258–65, a chancery clerk was careful to describe it in 1261 as 'the common eyre of the justices itinerant for the common pleas in the county'.[25]

The Meaning of 'Some Certain Place'

Clause 17 was enforced by standardizing the wording of royal writs. Henceforward every writ initiating a common plea stated, even if only in general terms, where the plea would be heard. The effect can be seen by comparing Glanvill's texts of writs (dating from late in Henry II's reign) with registers later than Magna Carta. Glanvill's writs of assizes of novel disseisin, mort d'ancestor and darrein presentment summon the jurors and defendant to be '*coram me vel iusticiis meis*', that is, before the king or his justices.[26] Later registers, on the other hand, (of which the earliest purportedly dates from 1227) replace this formula by '*ad primam assisam cum justiciarii nostri in partes illas venerint*', that is, at the first sitting when the king's justices come into those parts of the

---

[21] These references are poorly indexed in the printed rolls, but they are discussed by D. Crook, *Records (of the General Eyre)* (Public Record Office Handbook 20, 1982), p. 6 and listed in his footnotes eyre by eyre.
[22] *Historical Foundations of the Common Law*, second edition (London, 1981), p. 29.
[23] In *Close Rolls, 1242–47*, p. 356, the note of summons explicitly refers to the writ summoning *omnia placita* at Ibid., pp. 235–6.
[24] *Patent Rolls, 1247–58*, p. 227. Public Record Office, C. 66/64, membrane 16d.
[25] *Close Rolls, 1261–64*, pp. 93–4. Crook, *Records*, pp. 6, 127.
[26] Glanvill, pp. 167, 150, 161.

country.[27] This latter formula had been in intermittent use before 1215 and it now became standard. Before Magna Carta some litigants and jurors had obtained hearings in their own counties, but others had been required, by writs summoning them before the king, to follow the royal court up and down the country. (To what extent this was an abuse of royal power by King John is discussed in the last section of this paper.)

It had also been common, in the first half of John's reign and earlier, for litigants to resort to the tribunal at Westminster, which was already known as the 'Bench'.[28] But a striking feature of clause 17 is that it mentions neither Westminster, as the place of session for common pleas, nor the justices of the Bench. This was because prescribing Westminster would have had the drastic effect of prohibiting the eyre or any other commission to justices to hear common pleas in the counties. Clause 17 did not therefore assign Westminster but '*aliquo loco certo*', 'some certain place'. In the circumstances of 1215 these words did not refer to a fixed place in the sense of a stationery one, but to any (*aliquo*) place certified (*certo*) or stated in the writ initiating the plea. *Certus* was used in a similar sense in clause 14, where writs of summons were to specify each day and place of meeting of the tenants-in-chief.

Clause 17 laid down the general rule that some place must be certified for holding a common plea, while clause 18 elaborated this for the possessory assizes because there were the pleas which had suffered most from following the king's court; henceforward they were to be taken at regular intervals in the county courts. In intention and effect the two clauses were one, as is clear from the Articles of the Barons (the draft of Magna Carta) where they are designated as one in the manuscript.[29] Similarly in the first French translation of Magna Carta, which was probably made for the public reading of the charter in Hampshire in 1215, the phrase *en certain lieu* was included in clause 18 (although it was not in the Latin) in order to emphasize that this was a reinforcement of clause 17.[30]

By coupling *aliquo* with *certo*, clause 17 provided for flexibility as much as precision in the holding of common pleas. In the half century after Magna Carta, the jurisdictions of the Bench at Westminster and the eyre in the counties grew in symbiosis. Once King John was dead and a semblance of peace restored, an eyre began in 1218 on a scale

---

[27] *Early Registers of Writs*, ed. E. de Haas and G. D. G. Hall (SS, lxxxvii, 1970), 'Hib.' nos. 5, 8, 9, pp. 2–4. P. Brand argues in *The Irish Jurist*, xvi (1981), 103–6, that this register dates originally from 1210.

[28] B. Kemp, 'Exchequer and Bench in the later 12th Century', *English Historical Review*, lxxxviii (1973), 559–73.

[29] Holt, *Magna Carta*, p. 307, no. 8, and facsimile IVa.

[30] J. C. Holt, 'A Vernacular French Text of Magna Carta', *English Historical Review*, lxxxix (1974), 359. I. Short in *Semasia*, iv (1977), 53–63, confirms that this text is Anglo-Norman.

unprecedented for twenty years. There were eight simultaneous circuits, with the experienced justices of the Bench distributed among them.[31] No tribunal sat at Westminster during much of this eyre because priority was given to bringing the king's justice into the shires in the persons of the judges of his 'great court'.[32] To the minority of litigants who had pleas pending at Westminster this may have been an inconvenience, as their cases were adjourned to the shires.[33] Likewise, difficult cases could be adjourned from one county town to another and thence back to Westminster.[34] The eyre of 1218 established a model of practice for the next decades. Most common pleas business originated in the eyres (hence the description 'common eyre for the common pleas'[35]) and until 1249 the tribunal at Westminster was suspended during eyres because the Bench judges acted also as justices in eyre. In Henry III's reign 'the eyre on the civil pleas side was the Bench itinerant'.[36]

By Edward I's reign, however, arrangements for holding common pleas were changing. The volume and complexity of business had increased to such an extent that the eyre system fragmented. The two circuits which began in 1278 had not been completed by 1289, when they were abandoned because some of the judges were accused of corruption.[37] Then a revival in 1292 petered out in 1294.[38] The breakup of the eyre did not cause the inconvenience to litigants that it had done in John's reign, however, because there were now alternative arrangements. The second statute of Westminster in 1285 allowed other forms of inquiry by juries, in addition to assizes, to be held by commissioners in the counties, provided the parties agreed and 'a certain day and place' was assigned to them.[39] The judges of the Bench, on the other hand, now remained at Westminster during terms to deal with difficult cases; they generally went out into the shires only in vacation. The expertise of their central tribunal consequently increased in prestige at the expense of the county courts and a legal profession of counsel and attorneys concentrated in London. Westminster itself, graced by the palace and abbey of Henry III, had become the capital of a triumphant monarchy.

[31] Crook, *Records*, pp. 71–8.
[32] The term *magna curia* is used to describe the Bench in the rolls of the Lincs. and Yorks. eyres of 1218–19, ed. D. M. Stenton (SS, liii, 1934, lvi, 1937), indexed refs. under 'courts'.
[33] *Rotuli Litterarum Clausarum*, i (1833), 380 (writ to sheriff of Yorks.).
[34] 'Foreign pleas' of this sort are edited by M. T. Clanchy (SS, xc, 1973) and A. Harding (SS, xcvi, 1980).
[35] See note 25 above.
[36] *Crown Pleas of the Wilts. Eyre, 1249*, ed. C. A. F. Meekings (Wilts. Record Soc., xvi, 1961), pp. 2–3.
[37] Crook, *Records*, pp. 144–6, 29–30.
[38] *Ibid.*, pp. 170–1.
[39] *Statutes*, i (1810), 86, ch. 30.

These developments help to explain a case in 1290 which explicitly associated clause 17 with the jurisdiction of the Bench. Robert of Tilbury presented a bill claiming that he should not have to answer in the court *Coram Rege* on a plea of warranty of charter 'because this would be contrary to the form of the Great Charter (*Magne Carte*), in which it is contained that common pleas should be held in a certain place, that is, in the Bench'.[40] The *Coram Rege* judges rejected this claim by drawing on the royal prerogative: 'the king is supreme judge' and any case can be removed *Coram Rege* 'on account of difficulty or necessity'.[41] Nevertheless this judicial logic was not upheld, presumably because it had brought the *Coram Rege* judges into conflict with their fellows of the Bench. A note was added in the plea roll in the contradictory form: 'afterwards, before the aforesaid judgment was given, a discussion was held in the king's council'.[42] The judgment was therefore suspended and the council produced a non-committal opinion, which avoided offending the justices of the Bench: 'it seems that it can be safer to proceed in the Bench with this plea of warranty than in the court *Coram Rege*'.[43]

This victory for the Bench in 1290 marks the point at which clause 17 came to validate the court's jurisdiction. Magna Carta was the best weapon it had against the superior logic of the court *Coram Rege*. Robert of Tilbury's bill was not an isolated instance, as other similar cases followed in the 1290s.[44] The renaissance of Magna Carta in this decade culminated in its solemn confirmation in 1297 and the articles on Magna Carta (*Articuli Super Cartas*) of 1300.[45] The 'certain place' in clause 17 was understood thenceforward to refer to the Bench. The words could bear this interpretation provided the qualifying *aliquo* was ignored, or omitted as it had been in Robert's bill. Another significant point is that this bill identified the 'certain place' with the Bench and not with Westminster as such. This was because the Exchequer court likewise sat at Westminster and some litigants resorted to it; the *Articuli Super Cartas* prohibited the holding of common pleas at the Exchequer.[46]

The certainty of permanence rested in the Bench wherever it sat. Thus it was removed to York during Edward I's and Edward II's

[40] The *Dictionary of Medieval Latin*, i (1975), 179, in its definitions of *bancus*, mistakenly ascribes this to the year 1300; its reference to *Abbreviatio Placitorum* is superseded by *Cases in King's Bench*, ii (SS, lvii, 1938), 11.

[41] *Cases in King's Bench*, p. 12.

[42] *Ibid.*, p. 12. Public Record Office, K. B. 27/124, membrane 42d.

[43] *Cases in King's Bench*, p. 12. My translation differs from Sayles's.

[44] *Abbreviatio Placitorum*, (Record Commission, 1811) pp. 233 (Suffolk), 239 (Northants.). F. Thompson, *The First Century of Magna Carta* (Minnesota, 1925), pp. 44–6.

[45] A recent introduction to this is J. H. Denton, *Robert Winchelsey and the Crown* (Cambridge, 1980), pp. 136 ff.

[46] *Statutes*, i, p. 138, ch. 4.

Scottish wars without contravening Magna Carta.[47] The lawbook called 'Britton', which purports to contain a codification by Edward I (dating from the 1290s), requires justices to remain at Westminster 'or at such other place as we shall be pleased to ordain' to take common pleas.[48] A variety of venues is also suggested by documents from Edward I's reign which render the *loco certo* of clause 17 in the plural as *locis certis*, meaning in 'places specified'.[49] In the long term, however, it was with Westminster, and Westminster Hall in particular, that the courts of justice became specially identified.

Clause 17 was thus adapted to changing circumstances in Edward I's reign. By 1300 the eyre had fragmented, the Bench had become a permanent tribunal, and Magna Carta was interpreted more litigiously. The Bench and not the eyre was now the principal jurisdiction for common pleas and it was on the way to becoming that special but 'Common Place' familiar to Tudor and Stuart lawyers. There is a difficulty, however, with this explanation which is that Bracton's *De Legibus* appears to associate the jurisdiction of the Bench with clause 17 before Robert of Tilbury's bill in 1290. In S. E. Thorne's translation Bracton writes: 'There are also other permanent judges, sitting in a place certain, that is, in the bench.'[50] But the description of the judges as 'permanent (*perpetui*)' is omitted in a number of early manuscripts (no manuscript of Bracton is earlier than Edward I's reign, although much of the text was composed before 1236) and the Latin does not say 'that is (*scilicet*)' but 'as (*sicut*)'.[51] With these amendments, the text reads: 'There are also other judges, sitting in a place certain, as in the bench.' This passage may therefore have been doing no more than using the Bench judges as an example of *loco certo* jurisdiction, which would be consistent with the position in Henry III's reign when the Bench judges went on eyres.

King John's Administration of Justice

The question that remains to be considered is the extent of John's responsibility for the grievances which clauses 17 and 18 aimed to remedy. Every common plea was a plea 'of the king' and before 1215 writs were returnable before the king or his justices, as we have already seen.[52] John was therefore entitled to hear assizes and other common

---

[47] M. Hastings, *The Court of Common Pleas in 15th Century England* (Ithaca, 1947), pp. 20–2. *Reports of Sir John Spelman*, ed. J. H. Baker, i (SS, xciii, 1976), p. 21, no. 6; ii (SS, xciv, 1977), p. 62 of the introduction.

[48] Ed. F. M. Nichols (Oxford, 1865), i, p. 5, no. 8.

[49] *Councils and Synods, 1265–1313*, ed. F. M. Powicke and C. R. Cheney (Oxford, 1964), p. 970, no. 7. *The Mirror of Justices*, ed. W. J. Whittaker (SS, vii, 1893), p. 177.

[50] *De Legibus*, ii (Cambridge, Mass., 1968), p. 307.

[51] Thorne amends *sicut* to *scilicet*, p. 307, note 19.

[52] See notes 12 and 26 above.

pleas, either in person or through the justices *Coram Rege* who accompanied him. Indeed he had a duty to hear such pleas, because they concerned default of justice which the king's power alone could remedy. From Henry II's reign onwards litigants are found following the king up and down the country, and even across the Channel, in pursuit of justice, as described in Richard of Anstey's graphic account among others.[53] In feudal society justice was felt to be intensely personal, both by the lord (the king in this case) and his aggrieved man. But 'the king is made and chosen to do justice to all' (in Bracton's words) and he therefore has to delegate power to judges, as well as embodying justice himself.[54] By the time of John's accession a system had been elaborated which depended on a hierarchy of judges (appropriately called 'justices'), headed by the justiciar, and on writs in set forms. Two different approaches to justice were thus juxtaposed. Alongside royal power, which was essentially personal and arbitrary, there was placed the judicial machine regulated by bureaucracy. Both stemmed from medieval traditions: the king's power from ideals of lordship and patriarchal kingship, and judicial routine from respect for custom and the established procedures of local courts.

In John's first years as king he needed the judicial machine to control England, while he fought for his inheritance in France. Thus, during his absence from June 1201 to December 1203, the justiciar, Geoffrey Fitz Peter, presided during terms over the Bench at Westminster and supervised circuits of eyre justices who visited every county in England. When the king returned, his court *Coram Rege* supplemented the existing arrangements rather than replacing them. The justiciar continued to preside at Westminster (or sometimes at St Bride's in London) and other judges went on visitations in the counties.[55] The best evidence of the regularity and extent of the judges' activities are the dated copies of final concords (that is, agreements between litigants) made before them.[56] The plea rolls likewise, although they survive with less consistency, show justice being regularly administered and the king's concern about particular cases of personal or legal difficulty.[57]

In 1209 the final concords and plea rolls indicate a change, which

---

[53] P. M. Barnes, 'The Anstey Case', *A Medieval Miscellany* (Pipe Roll Soc., new series, xxxvi, 1960), pp. 1–23.

[54] *De Legibus*, ii, p. 305.

[55] F. West, *The Justiciarship (in England)* (Cambridge, 1966), p. 169, does not take account of final concords in his statement that the justiciar 'had done little or nothing since 1204'.

[56] Tabulated by D. M. Stenton in *Pleas before the King or his Justices*, iii (SS, lxxxiii, 1966). All my subsequent references to dates and places of court sessions derive from this source.

[57] C. T. Flower, *Introduction to the Curia Regis Rolls* (SS, lxii, 1943), pp. 21–2. D. M. Stenton, *English Justice (between the Norman Conquest and the Great Charter)* (London, 1965), pp. 93–4.

Magna Carta and the Common Pleas

needs describing in detail in order to appreciate its significance. Pleas from the justiciar's Bench at Westminster and from the eyres were all transferred to the *Coram Rege* court.[58] Trinity term consequently began on 31 May in the king's presence at Lewes in Sussex. The justiciar was there with him, as were the eyre justices and litigants who had been adjourned from Cambridge on 14 May. A month earlier Roger le Zuche, a defendant in a case before the justiciar, had vouched the king to warrant that 'no plea ought to be held at Westminster'.[59] Roger's case had accordingly been adjourned *Coram Rege* for 31 May, although the rule of holding no plea at Westminster was shortlived, as Simon of Patishall and other justices sat there in June 1209; sessions likewise took place there at the beginning of the judicial year in October 1210, 1211, 1212 and 1213. Nevertheless there had been a significant change, because the court which sat at Westminster at these times consisted of *Coram Rege* judges including the king (except in 1213); it was no longer the justiciar's Bench sitting regularly from term to term. Furthermore the justiciar himself, Geoffrey Fitz Peter, is not named among the judges on any final concord made after 31 May 1209 until 12 November 1212, although more than 250 concords exist from this period.

The difference in judicial routine is most marked during John's expedition to Ireland in the summer of 1210. Instead of transferring pleas to the justiciar's court, as was customary during royal absences, he adjourned them to await his return.[60] The pipe rolls and other evidence show that Fitz Peter commissioned justices in the counties while John was away, but the Dunstable annalist reports that 'the king on his return from Ireland intervened against many people because of the oaths which they had taken concerning disseisins in his absence'.[61] It looks as if John refused to endorse the assize juries commissioned by the justiciar. The pipe rolls for 1210 and 1211 record amercements imposed by a variety of justices: sheriffs, anonymous persons described as 'Autumn justices', royal judges sitting in their home counties, and magnates (the earls of Winchester and Salisbury) on circuits backed up by judges or household officials.[62] They raised large sums in fines but left no court records. By contrast with the court *Coram Rege*, no final concords nor plea rolls exist for any eyre or assize commission between June 1209 and February 1214. This suggests that the court *Coram Rege* was the sole court of record during this time. Fitz Peter's reinstatement

---

[58] Stenton, *English Justice*, p. 103. West, *The Justiciarship*, pp. 167–8, confuses the events of 1209 with those of 1210.

[59] *Curia Regis Rolls*, v, pp. v, 327.

[60] H. G. Richardson and G. O. Sayles, *The Governance of Medieval England* (Edinburgh, 1963), p. 385, note 3.

[61] *Pipe Roll 12 John* (Pipe Rolls Soc., new series, xxvi, 1949), pp. xv, 120. Stenton, *English Justice*, pp. 105, 212–13. *Annales Monastici*, iii (Rolls Series, 1866), p. 33, noted in *Pipe Roll 13 John* (xxviii, 1952), p. xxxvi.

[62] *Pipe Roll 12 John*, pp. xiv–xxii; *13 John*, pp. xxxiv–vi.

at Westminster in November 1212 had not brought a return to normality, as the king in March 1213 adjourned the courts until Michaelmas, purportedly because of the threatened French invasion.[63] Only with the appointment of Peter des Roches as justiciar in February 1214 (Fitz Peter had died in October 1213) did the king return to delegating jurisdiction during his absence and the Bench revert to regular terms at Westminster.

Why John made these changes in the judicial system is difficult to explain. A shortage of judges, caused by the papal interdict on clerics serving the king, has been suggested.[64] But no judge can be shown to have left the courts for this reason and between March and July 1209 negotiations were proceeding to lift the interdict.[65] There is better evidence for some rift between king and justiciar. As we have seen, Fitz Peter ceased to be named among the judges in final concords in 1209 and his judicial activities in 1210 were perhaps not endorsed by the king. In a final concord at the Tower of London in 1211 he was named as earl of Essex but not placed among the judges, which suggests that his judicial authority was in abeyance.[66] There are reports of strained relations in the *Histoire des Ducs de Normandie* and Matthew Paris.[67] But even if John had quarrelled with the justiciar, that does not explain why he suspended the eyre, along with the court at Westminster, in May 1209. His motives remain an enigma and are not necessarily attributable to a single cause. 'It may be', as Maitland wrote, 'that as John's troubles thickened around him, less and less justice was done, and that a larger fraction of what was done was done under his own eye'.[68] The Bench was suspended, the eyre of 1208–9 cut short with less than half the counties visited, and for months at a time in 1210 and 1213 the royal courts left no record. Attempts to mitigate litigants' difficulties, like Fitz Peter's irregular commissioning of justices in 1210, may only have caused further confusion. The court *Coram Rege* had always heard some common pleas, but it was new for it to be the sole court of record. Although it established some pattern in its movements (notably by being at Westminster in October) and adjourned some cases to litigants' home areas, it could not consistently accomodate their needs to the demands of the king's peri-

[63] Richardson and Sayles, p. 385, note 8.
[64] Holt, *Magna Carta*, p. 224.
[65] Eustace de Fauconberg did not cease judicial work in 1209 (*pace* Stenton, *English Justice*, pp. 97–8), as he took new amercements in 1210, *Pipe Roll 12 John*, p. 51. See also Richardson and Sayles, p. 384, note 5.
[66] *Curia Regis Rolls*, vi, pp. 150–1.
[67] The *Histoire*, ed. F. Michel (Paris, 1840), p. 116, is discussed by Stenton, *English Justice*, p. 104; Richardson and Sayles, p. 385; West, *The Justiciarship*, pp. 170–1. Matthew Paris, *Chronica Majora*, ii, p. 559, is discussed by V. H. Galbraith, *Roger Wendover and Matthew Paris* (Glasgow, 1944), p. 36.
[68] *Pleas of the Crown* (SS, i, 1888), pp. xv–xvi.

patetic way of life. John moved huge distances up and down England, leaving unfinished business in his wake.

Postponements of cases in the plea rolls from these years illustrate the difficulties which Magna Carta aimed to remedy. In 1211 for example Gilbert Fitz Reinfrey brought an action of right concerning his wife's inheritance against Henry of Dean in Cumberland.[69] The case was first set for hearing at Knaresborough (Yorks.), but then it was proclaimed at Horston (Derby) that pleas would be heard at Whitchurch (Salop.) on 8 July. Gilbert's attorneys missed this proclamation and appeared at Hereford on 18 November. The case was subsequently adjourned to Kingshaugh (Notts.) in January 1212, Clarendon (Wilts.) in April, Winchester (Hants.) in May, and then back up north to Durham in June. Here Henry got it adjourned for a further year by pleading sickness, but by the summer of 1213 the courts had been adjourned and Gilbert's wife was dead. Gilbert was a powerful man, being sheriff of both Lancashire and Yorkshire, and he had perhaps been deservedly outmanoeuvred.

Following the court benefited only those litigants who could take advantage of the king's restless itinerary to default their opponent's non-appearance. A remarkable instance of this is Roger de Reimes, who appeared on four successive days in December 1211 at Sutton (Surrey), Brill (Bucks.) Witham Friary (Somerset) and Gillingham (Dorset).[70] This is hard to credit, as the distance from Sutton to Brill is at least fifty-five miles and from there to Witham is seventy. Even if the reading is amended, as the manuscript is in poor condition, from Brill to Bramshill (east of Basingstoke), the distance of the next day's journey to Witham remains great at sixty miles. How John's court travelled so fast in winter is an unresolved problem. Roger was prosecuting an assize of mort d'ancestor for land in Somerset and in January 1212 he met delay when the jurors failed to appear at Kingshaugh (Notts.) and again in April at Clarendon and Westminster. Nevertheless they were surprisingly at Doncaster (Yorks.) in June to give their verdict in Roger's favour, as his opponent had failed to produce his warrantors from Somerset.[71] Of all common pleas, assizes were most affected by following the court because they required the presence of jurors, who could not be represented by attorneys, as well as the litigants and third parties. By paying one mark in 1213 Roger of St Martin brought an assize of darrein presentment against the prior of Durham into the court *Coram Rege* at Oxford. When the prior and jurors defaulted, the rule that 'pleas follow the court' was cited as

---

[69] *Curia Regis Rolls*, vi, pp. 156, 176, 194, 315, 343; vii, p. 36. See also J. C Holt, *The Northerners* (Oxford, 1961), concerning Gilbert.
[70] *Curia Regis Rolls*, vi, pp. 185, 187. Flower, *Introduction* (SS, lxii, 1943), p. 23.
[71] *Curia Regis Rolls*, vi, pp. 191, 246, 316.

justification for making a further adjournment to Reading.[72] This was the kind of practice that Magna Carta prohibited.

Clauses 17 and 18 were concerned with immediate problems arising from John's actions in his last years. They aimed to restore and reinforce the system of delegated jurisdiction as it had existed before 1209. Unlike later interpreters of clause 17, the makers of Magna Carta did not restrict their attention to the Bench at Westminster, important though that was. They looked at the country as a whole and especially at the regular holding of assizes by royal justices in the county courts. No longer should jurors from Somerset give their verdict at Doncaster, or the prior of Durham be adjourned to Reading. In fact such problems sometimes recurred after 1215, when pleas at Westminster were adjourned during eyres. Nevertheless clauses 17 and 18 were successful in restoring the jurisdiction of the Bench and eyre justices, as distinct from the court *Coram Rege*. Their authority grew so fast in the thirteenth century that later generations forgot what 'common pleas' had originally been and what 'some certain place' had meant to King John's contemporaries. When the eyre fragmented, clause 17 was appropriated by the Bench; ultimately it became the only court of common pleas. Without Magna Carta it could not justify its existence as against the *Coram Rege* and Exchequer courts. But this outcome should not be confused with the original purpose of clause 17. It did more than entitle the justices to their common place in Westminster Hall.

---

[72] *Ibid.*, vii, pp. 7, 35. K. Major, 'Blyborough Charters', *A Medieval Miscellany* (Pipe Roll Soc., new series, xxxvi, 1960), p. 204.

17

Titles to Orders in Medieval English Episcopal Registers

R. N. Swanson

In the ordination lists which bulk so large in surviving medieval English episcopal registers, one virtually constant feature is the recording of a 'title' for those ordained to the major orders of subdeacon, deacon, and priest. Possession of such a title – that is, of guaranteed financial support sufficient to maintain the dignity of his orders – was a basic requirement for the promotion of a clerk to holy orders.[1] Yet, although thousands of ordinations and titles are recorded, little attention has been given to what these titles actually represent. What follows attempts to fill the gap, offering a hypothesis which, while removing some problems, may well create others.

While all ordinands required titles, my main concern will be with the unbeneficed secular candidates. Possession of a benefice in itself provided a sufficient title; as did the vows of poverty taken by those entering religious orders. During the thirteenth century, there is a clear change in the nature of secular titles, with increasing numbers being ordained to a title of 'patrimony', of their own possessions as distinct from a benefice.[2] Ideally, these patrimonal titles were meant to serve as stop-gaps, until a benefice was obtained; but given the numbers so ordained by the end of the thirteenth century, and the comparatively small number of benefices available, for many the patrimonial title was clearly to be permanent. The fourteenth-century registers provide signs of a further change in titles: by the end of the century the majority of ordinands no longer

---

* The following abbreviations are used throughout: CYS = Canterbury and York Society; LJRO = Lichfield Joint Record Office; *Reg.* = *Register/Registrum*, etc.; WorcsHS = Worcesteshire Historical Society.

I am grateful to Mrs D. M. Owen and Dr H. C. Swanson for comments on earlier drafts of this paper, and to various correspondents who kindly replied to questions. For obvious reasons, the footnoting is not intended to be exhaustive.

[1] For a general statement on medieval titles, see R. Naz, 'Titre d'ordination', *Dictionnaire du droit canonique*, vii (Paris, 1965), cols. 1278–80.

[2] As permitted by X.3.5.c23.

presented titles derived from patrimony or individual patrons; now their titles were ostensibly provided by religious corporations – monasteries, nunneries, hospitals, guilds, university colleges, and collegiate churches. It has to be stressed immediately that this transformation was not wholesale, nor did it occur at the same rate throughout the country: at Lincoln the change was well under way by the end of the thirteenth century,[3] while for the see of Carlisle there is very little sign of it before the end of the fourteenth century,[4] and in Hereford diocese numerous candidates presented 'patrimonial' titles well into the fifteenth century.[5] Elsewhere, however, the change occurs with startling speed.[6]

The totality of this change, and the implausibility of the 'monastic' titles as guarantees of real financial independence if they are to be taken at face value, has provoked some debate. The most recent commentator on ecclesiastical administration in medieval England has condemned the whole system of titles – regardless of source – as spurious and fraudulent.[7] Others, however, have sought to defend the monastic titles, arguing that they represent the use of funds intended for chantry purposes.[8] There are suggestions that the 'monastic' titles were purchased (even hired) by the candidates, as a mere paper qualification required for ordination; and this thesis of mercenary arrangements between corporation and ordinand is now virtually part of the standard picture.[9]

However, none of these arguments has totally carried the field, and all can be opposed. Although there is evidence of fraudulent titles being used in the thirteenth and fourteenth centuries, so much so that the papal penitentiaries established a common form for the appropriate

[3] *[The Rolls and] Reg. [of Bishop Oliver] Sutton, [1280–1299*, ed. R. M. T. Hill], vii (Lincoln record society, 69, 1975), xii.
[4] R. K. Rose, 'Priests and patrons in the fourteenth century diocese of Carlisle', *Studies in Church History*, xvi (1979), 211–12.
[5] E.g. *Reg. Thome Millyng, episcopi Herefordensis, A.D. MCCCCLXXIV–MCCCCXCII*, ed. A. T. Bannister (C[anterbury and] Y[ork] S[ociety] xxvi, 1920), pp. 154–9; they appear fairly regularly in earlier registers.
[6] See below, p. 242.
[7] R. E. Rodes, *Ecclesiastical Administration in Medieval England* (Notre Dame, Indiana, 1977), p. 115.
[8] A. H. Thompson, *The English Clergy and their Organization in the Later Middle Ages* (Oxford, 1947), p. 143; H. S. Bennett, 'Medieval ordination lists in English episcopal registers', in *Studies Presented to Sir Hilary Jenkinson*, ed. J. Conway Davies (London, 1957), p. 29, is more circumspect. Something similar is suggested for those individuals who appear repeatedly as donors of titles at Carlisle: Rose, *ubi supra*, p. 213.
[9] J. E. H. Moran, 'Clerical recruitment in the diocese of York, 1360–1530: data and commentary', *Journal of Ecclesiastical History*, xxxiv (1983), 30; Bennett, *ubi supra*, 28–9.

resulting dispensation, not all patrimonial titles can have been invalid.[10] Canon law contained sufficient safeguards against fraudulence, and for the bishops to have connived at a system which would have involved ipso facto excommunication for all involved – including themselves as the ordainers – is going too far.[11] Nor can the arguments regarding the use of chantry funds really be accepted. Although it is not impossible that they apply in some circumstances (I have come across one instance of an individual being ordained to a title provided by a specific altar in a religious house),[12] it is impossible to envisage the system working on a large scale. Firstly, the chantries providing this income were clearly not technically benefices (otherwise they would themselves provide the specified title), but merely stipendiary donatives. Secondly, for such chantries the priest is most likely to have been hired *after* ordination rather than before; if he were not, their use to provide titles would require considerable prescience regarding vacancies. In any event, the sheer numbers involved militate against any universal application of such a solution.[13] Admittedly, and usually early in the period, ordination lists occasionally provide instances of individuals being supported en route to a chantry, or whose descriptions suggest that they were to serve as mass-priests, usually with a title provided by a guild or parishioners, but I doubt if these would really undermine the argument: the titles still suggest a permanent endowment rather than a

---

[10] On fraudulent titles, see [F. M. Powicke and C. R. Cheney], *Councils and Synods, [with other Documents Relating to the English Church, II, A.D. 1205–1313]* (2 vols., Oxford, 1964), pp. 373–4, 644, 1001; *The Reg. of John de Grandisson, Bishop of Exeter (A.D. 1327–1369): part 1, 1327–1330, with some Account of the Episcopate of James de Berkeley (A.D. 1327)*, ed. F. C. Hingeston-Randolph (London and Exeter, 1894), p. 384. For instances of dispensations granted by penitentiaries see *Reg. [Ade de] Orleton, [episcopi Herefordensis, A.D. MCCCXVII–MCCCXXVII]*, ed. A. T. Bannister (CYS, v, 1908), pp. 169, 268–9, 303–4; *Reg. [Johannis de] Trillek, [episcopi Herefordensis, A.D. MCCCXLIV–MCCCLXI*, ed. J. H. Parry] (CYS, viii, 1912), pp. 26–7; *Reg. Ricardi de Swinfield, episcopi Herefordensis, A.D. MCCLXXXIII–MCCCXVII*, ed. W. W. Capes (CYS, vi, 1909), p. 442; *[The] Reg. [of Walter] Reynolds, [Bishop of Worcester, 1308–1313*, ed. R. A. Wilson] (WorcsH[ist]S[oc], xxxix, 1927), pp. 81, 83–4; *[Calendar of the] Reg. [of Adam de] Orleton, [Bishop of Worcester, 1327–1333]*, ed. R. M. Haines (Worcs HS, n.s., x, 1979) no. 378.

[11] X.5.13.c45; see also [Johannes de Burgo], *Pupilla oculi* (Paris, 1513), 7.vi.T; also *Councils and Synods*, ii, pp. 373–4, 1001. That the canonical requirements on titles were well known is clear from the discussion of them in the early fifteenth century vernacular tract, *Dives and Pauper*, ed. P. H. Barnum, I.ii (Early English Text Society, O.S., cclxxx, 1980), 175, 181.

[12] *Reg. Henrici Woodlock, diocesis Wintoniensis, A.D. 1305–1316*, ed. A. W. Goodman (2 vols, CYS, xliii–xliv, 1940–1), ii, 812.

[13] Thus St Mary's hospital Bootham, provided seventy-six titles between 1398 and 1405: *A Calendar of the Reg. of Richard Scrope, archbishop of York, 1398–1405: part 2*, ed. R. N. Swanson (Borthwick texts and calendars: records of the northern province, xi, York, 1985), pp. xi, 143; see also below p. 242.

stipend.[14] There remains the final difficulty of the possible purchase of monastic titles. This is at present irresoluble, being an argument *ex silentio* on both sides: there appears to be no concrete evidence that titles were not sold or hired, but equally, and possibly more tellingly, no concrete evidence that they were.[15]

Faced with this uncertainty about what titles actually represent (particularly the 'monastic' titles),[16] further investigation seems appropriate. But, before considering monastic titles in particular, and the implications of the fourteenth-century changes, it is necessary to deal with the 'patrimonial' titles.

Although the majority of the early titles are 'patrimonial', their precise position in relation to ordination, and just what they mean, remains obscure. Although the canonists insist on possession of a title for ordination, they seem to give little thought to its content; and modern commentators have not exactly illuminated the shadows.[17] The title might take several forms, some of which at present appear more wishful thinking than formal guarantees of support. Any secure income, or prospect of a secure income, seems to have been considered sufficient: lands actually owned by the ordinand, annual pensions granted by laity or religious (sometimes with indications of assignment on a specific piece of property), rents, corrodies in religious houses, posts in episcopal households, schoolmasterships, etc.[18] Some sources of titles seem less secure than others, the most insubstantial being those based on papal provisions *in forma pauperum*, to be levied on specified religious institutions. Such dispensations are notorious for being no guarantee of a benefice, and unless the citation of a provision as title

---

[14] E.g. *Reg. Trillek*, pp. 499, 507, 518 (Thomas de Breyntone); Walter de Malleye at *Reg. Thome Charlton, episcopi Herefordensis, A.D. MCCCXXVII–MCCCXLIV*, ed. W. W. Capes (CYS, ix, 1913), pp. 179, 183, is a mass-priest, as are the instances in *The Reg. of Thomas de Cantilupe, Bishop of Hereford (A.D. 1275–1282)*, ed. R. G. Griffiths (CYS, ii, 1907), pp. 310–11.

[15] M. J. Bennett, *Community, Class, and Careerism: Cheshire and Lancashire Society in the Age of 'Sir Gawain and the Green Knight'*, Cambridge Studies in Medieval Life and Thought, third series, vol. xviii (Cambridge, 1983), pp. 138–9, on monastic titles in that region. I suspect that whatever mercenary arrangements there were would be reflected only in small agency fees, probably no more than a few pence per title: see also below, p. 244. The evidence adduced by Moran, *ubi supra*, p. 30 n. 52 is quite inconclusive.

[16] As I shall henceforth refer to titles derived from religious institutions. Other types of title will be generically described as either 'non-monastic' or 'patrimonial'.

[17] Compare the comments of M. Bowker, *The Secular Clergy of the Diocese of Lincoln, 1495–1520*, Cambridge Studies in Medieval Life and Thought, n.s., x (Cambridge, 1968), pp. 61–4, and Rose, *ubi supra*, pp. 211–15. See also *Reg. Sutton*, vii, xi–xiv.

[18] See, e.g. *Reg. Sutton*, vii, xi and refs.

gave such a guarantee, must often have been equivalent to being ordained without any title at all.[19]

It seems unlikely that the reality of these titles can be totally discounted. There is clear evidence for investigation of the title as much as of the personality of the candidate prior to his admission to orders; and this appears to have been no mere formality. There is some evidence of local inquisitions,[20] while the sheer precision of the figures occasionally returned suggests fairly rigorous investigation.[21] At times, the ordinand using a patrimonial title was even required to swear to continued possession of it at successive ordinations.[22] Moreover, when titles were investigated and found insufficient, the candidates could be required to show further sponsorship before receiving orders.[23] Where there were suspicions of a fictive title, even the grantor of the title might be required to swear not to interfere with the candidate's enjoyment of the property or income.[24] Bishops too might extract oaths from the candidates, not to enforce claims to sustenance against them should their titles prove insufficient.[25] These read like attempts to avoid the canonical requirements with regard to insufficiency or lack of title.[26] The canonists may have had doubts about such oaths, but the bishops clearly did not, and statements of the candidates' contentment with their titles appear to have been extracted almost as a matter of course. Not that they were necessarily invalid: John Acton, for one,

---

[19] E.g. *Reg. Pal[atinum] Dunelm[ense*, ed. T. D. Hardy] (4 vols., Rolls Series, 1873–8), iii, 187, 193–4; *Reg. Orleton*, ed. Haines, pp. 9–11, 20–1, 27–8. It is likely that some of the apparently monastic titles in the early ordination lists are obscured provisions: in the Lichfield list of Roger Northburgh individuals appear in some ordinations with a title apparently of provision, which is not noted as being such elsewhere, e.g. LJRO, B/A/1/1, ff. 175^r, 177^r (Robert de Marketon, John de Upton). For the failings of the papal provisions *in forma pauperum*, see C. Tihon, 'Les expectatives *in forma pauperum* particulièrement au XIVe siècle', *Bulletin de l'institut historique belge de Rome*, v (1925) pp. 91–4. The unreliability of such provisions may account for the case of Robert Schireve of Hatherop, who had such a provision on Hailes abbey, but also appeared with a title derived from Lechlade hospital (*Reg. Orleton*, ed. Haines, p. 11).

[20] *Reg. Sutton*, vii, 63.

[21] ibid., 6 (47s. 2½d.), 77 (42s. 8d.).

[22] *Reg. Reynolds*, pp. 102–22, 130–47, where titles are attested by deans and other officials. A marginal entry in the Ely register of Thomas de Lisle would also fit in the pattern of examinations: C[ambridge] U[niversity] L[ibrary], E[ly] D[iocesan] R[ecords], G/1/1, f.94^r [second series].

[23] LJRO, B/A/1/1, F.135^v (Walter de Cokton): 'et quia titulus videbatur minus sufficiens, dominus Ricardus de Norton manucepit pro sufficientiori'; *Reg. Pal. Dunelm.*, iii, p. 196.

[24] *Reg. Orleton*, ed. Haines, p. 42.

[25] E.g. *[A Calendar of the] Reg. [of Wolstan de] Bransford, [Bishop of Worcester, 1339–1349*, ed. R. M. Haines] (WorcsHs, n.s., iv, 1966), no. 726; *Reg. [Hamonis] Hethe, [diocesis Roffensis, A.D. 1319–1352*, ed. C. Johnson] (CYS, xlviii–xlix, 1948), pp. 178–9. Some of these seem to be additional sureties, in terms of the legal position set out in *Pupilla oculi*, 7.ii.Z.

[26] X.1.14.c13; X.3.5.c4; X.3.5.c16; X.4.3.c45; see also *Pupilla oculi*, 7.ii.X.

declared that such renunciations of future claims upon the bishops were lawful; but added the proviso that the sufficiency of the title should be proved beforehand by the appropriate documents.[27] Certainly, enforcement of titles was a concern for the bishops, and they did try to ensure that the clergy were duly provided for. Those ordained without title had their claims enforced against their diocesan for his failure; individuals ordained to a title from an Oxford college or a religious house gained episcopal support to enforce their claims to sustenance; and reluctant heirs found themselves lumbered with obligations granted by their precursors.[28]

There is only a hint that the system of enforcement continued into the fifteenth century.[29] Equally scarce is evidence for continued fictive or fraudulent titles, instances of penitentiary dispensations seemingly disappearing after 1345.[30] Quite possibly the decline in the need for enforcement is linked to the apparent change in the nature of titles, perhaps also to the drop in clerical ordinations after the Black Death: if this reduced the economic pressures forcing individuals into the clerical order, the pressure to produce fictive or collusive titles would also be reduced. But it is worth noting that in several dioceses the transformation of titles occurs prior to the plague; most notably at Lincoln, York and Lichfield.[31] It is to the motivations for that change that it is now necessary to turn.

The procedures for enforcing titles after ordination were fiddling and time-consuming; so too was the task of ensuring the validity of titles prior to ordination. The bishops seem to have attempted to keep things under control by retaining the original grant of title in their registries,[32] although precisely why is not clear. Title-checking was doubtless part of the usual process of examination prior to ordination and, not content with merely accepting the title-deed, some diocesans required formal

---

[27] *Constitutiones [legitime seu legatine regionis Anglicanae: cum subtilissima interpretatione domini Johannis de Athon]* (Paris, 1506), f. 9^r, gloss *et vero*.

[28] *Reg. Roberti Winchelsey Cantuarensis archiepiscopi*, ed. R. Graham, 2 vols. (CYS, li–lii, 1952–60),*i, 97, 197–8, 476–7, ii, 782, 1046–7, 1088–9; LJRO, B/A/1/3, f.19^v*; *Reg. Orleton*, ed. Bannister, p. 40.

[29] *Calendar of Entries in the Papal Registers Relating to Great Britain and Ireland, Papal letters*, iv, ed. W. H. Bliss and J. A. Twemlow (London, 1902), p. 463, contains implications of enforcement of a title by papal authority.

[30] The latest dated penitentiary dispensation which I know of is *Reg. Trillek*, ed. Parry, pp. 26–7 (dated 1345); but a papal dispensation for a fictive title dated 1429 is in *Calendar of Entries in the Papal Registers Relating to Great Britain and Ireland, Papal letters*, viii, ed. J. A. Twemlow (London, 1909), p. 90.

[31] For Lichfield and York, see below, p. 242; for Lincoln, above n.3.

[32] *[The] Reg. [of John de] Sandale [and Rigaud de Asserio, bishops of Winchester (AD 1316–1323)*, ed. F. J. Baigent] (London and Winchester, 1897), pp. 189, 195–6, 198–9, 206–9; CUL, EDR, G/1/2, f.118^{r-v}; *Reg. Sandale*, pp. 209–10, and LJRO, B/A/1/1, f.127^v (Nicholas le Mercer) indicate that copies might have been exhibited. Sometimes the title was incorporated into grants of letters dimissory: see *Reg. Sandale*, pp. 350–1; LJRO, B/A/1/1, ff.64^r, 70^v.

attestation of the validity of the title by a third party, most often in cases involving a patrimonial title.[33] The role of guarantor seems to merge into that assumed by a person whose participation in the ordination ceremony seems, for the most part, to have been overlooked: the presenter.

The available evidence for ordination procedures indicates that, apart from possession of a title, it was also necessary for the candidate to be presented for orders. This may have had to be done twice: once to the examining authorities, and then by the examiner to the ordaining bishop.[34] It is the first of these stages which seems particularly important for present purposes. Just as the freehold rights implicit in a title paralleled those acquired with a benefice, so, presumably, the presentation to orders paralleled presentation to a benefice, as an assertion (subject to later examination) that the presentee was a suitable person to receive orders, fulfilling all the requirements concerning his character which would allow him to assume priestly functions. Although as an action it was distinct from the title, nevertheless presentation and assertion of title could be combined in one document – and, when monastic titles became the rule, it seems that they were.[35] It is this combined character of the 'monastic title documents' which explains one of the apparent oddities of some of the registered ordination lists: the assertion that x was ordained *ad titulum y ad omnes ordines sibi concessum,* or *ad titulum y ad ordinem z tantum.* The grammar of surviving monastic title documents makes it clear that the limitation in fact applies only in terms of the act of presentation, rather than to the real title (which would, in any case, be canonically impossible).[36] The surviving lay equivalents to these monastic documents support this, all those that I know of (with one exception) being issued for advancement only to the next order in the general sequence of promotion.[37]

Nevertheless these lay letters of presentation do frequently include

---

[33] See above, n.22.

[34] On the procedure for presentation to the bishop, see *Pupilla oculi,* 7.ii.E; the first stage of the process appears to leave no discernible trace in the literature.

[35] See the grants of title in *Reg. Hethe,* p. 57; *Reg. quorundam abbatium monasterii S. Albani qui saeculo XV^{mo} floruere,* ed. H. T. Riley (2 vols, Rolls Series, London, 1872–3), ii, pp. 90–1; LJRO, RR.9; CUL, EDR, F5/32, f.40^v (I owe this reference to Mrs D. M. Owen).

[36] For the titles, see above: *Reg. Hethe,* p. 57 is in fact a title only for the diaconate and priesthood. On the problem, see *The Reg. of Edmund Lacy, Bishop of Exeter, 1420–55: Reg. commune,* ed. G. R. Dunstan (5 vols., CYS, lx–lxiii, lxvi, 1963–72), v, pp. xviii–xx; G. R. Dunstan, 'Some aspects of the register of Edmund Lacy, bishop of Exeter, 1420–1455' *Journal of Ecclesiastical History,* vi (1955), pp. 46–7.

[37] London, British Library, Cotton ch. iv. 2, Cotton ch. v. 38, Cotton ch, xi. 74–6, Add. ch. 19836; Stafford, William Salt Library, SD. Cornford. 116. This last is the exception, but in fact appears to have been used only for advancement to the subdiaconate: LJRO, B/A/1/1, f.107^r (John de Hulle) – a different presenter is named at his later ordinations, *ibid.,* ff.110^v, 115^r.

statements of title, although usually very vaguely worded. In most cases, these may approximate to pensionary titles.[38] But it seems that the letter of presentation was not identical to a title document, and, as far as the bishops were concerned, the principal importance of the presentation deeds may have been the financial arrangements outlined in such letters: not that the presenter was granting a title, but that he was acting as guarantor for whatever title the ordinand actually possessed. For all of the lay letters include a clause exonerating the bishop and his successors from any financial liabilities which might be incurred by his accepting the presentation.[39] Willingness to accept the presentation, and enforce the presentee's rights against his promoter, is apparent from a Hereford case of 1317, when bishop Orleton forced the executors of John de Kemeseye to continue to provide maintenance for John de Schyrebourne, who had been ordained on Kemeseye's presentation.[40]

Part of the problem posed by these letters of presentation-cum-title and their role in the ordination process is the ambiguity of their status, in part because there seems a likelihood that, officially, they were only a preliminary to proper examination, and could be rejected by the bishop.[41] But if the letters were taken as evidence of the candidate's character – testimonials, or references – then it is possible that they could have provided a short-cut in the overall examination procedure, easing the administrative burdens of the ecclesiastical officials. That ordinands were examined prior to receiving their orders is clear from a variety of sources, but precisely what this entailed is not always apparent.[42] Canonically, there was no real need for a stringent examination: good public reputation was sufficient guarantee. If the letter of presentation served as evidence of that repute, then it may be that, at the pre-ordination examination, that letter could be accepted as evidence of fulfilment of the requirements of character, together with the documents supporting the title.[43] There remained the possibility of full-scale examination, but, provided they were considered trustworthy, the presentation documents could have provided a convenient by-pass for the tedious process.

[38] All those mentioned in n.42, with the exception of Add. ch. 19836, include a statement of title, in four cases being 'ad titulum provisionis mee' or 'ad titulum presentacionis mee'.

[39] E.g. British Library, Cotton ch. v. 38 (concerning Nicholas de Bretford): 'de qua quidem provisione eidem Nicolao teneri ad exoneracionem vestram me et heredes meos obligo per presentes'.

[40] *Reg. Orleton*, ed. Bannister, p. 40.

[41] As suggested by British library, Cotton ch. xi. 74.

[42] Moran, *ubi supra*, 27–8 and refs.; see also the comments of Rodes, p. 116.

[43] D.24.c2; *Pupilla oculi*, 7.ii.G; see also L. E. Boyle, 'Aspects of clerical education in fourteenth century England', reprinted in his *Pastoral Care, Clerical Education, and Canon Law* (London, 1981), pp. 19–20.

Titles to Orders in Episcopal Registers 241

Apart from testifying to the candidate's personal characteristics, the presenter's financial undertakings were important, the exoneration clause perhaps implying that the presenter was himself examining and standing guarantor for the actual title (where it had not been provided by him in the first place).[44] In this sense, the function would be similar to, but not identical with, the attestation of titles undertaken in some dioceses by ecclesiastical officials as part of the process of formal examination – although a Worcester document of 1303 does suggest a more precise overlap.[45] If effective, this system could itself provide a bulwark against fictive titles and fraudulent reception of orders: if the ordinand needed such a guarantor, himself liable to financial sanctions if the title provided invalid, and with similar financial obligations if the priest (when ordained) was found to be canonically unqualified to receive a benefice, then the investigations of both character and title by the presenter are likely to have been fairly stringent.

That presentation and title could be combined in one document doubtless explains much of the ambiguity and uncertainty in the ordination lists themselves when it comes to distinguishing between the various actions involved;[46] and it is indeed one of the difficulties with the documents of title issued by religious houses that they seem to be more letters of presentation than real statements of title.[47] This doubtless made it easier, as an administrative convenience, and where there was a sufficient density of religious houses or hospitals, to adopt the policy of combining the processes of personal examination and examination of title before the candidate presented himself for ordination. The examining house would then issue the appropriate documents, which the registrars accepted and noted as the official titles in the ordination lists.

The evidence to support this hypothesis – and it is no more than that at present – is very slight. It is, moreover, difficult to envisage precisely how the system would work, especially when so many of the 'monastic' titles were provided by nunneries. Nevertheless, what evidence there is seems to me highly suggestive. In the first place, there is the totality of the change to the new type of title, when and where it occurs. In the second place, there is the evidence provided by the

---

[44] *Pupilla oculi*, 7.iv.H; Acton, *Constitutiones*, f.9^r, gloss *titulo*. Possibly the letters of presentation were intended to get round the provisions for examination by using the loophole outlined in *Pupilla oculi*, 7.ii.F.

[45] *The Reg. of the Diocese of Worcester during the Vacancy of the See*, usually called "*Reg. sede vacante*", ed. J. W. Willis Bund (WorcsHS, Oxford, 1897), p. 57: this is clearly the testimonial letter for his title referred to in *The Reg. of William de Geynesburgh, Bishop of Worcester, 1302–1307*, ed. J. W. Willis Bund (WorcsHS, xxii, 1907–29), p. 117.

[46] To justify this statement would require a massive amount of documentation. Suffice to say that the examination of ordination lists in preparation for this article has convinced me of its validity.

[47] Above, n.35.

sources of those titles. The richest houses notably fail to provide them; while apparently poor institutions provided large numbers.[48] Thus, Norwich cathedral provides few, but the nearby hospital provides hundreds; in York, the Minster and St Mary's abbey appear rarely, yet St Mary's hospital in Bootham appears exceedingly generous; at Lichfield, the hospital of St John dominates the lists, while the dean and chapter of the cathedral are almost totally absent.[49] It is almost as though certain houses were being designated to provide titles in particular localities. This, of course, would not prevent their being granted by other institutions, and for their own reasons,[50] but it may account for their notable concentration. The third piece of evidence to support the basic hypothesis is the speed of the changeover. This is not always readily apparent, much depending on the nature and survival of the evidence for different dioceses, but is glaringly obvious in two cases. At York, the change occurred at the start of 1349.[51] At Lichfield it took place in 1325: until then virtually all candidates for the subdiaconate offered patrimonial titles, or were ordained on 'presentations'; thereafter 'monastic' titles were the rule, with no presentations, and with patrimonial titles being confined almost wholly to incomers, usually from the Welsh dioceses.[52] In both instances, the only acceptable explanation is that the change had occurred with official sanction, if not prodding. The Lichfield lists support this idea: in September 1328, John Raven's patrimonial title was accepted, but he was instructed that he would need a monastic title to receive further orders.[53]

If this does confirm that the change in the nature of titles was an official policy – even if pressed only in individual dioceses – then how was the title to be arranged thereafter, and did it retain any reality? Initially, it was probably merely an administrative change, possibly a delegation of responsibility for examination to the religious institutions. Precisely why this occurred is unclear, but what seems to have happened is that the institutions acted virtually as clearing houses, checking on the personality and financial resources of the ordinand

---

[48] *Reg. Sutton*, vii, pp. xii–xiii; Rodes, p. 115.

[49] J. F. Williams, 'Ordination in the Norwich Diocese during the Fifteenth century', *Norfolk Archaeology*, xxxi (1957), p. 357; for York, above, n.13; for Lichfield, LJRO, throughout the episcopal registers.

[50] *Memorials of the Church of SS Peter and Wilfrid, Ripon*, iv, ed. J. T. Fowler (Surtees Society, cxv, 1908), p. 142.

[51] Moran, *ubi supra*, 30.

[52] The crucial change takes place at LJRO, B/A/1/1, ff.148^v, 150^{r-v}.

[53] LJRO, B/A/1/1, f.153^v; his ordination as priest is entered at f.156^v, to a title derived from St John's hospital, Warwick. A few later instances of patrimonial titles also refer to their being allowed 'by special grace'; e.g. *ibid.*, ff.158^v (John de Standisch), 159^v (William de Brissi). The case of John Tavener of Cardiff is perhaps analogous to Raven's (*Reg. Bransford*, pp. 236, 255).

before passing him on to the bishop. Once the administrative change was completed, the recording of independent presentations disappears almost totally, with the entries containing nothing beyond the record of the monastic titles.

The evidence for the activity of the religious institutions as clearing houses is decidedly scarce. In 1345 Bishop Bransford of Worcester ordained Walter de Dunstaple as subdeacon. The letter granting his title, from a layman, is entered in the register; but when ordained his title (according to the lists) derived from Holy Trinity hospital, Bridgnorth.[54] Worcester also provides indications of a possibly similar arrangement in 1329, when two individuals appeared for ordination with titles ostensibly derived from Lechlade hospital. But M. Stephen de Northeye, rector of Fairford 'acknowledged his responsibility for [their] titles . . . and promised to keep the bishop unharmed on that account'.[55] Presumably, the institution acted as repository for the letters of real title – charters, bonds, or whatever – after checking, where they were thus available for action if required. Whether this was actually the case is probably unproveable. But if there was any reality to this first stage of the proceedings, it might be possible to find evidence in the courts, whether in terms of *fidei lesio* actions in church courts, or pleas of seisin or debt in the secular forum. However, the actual identification of these particular cases as enforcement of title among the general mass of such actions – especially if they were merely bonds for payment of annuities – would prove extremely difficult.

All this is to some extent speculation, and doubtless will not be the last word on ordinations. Many nuances and anomalies demand further consideration. All I have been concerned to present is an hypothesis, which still needs considerable refinement. Whether the 'monastic' titles can be *proved* to have had any reality is doubtful. Such titles were, after all, only intended to be a temporary measure, until the ordinands acquired benefices. While it seems unlikely that patrimonial or pensionary sources were actually replaced as the real sources of income, they were administratively subsumed in the system of monastic titles, and remained so until the upheavals of the Dissolution. But, being thus obscured, what precisely was hidden? It is, in truth, impossible to say. There are, from the fourteenth century onwards, some complaints about the titles system, and suggestions that the legal fiction was a total fraud: that titles were no more than paper qualifications. The chief exponents of this view appear to have been Langland in the fourteenth century, and More in the early sixteenth.[56] But the opacity of the evidence precludes any firm conclusions. There were still patrimonial

---

[54] *Reg. Bransford*, nos. 725, 1063.
[55] *Reg. Orleton*, ed. Haines, p. 18.
[56] *Piers Plowman: an Edition of the C-Text*, ed. D. Pearsall (London, 1978), p. 227; for More see the quotation in Bennett, *ubi supra*, pp. 32-3.

and pensionary titles in the fifteenth century, which could involve quite considerable amounts of land and money.[57] But possibly the legal fiction of the monastic titles during these centuries covered a situation where individuals were, effectively, declaring a subsistence income: there seems to have been no national ecclesiastical legislation declaring the *minimum* amount needed for a title. Although five marks seems to have been considered (at least in the northern province) as the amount required to sustain a priest, with the diocese of Carlisle apparently producing its own local refinement on the system virtually amounting to a sliding scale for orders,[58] there seems to have been no formal requirement that titles should actually be so much. I suspect that many of the concealed titles would have been at the level of 40s. or so which was common in the early fourteenth century, and which itself was not necessarily the minimum.[59] Such sums would have been quite insufficient to secure existence without supplements. Possibly the examination or presentation system caused greater heart-searching than the question of titles: in 1532 Canterbury convocation established a system of testimonial letters for ordinands, which are clearly revisions to the presentation system. Interestingly enough, the fee stipulated for the new-style letters was not to exceed 4d., which suggests the sums the religious corporations might have been receiving as agents.[60] It is possible that, by then, the old problems of forged and fictive titles had reappeared, and the evidence for the early sixteenth century may not be applicable to the fourteenth and fifteenth. Certainly, when the Dissolution came, it brought a considerable change in ordination and title practice: numbers of ordinands dropped dramatically, while there was a reversion to the old forms of non-monastic titles – as would clearly have been necessary in the circumstances.[61] The connections (if

---

[57] E.g. pensions of 100s. derived from specified estates in 1455 and the early 1460s: *Reg. Johannis Stanbury, episcopi Herefordensis, A.D. MCCCCLIII–MCCCCLXXIV*, ed. A. T. Bannister (CYS, xxv, 1919), pp. 139, 152, 154; and in 1474 a title of the manors of Ashton, Stanage, Hampton Lovet, Toneke, and Laghton, belonging to Sir Thomas Cornewayle (*Reg. Myllyng*, p. 155).

[58] Rose, *ubi supra*, p. 211.

[59] LJRO, B/A/1/1, ff.143^{r-v}; *Reg. Reynolds*, pp. 107–22, 130–4, 138–42; lower figures sometimes appear among this last. Patrimonial titles in Lincoln diocese under Sutton averaged out at around 50s.: *Reg. Sutton*, vii, p. xi.

[60] D. Wilkins, *Concilia magnae Britanniae et Hiberniae* (4 vols., London, 1737), iii, p. 718: on the date see S. E. Lehmberg, *The Reformation Parliament, 1529–1536* (Cambridge, 1970), p. 142 n.4.

[61] M. Bowker, 'The Henrician Reformation and the Parish Clergy', *Bulletin of the Institute of Historical Research*, 1 (1977), pp. 34–5; W. Fergusson Irvine, 'The earliest ordination book of the diocese of Chester, 1542–7 and 1555–8', in *Miscellanies Relating to Lancashire and Cheshire*, iv (Lancashire and Cheshire Record society, xliii, 1902), pp. 29–115; *The Reg. of Cuthbert Tunstall, Bishop of Durham, 1530–59, and James Pilkington, Bishop of Durham, 1561–76*, ed. G. Hinde (Surtees society, clxi, 1952), pp. 79–82, 88–9; York, Borthwick Institute of Historical Research, Reg. 28, ff.197^r–201^r.

any) between these developments remain to be explored, as do later changes in the title system. Possibly an obscure bill presented to Parliament in 1539 would have resolved some of the problems, but nothing came of it and no details are known.[62]

Whatever the changes in the sixteenth century signify, it remains a possibility that, in the two preceding centuries, patrimonial and monastic titles to orders, even if not entirely sufficient to fulfil their supposed purpose, were not entirely fraudulent. They could have provided something of a financial safety-net for the unbeneficed clergy. They would still have had to celebrate masses, but their titular income could have provided a standby for periods of unemployment. Thus, although the titles recorded in late medieval ordination lists may be, for the most part, legal fictions, they may conceal the fact that the unbeneficed clergy in this period did have some independent financial security, with all that that implies for their social and economic positions.

---

[62] S. E. Lehmberg, *The Later Parliaments of Henry VIII, 1536–1547* (Cambridge, 1977), p. 82.

18

The Organization and Achievements of the Peasants of Kent and Essex in 1381

Nicholas Brooks

Few events in English history have seized the interest of public and of scholars alike so strongly as the 'Peasants' Revolt' or 'Great Rising' of 1381. For the medievalist it provides one of the very few episodes in which it is possible to detect something of the aspirations, both social and political, of the underprivileged bulk of the population. Some scholars treat the dramatic days of June in that year merely as a temporary aberration of unparalleled social unrest provoked by the political, fiscal and military incompetence of the government; others see them as the inevitable product of the exploitation that was inherent in a feudal regime. We should certainly not be surprised that the revolt should prove a litmus test of historians' own political creeds and favoured historical explanations. Writing this paper at a time when Arthur Scargill was bidding fair to become the Wat Tyler of 1984, it was more than usually apparent that revolutionary events or revolutionary threats make choices necessary – about the political morality of wealth, about the function of the law, about the legitimacy of political violence or of military force and about the role of the 'media' or reporting agents – choices which liberal bourgeois historians are normally happy to avoid. Whether it is a sign of this cowardice or not, it remains true that no full and critical account of the revolt has yet been written, despite the trickle of detailed studies engendered by the sixth centenary of the rising[1] and despite voluminous research into its manorial, administrative, fiscal, religious and military background.[2] Indeed the nearest approach still remains the incomplete masterpiece of André Réville, which was published posthumously and provided with an able but brief general survey by Charles Petit-Dutaillis in 1898.[3] It is

---

[1] *The English Rising of 1381* (Past and Present Society, 1981) reprinted with additions, ed. R. H. Hilton and T. H. Aston (Cambridge 1984); C. Barron, *Revolt in London: 11 to 15 June 1381 (Museum of London, 1981); Essex and the Great Revolt of 1381*, ed. W. H. Liddell and R. G. E. Wood (Essex Record Office Publication, lxxxiv, 1982); E. B. Fryde,, *The Great Revolt of 1381* (Historical Association Pamphlet, 1981); *The Peasants' Revolt in Hertfordshire 1381* (Hertfordshire Library Service, 1981).

[2] See the extensive bibliographies in R. B. Dobson, *The Peasants' Revolt of 1381* (second ed., London, 1983), pp. 404–19 and in Fryde, *Great Revolt* pp. 35–6.

[3] A. Réville, *Le soulèvement des travailleurs d'Angleterre* (Paris, 1898).

perhaps indicative of the English distaste for revolution as well as of unchanging inequalities in the distribution of English wealth that the 600th anniversary of William of Wykeham's foundation of Winchester College in 1382 should have received a far larger and more lavish celebratory volume than any of the cheaply bound and reproduced publications in honour of the revolt of the previous year.[4]

This essay is not an attempt to fill the major gap in the historiography of the rising, nor even to announce a programme for so doing, still less to sound a clarion for the history of revolutionary ideas in the Middle Ages. Instead it examines a neglected aspect of the 1381 rising that is vital for the general interpretation of the revolt. It is offered to Ralph Davis because, both by example and by teaching, he has encouraged the view that English history is far too important to be left to the acknowledged experts in any period; he has also repeatedly demonstrated how our understanding of particular historical events can be transformed by an appreciation of the local topography. For these reasons, an early medievalist is encouraged to venture far from his normal patch and to rush in where more sapient and angelic scholars have feared to tread.

Any attempt to understand the revolt needs to distinguish clearly the rising of the men of Essex and Kent, who moved simultaneously on London and sought to dictate their terms to the king and his government, from the sympathetic movements of local unrest that only occurred when news of the successes of the main rising had spread to Hertfordshire and to the East Midlands, to East Anglia, to Sussex and to Winchester, and even further afield to Somerset, to Worcester, to Lincoln and to Yorkshire. Some of these local and supplementary risings have been well studied and their background of bitter and long-standing grievances against local manorial or urban lords is now well understood.[5] Similarly there has been extensive research into the identities and the activities of the main bodies of the rebels in London itself, and into the demands that they presented to the king.[6] But astonishingly there has been little detailed study of the genesis of the revolt in Essex and Kent and of the actions of the rebels

---

[4] R. Custance (ed.), *Winchester College: Sixth-centenary Essays* (Oxford, 1982).

[5] For St Alban's and East Anglia see Réville, pp. 1–172 and E. Powell, *The Rising in East Anglia in 1381* (Cambridge, 1896); for Bury see M. D. Lobel, *The Borough of Bury St Edmunds* (London, 1935), pp. 150–5 and A. E. Levett, *Studies in Manorial History* (London, 1938), art. no. 4; for Cambridge and Cambridgeshire see *Victoria County History of Cambridgeshire*, ii (London, 1948), pp. 398–402 and iii (1959), pp. 8–12.

[6] R. Bird, *The Turbulent London of Richard II* (London, 1949), pp. 52–63; Barron, *Revolt in London*; A. J. Prescott, 'London in the Peasants' Revolt; a portrait gallery', *London Journal*, vii (1981), 125–43; G. Kriehn, 'Studies in the sources of the Social Revolt in 1381', *American Historical Review* vii (1901–2), 254–85, 458–84; B. Wilkinson, 'The Peasants Revolt of 1381', *Speculum* xv (1940), 12–35.

before they entered London on Thursday 13 June 1381.[7] Here modern scholars have reflected the ignorance of most of the chroniclers of the period, who concentrated on the events in London and on those subsequent local disturbances of which they had particular knowledge. This imbalance can only be partially redressed: Froissart certainly had knowledgeable informants, but he wrote at a distance and for an audience that required a good story rather than an accurate account, whilst the *Anonimalle Chronicle* whose detailed and plausible narrative has generally been followed is even less accurate for events in Kent and Essex than for events in London.[8] It is therefore scarcely surprising that the great rising has seemed 'too mysterious in its motivation and too complex in its ramifications for entirely satisfactory analysis'.[9] Even the modern scholar who has done most to elucidate the peasants' general demand for liberty, for an end to villeinage, to the labour laws and to the control of wages, has nonetheless supposed that the revolt was not centrally planned; any central organization like a modern revolutionary party is, we are told, 'inconceivable in the peasant and artisan society of south-eastern England in 1381'; the men of Kent and Essex reached London so rapidly 'that the local organization hardly had time to develop'.[10]

The impression is thereby created that the revolt developed almost unintentionally and that rural small-holders, bondmen and artisans were not capable of the elaborate planning necessary to realise their radical political and social aspirations. But organizing a rebellion is necessarily a secret operation, and in 1381 was all the more so because of the restrictions on the movement of the rural populace in the Statute of Labourers.[11] It is scarcely surprising that the narrative sources, which reflect the interests and knowledge of their aristocratic, monastic or governmental authors and patrons, tell us nothing of its planning. The other main source for the rising in Kent and Essex are the judicial records associated with the suppression of the revolt, above all the indictments of individual rebels and groups of rebels sworn by hundredal juries before the special commissions charged with

---

[7] Partial exceptions are C. C. Dyer, 'The causes of the revolt in Essex', and H. E. P. Grieve, 'The rebellion and the county town', in Liddell and Wood, *Essex and the Great Revolt*, pp. 21–36, 37–54 and A. F. Butcher, 'English urban society and the revolt of 1381' in *The English Rising* pp. 106–11.

[8] *Chroniques de Froissart*, x (*1380–2*), ed. G. Raynaud (Société de l'histoire de France, Paris, 1897); *The Anonimalle Chronicle 1333–81*, ed. V. H. Galbraith (Manchester, 1937).

[9] Dobson, p. 23.

[10] R. H. Hilton, *Bond Men Made Free: Medieval Peasant Movements and the English Rising of 1381* (London, 1973), pp. 215–16, 220.

[11] B. H. Putnam, *The Enforcement of the Statute of Labourers 1349–59* (New York, 1908), pp. 72, 156–60.

identifying and punishing the principal malefactors.[12] Indictments have their limitations as historical evidence: juries might be intimidated or bear grudges; their memory of dates or of places could be at fault; their knowledge might only extend to events in their own district; scribes made slips in recording so much repetitive material; and many of those indicted were subsequently acquitted. Nonetheless they do provide a mass of information about what acts of insurrection occurred and about some of the leading participants. For our purposes, however, it is important that they tell only about specific felonies – the urging or compelling of men to take up arms or the participation in particular acts of arson, pillage, theft, injury or murder. They do not record the planning of the revolt in outwardly peaceful smoke-filled rooms. We can therefore only assess the extent of whatever planning lay behind the revolt by examining what the men of Kent and Essex actually did and judging whether their acts reflect a disorganised and chaotic explosion of rural and urban anger or a consistent and disciplined plan of action; alternatively we may decide that the truth lies somewhere between these two extremes.

One indication that the revolt was more highly organized than the sources suggest could be seen in the astonishing speed with which it developed. It took but a fortnight from the first outbreak for the insurgents of Kent and Essex to enter London. The most detailed account, that of the *Anonimalle Chronicle*, agrees with the Essex indictments that the first sign of trouble, the spark from which the conflagration spread, occurred at Brentwood, apparently on Thursday 30 May.[13] The chronicler recounts that Thomas (*recte* John) de Bampton was presiding there over the commission set up to enforce

---

[12] The Kentish indictments were presented to a commission headed by Thomas de Holand, earl of Kent; those of West Kent were heard at Maidstone on 4–5 July 1381 (London, P[ublic] R[ecord] O[ffice], K[ing's] B[ench] 9 [Ancient Indictments] 43) of which extracts were printed by E. Powell and G. M. Trevelyan, *The Peasants' Rising and the Lollards* (London, 1899), pp. 1–12; those of East Kent at Canterbury on 8 July (P.R.O., Just[ices Itinerant] 1/400) were well translated by W. B. Flaherty, 'The great rebellion in Kent of 1381', *Archaeologia Cantiania*, iii (1860), 65–96. Some Essex indictments were presented to a commission of oyer and terminer under Sir Robert Tresilian at Havering (26–7 June) and Chelmsford (2–3 July) of which only fragmentary notes survive (P.R.O., KB 9/166/2), some parts of which were translated by J. A. Sparvel-Bayly, 'Essex in insurrection 1381', *Transactions of the Essex Archaeological Society*, i (1878), 204–19. A fuller range of Essex indictments presented to Thomas of Woodstock, earl of Buckingham, at Chelmsford (25 June), Colchester (3 July), Witham (22 July) and Brentwood (26 July) have not been printed (P.R.O., KB 145/3/6/1). These and other records have been magisterially surveyed by A. J. Prescott, *The Judicial Records of the Rising of 1381* (unpublished Ph.D. thesis, Univ. of London, 1984). I am most grateful to Dr Prescott for making his thesis available to me at short notice and for generously lending me his transcripts of the indictments of West Kent and of Buckingham's Essex commission.

[13] *Anonimalle*, p. 134/6: 'une iour avaunt le Pentecost' (= Dobson, p. 124) P.R.O., KB 9/166/2 m. 4 (=Sparvel-Bayly, *ubi supra in n. 12*, 218).

full payment of the unpopular three-groat poll tax of November 1380; the men of Fobbing refused further payments, and with fellows from Corringham and Stanford-le-Hope forced Bampton and his two sergeants-at-arms to flee to London. Doubts about this story arise when we find that the Essex commission, set up on 16 March 1381, in fact comprised the sherriff (Sir John Sewale), four justices with long experience in Essex and Suffolk (Sir John Gildesborough, Sir William de Wauton, Sir Richard de Waldegrave and Thomas Bataill) together with a clerk (Thomas de Wilford) and a single sergeant-at-arms (John de Asshewell). There is no trace of John de Bampton.[14] He may, indeed, have replaced one of the four justices in this unwelcome task; certainly it would not seem likely that his role at Brentwood has been entirely invented, though it may have been exaggerated or misunderstood. Bampton's property was to be one of the principal targets when the rising got under way.[15] Moreover an inquisition held before Sir Robert Tresilian at Chelmsford on 4 July 1381 records that on 30 May at Brentwood men, not only from Fobbing and Stanford but also from Mucking, Horndon, Billericay, Rawreth, Ramsden, Warley, Haverstock, *Ginge*, Bocking, Goldhanger, Rainham, South Weald, Bennington (Herts), and Ingatestone, assaulted 'John Gildesborough, John Bampton and other justices of the peace with bows and arrows, pursuing them to kill them.'[16] This is evidently the same occasion that the chronicler describes, though Gildesborough here takes precedence over Bampton. It is also instructive that both the chronicler and the indictment name Fobbing first amongst the villages involved in the resistance to the commission at Brentwood; for Henry Knighton's brief account of the inception of the rising specifies that Thomas Baker 'of Fobbing' was the 'first mover', the man who had had the courage to refuse the commission's demand for further payments and to encourage his fellow-villagers and men from other vills to follow suit.[17] The majority of the villages involved in the resistance at Brentwood were either (like Fobbing, Corringham and Stanford) in the hundred of Barstaple or on its fringes (Map 6). This may however tell us less of the organization of unrest at this seminal moment than of the

---

[14] *Cal[endar of] Fine Rolls, 1377–83* (London, 1926), p. 249. For the commissioners' previous experience as justices, commissioners of array etc., see *Cal[endar of] Pat[ent] Rolls, 1377–81*, pp. 23, 38, 40, 45, 59, 288, 304, 331, 358, 420, 472, 474, 514, 571, 575.

[15] Bampton's efforts to recover 'manors, houses, cattle, jewels and other goods led (8 August 1381) to a special Essex commission to enforce restitution; but he had died by that time (*Cal. Pat. Rolls 1381–5*, pp. 24, 76). For Gildesborough's licence to recover his properties, see *ibid.*, p. 24. Curiously the Essex indictments only refer to a single attack on a property of Bampton, at *Bermermersh* in Lawling (P.R.O., KB 145/3/6/1 unnumbered membranes).

[16] P.R.O., KB 9/166/2 m. 4 (= Sparvel-Bayly, *ubi supra in n. 12*, 218. The indictment does not include Corringham in its list of vills.

[17] Henry Knighton, *Chronicon*, ed. J. R. Lumby (Rolls Series, 1889–95), ii. 130–1 (= Dobson, p. 136).

particular business of the poll-tax commission on that day. Only Bocking, away in the north of the county, and Bennington in Hertfordshire – a shire that was normally linked with Essex in fiscal administration – fit ill with the other names.

After the initial outbreak at Brentwood events moved swiftly. The Essex indictments record a meeting on Whitsunday (2 June) in the north of the shire, significantly at Bocking, where men from not only Bocking itself but also from Great and Little Coggeshall, from Stisted, Ashen, Braintree, Dunmowe, Dedham, Little Henny and Gestingthorpe 'rose treacherously against the lord king' and swore to be of one mind 'to destroy divers lieges of the king and his common laws and all lordship' or 'to destroy divers lieges of the lord king and to have no law in England except only those they themselves moved to be ordained.'[18] It looks as if the men from Bocking who had been at Brentwood may have planned the spread of insurrection in their own part of the shire; for the Bocking men are named first in the indictments, and the others who took the oath all came from villages within easy reach, that is from the hundred of Hinckford and its immediate vicinity (Map 6). If the jurors reported accurately the nature of the oath taken at Bocking, then the aims of the Essex insurgents were already clear at this early stage: they wished to kill certain of the king's ministers or officials and they wished to achieve radical changes in the existing social structure and in the law which maintained it. We cannot fail to be reminded of the comparable demands made after the insurgents had entered London, namely that certain named 'traitors' be put to death, that there should be 'no law but that of Winchester' and that no man 'should be a serf, nor make homage or any type of service to any lord'.[19] These demands would seem to have been at the root of the revolt almost from its start.

On the same day (2 June) occurred the first recorded act of insurrection in Kent when Abel Ker (according to his confession) led a band of men from Erith and Lessness to the abbey of Lessness and forced the abbot to swear to be of their company.[20] It is unlikely to be chance that this oath to join the insurrection should have coincided with that taken in northern Essex at Bocking. The compulsion of the abbot made noteworthy what would otherwise have remained a secret and unknown occasion. That there was already an attempt to achieve a concerted rising in Kent and Essex is perhaps also indicated by the fact that on 3 June, Abel Ker and his group crossed the estuary of the

[18] P.R.O., KB 145/3/6/1: 'et ibidem iuraverunt essendum de uno assensu ad destruendum diversos ligeos domini regis et communes leges suas et etiam omnia dominia diversis dominis spectantia.'; '. . . essendum de uno assensu ad interficiendum et destruendum diversos ligeos domini regis, dicendum et iurandum quod noluerunt aliquam legem in Anglia habere nisi tantummodo certas leges per ipsos motas ordinandum.'

[19] *Anonimalle*, pp. 144–5, 147 (= Dobson, pp. 161, 164).

[20] Réville, pp. 183–4.

The Organization of the Peasants in 1381 253

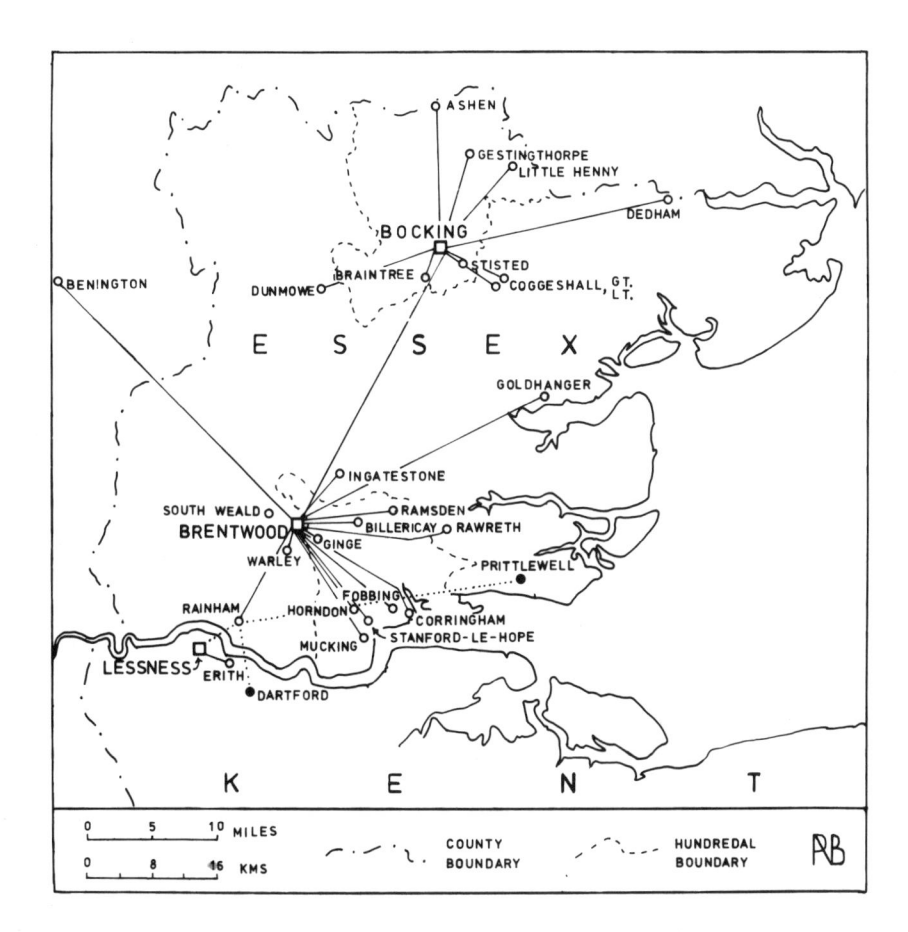

Map 6. The Beginning of the Revolt (30 May–4 June). Meetings at Brentwood (30 May), Bocking (2 June) and Lessness (2 June).

Thames into Essex, raised a sworn 'conventicle' of a hundred or more men there, and returned with them to Kent to Dartford on the following day (Tuesday 4 June).[21] Further light on Abel Ker's recruiting drive in Essex may be thrown by the jurors of Rochford hundred, who declared that John Chaundeler of Prittlewell was compelled against his will by 'the commons of Kent' to instruct Sir William Berland and John Prittlewell senior to rise and meet the commons of Kent at Rainham. Berland was currently a justice of the peace and Prittlewell had served as an assessor of the 1379 Poll Tax.[22] Once again it would seem that we only obtain information about the preparation of the revolt from the judicial records when members of the gentry happened to be affected. The village of Prittlewell is at least twenty-four miles from Rainham which itself lies conveniently just across the Thames from Erith and Dartford (Map 6); the hundred or so Essex men who gathered at Rainham to join the rising in Kent may (to judge from Prittlewell) have been drawn from villages quite widely spread in southern Essex.

Dr A. J. Prescott has recently demonstrated that whilst these preparations were under way in Essex and Kent, Sir Robert Belknap, the chief justice of Common Pleas, had been holding routine sessions of the assizes in both shires: at Stratford Longthorne (Essex) on 30 May and at Dartford (Kent) where he sat with William Topclyve on 3 June.[23] The record of these assizes gives no hint that they met any disturbance, though they may well, of course, have aroused resentment amongst some litigants. The fact that Belknap's assize at Dartford was so closely followed by the return of Abel Ker's band with its reinforcement from Essex and by a day and a half of insurrection that then ensued in the same township (5–6 June) appears to have muddled the author of the *Anonimalle Chronicle*. He recounts erroneously that Belknap's assize was a commission of trailbaston intended to suppress those who had driven Bampton from Brentwood, that a similar trailbaston commission was at work in Kent accompanied by a royal sergeant-at-arms, John Legge, and that both commissions were turned back by the rebels.[24] This is an astonishing mixture of half-truth and conjecture resulting in total error. There were no trailbaston commissions in Kent or Essex at this time; John Legge was indeed a sergeant-at-arms assigned to a commission sent to Kent, but it was the unpopular commission to check upon the assessment and collection of the 1380 poll tax – a commission which had only been set up for Kent on 3 May – not a commission of trailbaston. Legge's objectionable activities on the Kentish poll-tax

[21] *Ibid.*, pp. 183–4.
[22] Prescott, *Judicial Records*, p. 143 citing P.R.O., KB 145/3/6/1. For Berland's and Prittlewell's earlier offices, see *Cal. Pat. Rolls 1377–81*, pp. 348, 358, 514, 591; *Cal. Fine Rolls 1377–83*, p. 147.
[23] Prescott, *Judicial Records*, pp. 128–9 citing P.R.O., Just. 1/1491.
[24] *Anonimalle*, pp. 135–6 (= Dobson, p. 125).

commission, above all his determination to allow the exemption due to those under fifteen only to those young girls whose virginity he established by personal examination and touch, aroused such hatred in Kent that public opinion even held him responsible for the initial suggestion that the poll-tax commissions should be set up; he was later to be one of the 'traitors' beheaded upon Tower Hill on Friday 14 June.[25] It seems clear that in Kent, as in Essex, the poll tax and the government's attempts to tighten its assessment and collection was one of the main roots of the uprising.

A new stage in the development of the revolt seems to have been reached in both shires on Thursday 6 June. By then the period of sworn 'conventicles' in secret was over and we hear instead of open acts of insurrection and of the public proclaiming of the rising. The men who had sworn the oath at Bocking on 2 June gathered once more and went to Great Coggeshall to the house of Sir John Sewale, the sheriff of Essex, and there did such 'insult' to him and to Robert de Segynton, an exchequer clerk, that they despaired of their lives.[26] The purpose of this episode is unclear; it may have been a trial run for the actions of 10 June; it may have been an attempt to seize the sheriff's records which failed, or it may have been a successful but inadequately recorded effort to intimidate the sheriff and prevent him from taking action to curb the revolt as it gathered momentum during the ensuing days. What emerges clearly from the Essex indictments, however, is that the days from 6 to 9 June saw in southern and central Essex a crescendo of public proclamations in which the inhabitants of village after village were urged or coerced to join the sworn company of the insurgents (Map 7). We receive an uneven record of the communications from one village to another in this process, but the names of some of the principal inciters stand out clearly: Robert Berdon of Orsett (the most active of all), Ralf Spicer and John Messager of Prittlewell, John Glasier of Rochford, John Newman of Rawreth, William Roger of South Ockendon, John Cukholz of Great Wakering, Peter White of Canewdon, John 'Frost' of Chipping Ongar. Behind such men (the 'flying pickets' of 1381) lies the organizing activity of Thomas Baker of Fobbing who is said to have sent Robert Berdon to proclaim the rising at Rayleigh on Friday 7 June.[27] The man who had started the insurrection at Brentwood was evidently still involved with its dissemination.

In Kent the indictments do not normally record the proclaiming of

[25] For the commission of 3 May, see *Cal. Fine Rolls 1377–83*, p. 250; Knighton, *Chronicon*, pp. 129–30, 133–5 (= Dobson, pp. 135–6, 182); *Anonimalle*, p. 145 (= Dobson, p. 162).

[26] P.R.O., KB 145/3/6/1.

[27] *Ibid.*: '. . . quod Thomas Bakere de Fobbyng et Willelm Goldebourn felonice miserunt Robert Berdon de Orsete ut nuntium eorum ad villam de Reyle die veneris proxima sancte Trinitati . . . ad levandum homines ville predicte contra pacem regis.'

the rising, but they do make clear the growing momentum of open insurrection between Thursday 6 June and Trinity Sunday (9 June). The insurgents from Erith and Lessness and from Essex who had assembled at Dartford were joined on the Thursday by men not only from Dartford itself but also from Maplescombe, Farningham, Kingsdown, Brenchley, Wrotham, Stoneham, Maidstone, Strood and Rochester (Map 7).[28] Their first recorded action might seem to have had purely local motives. They besieged Rochester castle and released from gaol (purportedly against his will) a prisoner named Robert Belling, who may be identified as the subject of a story in the *Anonimalle Chronicle*: an inhabitant of Gravesend, he had been claimed as a serf by (*recte* on behalf of?) Sir Simon Burley on 3 June and had then been imprisoned at Rochester because he was unable to pay the exorbitant sum demanded for his enfranchisement.[29] We should not underestimate the symbolic importance of the release, willingly or not, of the imprisoned serf. It suggests that even in Kent the demand for the abolition of villeinage was a potent rallying cry. But the capture in a single afternoon of a major royal castle was, like the attack on the sheriff of Essex at Coggeshall on that same day, a vivid demonstration of the insurgents' power. It must have made the work of spreading the revolt in the ensuing days very much easier. This would have been all the more so if there is any factual basis to Froissart's story of their compelling the castellan, Sir John Newton to accompany them and be of their number.[30] From Rochester the Kentish insurgents moved on to Maidstone (7 June), to North Cray and Dartford (8 June) and back to Rochester again on Sunday 9 June (Map 7). On each day they broke into and sacked the manors or houses of certain selected targets or victims whose records, rolls and other muniments were destroyed. These activities culminated in the ceremonial burning in Rochester on Trinity Sunday of all the 'evidences' of the escheator for the county of Kent, Elias Reyner, which he had been compelled to hand over at his home at Strood that same day.[31]

The indictments do not entitle us to assume that all the insurgents, or even the bulk of them, completed every stage of this round trip of northern and western Kent; nonetheless, the distance of sixty-four miles covered in four days, whilst they disposed of selected targets, suggests that we should not underestimate the organization that underlay it. Even at this preliminary stage the Kentish 'peasants' of 1381 were operating at a speed which compares very favourably with

---

[28] Réville, pp. 184–7; P.R.O., KB 9/43 (Powell and Trevelyan, pp. 1–12); P.R.O., Just. 1/400 m. 19 (Flaherty, *ubi supra in n. 12*, 90); *Anonimalle*, pp. 136–7 (= Dobson, pp. 126–7).

[29] Réville, p. 187; *Anonimalle*, pp. 136–7 (= Dobson, pp. 126–7).

[30] Froissart, *Chroniques*, x. 101 (= Dobson, p. 140).

[31] P.R.O., KB 9/43 m. 7 (Powell and Trevelyan, p. 6).

The Organization of the Peasants in 1381

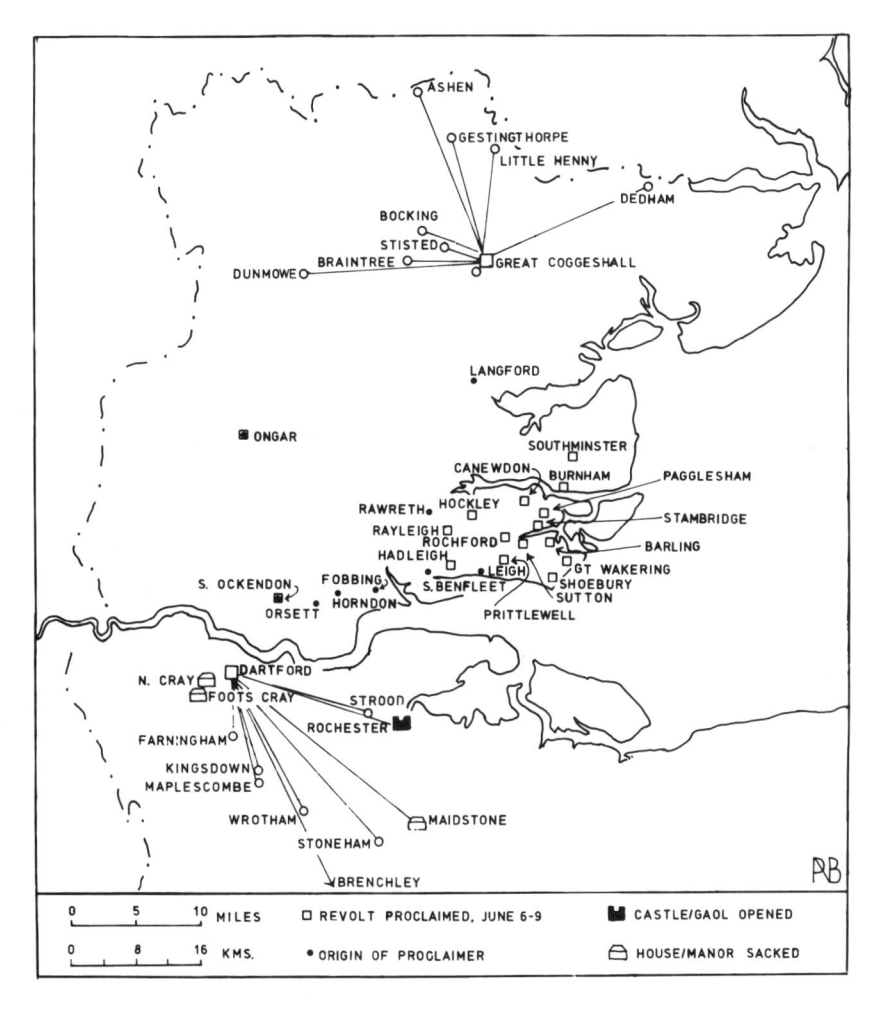

Map 7. Preparation and Dissemination of the Revolt (6–9 June).

that of the later popular risings with which it is natural to compare them,[32] or with that of the most highly trained infantry armies of later times.[33] It is instructive that it is during these days that we first hear of new leaders of the rising. According to the *Anonimalle Chronicle* it was after the attack on Rochester Castle and the participation there of men from Maidstone that the insurgents chose Wat Tyler 'of Maidstone' as their leader. Partial confirmation of this story is provided by the indicting jury of Maidstone hundred which, after describing events of 7–9 June, declared that Wat Tyler 'of Colchester', John Abel of Dartford, John Hales and William Apouldre of (East) Malling and William Heneke were the 'first malefactors and maintainours of the malefactors and perturbers of the peace'. Other jurors, from hundreds in East rather than West Kent, were to refer to Tyler as 'of Essex' and this local information must be preferred to that of less well placed sources which assumed from his leadership of the 'commons' of Kent that he had originated there.[34] We might seek to reconcile the sources by supposing that Tyler was a Colchester man who had been resident for a time at Maidstone; but it is equally possible that he was one of the men whom Abel Ker had recruited in Essex and that he only came to prominence at the siege of Rochester Castle. On either interpretation, the prominence amongst the Kentish insurgents of a man from Essex is another sign of how closely the risings in the two shires were interrelated and interdependent.

Certainly from Monday 10 until Wednesday 12 June, the risings in Kent and Essex have all the appearance of a most carefully planned and synchronized insurrection. We need to bear in mind that though the

---

[32] Jack Cade's 1451 rising took 4 or 5 days to travel from Canterbury to Blackheath (59 miles via Rochester); Kett's Norfolk rising of 1549 took 2 days to travel 6 miles from Hethersett to Bowthorpe near Norwich; Wyatt's rebellion of 1554 took 5 days to march from Rochester to London; Monmouth's 'army' in 1685 when moving at maximum speed but by a circuitous route, travelled 73 miles from Taunton to Frome in 7 days. See R. A. Griffiths, *The Reign of Henry VI* (London, 1981), pp. 610–16; W. K. Jordan, *Edward VI: the Young King* (Cambridge, 1968), pp. 480–1; D. M. Loades, *Two Tudor Conspiracies* (Cambridge, 1965), pp. 63, 68; G. Roberts, *Life of Monmouth* (London, 1844), chs xviii–xxi *passim*. I owe most of these references and those in n. 33 to the kindness of Professor J. P. Kenyon.

[33] Cromwell's New Model Army could average 10 miles a day for a week and achieve up to 13 miles on a single day; Marlborough achieved no improvement, but Frederick the Great's reform of training boosted the average to 22 km. (15 miles) a day. See C. H. Firth, *Cromwell's Army* (London, 1902, reissued 1962), pp. 106–8; W. S. Churchill, *Marlborough his Life and Times* (London, 1954), ii 364; J. Childs, *Armies and Warfare in Europe, 1646–1789* (Manchester, 1982), p. 115.

[34] P.R.O., KB 9/43 m. 12 (= Powell and Trevelyan, p. 9); P.R.O., Just. 1/103 m. (= Flaherty, *ubi supra in n. 12*, 92–3); the continuator of the *Eulogium Historiarum* (iii 352) describes him as 'unus tegulator de Estsex'; but in *Rot[uli] Parl[iamentorum]* (London, 1783), iii 175 he is 'Wauter Tylere del countee de Kent', and in *Anonimalle*, p. 137 'Watt Teghler de Maydenstoun' (= Dobson, p. 127).

The Organization of the Peasants in 1381

methods of the 'peasants' of 1381 were to provide the classic model for English popular risings in subsequent centuries, they themselves had no such pattern to follow, at least not in England.[35] On any reckoning, to bring men out from communities throughout the two counties in open and simultaneous revolt and to concert the movement on London of sufficient forces to overrun the capital, to capture the Tower of London and seize and behead the leading ministers of the crown was an astonishing and impressive achievement. Even though the chroniclers' figures of 50 and 60,000 men arriving at Blackheath and at Mile End respectively on 12 June are probably conventional exaggerations, which should perhaps be divided by ten or even more, it is clear from the judicial records that we should at least be thinking in terms of a few thousand men from both shires.[36] Even if we suppose that most will have travelled light, have had only the simplest weapons or armour and will have relied on being provided with food by sympathisers or on seizing it as needed, the rising remains a formidable logistic accomplishment. The main forces assembled in both shires on the morning of Monday 10 June. The 'commons' of Essex, who gathered in the north of the county at Cressing Temple before moving to Coggeshall, can be shown from the indictments to have been drawn from over forty parishes from almost every part of the shire (Map 8). Then on the following day they moved on to the county town, Chelmsford, and on Wednesday 12 June they reached the outskirts of London at Mile End and encamped there. In Kent we find a very similar pattern. On the morning of 10 June, Wat Tyler, John Hales of Malling and the Kentish insurgents who had been at Rochester the previous day, arrived in Canterbury and were met there by men from villages throughout East Kent; the following day, thus reinforced, they moved on to the county town of Maidstone; on 12 June they reached

---

[35] E. J. Hobsbawm, *Primitive Rebels* (Manchester, 1959); G. Rudé, *The Crowd in History* (London, 1964). For earlier peasant unrest in England, see R. H. Hilton 'Peasant movements in England before 1381', *Economic History Review*, second ser., ii (1949), 117–36; for comparable European risings from 1378 see M. Mollat and P. Wolff, *The Popular Revolutions of the Middle Ages* (London, 1973), pp. 138–84, and G. Fourquin, *Les soulèvements populaires au moyen âge* (Paris, 1972), p. 197–209).

[36] *Anonimalle*, p. 139 (= Dobson, p. 129) has 50,000 of the commons of Kent gather at Blackheath and 60,000 of Essex north of the Thames; Thomas Walsingham, *Historia Anglicana*, ed. H. T. Riley (Rolls Series, 1863–4), i 455–6 (= Dobson, p. 134) has 100,000 of Kent and Essex gather at Blackheath; Froissart, *Chroniques*, x 110 (= Dobson, p. 190) has 60,000 at the Mile End meeting of 14 June. According to A. J. Prescott, 'Some Essex Rebel Bands in London', in Liddell and Wood, *Essex and the Great Revolt*, p. 56 private trespass actions against the insurgents provide the actual names of nearly a thousand rebels from Essex. For comparisons of Froissart's and other chronicler's figures for fourteenth-century armies with the numbers actually mustered, see J. H. Ramsey, 'The Strength of English Armies in the Middle Ages', *Eng. Hist. Rev.*, xxix (1914), 221–7 and F. Lot, *L'Art militaire et les armées au moyen âge*, i (Paris, 1946), pp. 336–7.

Blackheath, just five miles from London (Map 8). The synchronized assembly and movement of the insurgent forces in the two counties did not fit by chance into so neat a pattern. Decisions had to be taken and orders sent about meeting places, about dates and about targets; these decisions had to take account of the distances to be covered by each band on each day and of the time that would be needed to open gaols and to break into properties and destroy records. Every vill that sent men to the assembly-points had to be contacted in advance. To judge from the Essex indictments there are likely to have been preliminary secret oath-taking meetings, followed on a predetermined day by the public proclamation of the revolt and the setting out of the insurgents for Cressing Temple or for Canterbury. We cannot, of course, be certain how many of the individual acts of pillage or terrorization were predetermined and how many were decided on the spur of the moment. But the fundamental plan for bringing out the two shires simultaneously and moving next day to the county towns and to London on the following day must have been planned in advance by some form of central high command. Whether it was men like Thomas Baker of Fobbing or Wat Tyler of Colchester who planned it, or rather some anonymous revolutionary committee, the reality of the planning can scarcely be doubted.

A very similar conclusion may be drawn if we consider the targets of the insurgents in the days leading up to their arrival in London. In both counties the sheriff was captured on Monday 10 June: Sir John Sewale of Essex at his house in Great Coggeshall, Sir William Septvans of Kent when Canterbury Castle was successfully stormed. We learn that Sewale was abused, his clothing torn and his house pillaged, and that the rebels then removed 'all writs and summs of the lord king of the green wax' or 'divers writs of the lord king and the rolls of the same', and carried them to Chelmsford the next day where they were publicly burnt.[37] Septvans was taken from Canterbury by Wat Tyler, John Hales of Malling, Abel (Ker) of Erith and many others to his manor some two miles to the south of the city at Milton, where he was forced to hand over 'fifty rolls of the pleas of the county and of the crown', together with whatever royal writs were in his custody; these were taken back to Canterbury and burned there that same day.[38] The desire to destroy documents sealed with green wax, for which we have evidence in Kent as in Essex, reflects the fact that this was the colour used for documents issued from the exchequer. For largely illiterate insurgents 'green wax' was an easy way of identifying documents that might concern taxation. It is clear that these simultaneous attacks on the sheriffs of Essex and Kent represent a deliberate attempt to destroy the current records of the fiscal and judicial administration of the two

---

[37] P.R.O., KB 145/3/6/1.
[38] Flaherty, *ubi supra in n.* 12, 89, 92–3.

The Organization of the Peasants in 1381 261

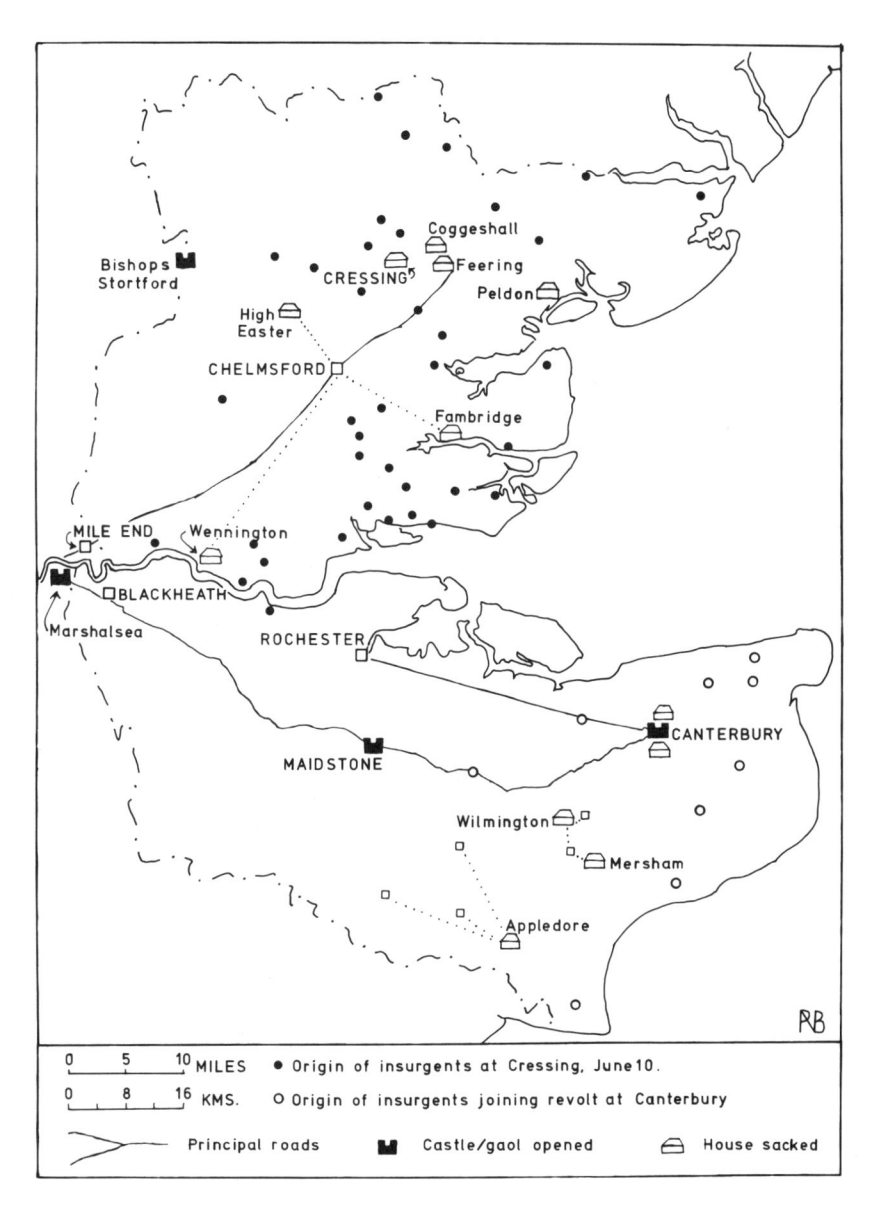

Map 8. *The Approach to London (10–12 June).*

shires. They imply both careful planning and accurate knowledge of the sheriffs' whereabouts and likely movements.

The indictments establish that in both shires not only the sheriffs but also the escheators were especial targets. We have already seen that in Kent Elias Reyner had been compelled to hand over the records of his escheatry on Sunday 9 June and that they had then been burnt at Rochester. On the following day the Essex insurgents seized and killed the escheator John Ewell (or John Clerk of Ewell) at Coggeshall at the same time as they were seizing the sheriff. We do not know whether he was killed because he was less compliant than the sheriff or whether he was particularly hated in the shire; but after he was slain a detachment went on to Ewell's house at Feering, just two miles to the south of Coggeshall, and broke in and carried away 'the writs and muniments pertaining to his office'.[39] They were presumably burnt at Chelmsford along with the shrieval records on Tuesday 11 June. That same Tuesday a group of Kentish rebels from Longbridge and Mersham, apparently acting separately but presumably in sympathy with and perhaps at the orders of the main body of the Kentish commons, broke into the manor-house of John Brode in the south of the county at Mersham (Map 8). Brode had been escheator of Kent from 1377 until he was replaced by Elias Reyner in October 1380; on demitting office he was soon appointed as an assessor of the poll tax. At Mersham the rebels destroyed not only his escheat roll but also the roll 'of the receipt of the subsidy of three groats'.[40] There is no doubt that the escheators were targets in 1381 precisely because they were the local officials most closely involved with the poll tax: in every shire they had been appointed to survey and control the assessment of the tax; in January 1381 when there was already governmental concern at low returns, the escheator and sheriff were established as a two-man commission in every shire to enquire into *and record* the name, abode and class of every person over 15; a few months later the escheators were normally members of the enlarged commissions charged with identifying tax-evaders and securing full payment of the three-groat poll tax.[41] In view of the initial stand against further payments of tax taken by Thomas Baker of Fobbing at Brentwood, it is not surprising that the insurgents took such care to destroy any records which made it possible to identify those who had paid (and therefore also those who had not paid) the tax.

Indeed a concern to wipe out all traces of the poll tax and to punish those responsible for it explains a high proportion of the actions of the

---

[39] P.R.O., KB 145/3/6/1.

[40] Flaherty, *ubi supra in n. 12*, 84.

[41] *Cal. Fine Rolls 1377–83*, pp. 224–34, 248–50; *Cal. Pat. Rolls 1377–81*, pp. 627–8; T. F. Tout, *Chapters in the Administrative History of Mediaeval England* (Manchester, 1920–33), iii 359–64. For Wat Tyler's alleged view that all the escheators should be beheaded, see Walsingham *Historia Anglicana*, i. 464.

Kent and Essex commons before they reached London. In Essex the insurgents had assembled at Cressing Temple in order that their first action on Monday 10 June could be the sacking and destruction of the preceptory of the order of the knights of the Hospital of St John of Jerusalem. The hospitallers were not themselves in any way such notorious lords to have merited this attention, but their prior, Sir Robert Hales, had been appointed as treasurer on 1 February 1381.[42] He had, therefore, not himself been responsible for devising the 1380 poll-tax, but he had inherited responsibility for it and he had been in office when the notorious commissions to enforce payment and identify evaders had been established. He was therefore one of those whose head was demanded by the insurgents when they reached London, and was one of the 'traitors' summarily beheaded on Tower Hill on Friday 14 June. The admiral, Sir Edmund de la Mare, whose manor at Peldon was sacked on Wednesday 12 June and whose documents were carried to Mile End on a (pitch) fork, seems likewise to have been a target simply as a minister of the government responsible for the poll tax, though he may also have been held accountable for the vulnerability of the channel ports to naval attack.[43] The other main target of the Essex insurgents was Sir John Gildesborough, whose three manor-houses at Fambridge, High Easter and Wennington were sacked and the documents found therein destroyed in simultaneous attacks by different detachments on Tuesday 11 June. The first two of these manors lay at convenient distances of ten and twelve miles from the main assembly of the rising that day at Chelmsford, but Wennington was over twenty miles away to the south-west (Map 8). Once again when we piece together the fragmentary evidence of the indictments we find that an impressive degree of organization must lie behind the recorded actions of the insurgents on a single day. Gildesborough was an Essex landowner and justice of the peace, who had been a member and indeed also the speaker of the Northampton parliament of November 1380, which had reluctantly consented to the three-groat poll tax; he had also been a member of the Essex commission of 16 March 1381 to enforce payment of the tax and he had been presiding over this commission's session at Brentwood when the insurrection had started.[44] No one in Essex was therefore more closely associated in the popular mind with

[42] *Cal. Pat. Rolls, 137781*, p. 589.
[43] P.R.O., KB 145/3/6/1: 'Item presentant quod Radulfus atte Wode de Bradewell . . . die mercurii tunc proxima sequente domum, Ed*mundi* de la Mare fregit apud Peldon, . . . et libri domini Regis a domo . . . usque le Mile End super unum longum furcum felonice portavit . . . ' See also Sparvel-Bayly, *ubi supra in n. 12*, 217. For the neglect of coastal defence, see, E. Searle and R. Burghart, 'The Defence of England and the Peasants' Revolt', *Viator: Mediaeval and Renaissance Studies* iii (1972), 365–88.
[44] *Cal. Pat. Rolls, 1377–81*, p. 571; *Rot. Parl.*, iii 71–3, 88–90; for the poll tax commission, see *Cal. Fine Rolls, 1377–83*, p. 249; and Sparvel-Bayly, *ubi supra in n. 12*, 218; for attacks on his properties, see, P.R.O., KB 145/3/6/1.

the poll tax than he, and there can be no doubt that this was why his properties were selected as a target.

In Kent too, the poll tax lies behind many of the actions of the insurgents. Of the members of the commission to enforce payment of the tax, set up for Kent on 3 May 1381, we have already noted that the sheriff (Septvans), the escheator (Reyner) and the king's sergeant-at-arms (Legge) were in different ways principal targets. Another member was the justice of the peace, Sir Nicholas Heryng, whose manors at North Cray and Foots Cray were sacked and his records destroyed on Saturday 8 June and whose town-house in Rochester received similar treatment on the following day.[45] He was perhaps the nearest Kentish equivalent to Gildesborough. Two other commissioners, James de Peckham and John de Farningham, were amongst the gentry who when captured by the 'commons' were prepared under duress to accompany them and to swear to be of their number and to support their aims.[46] In Canterbury, where a separate commission of three had been set up on 20 May to enforce the tax in the city, we find a similar pattern: Thomas Oteryngton's house in the city was sacked on 10 June, whilst John T(y)ece who had evaded the insurgents on that day was killed on Saturday 15 June by a group of Canterbury men returning from London.[47] It is of course impossible to know how far it was their membership of the poll-tax commissions that made such men targets and how far it was their participation in local judicial, administrative, political and business activities as jurors, bailiffs, aldermen, stewards and the like. Certainly in Canterbury, as elsewhere, it seems likely that the insurgents often had local and personal grievances and scores to settle as well.[48] One feature that appears to distinguish the Kentish rising from that of Essex is that the 'commons' of Kent do not seem to have attacked any central governmental targets before they reached London. There is no Kentish equivalent to the assaults on Cressing Temple and Peldon, even though the archbishop of Canterbury, Simon Sudbury, had been chancellor since January 1380 and was the principal target of the rebels when they broke into the Tower on 14 June. He is likely to have been regarded as one of the 'traitors' held responsible for the poll tax from the start of the uprising; yet neither the archiepiscopal palace at Canterbury nor the cathedral priory at Christ Church was attacked on 10 June, nor were any of the numerous archiepiscopal manors in northern Kent during the days when the Kentish insurgents were on the move from 6 to 12 June. This suggests an element of discipline and planning in the actions of the Kentish insurgents that was

[45] Powell and Trevelyan, pp. 4, 7, 9; Réville, pp. 185, 187.
[46] Réville, pp. 185, 187.
[47] Flaherty, *ubi supra* in n. 12, 74–6, 87, 93.
[48] Butcher, *ubi supra* in n. 7, 28–31. Compare the settling of local scores in London instanced by A. J. Prescott, *ubi supra* in n. 6, 136–7.

The Organization of the Peasants in 1381   265

based on the knowledge that the main residence of the archbishop (which was used when he needed to be in London) was at Lambeth on the south bank of the Thames. They probably also knew that Lambeth was already the main archiepiscopal archive; certainly Lambeth Palace was one of the first targets when the insurgents reached the outskirts of London, though it remains uncertain whether it was sacked on the evening of Wednesday 12 June or on the following day. Amongst much general pillage and destruction we learn that those attacking the palace burnt 'all the books of registers and the chancery remembrancer rolls' that they found there.[49] That is to say they destroyed not only the archbishops' manorial records but also whatever governmental records Sudbury had stored there.

Apart from the chief officers of state ('the traitors') and from all those connected with the poll tax, there is one other clearly identifiable category amongst the victims of the revolt in Kent and Essex during the first fortnight of June 1381, namely men of the law. The chroniclers write of a plan, associated especially with Wat Tyler, to kill all lawyers, jurors and justices as a preliminary to the rebels' intentions to abolish all the laws of the realm.[50] The indictments reveal that in reality very few individuals were killed by the insurgents in Essex (6) or in Kent (8).[51] With the exception of John Ewell, the escheator of Essex, they seem to have all been men of little social or political standing and it is entirely likely that several of them may have earned popular hatred as 'questmongers' (that is by constantly serving on juries of inquisition), for jurors might reveal critical information to the detriment of their neighbours.[52] But if the chroniclers grossly exaggerated the killing, they were correct in supposing that the insurgents regarded the law as an instrument of social repression, as the means by which the landed gentry maintained the economic and social dependence of the bulk of the rural populace. That is implicit in the secret oath sworn at Bocking on 2 June to destroy the common laws and all lordship. Moreover both

[49] *Anonimalle*, p. 140 (= Dobson, p. 155); for the confusion of the chronology, see *Anonimalle*, pp. 194–5. The earlier date is however supported by the only other account of the attack on Lambeth. See *The Westminster Chronicle, 1381–94*, ed. L. C. Hector and B. Harvey (Oxford, 1981), p. 2 (= Dobson, pp. 199–200).

[50] *Anonimalle*, p. 135 (= Dobson, p. 125); Walsingham, *Historia Anglicana*, i 455, 463–3, 468 (= Dobson, pp. 133, 177, 270).

[51] In Kent: John Southalle (Stonhelde) killed at Maidstone (Réville, pp. 185, 187), John Charlet killed at Chatham, John Glovere at Rochester, John Godwot at Borden (Powell and Trevelyan, pp. 7, 11–12), John Tebbe and John Tyece at Canterbury, John Hemynherst at Mersham, William Wottone at Wootton (Flaherty, *ubi supra in n. 12*, 74–5, 84–7, 93–4). In Essex: John Ewell at Coggeshall, John Preme (a Fleming) at Maldon, Nicholas Davenant an auditor of Aubrey Vere, the acting chief-chamberlain, at Brentwood, John Bernard a potter at Danbury, 2 clerks of John Ewell killed by men from Tendring hundred (P.R.O., KB 145/3/6/1).

[52] Compare the fate of the questmonger Roger Legat in London; see Prescott, *ubi supra in n. 6*, 133–6.

in Essex and in Kent, a high proportion of the properties attacked and records destroyed in the days before the rebels reached London belonged to men who had been commissioned as justices of the peace the previous spring or autumn: in Essex – Walter FitzWauter, Thomas Tyrell, John Gildesborough, William Berland, Clement Spice, Geoffrey Dersham, Robert Rikdon and John Bampton; and in Kent – Thomas de Cobham, William Horn of Appledore, William Topclyve, Thomas de Shardelowe and Nicholas Heryng.[53] Seen in this light the rebels' attacks on properties at this time are not simply a general but random assault on manorial lordship – for they left the vast majority of manors untouched at this time – but a specific and selective assault on the judicial establishment in the two counties. The point is reinforced when we find that the other targets in Kent on these days were the houses and 'evidences' of the sub-sheriff, Sir Thomas Holt,[54] of former justices, commissioners of oyer and terminer and members of parliament, Thomas Fogg, Nicholas atte Crouch and Thomas Garwynton;[55] and of two of the county coroners of Kent (William de Medmenham and John Colbrand of Wilmington) whose 'rolls of green wax' or estreat rolls – that is rolls of extracts from exchequer records of outstanding fines and amercements – were the particular objective of the insurgents.[56] It is clear that between 6 and 12 June the rebels in Kent and Essex delivered a shattering blow to the judicial, as to the fiscal, administration of the two counties. It is likely that some degree of common planning and direction lay behind all the attacks upon the judiciary, whether they were made by the main bodies of the insurgents, by detachments from them or by separate groups who operated at the other end of their shires but at the same time. Just occasionally we have proof that this was so. On Monday 10 June the insurgents, who were then assembled at Canterbury, broke into the house of the coroner, William de Medmenham, without apparently discovering there any of his records. Three days later on the Isle of Thanet a proclamation was made in the church of St John 'by commission of John Rakestraw and Watte Tegheler' and as a result a force of two hundred local men was raised who broke into William de Medmenham's house on the Isle and destroyed his coroner's rolls and the estreat rolls they found there.[57] We do not know at what stage en route for London, Jack Straw (assuming he is meant) and Wat Tyler acquired or extorted the information about the whereabouts of

---

[53] For their appointment as justices, see *Cal. Pat. Rolls, 1377–81*, pp. 571–2; for the attacks on their records, properties and persons, see the sources listed in n. 12.

[54] Flaherty, *ubi supra in n. 12*, 74; Powell and Trevelyan, p. 9.

[55] Flaherty, *ubi supra in n. 12*, 75–6, 86–8, 93. For their offices, see *Cal. Close Rolls, 1377–81*, pp. 326, 356, 406, 497; *Cal. Pat. Rolls, 1377–81*, pp. 92–3, 166, 360, 467, 471, 574.

[56] Flaherty, *ubi supra in n. 12*, 73, 76, 83–4.

[57] *Ibid.*, 76.

The Organization of the Peasants in 1381

Medmenham's records; but it is a signal demonstration of their authority that whilst they were gaining entry into the city of London and forcing the king to meet them, their orders were being obeyed over eighty miles away in Thanet.

One of the most remarkable aspects of the 1381 rising, especially in Kent, was the ability of the insurgents to break into major castles and gaols at will. The list is an impressive one: Rochester castle on Thursday 6 June, Canterbury castle on Monday 10 June, the archbishop's castle and gaol at Maidstone on Tuesday 11 June, the bishop of London's gaol in the castle at Bishops Stortford (Hertfordshire) opened by a detachment of the Essex insurgents on the same day,[58] the Marshalsea prison at Southwark opened on Wednesday 12 or Thursday 13 June[59] and the Tower of London on 14 June. None of these fortifications offered significant resistance, even though there is no reason to suppose that the 'commons' of Essex and Kent would have wished or been able to mount an effective siege. The fall of these monumental symbols of governmental and episcopal authority to the rebels may indicate that many of the servants, minor officials and men-at-arms within the castles sympathised with the insurgents so that resistance was impossible; it also reflects the boldness of the planning of the revolt and the speed of its execution which gave local and central government no time to respond; but above all it is a witness to the terror they inspired and to the collapse of the credibility of the ruling class in a world turned upside down. This was achieved not so much by the burning of manor-houses as by the treatment of those members of the county gentry whom they succeeded in capturing. The indictments and other judicial records provide the names of a significant number of gentlemen who were compelled under threat of death and of the destruction of their property to make substantial payments to the insurgents, to ride with them and to become sworn members of their conspiracy.[60] Thomas Walsingham informs us that this revolutionary technique of not allowing any gentleman to stay in his home and of forcing them to aid the rising was adopted by the St Albans insurgents (about whom he is well informed) because it was the particular method taught by Wat Tyler.[61] Since this policy was followed at least from the

---

[58] P.R.O., KB 145/3/6/1: 'Item iidem jurati presentant quod Johannes Bowyers de Plesshy . . . die martis supradicto . . . gaolam episcopi Londinii apud Storteford fregit et quondam fratrem Andream de ordine Carmeli ac Johannem Balle proditorem in eodem castro pro diversis feloniis convictos existentes proditorie abduxit . . . '

[59] *Anonimalle*, p. 140 (= Dobson, p. 155).

[60] For example Willian Berland, and John Prittlewell (above p. 254) and Robert Rikdon in Essex (P.R.O., KB 145/3/6/1), and in Kent Thomas de Shardelowe, Thomas Tryvet, Thomas de Cobham, John of Farningham, James of Peckham (Réville, pp. 185–7), Thomas Holt (Powell and Trevelyan, p. 9) and Richard Bertelot of Ospringe (Flaherty, *ubi supra in n. 12*, 90).

[61] Walsingham, *Historia Anglicana*, i 470 (= Dobson, p. 273).

time that Abel Ker's men coerced the abbot of Lessness to join them on 2 June, we have another indication of a degree of tactical planning from the inception of the revolt.

Much the most impressive evidence for the degree of organisation that lies behind the revolt, however, is to be found in the astonishing speed of their concerted movements. In Essex many of the men who responded to the proclamations of 9 June gathered the following day at Cressing Temple after a journey of 20, 30 or even 40 miles. Yet they had time to sack the hospitallers' priory and carry off much loot, to move on 4 miles to Coggeshall and capture the sheriff, carry off his records and destroy his house, to kill the escheator whilst others then moved on to Feering (2 miles) to seize the escheatry records there. The following day, Tuesday 11 June, the insurgents were at Chelmsford (some 16 miles from Coggeshall) and burnt the shrieval and escheatry records there, whilst others attacked Gildesborough's properties which lay 10, 12 and 20 miles away. The next day (Wednesday 12 June) the insurgents reached Mile End, a full 29 miles from Chelmsford. There can therefore have been few Essex rebels who had not covered 70 miles in three or four days; many will have done more. If we ask how they managed to move so far so quickly, the answer of the indictments is clear: they rode. Thus a jury before Tresilian's commission at Chelmsford testified that a band of men from Hadleigh, South Benfleet, Bowers Gifford, Rayleigh, and Leigh 'all *rode* about armed . . . with the company . . . to Cressing and to the house of John Sewale of Coggeshall'; they also swore that John Geffrey, bailiff of East Hanningfield, caused all the men of five neighbouring vills to swear 'that they would *ride* against the king whenever he (*Geffrey*) summoned them'; they also testified that the substantial body of men from sixteen different vills, who had first resisted the poll tax commission at Brentwood on 30 May, subsequently attacked the sheriff's house at Coggeshall 'and afterwards they *rode* about armed in a land of peace and did many ill deeds'.[62] Nor is the evidence restricted to Tresilian's commission, for the jurors of Chafford hundred testified before Buckingham's commission that John Frost of Chipping Ongar after the burning of the records at Chelmsford on Tuesday 11 June, entered the house of Robert Rikdon at Witham (9 miles away) and forced Robert to ride (*equitantem*) with them to Chelmsford and to join their conspiracy to 'destroy divers lieges of the lord king'.[63] Nor may we suppose that it was just the leaders or the coerced members of the gentry who were horsed, for Thomas Walsingham recounts how on 28 June in the suppression of the rising the earl of Buckingham killed no less than 500 rebels at Billericay and

[62] Sparvel-Bayly, *ubi supra in n. 12*, 217–19.
[63] P.R.O., KB 145/3/6/1 m. 5: '. . . ita quod ipsum Robertum abinde usque Chelmersford contra voluntatem suam equitantem fecit cum predictis inimicis ad destruendum diversos ligeos domini Regis etc . . .'

captured 800 of their horses.[64] Even if the numbers are exaggerated, they indicate that a contemporary had no difficulty in supposing that the insurgents had horses.

In Kent the insurgents can be shown to have moved even faster than those of Essex, though the Kentish indictments do not specify how they travelled. Thus the insurgents led by Wat Tyler, John Hales of Malling and others were at Rochester on Sunday 9th June, but had reached Canterbury, 26 miles away, before noon on the following day; there they proceeded to break into the castle, release the prisoners, capture the sheriff, seize his records at Milton (2 miles) and destroy some six other houses either in the town or some 2 or 3 miles distant. Yet the following day they had reached Maidstone, 27 miles away, in time to break into the archbishop's gaol. The next day, Wednesday 12 June, the commons of Kent were at Blackheath, a distance of 31 miles, in time to conduct negotiations with the king's emissaries in order to arrange a meeting with him; some groups of Kentish rebels even pushed on the remaining 5 or 6 miles to Southwark and Lambeth that same evening.[65] It must be apparent that Tyler and his men could not have 'marched' the 85 miles from Rochester via both Canterbury and Maidstone to Blackheath in three days whilst also breaking into three gaols, destroying key records, sacking many manor-houses and compelling several of the county gentry to accompany them. No infantry force in history travelled at 25–30 miles a day whilst tackling major military targets en route. Indeed a speed of 30 miles a day was in the Middle Ages attained only by individual well-mounted travellers who had no military distractions – long-distance pilgrims or express riders on royal business.[66] Fortunately in Kent we do have one specific witness that the commons were mounted. In the royal pardon to Thomas atte Raven of Rochester we learn that Thomas 'with other unknown malefactors' on Wednesday 12 June came riding (*equitans*) to Southwark and there attacked the prison houses of the Marshalsea.[67] Of course one could argue that Thomas alone was mounted, though it would then be difficult to know how the other 'malefactors' kept pace with him; but we cannot suppose that the commons of Kent were fitness fanatics who accomplished a marathon (26⅓ miles) and more on foot on each of three successive days before attacking their fiscal, judicial and governmental targets.

It is not the medieval chroniclers (who are entirely silent on the matter) but modern historians who have repeatedly referred to the 'march', the 'long walk' or 'the wonderfully quick march' on London

---

[64] Walsingham, *Historia Anglicana*, ii 20–1 (= Dobson, pp. 311–12).
[65] Above, p. 265, n. 49; Réville, p. 186.
[66] L. Landon, *The Itinerary of King Richard I* (Pipe Roll Soc., li, 1925), pp. 184–8.
[67] Réville, p. 186.

of the commons of Kent and Essex.[68] It is a revealing assumption which reflects the lack of attention to the inception of the revolt and an unwillingness to suppose that fourteenth-century peasants were capable of organizing a co-ordinated rising with military precision. No one would pretend that every recorded action of the insurgents of Kent and Essex fits into a neat and readily comprehended master-plan. But if we allow that the insurgents raised a mounted force in each shire that struck with devastating speed in accordance with a carefully synchronized plan at the chief castles and gaols, at the fiscal and judicial government of the two counties and also at the leading officers of state, then we shall be less surprised at their success in overrunning the capital and at the discipline and selectivity of their targets there.[69] Theirs was an astonishing administrative achievement. If they did not succeed in bringing serfdom and seignorial lordship to an end at a stroke, they did deliver a salutary shock to the ruling class and they ensured that the poll tax – productive but grossly inequitable – was abandoned as a tax that was politically unacceptable. It is time that Wat Tyler, Thomas Baker, Abel Ker, John Hales and many others got the recognition they deserve not only as the champions of an egalitarianism that has scarcely yet been achieved, but also as the leaders of a bold and superbly planned insurrection.[70]

[68] C. Oman, *The Great Revolt of 1381* (Oxford, 1906), pp. 45, 47; Dobson, pp. 23–4; Hilton, *Bond Men Made Free*, p. 138.

[69] Barron, *ubi supra in* n. 1, p. 2.

[70] I am indebted to my colleagues, Miss A. J. Kettle and Dr C. Given-Wilson, and above all to Dr A. J. Prescott, for guiding a novice through unfamiliar territory, but am alone responsible for the conclusions reached and any errors perpetrated.

19

How Much did it Cost to Found a Jeronimite Monastery in late Medieval Spain?

J. R. L. Highfield

Founding a monastic or religious house of any order in the late Middle Ages often presented that order and its benefactors with problems in the course of whose solution revealing documents were produced. In the early Middle Ages the extent of the generosity of founders is usually a matter of guesswork, based on the amount of land with which a particular house was endowed by a specific founder or by the scale of such buildings as those of Cluny or Poblet, Fountains or Rievaulx. By the end of the fourteenth century in Aragon and Castile, however, problems of foundation were posed afresh by the popularity of old orders renewed, such as the Observant Franciscans, or of a new order like the Jeronimites, and a few figures begin to appear. It is proposed in what follows to examine some of the incidental quantitative and revealing documents which began to show themselves as problems of founding Jeronimite houses arose between the establishment of the order in 1373 and the death of Ferdinand in 1516.[1] For Catalonia for the second half of the fourteenth century this evidence can be placed beside that recently made available for the endowment, building expenses and running costs of eight different city hospitals in Barcelona (and of the consolidated city hospital which replaced them in 1401)[2] and for the years 1355 to 1598 beside figures based on architectural contracts described in documents from the Catalan notarial archives, published or calendared by Sr Madurell Marimón.[3] It is, of course, realized that where Castilian

---

[1] Josemaría Revuelta Somalo, *Los Jerónimos* (Guadalajara, 1982), pp. 129–36; for the Jeronimites in general, see J. R. L. Highfield, 'The Jeronimites in Spain for their patrons and success, 1373–1516', *Journal of Ecclesiastical History*, 34 (1983), 513–33.

[2] U. Lindgren, *Bedürftigkeit, Armut, Not*, Spanische Forschungen, second ser., xviii (1980), cf. also J. M. Doñate Sebastiá, 'Salarios y precios durante la segunda mitad del siglo xiv', in *7° Congreso de Historia de la Corona de Aragón*, 3 vols. (Barcelona, 1962), ii, 417–506. I am most grateful to Mr P. Rycraft for drawing my attention to these two works and for helping me with references to the history of the Crown of Aragon. I have marked these references with his initials thus (PR).

[3] J. M. Madurell Marimón, 'Los contratos de obras en los protocolos notariales y su aportación a la historia de la arquitectura', in *Estudios históricos y documentos de los archivos de protocolos* i (Barcelona 1948), 105–199 (PR).

costs and the money of account is concerned – the schizophrenic maravedí, as it has been called – a separate problem lies in the interpretation of the figures themselves.[4]

In the early years of the Jeronimite Order apart from the supervision of the ordinary, the machinery to ensure that the houses would be properly funded was inadequate. There was also the danger, particularly pronounced in an eremitical order like the Jeronimites, that the new houses might not maintain enough monks to ensure continuity. We know that Francisco García. vicar-general of the diocese of Burgos, granted license for the foundation of the monastery of Santa Catalina de Monte Corbán in Asturias on 3 March 1407, when he was satisfied that it had enough rents to sustain a prior and four monks.[5] In the event he was right and the monastery took root, but the risk had been there. The fact that the founders of the Order itself, Canon Yáñez de Figueroa and the Pecha brothers, had set an example of strict austerity meant that the Order not only exerted a special charisma on lay society but also that its houses might prove comparatively cheap to found or to endow. We learn, for example, that when the Infant Fernando de Antequera endowed the house of La Mejorada, near Olmedo, in 1409 in answer to the request of its third prior, Fray Juan de Sotovenado, he did so not with the magnificence which might have been expected from a prominent member of the royal house, but in accordance with the poverty and condition of the holy fathers who were content with humble and poor things.[6] Jeronimite houses could nevertheless be founded on a grander scale.

In 1376 a house had been founded in the kingdom of Valencia at La Plana de Javea on the Levant coast. A year later Peter IV of Aragon granted goods to the value of 40,000 sueldos with the right to mortgage them and subsequently the gift of one hundred Valencian pounds.[7] However, the exposed position of the monastery resulted in 1386 in the capture of the monks by Muslim pirates operating out of Bougie in North Africa. Nine of those who survived this ordeal were rescued by Alfonso, count of Denia, grandson of James II of Aragon, and one of the original benefactors of La Plana. In 1388 he not only ransomed the nine survivors but subsequently set them up again in a safer place inland at **Cotalba** to which the monks were transferred. He bought the new

[4] A. MacKay, *Money, Prices and Politics in Fifteenth-Century Castile*, Royal Historical Society Studies, no. 28 (London, 1981), p. 51.

[5] A(rchivo) H(istórico) N(acional), Clero, Libro 11,455, no. 30 in Revuelta, p. 276.

[6] B(iblioteca del) E(scorial), MS.Ç.III.4, fo. 209.

[7] In 1375/6 at Villarreal or its neighbourhood, 59 km. from Valencia, a day labourer, carrying away earth from a ditch with a horse, was paid 2/6 d.p.d.; a mason was paid at the same rate; in 1376/7 a pair of trousers cost 7/–; in 1377/8 a pair of rabbits 10d. (Doñate, *op. cit.*, pp. 447, 425, 451, 471). For the Valencian currency see also Earl J. Hamilton, *Money, Prices and Wages in Valencia, Aragon and Navarre, 1351–1500* (Cambridge, Mass., 1936), especially pp. 23–4.

site from eight 'mudéjas' proprietors for 2,550 Valencian sueldos[8] and secured permission to spend 35,547 sueldos of Barcelona on the buildings of Cotalba. In 1395 his wife, Violante, added the perpetual lease worth 240 sueldos p.a.[9] In 1403 Alfonso himself, by now duke of Gandía, gave orders to his proctor general to hand over 2000 florins (or about 22,000 sueldos, reckoning the florin at 11 sueldos)[10] for the works at Cotalba. When he died on 5 March 1412 he left to the monastery all his perpetual leases in the towns of Gandía and Denia and his rights in the property of the archdeacon of Valencia, whose universal heir he was. This brought to Cotalba the lordship of Rascana.[11] In addition Martin I granted to Guillermo Martorell,[12] presumably as an intermediary, the right to hand over to the monastery 13,934 sueldos which the King had given him. Between 1388 and 1412 it seems that we can account for over 55,547 sueldos which had been spent on the monastic buildings. All this meant that this house was well enough endowed to have already a prior and twenty-four monks.[13]

Much less happy was the example of **Sant Jeroni de la Vall d'Hebron**, another house patronised by a member of the Aragonese royal house. There the queen of Aragon, Violante de Bar, became interested in 1391 in a hermitage which she wished to transform into a new Jeronimite monastery. In the following year she began to offer endowments for the prospective house. Firstly she gained a license to give it B£575 p.a. With a further 500 sueldos of Barcelona on the constableship of Tortosa, 400 sueldos of Jaca on the commandery of 'Guarden'[14] and the city of Lérida and 500 sueldos of Jaca on the commandery of Lérida in the Order of St John. Then she gave it a further 3,300 sueldos of Barcelona, secured on the rents of Tortosa. She promised 1,000 sueldos more by 1394 and had faculty to spend 6,000

---

[8] In 1388/9 twelve bushels of corn (a 'cahiz') cost 40/– (Doñate, p. 498).

[9] In 1395/6 a cleaner of wells was paid between 1/6 and 2/– p.d; a day labourer, carrying earth from a ditch with a horse, was paid 2/6 p.d., twelve bushels of corn cost 41/– (*Ibid.*, pp. 447, 498).

[1²] This was true, for the most part, internally, cf. M. Llop Catalá, 'Fluctuaciones del Florín en Valencia en el siglo xv', *Primer Congreso de la historia del país valenciano*, 4 vols. (1973–80), ii, 727–39, though by 1415 the florin externally was appreciating against the French currency (PR).

[11] AHN (Osuna), leg. 538, fo. 3ᵛ. The second duke's accounts for 1418–19 (Ibid., leg. 809, no. 2) raise doubts as to whether the monastery received all of this benefaction (PR).

[12] He had been the king's receiver-general in Valencia, but was listed among the household of Queen Violante in 1410 (A(rchivo de la) C(orona de) A(ragón), R(eal) P(atrimonio), R(eg), 407, fo. 52; R. 2060, fos. 144–6) (PR).

[13] Revuelta, *op. cit.*, pp. 280–9.

[14] Presumably the ex-Templar commandery of Garden *viz* Gardeny (PR).

florins (or about 66,000 sueldos) or more on the buildings.[15] Fray Jaime Ibáñez, prior of Cotalba, took the view that the endowments by August 1393 were sufficient for the monastery to be set up. The assignment of the revenues in the diocese of Lérida received the approval of the ordinary of that see, Gerardo de Requesens. But when in 1396 the death of John I of Aragon cut the queen off from her source of funding, the house was still unfinished, even if we know from an account-book that between 1394 and 1397 B£6,842.19s.8d. were spent on the buildings.[16] Interestingly enough, as Revuelta has pointed out, a merchant of Barcelona, named Bertrán Nicolao who, unusually for a man of his class, had been attracted by the Jeronimite Order offered to complete the monastery in 1413. To do this he proposed to give 90,000 sueldos (or about 360,000 maravedis) to buy rents and B£2,000 (or about 160,000 m.) to build and endow six cells for monks each saying a daily mass.[17] Thus by his estimates it cost B£333 (or 26,640 m.) to build and endow a cell for a monk saying a daily mass in Catalonia in 1413.[18] The queen dowager turned down the offer thinking it unworthy for a royal foundation to be dependent on a merchant for its completion. This did not deter Bertrán from founding another Jeronimite monastery himself at **Monte Olivete**, later moved to **La Murta** also near Barcelona. The site of Monte Olivete was then bought for B£4,570. The monastery itself was erected in 1413 and endowed with B£14,000 (about 1,120,000 m.). This was thought adequate support for a prior and twelve monks.[19] The same benefactor founded a monastery for the Augustinians and this he endowed not quite so well with 14,000 écus.[20]

---

[15] Revuelta, pp. 192–3. In 1387 her total revenues in Aragon have been estimated at 90,000 sueldos of Barcelona and 37,516 sueldos of Jaca (M. A. Ledesma Rubio, 'El patrimonio real en Aragón a fines del siglo xiv' in *Aragón en la Edad Media*, 3 vols. (Saragosa, 1977–80) ii. 135–69; Jaca and Barcelona currencies were expected to circulate at par. For this monastery see also A. Durán y Sampere, 'Santa Jeroni de la Vall d'Hebron', *Barcelona i la Seva Historia*, i (Barcelona, 1972), 698–706 (PR).

[16] B.Esc. Ç.III.3, fo. 294 in Revuelta, p. 295 and n. 1, 175.

[17] In 1415 the Generalitat worked on a basis of 10 maravedis to 2 sueldos 6 denarios (Barcelona) (ACA Generalitat, 634, fo. 44) (PR).

[18] Revuelta, pp. 295–6. In 1362 a citizen of Javea in the kingdom of Valencia had endowed a perpetual chaplaincy with 200 sueldos p.a. (*Ibid.*, p. 285).

[19] Ironically enough when in 1431 San Jeroni de Vall d'Hebron was still in difficulties and there were only six monks, a proposal was made to join it up with La Murta which at that time had fourteen. But it came to nothing, and it was not until 1467 that we learn of the completion of the cloister for B£182, thanks to the patronage of Queen María, wife of Alfonso V (J. M. Madurell Marimón, 'Contratos . . .', pp. 126–7 and app. no. 7 p. 152; cf. A. Durán i Sampere, 'Bellesguard, residenci de reis' in *Barcelona i Seva Historia*, i. 713 n. 10, quoting 'Arxiu de la Comunitat de San Just, Fons Gualbes, perg. no. 3 and Reg. Gualbes, Bellesguard, fo. 204' (PR). For La Murta building contracts in 1478–9 see Madurell, *op. cit.*, pp. 127–33.

[20] That is the equivalent of B£12,900, reckoning the écu at 17 sueldos (1415); it was 17 s. in 1417; cf. also Revuelta, pp. 296–7 and Bibl. Esc. MS & II. 23, fo. 175 in *ibid.*, p. 296, n. 1, 186.

By 1415 the Order of the Jeronimites had secured the position of an exempt order and the first Chapter General met at Guadalupe. Fray Diego de Alarcón, Prior of San Bartolomé de Lupiana, was elected the first General and two houses were suppressed, probably because their endowments had proved inadequate. These were Santa María de Tolonio in Alava[21] and Santa María de Villavieja in Rioja.[22] Similarly El Abadía, a daughter of Guadalupe never made good its foundation.[23] Another daughter house, Corralrubio, which had been founded from Guisando in 1384 was subsequently united with the neighbouring house of La Sisla in 1418.[24] The seriousness with which the new Chapter General took the matter of endowment is illustrated by the case of San Jerónimo de Buenavista, near Seville. Four times its supporters had to put forward its claims to successive Chapters General before it was finally accepted at the Private Chapter of 1426.[25]

Important information on the subject of endowment is also provided by an episode soon after 1425 when John II had seized 50,000 florins belonging to Cardinal Pedro de Frías, destined, it would seem, for the monastery of **La Espeja**, in the province of Soria, near Coruña del Conde, of which he had been the founder in 1402. The king had thus deprived the monks of substantial additional income intended for them by their patron. The house of twenty-five monks was asked what it needed in compensation. The answer given was distinctly modest. They replied that twenty-five thousand maravedis in perpetual rent would satisfy them (the annual revenue of Burgos cathedral at this date was 229,468 maravedis a year); each monk would thus receive, in addition to his existing income, no more than 1,000 maravedis a year (at this time a workman might earn 2,000 a year and a carpenter 3,500). But unless one calculates the rent in terms of, say, one hundred years purchase, the sum secured was in no way the equivalent of 50,000 florins, which in 1425 was worth some 2,600,000 maravedis.[26]

However, soon the cost of endowment was to increase superficially as a result of the series of debasements initiated by John II in 1429–30.[27] In the midst of them in 1435 a would-be founder of a Jeronimite house, Ruy González de Avellaneda, lord of Langa, Ovadero, Rejas and other places in the province of Soria, was faced with the difficulties which come upon a man who knows that he will not live long enough to implement his

---

[21] Ibid., p. 270 (in 1417).
[22] Ibid., p. 269.
[23] Ibid., pp. 220–1.
[24] Ibid., p. 164.
[25] Ibid., p. 280; José de Sigüenza, *Historia de la Orden de San Geronimo*, ed. J. Catalina García (Nueva Biblioteca de Autores Españoles), 2 vols., (Madrid, 1907–9), i. 304.
[26] Cf. Revuelta, p. 246, MacKay, pp. 148, 150–1, (Dr. MacKay has kindly supplied me with the figure for the revenue of Burgos Cathedral), M. A. Ladero Quesada, *La Hacienda de Castilla en el siglo xv* (La Laguna, 1973), p. 42.
[27] MacKay, p. 62.

wishes himself. He set his aspirations out in the will which he drew up on the 30th August 1436.[28] He asked that when he died his body should be temporarily buried in an alabaster tomb in the Jeronimite monastery of La Espeja, which had been founded in the hermitage of Santa Agueda by Cardinal Pedro de Frías, already referred to. His body was subsequently to be moved to the monastery which he wished to found. Having made a bequest of 1,000 doblas 'valadís' (or about 100,000 maravedis)[29] for releasing from captivity seventeen captives (five in honour of the wounds of Christ and twelve more in honour of the twelve apostles) and further donations of 10,000 maravedis in all to the house of San Agustín, Burgos, to the five Franciscan houses of San Esteban de Gormaz, Santo Domingo de Silos, Ayllón, Peñafiel and Cuéllar, and to the Jeronimites of La Espeja, he turned to making proper arrangements for the maintenance of his wife Isabel de Avila. He did so on the understanding that she would supervise the foundation of a Jeronimite monastery at the hermitage of **Santa María de Viñas** near Aranda de Duero. Failing that, the monastery was to be placed at Langa, where a free site could be provided on his own lands, or finally, wherever else the Jeronimites would be happy to put it in the region. She was to spend 10,500 maravedis a year on the building provided from a 'juro' to that amount secured on the city of Burgo de Osma and its land until its completion. After her death, the lands, including Langa, Ovadero and Rejas, three towns near San Esteban de Gormaz, whose usufruct she had enjoyed, should pass to the new monastery. After a wide variety of other bequests totalling in cash alone over 50,000 maravedis, he named as his executors his wife, his nephew, Ochoa de Avellaneda, Fray Rodrigo, a Jeronimite of La Espeja and the Guardian of the Franciscan house of Santo Domingo de Silos. The notary public who drew up the will was Pedro Sánchez of Aranda de Duero and the seven witnesses were all inhabitants of Aranda. But it was not at Aranda that the new monastery was built.

In little over a year from the date of the drawing up of the will, Ruy González de Avellaneda was dead and his widow had exchanged four of his properties for a 'juro' worth 30,000 maravedis a year with Alvaro de Luna,[30] Constable of Castile since 1423, and still in 1437 at the height of his power. Isabel gave the endowment to a different if recently founded Jeronimite house, which Dr Roberto de Moya, abbot of Valladolid, was setting up at the hermitage of **Santa María de Prado**, near that city. The true reasons for this change can be guessed at. Was the site of Santa María de Viñas unsuitable? What was the role of Don Alvaro? We know that the

---

[28] AHN Clero, carpeta 3512, no. 18. This was not the first time that an attempt had been made to found a Jeronimite monastery at Santa María de Viñas. Cardinal Pedro de Frías in 1401 had himself started by wanting to found a monastery there, but eventually did so at La Espeja (Revuelta, p. 245). For the difficulty involved in working out salaries cf. MacKay, p. 89 and for the 'dobla valadí' in 1442, *ibid.*, p. 50.

[29] Cf. MacKay, p. 50.

[30] AHN Clero, carpeta 3512, no. 19, dated 9 September 1437.

faction of the king of Navarre and the Infant Don Henry sent a memorial to John II in which they complained specifically that Don Alvaro 'wishing in the same way to increase his wealth in land and vassals, being discontented with those which he had received from Your Worship, had managed and exercised great force and has exacted rewards for money . . . '.[31] This had been the case with the 'villa' of San Martín de Valdeiglesias which Don Alvaro had exchanged with the abbot and convent of the Cistercian house of Valdeiglesias for a 'juro' of 30,000 maravedis a year which would be subject to the sharp devaluation of c.1430–c.1441.[32] The town was then named by Don Alvaro in the mayorazgo whose foundation was licensed by John II on 26 February 1438. Since we learn that among the seventeen 'villas' there named were three which had belonged to Ruy González de Avellaneda, namely Langa (de Duero), Ovadero and Rejas (de San Esteban), it seems highly likely that it was also Don Alvaro who had brought about the transfer of these lands from the possession of the widow of Ruy González. The new monastery of Santa María de Prado, it is true, will have received an endowment of well over 30,000 maravedis a year, but this too will have been affected by devaluation since it was largely in the form of a 'juro'.[33] The tomb of Ruy González must have remained permanently with those of other members of his family at La Espeja.[34]

Ten years later the policies of the disturbed reign of John II still prevailed. Would-be donors on this occasion were no less important persons than Juan Pacheco, later marquis of Villena, and his patron, Henry, prince of Asturias, born in January 1425 and now a young man of twenty-two. Pacheco and prince Henry were at odds with Don Alvaro and John II. Although an agreement had been reached between these rival groupings at Astudillo in 1446, the situation remained extremely precarious.[35] Moreover, Pacheco had chosen as the site for a new monastery the scene of a successful fight in which he had defeated three opponents. This was the hermitage of **Santa María de El Parral**. Since it belonged to the dean and chapter of Segovia, the first essential was to buy the site. The process was complicated by the role of prince Henry in the purchase. Sigüenza tells us that the king did not want his son to erect buildings in his lifetime.[36] Pacheco offered to buy the site, together with

---

[31] *Cronica del halconero de Juan II*, ed. J. M. Carriazo (Madrid, 1946), p. 326 and cf. J. Pérez-Embid Wamba, 'Don Alvaro, los monjes y los campesinos . . .' in *En la España Medieval. Estudios en memoria del professor D. Salvador de Moxó*, ed. M. A. Ladero Quesada, iii (Madrid, 1982), 238.

[32] *Cronica de don Alvaro de Luna*, ed. J. M. de Flores (Madrid, 1784), pp. 408–9 and cf. Ladero Quesada, op. cit., iii, 234 n. 7.

[33] For the devaluation cf. MacKay, p. 57.

[34] Sigüenza, i. 348.

[35] W. D. Phillips Jr., *Enrique IV and the Crisis of Fifteenth-Century Castile, 1425–1480* (Medieval Academy of America, Cambridge, Mass., 1978), p. 40.

[36] Sigüenza, i, 348.

all its appurtenances, for 10,000 maravedis a year of 'juro' secured on the alcavalas of Aguilafuente, a town situated on the Pacheco lands between Cuéllar and Sepúlveda. This proposition gave the dean and chapter pause and lengthy negotiations followed. Firstly, they wanted any agreement which they might make confirmed by the administrator of the diocese, Juan de Cervantes, cardinal bishop of Ostia. So much they secured through the efforts of Alfonso García, archdeacon of Cuéllar, although the cardinal stipulated that 10,000 maravedis should first be applied to the construction of the fabric of the buildings[37] and to the necessary ornaments which were lacking at the hermitage. Noting that there were other claimants on the alcavalas of Aguilafuente, the dean and chapter wanted Henry to ensure that their claim should have precedence, and in default of revenue from this source, should be met from another. Eventually on 16 September, the dean and chapter were given permission to proceed by the provisor of the diocese, Nuño Fernández de Peñalosa, bachelor in laws, canon of Segovia and Vicar-General. On 7 December the dean and chapter received from Alfonso Gómez de la Hoz, secretary of prince Henry and an alderman of Segovia, the privilege of 10,000 maravedis a year, secured on the alcavalas of Aguilafuente. Fray Rodrigo de Sevilla, prior of the Jeronimite house of San Blas de Villaviciosa, who represented the Jeronimites, brought a letter from Fray Estevan de Léon, General of the Order, dated from Lupiana on 7 August, giving his approval. It was then agreed that the formal ceremony should take place on the first Sunday following, which was 10 December. On that day prince Henry and Juan Pacheco were personally present, together with Fray Estevan de Léon, Pedro Girón, Master of Calatrava (and younger brother of Pacheco), the bishop of Ciudad Rodrigo and many 'caballeros', squires, aldermen and clergy of Segovia. Towards paying for the new buildings Pacheco himself gave a rent of a 'juro' worth 15,000 maravedis a year secured on the alcavalas of wine of Segovia and a water mill with two wheels on the banks of the river Eresma.[38] Two friars were to work on the buildings whose labour was presumably free. They were to have their food, and 8,000 maravedis a year were to be spent on the construction of the new monastery until it was completed. Prince Henry agreed to meet the whole of this cost. But building only began, properly speaking, in 1459 four years after Henry became king. The design was entrusted to Juan Gallego, a citizen of Segovia. A 'greater cloister' and a 'lesser cloister' were built as a hospice. Pacheco had some small houses – 'casillas' – constructed, just adequate to give the earliest monks some basic shelter. But the disturbances of Henry's reign and Pacheco's evident unwillingness to unbelt further coincided with the disastrous fall in the maravedí during the anarchy from

---

[37] AHN Clero, carpeta 1968, no. 10, fo. 3.
[38] *Ibid.*, fo. 5^v.

1463 onwards.[39] In 1472 the 'greater cloister' was entrusted by Pacheco to Juan and Bonifacio Guas of Toledo and to the 'converso' Pedro Polido of Segovia.[40] But twenty years after Henry's accession to the throne the vaults of the main building were still incomplete. In the end Ferdinand and Isabella undertook the completion of Santa María de El Parral from c.1485 onwards. In 1495 they endowed it moderately with a single payment of 100,000 maravedis.[41] We may note that in the following year a cantor in the royal chapel was being paid 25,000 maravedis a year, a mule cost between 11,000 and 16,000 and a horse 17,000.[42] In the same year Sebastián de Almonacid carved statues of the Twelve Apostles at 1,900 maravedis each and Francisco Sánchez de Toledo the two great shields over the entrance at 2,800 maravedis a shield. The retable was finished in 1528 and the tower three years after that.[43]

In the end of the fifteenth century when a particular wealthy benefactor wished to found a Jeronimite monastery in Andalusia, the procedure was much more cut and dried. Francisco Enríquez de Ribera, son of Pedro Enríquez, lord of Tarifa and uncle of Ferdinand was a big fish indeed. Adelantado Mayor of Andalusia and of Seville, lord of Alcalá de los Gazules, of Tarifa, Cañete, Bornos and many other places, he was a devotee of the Jeronimite Order who wished to found a monastery on a convenient site near his town of **Bornos**. This time the site was provided by the founder on his own land. On 15 September 1493 an agreement was reached between the prior of Montamarta, Fray Daniel, and three proctors of Francisco Enríquez, according to carefully stated conditions.[44] The site was to be between the mills and the town of Bornos together with an orchard and all other offices required. These were to be in as good a style as those at the monastery of San Jerónimo de Buenavista at Seville (founded in 1426 with money from Nicolas Martínez de Medina, treasurer and contador mayor of John II of Castile). Francisco Enríquez de Ribera agreed to fit out the monastery church with everything needed for the divine cult, namely chalices, crosses, wine vessels for mass, retables, organs, wall-hangings and bells. There was to be a clock, a library and everything necessary for the refectory. For the dormitory there were to be beds with cloths and linen. Iron implements were to be made for the kitchen, vessels for the bodega, an oven with its fittings; two mules and two beasts of burden were to be added. An endowment of 100,000 maravedis per year was to be made and this was

---

[39] MacKay, p. 89.
[40] José M. Quadrado, *Salamanca, Avila y Segovia* (1865–72, repr. Barcelona, 1979), p. 642, and cf. L. Torres Balbas, *Ars Hispaniae*, vii (Madrid, 1952), 343.
[41] *Registro General del Sello*, x (Jan.–Dec. 1493), no. 196, p. 42 (27 Jan. 1934).
[42] *Cuentas de Gonzalo de Baeza*, ed. A. and E. A. de la Torre, 2 vols. (Madrid, 1956), ii. 317, 326, 338. The court was at Almazán in the neighbouring province of Soria when these prices were paid.
[43] Quadrado, *op. cit.*, pp. 643 and 644 n. 1.
[44] AHN Clero, Libros, 18, 989, fo. 2 v.

to be secured on the taxes of the town of Bornos whence it could no doubt be raised with convenience.[45] We may note that two years earlier in neighbouring Jaén skilled troops like 'caballeros' and arquebusiers were paid 62 maravedis a day, artillerymen and auxiliaries 35 maravedis a day and archers or lancers 31 maravedis a day.[46]

The monastery was also to be allowed to graze its stock on the lands and territory of Bornos up to a maximum of fifty pigs, one hundred sheep, fifty goats and ten cows, free of charge. There were to be four 'aranzadas' of land for a vineyard (an 'aranzada' was forty to fifty square metres). Although Francisco Enrique's intentions were indicated to a private chapter of 1493, Bornos was not officially accepted until the chapter general of 1495. In the meantime four monks had arrived from Montamarta, four more from Guadalupe and one from Guisando. So Bornos started with a complement of nine. However, the endowment was designed to support twenty-five and evidently there were often as many as thirty in the early sixteenth century. The buildings also reflected the wealth of the founder. There was one cloister, one hundred and ten feet wide, adorned with pillars of Genoese marble, and another equally large to serve as a guest-house. The donor died in 1509 having asked to be buried in the monastery without pomp but just as if he were a monk. In his will he left the monastery the valuable gift of the town of Bornos and made it his universal heir. Sigüenza reckons that the value of the rents which he left to his foundations were worth 16,000 ducats or 6,000,000 maravedis a year.[47] In the same year two of the three more important towns on the estates of the count of Benavente brought him together about 2,000,000 maravedis,[48] so that if Sigüenza is right, the monastery of Bornos had rents equivalent to that of five or six prosperous small towns. Even taking into account the debasement of the maravedí, this was a very substantial endowment.

More substantial endowments were yet to come. This survey has concentrated on six monasteries, three in the kingdoms of the Crown of Aragon and three in Castile, whose records have provided quantitative or revealing evidence from the late fourteenth, fifteenth or

---

[45] *Ibid.* This guaranteed the equivalent of c.400 florins per year as a basic minimum for twenty-five monks without prejudice to additional generosity. This compares with the equivalent of c.481 florins per year as the additional endowment of La Espeja in 1425, see above n. 26.

[46] P. A. Porras Arboledas, 'La sociedad de la ciudad de Jaén a fines del siglo xv', in *En La España Medieval*, iii, 314. These were wages for troops on campaign. They work out at 22, 630, 12, 775 and 11, 315 m.p.a. For other evidence on wages during the Granada campaign see M. A. Ladero Quesada, *Castilla y la Conquista de Granada* (Valladolid 1967), *passim*.

[47] Sigüenza, ii. 60.

[48] J. R. L. Highfield, 'The De la Cerda, the Pimentel and the so-called "price revolution"', *English Historical Review*, lxxxvii (1972), 511.

How Much did it Cost to Found a Jeronimite Monastery? 281

early sixteenth centuries.[49] The foundation of the Escorial was to produce a wealth of evidence in the later sixteenth century and is a subject in itself.[50] By then evidence on costs and prices was becoming much more freely available and the movement for new foundations itself, in part no doubt because of the very prosperity of the Order, was fast ebbing away.

---

[49] Some information, though not so extensive is available for other Jeronimite monasteries such as Frex de Val, Valparaíso, and Guisando.

[50] G. Kubler, *Building the Escorial* (Princeton University Press, 1982) and cf. review by G. Parker in *EHR*, xcix (1984), 378–9.

20

War and Peace in Fifteenth-Century Castile: Diego de Valera and the Granada War

John Edwards

Whether or not it is possible to draw lessons from history, it seems to be undeniable that the problem of controlling human aggression, now posed in the acute and possibly terminal form of the possession and use of nuclear weapons, has demanded consideration throughout the recognisable history of Europe. Of this Ralph Davis, as a historian of the warlike Normans with strong peace-loving convictions of his own, is able to be acutely aware. The teachings associated with the concept of the 'just war', which formed the basis of medieval attempts to tackle this question, provided, in accordance with the intellectual habits of the period, a framework for the analysis of any specific conflict which might arise, within or between states. In theoretical terms, the question was both philosophical and religious, and its answer was perceived to lie in the customary scholastic combination of Judaism, as seen in the distorting mirror of Christianity, New Testament teaching, and the ideals and practice of Greek and Roman political thought and government. Fundamentally, the issue was always the characteristic nature of human beings. Were they naturally violent, in which case the best hope was an efficient police force, or were they capable of avoiding aggression altogether? The accumulated wisdom of medieval theologians and political theorists, who were often the same people, indicated that the only realistic aim was to control warfare and make it 'just'. This relatively simple human impulse was expressed in a complex mixture of Christian notions of the love of one's neighbour, and Greek and Roman concepts of political society, seen as an uneasy combination of the Greek city state and the Roman empire, adapted awkwardly to the realities of a 'feudal' monarchy. The consequence was a refinement of Roman monarchy, with the added divine sanction of Jewish kingship, leading to the adulation of state power and, at the same time, at least theoretical respect for the essentially non-political evangelical impulses of Jesus's teachings.[1] It was never possible,

---

[1] Frederick H. Russell, *The Just War in the Middle Ages* (Cambridge, 1975), pp. 1–26, 41–69, 84–99, 128–61, 215–44, 258–308; Maurice Keen, *The Laws of War in the Late*

Continued

however, to treat the question in an entirely theoretical way, and fifteenth-century Castile is a striking example of the demands which political realities made of medieval political theory and moral philosophy. During the reigns of John II (1406–1454) and Henry IV (1454–1474), this kingdom was faced, not only with the hostility of its Iberian neighbours, Portugal, Navarre, Aragon and Granada, but also with internal conflict in the form of a battle, mainly between aristocratic factions, for control of royal patronage.[2] Yet under all these internal and external problems lay the imperative of the Reconquest, the long-term aim of restoring to Christian hands all the Iberian territory still under Muslim rule. By the fifteenth century, this war, whether potential or actual, had acquired the attributes of a crusade, a war for the faith to which the flimsy restraints of the 'just war' doctrine scarcely applied.

Diego de Valera's writings provide a valuable insight into the problems and tensions of Castilian politics and society in this period. Diego lived from 1412 until, probably, 1488. There are doubts both about his origins and about the last years of his life, when he had withdrawn from the Court, though for most of his career he shone in a wide range of political, military and cultural activities. In the present century, Diego has attracted a series of biographers, but, while it seems to be established now that his father was Alfonso Chirino, physician to John II of Castile, it is not certain whether his mother was Chirino's first wife, María de Valera, as his name, adopted later with royal approval, would suggest, or the second, Violante López. It has been suggested by some authors that the Chirino/Valera family, despite Chirino's great-great-grandfather, Payo Gómez, having been admiral of Castile, was of Jewish origin, though the evidence in Diego's writings of a pro-*converso* stance is far from conclusive. In any case, Diego was born in 1412, probably in Cuenca, and eschewed not only his father's profession of medicine but also other non-military careers which were typical of *conversos*, such as the Church and service in the royal administration. He became a royal page, according to his own account, first of John II and, after 1429, of prince Henry, later Henry IV, and thus trained as a *caballero*, or knight. In this capacity he went on John's largely abortive campaign in the kingdom of Granada in 1431,

---

Continued

Middle Ages (London, 1965), pp. 64–75, 103–33, 189–91, 239–47; Jonathan Riley-Smith, 'Crusading as an act of love', *History*, lxv (1980), 177–92; Louise and Jonathan Riley-Smith, *The Crusades. Idea and Reality, 1095–1274* (London, 1981), pp. 68–9 (a sermon by Jacques de Vitry, apparently delivered to a military order in Outremer).

[2] J. N. Hillgarth, *The Spanish Kingdoms, 1250–1516, ii, 1410–1516. Castilian Hegemony* (Oxford, 1978), 300–47; Angus MacKay, *Spain in the Middle Ages; from Frontier to Empire, 1000–1500* (London, 1977), pp. 145–59, 173–87.

and was present at the battle of La Higueruela. In 1435 he was with Gonzalo López de Estúñiga in an attack on Muslim-held Huelma, and was dubbed a knight. In 1437, he started his travels abroad, undertaking minor diplomatic missions in France and Bohemia and taking part brilliantly in chivalric events, such as jousts, in Burgundy and elsewhere. In the 1440s, as will become clearer from a more detailed examination of some of his writings, he became active in the tortured politics which surrounded the Castilian monarchy. Under Henry IV, after 1454, although he held the honorific post of *maestresala*, or steward of the royal hall, Diego increasingly withdrew from the Court, living mostly in Cuenca, but in 1467 he received an important post in the service of the ducal house of Medinaceli, as *alcaide*, or governor, of Puerto de Santa María, a small but economically important seignorial port on the bay of Cádiz, at the mouth of the Guadalete river. Soon after this, he became involved with the future Catholic Monarchs, Ferdinand and Isabella, who were then still far from the political eminence that they were to achieve five years later. He became *maestresala* to the newly-married couple, and thus began the final phase of his career, which is of most concern here, living for the most part in Puerto de Santa María, even after he had handed its governorship over to his son Charles (*sic*) in about 1478. Diego was given one more important Crown post by Ferdinand, as *corregidor*, or chief magistrate and royal representative, of Segovia in 1479, but the enterprise was unsuccessful, and the old warrior seems to have made no further major sallies from south-western Andalusia, though, as will be seen, he not only continued to heap political and military advice on his king, but also played a practical role in events in that area.[3]

Throughout his career, Diego de Valera sustained a varied, and often distinguished, literary output. He is best known to historians as a chronicler, his major works being the *Memorias de diversas hazañas*,[4] devoted to the reign of Henry IV, and his *Crónica de los Reyes Católicos*, covering the first part of their reign.[5] However, he also wrote a series of treatises, including a pro-female contribution to the mysogynist-feminist literary debate, the *Tratado en defensa de virtuossas mugeres*,[6] a valuable work on the nature of nobility, entitled the *Espejo de verdadera*

---

[3] Juan de Mata Carriazo, introductory study to his edition of Valera's *Crónica de los Reyes Católicos* (Madrid, 1927), pp. xiii–lxxiii; A. González Palencia, 'Alfonso Chirino, médico de Juan II y padre de Mosén Diego de Valera', *Boletín de la Biblioteca Menéndez Pelayo*, no. vol. (1924), 42–62; Hipólito Sancho de Sopranis, 'Sobre Mosén Diego de Valera: notas y documentos para su biografía', *Hispania*, vii (1947), 531–53; M. Penna, introductory study to his edition of some works of Valera in B[iblioteca de] A[utores] E[spañoles], cxvi, pp. xcix–cxxvi.
[4] Ed. Carriazo (Madrid, 1941).
[5] *Ed. cit.* by Carriazo (Madrid, 1927).
[6] Ed. Penna, *BAE*, cxvi, 55–76.

nobleza,[7] a treatise on heraldry (*Tratado de las armas*)[8] and a conventional work on government and monarchy, the *Doctrinal de príncipes*.[9] As well as writing other short treatises and occasional pieces, generally for noble patrons, Diego dabbled in poetry, composing mediocre lyrics and even erotic parodies of the Penitential Psalms and Litanies of the Church.[10] His views on peace, however, are largely to be found in his letters,[11] which were described by the nineteenth-century literary critic, Marcelino Menéndez y Pelayo, as 'one of the most precious documents of the Castilian language of the fifteenth century',[12] and in his systematic treatise, the *Exhortaçión de la pas*,[13] and both of these texts will now be examined, with a view to determining Valera's views on peace and war.

In many respects, the *Exhortaçión*, although its author's only known major work on the subject, is of less theoretical interest than the letters. It is addressed to John II himself and seems to have been written in or around the year 1445. The quotations in the text itself, together with the references provided by the author, clearly indicate its derivation from the amalgam of Christian and classical sources to which allusion has already been made. Works of St Augustine of Hippo, including the *City of God*, are quoted frequently and directly, as to a lesser extent are St Bernard and St Ambrose, as well as a sentence from the biblical book of Proverbs, conventionally ascribed to Solomon. The main classical authors quoted are Cicero and Seneca, though others, such as Plato, Aristotle and Horace, also appear. It is worth noting, in view of the controversy which surrounds the level of classical learning in fifteenth-century Castile,[14] that all these quotations are in Latin. The content of the treatise, however, is largely abstract and unremarkable, praising the virtues of peace, concord and justice, and using historical examples to illustrate the dangers, to societies in general and monarchies in particular, of a failure to secure them. The main interest of the work lies in its chronological and political context. Between 1438 and 1445, when the *Exhortaçión* was apparently published, Castile was in a state of civil war in which, as in the case of the English wars of the Roses, there was

---

[7] *Ibid.*, 89–116.

[8] *Ibid.*, 117–39.

[9] *Ibid.*, 173–202.

[10] Ed. Lucas de la Torre in 'Mosén Diego de la Valera. Su vida y obras', *Boletín de la Real Academia de la Historia*, lxiv (1914), 249–76.

[11] The two standard editions are J. A. de Balenchana, *Epístolas y otros varios tratados de Mosén Diego de Valera* (Madrid, 1878) and Penna, *ed. cit.*, *BAE*, cxvi, the latter being used here.

[12] *Antología de poetas líricos*, ii (Santander, 1944), 232.

[13] *BAE*, cxvi, 77–87.

[14] See, for example, Hillgarth, *op. cit.*, ii, 170–89 and Helen Nader, *The Mendoza Family in the Spanish Renaissance, 1350–1550* (New Brunswick, 1979).

far more intrigue and negotiation than fighting. The issue was primarily the role of the constable of Castile, Don Alvaro de Luna, in the government of the kingdom, and the attempt by some members of the upper nobility to unseat him and gain control of John II and his patronage for themselves. Valera saw this period of conflict, which culminated in the first battle of Olmedo, the only major battle of the war, on 19 May 1445, in which Luna defeated his enemies with the help of the chronicler's master, Prince Henry, partly from abroad and partly from the vantage-point of the heir to the throne's household. In the future, Alvaro was to fail to exploit his victory and eventually to die by execution on the orders of his old master, John II, in 1453, but in the meantime Diego urged the king to heal the wounds of the kingdom by means of clemency towards his opponents.[15]

The *Exhortaçión* thus has a much more practical purpose than might superficially appear, but it is also important to note that the treatise fitted into a series of letters, written to John II at various times in the 1440s, in which Valera urged upon his monarch the virtues of peace and the evils of war. During a brief revival of the fortunes of Alvaro de Luna in 1441, before the king was captured at Medina del Campo by the Trastamaran princes of Aragon, namely John, who was also king of Navarre, and Henry, Valera wrote to John II at Avila, urging him, somewhat misguidedly as it turned out, to avoid at all costs a military settlement of his and his constable's quarrel with the aristocratic opposition. Diego wrote that he would like those who were keen for war, or would allow no place for peace, to say 'what is the cause which moves them'. 'These people ought to consider how doubtful is victory and how much more valuable it is to have certain peace than doubtful victory.' He went on to mention the defeats, in the past, of monarchs or leaders who were fighting for the righteous cause, such as Pompey, who was defeated by Julius Caesar, although Pompey was 'fighting for liberty', and Louis IX of France, who was defeated and lost most of his army, although he was 'fighting against the enemies of the Holy Faith'. Valera's explanation of these apparent triumphs of the wicked over the good was based on the example of the Old Testament. The people of Israel, 'having most just reason to fight', were nonetheless defeated twice, on unspecified occasions, but 'the prophet' told them 'that it was right that their sin should be purged in blood'. Admonished a third time, they duly achieved victory, but only at heavy cost. Diego's message to his sovereign was clear. 'Seek, my lord, every way so that these matters do not come to the ultimate remedy of battle.'[16]

In March 1448, Valera returned to the theme of peace and concord, apparently in more propitious circumstances, when a temporary reconciliation had taken place between the king and Prince Henry, at

[15] Hillgarth, *op. cit.*, ii, 313–14; Penna, *op. cit.*, pp. cvi–cx.
[16] *Ibid.*, no. i, 3–5.

Tordesillas. On this occasion, Diego wrote to John under the heading, in Latin, 'Give peace in our time, O Lord'. Once again, he described the horrors which resulted from war, using the phrases of the Lamentations of Jeremiah concerning the desolation of Israel, and the Psalms of David on the isolation in which a sinful monarch found himself. The failings of Castilian society were, remarkably, blamed on the king, as 'prince and leader' (*principe y caudillo*), and Diego urged that the only weapons John should use were 'good counsel, mercy and clemency, seeing that you have tried iron and rigour, from which what else emerged but the deaths of innumerable men, the depopulation of cities and towns, rebellions, violent acts and robberies'. Valera's letter apparently went down badly with the king, and at the end of March he wrote a further letter in reply to a courtier who had rebuked him for the advice he had proffered to his sovereign. He stood his ground, refusing to abandon his pacifist views and rebuking his courtier friend, in turn, for 'following the common opinion of the people, which believes such a [pacifist] view to be appropriate only for religious and counsellors'. While recognising 'the lowness of my estate and person and the roughness of my rude speech', he still urged the programme of reconciliation which he had put before the king in his previous letter, 'entire concord between you and the prince [Henry]', 'restitution of the absent knights' (the dispossessed opponents of the Luna regime), 'deliverance of the prisoners' (those captured on the constable's orders), and 'a general pardon of the guilty'.[17] The almost foolhardy openness with which Valera advised his king is noticeable. Even allowing for his membership of the household of Prince Henry, who so often opposed his father politically, it hardly seems surprising that he should have received the rebuke which led to his second 1448 letter. This independence of mind was also to be a feature of his conduct during the succeeding reigns of his former master, as Henry IV, and of his adopted master, Ferdinand. J. N. Hillgarth has commented that, as a historian, Valera was 'capable of independent judgement', and says of his *Doctrinal de príncipes*, probably written about 1470, in which resistance to tyrants is justified, that 'These views were in sharp contrast to the monarchical propaganda which, spreading out from Castile, gradually swamped the whole peninsula'.[18] Whether or not this lurid imagery is justified, Diego's independence of mind is still discernible in his written exchanges with Ferdinand, receiving in the new reign, as will become clear, its supreme test.

On 10 February 1482, the former governor of Puerto de Santa María wrote to the king after the capture of Zahara by the Moors, the event

---

[17] *Ibid.*, no. ii, 5–7 (the letter is dated 1447 in this edn.).
[18] Hillgarth, ii, 320, 204; *BAE*, cxvi, 173–202.
[19] *Ibid.*, no. xvi, 20–2.

which sparked off the war which finally led to the conquest of Granada.[19] Assuming that Ferdinand intended to attack the Muslim state in the summer of 1482, Diego offered his advice on the methods to be followed. Firstly, the export of grain from all the Catholic Monarchs' kingdoms should be completely banned, then all available food supplies from Andalusia and Extremadura should be assembled on the boundaries of the kingdom of Granada. Ship's biscuit (*bizcocho*) would be particularly valuable, being a less perishable foodstuff. Diego laid great stress on the importance of naval warfare. A fleet should be assembled with sufficient strength not only to secure the straits between Europe and Africa, but also to patrol the coast of Granada and the Barbary coast. Siege engines and artillery should be obtained from as far afield as Galicia, Vizcaya, Asturias and Brittany, and the Genoese and Venetians should be urged to abandon all trade with the Muslim kingdom. Then, all available cavalry and infantry forces were to be assembled from the Catholic Monarchs' kingdoms and the campaign should begin. It should include *talas*, or *chevauchées*, into Granadan territory, but the crucial step was to be the capture of Málaga, because, given that town's geographical, military and economic role, as Valera told the king, 'with Málaga taken, Granada is yours'. He then proceeded to outline a detailed plan for the siege, involving the artillery bombardment of the city from two batteries, to be set up one at Gibralfaro and the other on the coast near the city. In addition to these two land batteries, blockships should be placed offshore, from which ten or twelve guns would bombard the coastal defences, 'which are no more than four feet thick and will be destroyed very quickly'. At this point, 'it would be convenient if heavily-armed infantry were ready to enter'. The Custom House would then be captured, after which the city and its surrounding lands would soon fall. In addition, Diego advocated another assault from the opposite direction, by the *adelantado*, or governor, of Murcia, on the east coast of Spain, against the eastern Granadan port of Almería which, being weakly defended, would fall to an artillery bombardment from the mountains in its hinterland, without the need for elaborate naval operations. Following past precedent, the financial aid of the Church should also be sought for these expensive proceedings. Once again, it appears that Valera's advice was not received with universal delight at Court, and on 10 April he wrote again to his sovereigns, underlining his earlier advice and stressing the superiority of his proposals over the traditional *tala* methods of Christian and Muslim frontier warfare, involving the destruction of crops and theft of livestock. He pointed out that if their crops on fertile lands were destroyed, the Moors were always capable of sowing in the mountains, which were extremely difficult to raid, while the great advances of the Christians in the Reconquest, as in the cases of Alfonso IX, Ferdinand III and Alfonso XI, had always been achieved by a combination of land and naval forces, with the clear intention in mind, not merely of raiding Muslim territory but of conquering it.[20]

At about this time, Valera set out in a memorandum, apparently at the request of the king and queen, his views on how the fleet in the straits of Gibraltar and off the Granada coast should be organised. The purpose was to blockade Muslim territory, and Diego specified the number and types of ships to be used, the level of manning, the remuneration of the sailors and the command structure. The ex-governor's advice was extremely practical. He advocated the use of ships, mainly carracks and carvels, rather than galleys, on the grounds that the blockade would have to be kept up all the year round, and galleys were 'very expensive and not suited to the seas round here' (i.e. the south-western tip of Spain). The galleys would not be able to sail in winter, when naval patrols would in fact be most necessary, 'because the Moors are always accustomed to cross [the straits] more in winter than in summer'. However, Diego foresaw that the Moors would resort to two tactics in order to keep Granada supplied. They would use their own ships, 'which are so small and so subtle (*sic*) that . . . they cross with the first Levante [the well-known east wind in the straits of Gibraltar]', and which would not be caught by large ships, but they would also put their goods on the larger vessels of the Genoese, Venetians and Florentines, 'or perhaps the Portuguese'. To deal with the Moorish ships, carvels would be used in winter and galleys in summer, while carracks, balingers and other large ships would deal with the Italians. Valera was concerned, not only that the sailors should be well paid, with the admiral of Castile as arbitrator of disputes, but that the ships should be properly supplied with biscuit, bread, wine, meat, fish, cheese, onions and vegetables, 'and such things with which ships should always go well supplied'. In addition to this stress on vegetables, many years before Captain Cook, Diego urged that olive oil and vinegar should not be forgotten, 'which are two very necessary things at sea, because sea voyages are very doubtful, and are sometimes longer than men think, and for this reason it is fitting that they should have some victuals to spare'. He was also worried that the commanders might be inexperienced, and not have access to expert advice. The captain-general in charge of the fleet should therefore not only take care to choose experienced masters for the vessels, 'because very often these captaincies are sought after by men who think they are adequate for them, and although they may be very valuable for other things, for the sea they are worth little, and when they find themselves in this case, they wish they had not taken the job', but also make sure to have three or four experienced pilots, with knowledge of the relevant waters, on his flagship. Finally, with his customary courage, he urged that 'Your Majesty should take counsel from people who have more experience of

[20] *Ibid.*, no. xviii, 23–4.

naval matters', and that these plans should be put into effect without delay, 'because other losses may receive recompense but time never, and the same [is true] for errors committed in war, because the punishment quickly follows the error'.[21]

From his base in Puerto de Santa María, Diego de Valera was in an ideal position to acquire knowledge of maritime activity, including that of foreign vessels. His town was not only in conflict with the inland royal town of Jerez de la Frontera, among other things, over control of navigation on the river Guadalete, but also with the neighbouring seigneurial ports of San Lúcar de Barrameda, lynchpin of the vast Andalusian estates of the Guzmán, dukes of Medina Sidonia, and Rota and Cádiz, which were in the hands of the rival family of Ponce de León. In addition, the Crown coveted all these wealthy ports in an area of economic growth, based on both Mediterranean and, more particularly, Atlantic trade, around the bay of Cádiz. The records of Jerez municipal council contain many references to conflicts over international trade, as well as more local agricultural and pastoral problems, between that town and Puerto. In these disputes, in the words of Hipólito Sancho, Diego, when *alcaide*, acted as a 'diplomatic man and a character opposed to violence'.[22] His observations of naval activity off the western Andalusian coast had already been placed at Ferdinand's disposal in a letter dated 17 August 1476, and a sequel, in which he gave an account of the destruction by a Genoese and Castilian patrol, in the bay of Cádiz, of a French fleet supporting the Portuguese attempt to remove Isabella from the throne of Castile. This engagement, in Valera's opinion, was the incident which brought Andalusia over to the Catholic Monarchs' side.[23] In 1482, Ferdinand gave Diego a chance to be more than an observer. In response to letters from Diego himself and from his son Charles, the king put them in charge of naval activities in the straits. A royal document in Jerez's municipal archive, dated 25 May 1483, instructed all the ports and towns of the region to give full assistance to the fleet, which was under the command of the two Valeras and also of Juan Sánchez de Cádiz, who was *alcaide* of the marquis of Cádiz's port of Rota, and of one Antón Bernalte de Cádiz.[24] This fleet, according to a later history of the Granada war, consisted of carvels, two of them in particular, from Puerto de Santa María and under Charles's command, succeeding, among their other exploits, 'while patrolling off the coasts of Africa and

---

[21] *Ibid.*, no. xxii, 28–9. On types of ship, Wendy R. Childs, *Anglo-Castilian Trade in the Later Middle Ages* (Manchester, 1978), pp. 158–9.
[22] Sancho, *op. cit.*, 538–9.
[23] *BAE*, cxvi, no. vii, 12–13, no. ix, 13–15.
[24] Sancho, *op. cit.*, 541–5, 548–9 (text).

Granada', in capturing over thirty Moorish ships, which were crossing the straits.[25]

It is clear from this evidence that at least part of Valera's advice was indeed put into practice when the Granada war actually began, but his 1482 plan was intended to be comprehensive, and it is therefore necessary to look more closely at the overall strategy of the war, in relation to his views. Modern work has tended to support Diego's proposals, and Ladero goes so far as to say that, if his scheme had been properly applied, Málaga would have fallen in 1482, not 1487, as in fact occurred. In general, despite the activity of the Andalusian fleet in the straits, little use was made of naval forces in the campaigns. This was not due to a shortage of ships, but rather to a lack of strategic awareness at Court, of precisely the kind referred to by Valera in his letters. In fact, the war was not planned in an organised way, but developed more or less spontaneously after the capture of the inland fortress and town of Alhama, which was of no great military importance, but nonetheless wasted three years and was hard to hold.[26] Valera had urged that naval forces should be used, not only to blockade Granada, but also to carry infantry reinforcements and equipment from northern Spain. Both royal and municipal documents show the immense burden, in finance, manpower and materials, which was in the event placed on communities all over Castile, by the Crown's failure to heed this advice. In the case of naval power, only the blockade proposals were taken seriously. Aragonese merchant ships, for example, were allowed to continue their trade with the Barbary coast, but not in the straits or off the coast of Granada, while, more significantly, Aragonese warships were diverted from defence against the Turks in the central Mediterranean to duties further west. However, when the siege of Málaga eventually began, it did to a considerable extent conform to Diego's plan. In military terms, the outlying fortifications of the city were in a poor state to resist a long conventional siege, let alone the artillery bombardment which eventually came. The geographical protection of the city, in the form of mountain chains, had long since been breached, above all by the Castilian capture of Antequera in 1410, which opened up the *sierras* round Ronda, and the hinterland (*tierra*) of Málaga itself, to Christian raids. Valera was not alone in advocating naval attacks on the port, as his contemporary, the chronicler Alfonso de Palencia, criticised Henry IV for not having adopted a naval strategy during his attempted attack on Málaga in 1456, but it was only in 1486 that Diego's blockade policy was adopted in full, despite the efforts made since 1482. It is possible that the marquis of

---

[25] M. Ximénez de Espada's history, ed. under the title *La guerra del moro a fines del siglo XV* by Hipólito Sancho (Ceuta, 1940), pp. 17–18.

[26] Miguel Angel Ladero Quesada, *Castilla y la conquista del reino de Granada* (Valladolid, 1967), pp. 146–7.

[27] *Ibid.*, pp. 147–8, 169–75.

Cádiz played a leading part in the decision to attack Málaga, but, in any case, Valera's stress on the city's economic vulnerability seems to have been fully justified. The famous Castilian traveller, Pedro Tafur, had seen this as early as 1435, and Palencia was of the same opinion. The apparent prosperity of Málaga was, in the words of its most recent historian, López de Coca, 'no more than a screen masking the true weakness of the hinterland [and] its enormous dependence on imports for subsistence commodities, so that a generalised conflict might bring about its total collapse in a brief interval'.[28]

This 'screen' was largely provided by Italian merchants, most of them Genoese, and here again Valera pinpointed the true weakness of the economy, not only of Málaga but of the kingdom of Granada as a whole. Málaga, and to a lesser extent the rest of the kingdom, played an essential part in the Genoese economic system. Not only had Genoese merchants established a colony in Málaga, for the export of Granadine silk and other textiles, sugar, fruit and paper, but the port was a vital link in the transfer of African gold in Europe, which helped the Genoese to compensate for their inability to control the silver production of central Europe, which was dominated by their Venetian rivals. Some have argued that, without Genoese support, the Nasrid kingdom of Granada would never have been so long-lived, and the high value placed by the Genoese on their Malagan and Granadan contacts is indicated by the speed with which the Italians became naturalised as Castilian subjects after the war. Once again, Diego de Valera had correctly analysed the situation, even if the ingenuity of the Genoese merchants defied the Crown's efforts to control them.[29]

In view of this perspicacious and fairly bellicose advice, it may well be asked what had happened to the pacifist views so eloquently put forward by Valera in the 1440s. A letter written to Ferdinand from Puerto de Santa María on 10 May 1483, after the capture by Cordoban nobles of the Muslim king Boabdil in the battle of Lucena, indicates that, despite his clear notion of the best strategy for the capture of the

[28] José E. López de Coca Castañer, *La tierra de Málaga a fines del siglo XV* (Granada, 1977), pp. 51–9.
[29] Felipe Ruíz Martín, introduction to F. Melis, *Mercaderes italianos en España, siglos XIV–XVI* (Seville, 1976), pp. xxi–xxviii; Jacques Heers, 'Portugais et Génois au XVe siècle; la rivalité atlantique-méditerranée', *Actas do III Coloquio Internacional de Estudos Luso-Brasileiros*, ii (Lisbon, 1960), 138–47, 'Les hommes d'affaires italiens en Espagne au Moyen Age: le marché monétaire', in *Fremde Kaufleute auf der iberischen Halbinsel*, ed. H. Kellenbenz (Cologne and Vienna, 1970), pp. 74–83, both reprinted in *Société et économie à Gênes (XIV–XVe siècles)* (London, 1979); 'Los genoveses en la sociedad andaluza del siglo XV: orígenes, grupos, solidaridades', in *Actas del II Coloquio de Historia Medieval Andaluza (Seville, 1981)*, (Seville, 1982), pp. 419–44; 'La mode et les marchés des draps de laine. Gênes et la montagne à la fin du Moyen Age', *Annales E.S.C.*, 26e année no. 5 (1971), 1108; Rachel Arié, *L'Espagne musulmane au temps des Nasrides (1232–1492)* (Paris, 1973), pp. 319–20, 361–3; Angus MacKay, *Money, Prices and Politics in Fifteenth-century Castile* (London, 1982), pp. 38–40.

kingdom of Granada, Diego had not abandoned his former moralistic and humane view of war. Balancing the victory at Lucena against the equally spectacular defeat, in March 1483, of the master of the military order of Santiago, Alonso de Cárdenas, together with the marquis of Cádiz and other Castilian nobles, in the Ajarquía, or mountains behind Málaga, Valera drew the moral that all excessively violent and overweening warriors would be judged by God. The defeat in the Ajarquía was compared to the Fall of Man and his expulsion from the garden of Eden, and to the collapse of the tower of Babel. Even David's pride was not permitted by the Lord, 'for which seventy-two thousand of his men were suddenly done to death' (2 Sam. 24), 'and it is written, that God resists the proud and gives grace to the humble'. The Lord 'is more accustomed to show his power in battles than in any other thing, and in them he is accustomed sometimes to punish sins very harshly, as appears in various parts of Holy Scripture', and both the Christians in the Ajarquía of Málaga and the Moors at Lucena came under this same condemnation.[30]

Nonetheless, it is clear from this, as from other writings of Diego de Valera, that he regarded the Granada war as a crusade, 'this holy and necessary war', even if it was not to be prosecuted in an indiscriminate fashion. Apparently, even before his accession to the Aragonese throne, Ferdinand was seen by Diego as having some kind of divinely-sanctioned aim. In the preface to his *Doctrinal de príncipes*, he writes of Prince Ferdinand that 'it has been prophesied for many centuries that you will not only be lord of these kingdoms of Castile and Aragon, which belong to you by all right, but you will have the monarchy of all the Spains, and will reform the imperial seat of the illustrious blood of the Goths from which you come . . . '.[31] Valera is in fact a notable example of the metamorphosis which was experienced by many leading Castilians after the accession, and more particularly the victory in the ensuing civil war, of Ferdinand and Isabella. It seems clear that, for Diego and his Andalusian friends, whether soldiers or sailors, or both, the inauguration of the royal campaign against the Muslims of Granada in 1482 was in a sense a liberation, an opportunity to employ the skills in which they were trained and which they valued above all others. It would be wrong to attribute the apparent contrast between Diego's earlier and later writings to pragmatism, let alone opportunism. Neither his successive sovereigns nor modern scholars seem ever to have accused him of sycophancy. Instead, he may be seen

[30] *BAE*, cxvi, no. xxi, 27–8.
[31] *Ibid.*, 173.

as a true representative of the Augustinian and scholastic theory of the 'just war', together with a proper admixture of fifteenth-century Spanish classical learning. Idealism, for the crusader of the Granada war, still, despite everything, retained considerable force, as the Muslims discovered to their cost.

21

Did Politics Change in the late Middle Ages and Renaissance?

Denys Hay

May I begin the following brief reflections by glossing my title? 'Politics', I presume is self-evident in its meaning, but 'late Middle Ages and Renaissance' is a clumsy attempt to deal with the chronological problems thrown up by these two unavoidable expressions which are, to add to the confusion, often used to refer to periods contrasting with each other. In the north of Europe the Middle Ages are traditionally regarded as coming to an end about 1500, when they are followed by a period commonly termed Renaissance, except in Italy where the features of the new cultural attitudes manifest themselves in the course of the fourteenth century and dominate the Peninsula in the fifteenth. The Renaissance is reasonably applied to the rest of continental Europe, including the countries generally called Britain, in the sixteenth century. Hence if these terms are used to delimit epochs, what is medieval in the North corresponds with the Renaissance south of the Alps. The matter is further complicated since for many non-Italian scholars and students the northern Renaissance is treated as a sort of curtain-raiser to the Reformation, and in Germany a very short curtain-raiser. Such assumptions directly invite the pursuit in pre-sixteenth- century times of predecessors, of 'morning stars', of the Renaissance, such as may be seen in the writings of Franco Simone on France and Roberto Weiss on England. None of these terminological abstractions posed obtrusive problems so long as historical narrative stuck to politics, narrowly defined. There is nothing about cultural change in the old Longmans History of England in the volumes contributed by Sir Charles Oman and H. A. L. Fisher (both published in 1906), although the latter has a brief chapter, not integrated into the rest of the book. Even more surprising is the virtually total absence of any reference to Italian literary and artistic innovations in the standard and valuable *Le signorie*, Luigi Simeoni's two volume contribution to the 'Storia politica d'Italia' which came out in 1950. True, like the Italian series, the Longmans' volumes were explicitly political. So long as one adheres to *l'histoire événementielle*, it might be thought, the rest of human activity can remain marginal.

Burckhardt inserted political history into his great survey of the Renaissance in Italy as early as 1860. In the last half-century the moral aspects of humanist thought, the concept of 'civic humanism' as elaborated by Hans Baron and Eugenio Garin and others seem to make it inevitable that the divorce between cultural aspects and the hunt for power, which is what politics is about, should be annulled and I believe most historians would feel that all activities of a period should be related to one another. I certainly accept such a point of view, and I am aware that it presents many dangers.[1] It would be tempting to deal with civilization fractionalised into the compartments of familiar states, towns, dynasties, and such work is indeed being pursued. Perhaps one should wait until more of this has been finished before venturing on generalizations. What I have tried to do below is to see some of the ways in which recent scholarship has related in concrete fashion trends and tastes which would have seemed peripheral to political narrative a century ago, or even later; when I suggested at Oxford in 1935 I might read for the 'Special Subject' the Renaissance my tutor V. H. Galbraith vetoed the idea by remarking that only girls did such options: I must do 'Church and State under Edward I' with F. M. Powicke. I leave to the concluding lines of my short essay an indication of my view regarding the connection of culture and politics and will begin by reminding the reader of much stimulating research recently devoted to patronage of the arts or literature, painting, sculpture and architecture, and the integration of all these arts in public display. This 'interdisciplinary' study brings together in a way which seems to me extremely significant both the attitude of men and women in all ranks of society and the few creative authors and artists who were caught up in gestures big and small organised by communities and 'governors' – town councils, princes, kings, popes and cardinals.[2]

There are elements in some manifestations of this interreaction which look backwards in time. Florence's unavailing efforts to secure the relics of Dante (buried in Ravenna) and Petrarch (buried at Arquà in the Euganean hills) recall the ruthless way in which saints' bones were subject to theft in an earlier period and were trafficked in by the Vatican in the early twentieth century (on this last I refer the reader to R. Peyrefitte's entertaining but alas mainly accurate book *Les clefs de Saint*

---

[1] A very different version of this brief essay was originally delivered in French at the twenty-fifth anniversary of the Centre d'Études Supérieures de la Renaissance at the University of Tours in December 1981: 'La Renaissance et la politique, hier et aujourd'hui'. I must here thank Professor J. C. Margolin for many kindnesses on this occasion. In re-writing it for Ralph Davis's *Festschrift* I repay inadequately a debt to an old friend who taught me a lot as my first pupil. The annotation in what follows is highly selective and mainly restricted to recent literature.

[2] There has been much research recently into public display and government. Cf. the bibliographies in A. G. Dickens (ed.) *The Courts of Europe* (London, 1977) to his own chapter and the chapter by Dr Sydney Anglo; a recent work of relevance is Gordon Kipling, *The Triumph of Honour. Burgundian Origins of the Elizabethan Renaissance* (Leiden, 1977). I have to thank Professor André Chastel for drawing my attention to this book.

Pierre, 1955). We may dismiss this latest, perhaps last, use of relics as totems or bread-winners, and remember that we do not know the splendour which might have attended the reception in Florence of those two laureates Dante and Petrarch. But we do know the panoply which attended the reception in Rome of the head of St Andrew, for we have the description from the pope himself who received it in 1462: Pius II.[3] There is little doubt that this event was orchestrated to appeal not just to clergy but to the people of Rome, as were the regular events associated with the *possesso*, the ritual procession of a new pope from the Vatican to the Lateran. And we may be certain that Paul II's reorganisation of the carnival in Rome in 1465 was designed to please the populace as well as the Curia, the senior members of which delighted in it in later times; indeed Paul's carnival was designed to replace other even less respectable festivities in the City.[4]

Such demonstrations of the arts and literature in the service of a government are of course found all over Europe in the majestic ceremonies of the marriages and deaths of the great and especially of monarchs. And every country witnessed the *joyeuses entrées* into large cities. These spectacular displays were often garnished with literary allusions which must have been mysterious even to many tolerably well educated courtiers let alone the majestic personages, whose advisers contrived to mount them in conjunction with local councils which also often had to foot the bill. And not only for princes but for all the great and well-endowed birth, marriage and death were occasions for parties in which the generality participated. If the Latin inscriptions and Latin orations were beyond them, every one would enjoy the music which from the fifteenth century began to figure largely in such festivities in most European cities.

As for the Latin oration, it became *de rigueur* in the Italy of the fifteenth century, and the propaganda value of the modern good style begins really earlier in Florence with Coluccio Salutati, chancellor of the Republic from 1375. One of the interesting features of this literary development is that Italy was prolific in its public use of notaries. Notaries, indeed, were found everywhere although more numerously in the regions of Europe bordering on the Mediterranean, a result of the Roman inheritance, doubtless. The notaries of Italy and their cultural influence deserve more attention than they have as yet received. The small Tuscan town of Arezzo, which produced so many of them, is a case in point: it would not be going too far to say that the grammarians of Arezzo had more influence on the literary Renaissance in Italy, at any rate down to the mid-fifteenth century than all the splendid legists, doctors of civil law or of canon law or, the cream, *Doctores utriusque iuris*

---

[3] The whole affair is described in book VIII of Pius's *Commentaries*, ed. Gragg and Gabel, *Smith College Studies in History*, xxxv (1951), 523–542.
[4] L. Pastor, *History of the Popes*, trans. Antrobus, iv. 31–2.

from Bologna, Padua and elsewhere.[5] Salutati had fulfilled a number of unimportant administrative posts in small communes before his Latin talent caused him to be made chancellor or secretary of the Signoria at Florence. It is true, one may admit, that no one involved in his appointment realised that his cultural influence was to become so great by his death in 1406 that the republic found it desirable to have further humanist chancellors, including the great Leonardo Bruni, down to the point where the Medici moved to the front of the political stage with Lorenzo after the Pazzi conspiracy.[6] But if the Florentine businessmen, hard-headed, jealous, politicians in all the bad senses as well as the good, did not realise that with Salutati they were inaugurating cultural innovation, nor, we must suppose, did the Pazzi who commissioned Brunelleschi to build a chapel for them at Sa. Croce, nor the Brancaci when they employed Masaccio for their chapel in Sa. Maria del Carmine. These gestures may have been incidental but they were to change the whole direction of architecture and art, just as Bruni and his contemporaries in Italian courts and communes, and the papal Curia also (where Bruni had previously worked) were to make it essential for governments everywhere to employ 'Latin secretaries' (i.e. Latin of the new sort, including the new scripts) in order to deal with Italian and international affairs. Later the royal library needed a librarian. Sometimes we find a historiographer with an official appointment, the equivalent of the poets laureate and propagandists for the governments who employed them.

This was not, we should remember, the innovation solely of the Italian humanists. The intense patriotic rivalries in northern Europe also threw up their share of propagandists. A signal example was the famous *Débat des Héraults d'Armes* in which a French apologist, writing about 1460, castigated English pretensions; the episode is interesting because a century later the whole argument was stood on its head in a pro-English version which was printed in London in 1550.[7] And similar broadsides were delivered at the Council of Constance where the traditional four nations of the medieval university formed the subdivisions and were thrown into disarray by the arrival of a fifth nation, the Spanish. This well known episode is obviously less surprising in a collection of clergy who were educated both in debate and Latin, *literati* in the good and the bad sense, one might say, rather like the deliberative bodies of a modern university. What is new about the *Débat* and propagandists like Gaguin in France or Polydore Vergil in

[5] I understand that Dr Robert Black will discuss the schools of Arezzo in his forthcoming *Benedetto Accolti and the Florentine Renaissance*; he plans further studies on Aretine learning.

[6] See E. Garin's essay, 'I cancellieri umanisti della repubblica fiorentini', now reprinted in his *Scienze e vita civile nel Rinascimento Italiano* (Bari, 1965) pp. 1–21.

[7] Both the French and English texts in *Le Débat des Héraults d'Armes*, ed. L. Pannier, Societé des Ancien Textes Français (Paris, 1877).

England, the Latin secretaries, the pompous speeches and diplomatic exchanges, is that by the early sixteenth century the way to get on in the world of politics was to have an education in grammar, i.e. Latin. One recalls the famous story of Richard Pace in his *De fructu* where the 'huntin' and shootin'' gentlemen are shown to be useless to a prince, who did not want a visiting ambassador greeted by a hunting horn but by eloquence in the approved style.[8]

It was indeed from about this time and very generally all over western Europe that the grammar schools began to be endowed to which young men were sent by families who could not afford to employ, as the very rich did, a private tutor. So deeply ingrained did this education at *gymnasia, lycées*, academies and grammar schools become that it was to last into the nineteenth century, and become part of the process of growing up rather than the preparation for a public career, although it was the essential hurdle to be cleared by those anxious for state promotion.[9]

There are indeed some curious paradoxes in the process. Castiglione in his *Courtier* described in detail the humanist servants of a prince and their importance in enhancing the reputation of his court. Yet at much the same time that Castiglione was recalling the wit and wisdom of Montefeltro Urbino, Thomas More compiled the *Utopia*. This work is curious in two ways. It criticised everything that Castiglione had admired, and especially in its first book (clearly the second to be written) arrived at the conclusion that no wise man should serve a prince. Yet not only is this written in Latin by the greatest English humanist (who, incidentally, had never visited Italy) but by a man who was shortly to do the opposite of what he had prescribed in the book.[10] Thomas More was to climb steadily to the top of the conciliar structure almost until his execution, when he did give sincere advice to Henry VIII and refused to retract it.

If More remains unique and, to the end of his days, enigmatic, his life does display the conjunction between a new educational programme and a steady increase in the number of laity in all countries of Europe who attained positions of importance in government. This was a

---

[8] *De Fructu qui ex Doctrina Percipitur*, ed. and trans. F. Manley and R. S. Sylvester (New York, 1967) pp. 23–5. The original and only earlier edition of Pace's work itself was printed by Froben at Basel in 1517.

[9] Curiously enough very little systematic work has been done on these developments, so far as I am aware, in Italy or France; England has been well served, latterly by Nicholas Orme, e.g. in *The English School in the Middle Ages* (London, 1973).

[10] For the composition of Utopia see J. H. Hexter, *More's Utopia: the Biography of an Idea* (London, 1952) and at greater length in his share of the introduction to the edition with Edward Surtz, S. J. of *Utopia* in the Yale 'Complete Works' (New Haven and London, 1968). A splendid catalogue of an exhibition (1977–8) in the National Portrait Gallery, London, '*The King's Good Servant*'. *Sir Thomas More*, ed. by J. B. Trapp and Hubertus Schulte Herbruggen, contains many recent references.

development full of contradictions. On balance the universities took small part in it, either in Italy or the North; in Italy the law (and not the mastery of Latin which notaries acquired at grammar schools and from *artes dictaminis*) and in the great centres of the North such as Paris, Oxford, Cologne, divinity and above all theology were senior and dominant. There were pockets of novelty such as Busleyden's Trilingual college at Louvain[11] where the University itself was the home of rigid orthodoxy and censorship as ruthless as was the Sorbonne's. In France the Crown had later to establish the Collège de France to give the new humanist disciplines a platform; and in Oxford the idiosyncratic foundation of Corpus Christi College – not by a civil servant like Busleyden but by a bishop (Richard Fox, who had, not surprisingly, been a royal administrator too) which was in its way a kind of mini-Trilingual – had to be bolstered up by More and Henry VIII against the attacks of the Oxford conservatives, who were against Greek on principle one might say, and hostile to 'literature' in its new and growing sense, a sense which also appealed to the butcher's son Wolsey, apparently a reader of Machiavelli's *Prince*.

It is tempting to see these European developments as part of the victory of laity over clergy. In some ways they were. In Herbert Butterfield's phrase 'there was a wind blowing on the side of kings' and kings wanted to demonstrate their ability to keep up with the sophisticated Italians; rulers in the north were much richer and more powerful, but they found it desirable to play the international game according to Italian rules. Why was it so desirable? There is a big unanswered question here, but part of the answer may lie in the development of the papal Curia at this time. For although popes were pitifully lacking in muscle, Rome was to remain, until the Reformation finally obliterated its influence in the later sixteenth century, the sounding board of European political activity and, so long as the Roman church remained undivided, Rome was necessary for the senior clergy in all principalities as the tree on which the sweetest plums grew.

If a secular spirit was evidently developing in normal circumstances, it may be harder to discern in the abnormal 'state' of the church, not only in the 'States of the Church' but also in the Christendom of which the pope claimed to be, and, however little it helped the holders of the office, was accepted as being a different and superior ruler. The Curia was, however, changing and helping the wind in the world. This is not easily discernible because the upper rungs of papal administration were composed of men who were, at any rate technically, celibate, and who looked towards ecclesiastical rewards of a rich kind: commendams of wealthy abbeys, archdeaconries and canonries of substance, bishoprics and even cardinalates. It is true that in the midst of this great company

---

[11] For Jerome de Busleyden (1470–1517) and his Trilingue see Henry de Vocht, *History of the Foundation . . . of the Collegium Trilingue Lovaniense*, vol. i (Louvain, 1951).

the highest officers, the cardinals were often the least influential. The pope was not saddled, or aided, by the sort of council to whom princes turned; for one thing the pope was normally a compromise candidate, disliked and distrusted by the men who had elected him, anxious to appoint others, including some relatives, on whom he felt he could depend. But the consistory, when the pope presided over the cardinals, and which was often attended by other and perhaps more influential curialists, was seldom asked for its advice in any meaningful sense. The pope may have been a puny figure among the rulers of Christendom but in his own narrow territory he was in theory an absolute monarch. He had no need himself to invoke those comfortable civilian doctrines that the will of the prince has the force of law, *salus populi suprema lex, rex imperator in regno suo.* Powerless many popes were, their anathemas ignored, their funds small even compared with those of other Italian rulers, but they clung to the shreds of spiritual sovereignty. Powerless occasionally even in Rome itself[12] they could sometimes strike a bargain with noble families to benefit their own kinsfolk, and play tricks of a cynical kind such as freeing Cesare Borgia from his clerical status as a cardinal so that he might become a prince in central Italy. The strongest, almost the only, lever the cardinals had at their disposal was the threat of another schism – and here again the lay rulers of Europe behaved in similar fashion. In short the clergy in the Curia may have been ordained, and some even well-educated in the older disciplines of theology and canon law, but they were virtually indistinguishable in attitudes, in morals, in style of life, from the courtiers elsewhere in Italy and in Christendom.

Nevertheless celibacy is an important feature of the administrators in many parts of Europe in the medieval period and after. It was not only popes who promoted clerks, but civil governments as well. In practice a king made (as he had for centuries) bishops of whom he pleased; so did dukes of Burgundy or of Brittany (the latter styling himself *dux dei gratia*); and one of the bribes popes offered in their negotiations was the right to nominate for a period to a certain number of benefices, which might be very large. It was bargaining like this that enabled the pope to detach the emperor from the council of Basel. Thus the wealth of the church largely financed the administration of the state and this posed problems, especially in Protestant areas after the Reformation, when crown servants expected to have 'tenure' and, indeed, like their clerical predecessors, the right of handing on their offices to children or other relatives. But this was a problem which had hardly emerged by the mid-sixteenth century. Purchase of office, initiated by the popes at Avignon, was no new thing. In northern Europe it went side by side

---

[12] That the pope could not always get his way, even in Rome itself, see the extraordinary account of the so-called Lateran Canons in Philip McNair, *Peter Martyr in Italy* (Oxford, 1967).

with purchase of titles of honour. But the lesser men climbing the ladder by service were hardly affected (until they made their pile) by such procedures.

Did these developments affect the character of government, of politics? One may feel that, though the changes are important, they hardly affected the structure of power. Senior clergy had looked to their lay masters to protect them if possible from the predatory claims of the *Camera Apostolica*, common services and annates. The clergy hoped, despite frequent deceptions, that the lay power's rapacity would be tempered by the pope. In the end the sixteenth century was to see a division of the cake, an illustrious example being the Concordat of Bologna in 1516. It remained for the clergy almost everywhere to use their cloth in a more discreet way – to avoid tiresome legal process, or even lynching. But the *privilegium fori* was everywhere in decline. It is fascinating to see this dilemma in the heart of the Papal States, where a papally appointed bishop had to face another notable clerk, who was governor in temporalities, over the question of the rights of the clergy and the punishment of their wrongs. The case of Bologna has been the subject of just such a study.[13]

The steady change towards a lay administration paid by the state brought in its train various consequences. The lay purchaser of office felt a proprietory interest in it, felt that he should be able to transmit it to an heir. This proprietorial sentiment was deeply ingrained in medieval habits and it seemed entirely reasonable that a man should do his best for his relatives. Hence the fourteenth and fifteenth centuries saw the mechanism of the *resignationes in favorem* and the *regressio* develop, permitting a prelate to hand on his benefices to a successor chosen by himself; contemporaries regarded this (despite its perilous proximity to simony and its undoubted encouragement of corruption in the administration of diocesan and monastic clergy) as a perfectly understandable practice.[14] Here again the similarity of clergy to laity is evident. Just as a barony descended for generations in the same family, so did many a bishopric.

None of all this was in any way directly attributable to the changing educational patterns so pronounced in Italy by about 1400 and influential everywhere a century later. It meant that money to pay for administration had to come (from the church, where else?) by a different route, even if that involved a dissolution of the monasteries or parallel acts of a draconian kind. The new style of public splendour did however make for heavy charges falling on lay princes and their lay subjects. Here the Italians were unquestionably leading the fashion, with palaces dressed, one might say, overall, like the ducal palace at Urbino or the ceremonial rooms at the Vatican. The tournament and jousting in cities

[13] In the admirable study of Paolo Prodi, *Il sovrano pontefice*, (Bologna, 1982).
[14] A. Clergeac, *La Curie et les bénéfices concistoriaux* (Paris, 1911).

to entertain gentlemen participating also served to please the plebs (and let us remember jousting was found in all the bigger Italian towns during the Renaissance); even an artistically unimportant centre like London had by the sixteenth century its band of musicians, although they could not compare with the choirs of foundling children for whom Venetian composers were creating masterpieces in the sixteenth century. By 1500 Rome and Venice had parallels in the grandeurs of Mantua and Ferrara.[15] It was to be long before northern Europe created spaces for urban pomp to be fully displayed just as one did not (outside Italy) deliberately build new cathedrals to replace the old ones. A new St Paul's in London had to await the Great Fire of 1666, and the Sack of Rome in 1527 doubtless encouraged the construction of new *piazze*, and straight thoroughfares, the destruction of the old streets where porticos invited crime: but St Peter's was being rebuilt well before 1527.[16]

But we may wonder if the Italy of the time of Leonardo da Vinci and Michelangelo did not witness the introduction of a new and sharper attitude in government. This, I suppose, is the traditional defence of regarding the changes in the state around 1500 as constituting a watershed. Had not the political speculation of the Middle Ages been expressed in treatises which aimed to set out what princes and governors should do to be good, to obey, and cause to be obeyed, the laws of God? The *de regimine principum* of Aquinas and other similar works were now challenged by a more pragmatic theory, whose most illustrious example was Machiavelli, especially in *The Prince*. Of course there had been earlier attempts to define sovereign power and the power of the executive. Marsiglio of Padua was groping towards this in his difficult *Defensor Pacis*; as we have noted above, Fortescue in England, with his analysis of the problems posed by the over-mighty subject, was edging towards greater political realism; and in France Commynes in several reflective passages in his *Mémoires* ventured beyond narrative into precepts to secure effective government. There is an astringency in Machiavelli which some contemporaries found shocking. Yet the former chancellor of Florence longed to have a post under the re-established Medici and it is clear that *The Prince* is not advocating a general political programme but dealing with a particular situation. Machiavelli was a Florentine republican as we can see in his *Discourse on the First Decade of Livy*, and a Florentine republican meant an advocate of the mixed balance of forces which precariously survived in the city till the re-introduction of the Medici in 1512.[17] The rich

---

[15] Cf. *Splendours of the Gonzaga*, catalogue ed. by David Chambers and Jane Martineau of the Exhibition at the Victoria and Albert Museum, London, 1981–2.

[16] On the Sack of Rome see now André Chastel's Mellon Lectures for 1977, with that title (Princeton, 1983).

[17] The last stages of the Republic are now analysed by J. N. Stephens, *The Fall of the Florentine Republic* (Oxford, 1983).

bourgeoisie were in control of the tortuous administration. Much the same was the viewpoint of the rich bourgeois Guicciardini, who, like Machiavelli, lost power with the advancing autocracy of the Medici, who in his day really did become princes. The two men were of course very differently composed. Machiavelli was an optimist, and envisaged a society which could be remade along sensible lines if men would only follow good principles of government – a citizen army rather than mercenaries and so on. Guicciardini was a pessimist. He knew that the basis of life, and especially of political action, was that whatever a statesman did was bound to prove mistaken in the end. 'Nevertheless one must do one's best'. A truly patrician view.

Does any of this matter, save to students of ideas? Did men of power wait to exercise it until their theorists could produce moral or any justification? That they did not was precisely the reason for Thomas More's criticisms in Book 1 of *Utopia*, referred to earlier in this paper. Charles V, Henry VIII, Francis I acted first and then, if it was unavoidable, argued later; as the scope of national governments widened, so principles tended to dwindle. The famous debate between Sepulveda and Las Casas in Valladolid in 1550, even if it produced official sympathy for the Dominican case, did not have much effect on the aggressive settlers, remote as they were from Spain. Both in Germany and in America the emperor pursued what were normally pragmatic policies. And so (when he could bring himself to action) did Pope Clement VII. Earlier we may wonder if Edward I of England waited to obliterate an independent Scotland till he had collected from the monastic chronicles the justification of his annexation. And, at about the same time, Pierre Flotte (speaking for his master King Philip IV) told Pope Boniface VIII, 'You have verbal power, we have real power'. And so it was. Kings (and in certain circumstances urban authorities) made and if necessary broke clergy. Even an archbishop could be executed for treason; even a cardinal could end his days in the Castel S. Angelo. Everywhere at the lower level there was *peine forte et dure*, and the threat of employment of popular violence. Everywhere in vernacular tales the clergy are treated with contempt, sometimes all the ruder from being humorous. So it is in the *Fabliaux*, in Boccaccio, in Chaucer, and a little later in Scotland in *Ane Satyre of the Thrie Estaites*. No one dared to write of kings or town councils in such a contemptuous manner. There is no anti-laicism to balance the anti-clericalism. Was there a 'Renaissance State'? Federico Chabod asked himself, and concluded that there was not.[18]

[18] Federico Chabod, 'Y-a t'il un état de la Renaissance?' in *Actes du Colloque de la Renaissance 1958* (Paris, 1962); cf. my 'Renaissance education and its influence on the "Gouernours"', in *Per Federico Chabod, 1901–1960*, atti del seminario internazionale, ed. Sergio Bertelli, Annali della Facoltà di Scienze Politiche, Perugia 1980–1 (Perugia, 1982).

Referring to Burckhardt's celebrated section on 'The State as a work of art', Chabod described it as 'an elegant formula . . . but quite superficial'. Much criticism could be levelled at Burckhardt's treatment of the subject. Its chief significance, in my view, is that it completed the slow progress of the concept of the Renaissance from literature, to art, to politics. But on the main issue, Chabod, who (be it remembered) was a formidable politician as well as a formidable historian, was surely right. The style and manifestation of politics were altered. The bureaucrats, even when still clergy, were by the mid-sixteenth century educated in the new manner. The humanities all over Europe, and in the seventeenth century in North America too, were the way in which one was trained to run the world. 'Floreat domus de Balliolo' is ugly Latin, but its disciples (among whom Ralph Davis and I must be numbered) encouraged public service as a function or justification of education. Humanists, if I may quote myself, are all educators. I do not believe there is a nobler calling.

LIST OF SUBSCRIBERS

Mrs JUDITH ATKINS, 52 Davenant Road, Oxford OX2 8BY

Professor FRANK BARLOW, Middle Court Hall, Kenton, Exeter EX6 8NA
Dr CAROLINE M. BARRON, 9 Boundary Road, London NW8 0HE
Professor G.W.S. BARROW, Dept. of History, Edinburgh University, Edinburgh EH8 9JY
STEVEN BASSETT, School of History, Birmingham University, Birmingham B15 2TT
Dr B.S. BENEDIKZ, Main Library, University of Birmingham B15 2TT
W.J. BLAIR, The Queen's College, Oxford OX1 4AW
J. BOSANKO, School of Education, St Luke's, Exeter EX1 2LU
Dr J.M. BOURNE, School of History, Birmingham University, Birmingham B15 2TT
Professor and Mrs C.N.L. BROOKE, Faculty of History, West Road, Cambridge CB3 9EF
Professor NICHOLAS BROOKS, School of History, Birmingham University, Birmingham B15 2TT
Professor A.L. BROWN, Dept. of Medieval History, Glasgow University, Glasgow G12 8QQ
Professor ANTHONY BRYER, Dept. of Byzantine Studies, Birmingham University, Birmingham B15 2TT
Dr KATHLEEN BURK, Dept. of Humanities, Imperial College, London SW7 2AZ
Dr C.S.F. BURNETT, Warburg Institute, Woburn Square, London WC1H OAB
R.R.J. BURNS, 4 Spylaw Avenue, Edinburgh EH13 0LR
GRAHAM BYRNE HILL, 26 Lawn Crescent, Richmond TW9 3NS

Professor R.C. VAN CAENEGEM, Veurestraat 47, B9821 Gent-Afsnee, Belgium
JAMES CAMPBELL, Worcester College, Oxford OX1 2HB
N.G. CAMPBELL, 15 Warriston Crescent, Edinburgh
PATRICK CAVENDISH, 17 Kensington Square, London W8
Dr PIERRE CHAPLAIS, Wadham College, Oxford OX1 3PN

List of Subscribers

Dr M.T. CLANCHY, Dept. of History, Glasgow University, Glasgow G12 8QQ
Dr C.H. CLOUGH, Dept. of History, Liverpool University, Liverpool L69 3BX
H.E.J. COWDREY, St Edmund Hall, Oxford OX1 4AR
D.B. CURTIS, 15 Upper Oldfield Park, Bath, Somerset

Professor R.R. DAVIES, Dept. of History, University College of Wales, Aberystwyth SY23 3DY
Professor R.B. DOBSON, Dept. of History, University of York, York YO1 5DD
JEAN DUNBABIN, St Anne's College, Oxford OX2 6HS
EUAN DUNCAN, Gable Barn, Lower End, Leafield, Oxon. OX8 5QG
A.C. DYBALL, Arkady, Clunbury, Craven Arms, Salop, SY7 OHE
Dr CHRISTOPHER DYER, School of History, Birmingham University, Birmingham B15 2TT

R.G. EALES, Eliot College, University of Kent, Canterbury CT2 5BG
JOHN EDWARDS, School of History, Birmingham University, Birmingham B15 2TT
Professor G.R. ELTON, Clare College, Cambridge CB2 1TL
Lt Cdr P.R. ENGEHAM R.N., H.M.S. Illustrious, B.F.P.O. (ships), London
HENRY N. ESS III, 250 Park Avenue, New York, N.Y. 10177, U.S.A.

A.J. FLETCHER, Dept. of History, Sheffield University, Sheffield S10 2QN
Dr R.F. FRAME, Dept. of History, Durham University, Durham DH1 3EX
PAUL H. FROGGATT, 14 Ashby Street, London EC1
Professor EDMUND FRYDE, Preswylfa, Trinity Road, Aberystwyth

DAVID GANZ, Dept. of Classics, University of North Carolina at Chapel Hill, Chapel Hill, N.C. 27514, U.S.A.
GEORGE GARNETT, St John's College, Cambridge CB2 1TP
Dr MARGARET GIBSON, Dept. of History, Liverpool University, Liverpool L69 3BX
Dr JUDITH GREEN, Dept. of Modern History, Queen's University of Belfast, Belfast BT7 1NN

BERNARD HAMILTON, Dept. of History, Nottingham University, Nottingham NG7 2RD

List of Subscribers

Professor ALAN HARDING, Dept. of History, Liverpool University, Liverpool L69 3BX
BARBARA F. HARVEY, Somerville College, Oxford OX2 6HD
Professor DENYS HAY, Dept. of History, Edinburgh University, Edinburgh EH8 9JY
THOMAS HEAD, The School of Theology at Claremont, Claremont, Ca. 91711, U.S.A.
R.H. HELMHOLZ, 1111 E. 60th Street, Chicago, Il. 60637, U.S.A.
Dr. J.R.L. HIGHFIELD, Merton College, Oxford OX1 4JD
Professor CHRISTOPHER HOLDSWORTH, Dept. of History and Archaeology, Exeter University, Exeter EX4 4QH
Professor C. WARREN HOLLISTER, Dept. of History, University of California at Santa Barbara, Santa Barbara, Ca. 93106, U.S.A.
Professor J.C. HOLT, Fitzwilliam College, Cambridge CB3 ODG
RICHARD HOLT, School of History, Birmingham University, Birmingham B15 2TT
ANNE HUDSON, Lady Margaret Hall, Oxford OX2 6QA
MICHAEL HURST, St John's College, Oxford OX1 3JP
Dr MICHAEL JONES, Dept. of History, Nottingham University, Nottingham NG7 2RD
B. JUBB, Sidney Jones Library, Liverpool University, Liverpool L69 3DA

FRANK KELSALL, Room 208, Chesham House, 30 Warwick Street, London W1R 6AB
M.J. KENNEDY, Dept. of Medieval History, Glasgow University, Glasgow G12 8QQ
ANNE J. KETTLE, Dept. of Medieval History, St Andrews University, St Andrews, Fife, KY16 9AJ
SIMON KEYNES, Trinity College, Cambridge CB2 1TQ
EDMUND KING, Dept. of History, Sheffield University, Sheffield S10 2TN

Dr JOHN LAW, Dept. of History, University College, Swansea SA2 8PP
ROGER LAUGHTON, 286 Sandycombe Road, Richmond, Surrey TW9 3NG
Professor KARL and Mrs HENRIETTA LEYSER, Manor House, Islip, Oxon.
IFAN LLOYD, 24 Wieland Road, Northwood, Middlesex
D.W. LOMAX, Dept. of Spanish, Birmingham University, Birmingham B15 2TT
CATHERINE LORIGAN (née DODDS), 2 St David's Close, Caversham, Reading, Berks., RG4 7PX
Professor H.R. LOYN, Westfield College, London NW3 7ST

Dr A.K. MCHARDY, Dept. of History, Aberdeen University, Aberdeen AB9 1FX
Dr R. MCKITTERICK, Newnham College, Cambridge CB3 9DF
ANDREW MALIPHANT, 6 Horwood House, Davey Lane, Alderley Edge, Cheshire, SK9 7NZ
Professor R.A. MARKUS, Dept. of History, Nottingham University, Nottingham NG7 2RD
Dr HENRY MAYR-HARTING, St Peter's College, Oxford OX1 2DL
Mr and Mrs. J.R.S. MILL, 35b Gloucester Avenue, London NW1 7AX
EDWARD MILLER, 36 Almoners Avenue, Cambridge CB1 4PA
LENNOX MONEY, 193 Pimlico Road, London SW1W 8PH
R. I. MOORE, Dept. of History, Sheffield University, Sheffield S10 2TN
Professor COLIN MORRIS, Dept of History, Sothampton University, Southampton S09 5NH
ROSEMARY MORRIS, Dept. of History, Manchester University, Manchester M13 9PL

JANET L. NELSON, Dept. of History, King's College, London WC2R 2LS
Dr P.A. NEWTON, King's Manor, York YO1 2EP

ROBIN S. OGGINS, Dept. of History, S.U.N.Y. at Binghamton, Binghamton, N.Y. 13901, U.S.A.
Mrs D.M. OWEN, University Library, Cambridge CB3 9DR

D.J.H. PAGE, 67 Ruskin Walk, London SE24 9NA
Dr D.M. PALLISER, Dept. of History, Hull University, Hull HU6 7RX
J.H.M. PARRY, Snuff Mill Cottage, Kentshars Lane, Winford, Bristol BS18 8HA
Dr DAVID PELTERET, New College, 21 Classic Avenue, Toronto, Ontario M5S 2Z3, Canada
R.G. PRICHARD, Dymchwa, 2 Fford Iago, Y Groeslon, Caernarfon, Gwynedd, LL54 YDH

Professor A. COMPTON REEVES, Dept. of History, Ohio University, Athens, Ohio 45701-2979, U.S.A.
S.M.G. REYNOLDS, 26 Lennox Gardens, London SW1X ODQ
J.M. ROBERTS, Merton College, Oxford OX1 4JD
MARTIN ROBERTS, Cherwell Upper School, Oxford
Mrs J.E. ROBINSON, The Library, Keble College, Oxford OX1 3PG

List of Subscribers

D.W. ROLLASON, 43-5 North Bailey, Durham DH1 3EX
W.G.G. ROLLASON, 43-5 North Bailey, Durham DH1 3EX
Professor CONRAD RUSSELL, University College, Gower Street,
    London WC1E 6BT
PETER RYCRAFT, Dept. of History, York University, York YO1 5DD

M.J. SANDS, 10 Grosvenor Court, Fairfax Road, Teddington,
    Middlesex, TW11 9BT
KAY SAUNDERS, 31 Manton Street, Plumstead, London SE2 0JE
HILARY SAYLES, Warren Hill, Crowborough, Sussex
JAMES M. SCHIBANOFF, 1610 Luneta Drive, Del Mar, Ca, U.S.A.
Dr E.I.M. SHEPPARD, Quantock House, Park Lane, Bath, Somerset
Col. G.T.F. SHEPPARD, Herne House, Weston Road, Bath, Somerset
Dr GRANT G. SIMPSON, Dept. of History, King's College, Old
    Aberdeen AB9 2UB
R.C. SMAIL, Sidney Sussex College, Cambridge CB2 3HU
Sir RICHARD SOUTHERN, 40 St John's Street, Oxford
CHRISTOPHER SUTCLIFFE, 2 Low Green Terrace, Bradford,
    West Yorkshire BD7 3NA
Dr R.N. SWANSON, School of History, Birmingham University,
    Birmingham B15 2TT

Dr ARNOLD TAYLOR, Rose Cottage, Lincoln's Hill, Chiddingfold,
    Surrey GU8 4UN
KEITH THOMAS, St John's College, Oxford OX1 3JP
Dr J.A.F. THOMSON, Dept. of Medieval History, Glasgow University,
    Glasgow G12 8QQ

Miss L.E.M. WALKER, University Hall, Kennedy Gardens, St Andrews,
    Fife, KY16 9DL
BREFFNI M. WALSH, Bracken, 16 Bearswood End, Beaconsfield,
    Bucks., HP9 2NR
Professor W.L. WARREN, Dept. of Modern History, The Queen's
    University, Belfast BT7 1NN
Dr C.J. WICKHAM, School of History, Birmingham University,
    Birmingham B15 2TT
C. PATRICK WORMALD, 60 Hill Top Road, Oxford OX4 1PE